The Harmonious Garden

The
Harmonious Garden

Color, Form, and Texture

Catherine Ziegler

Timber Press
Portland • Cambridge

Timber Press, Inc.   Timber Press
The Haseltine Building   2 Station Road
133 S.W. Second Avenue, Suite 450   Swavesey
Portland, Oregon 97204-3527, U.S.A.   Cambridge CB4 5QJ, U.K.

Please send e-mail to: orders@timberpress.com
and visit our Web site: www.timberpress.com

Library of Congress Cataloging-in-Publication Data

Ziegler, Catherine
The harmonious garden : color, form, and texture / Catherine Ziegler.
        p.   cm.
Includes bibliographical references and index.
ISBN 0-88192-597-7 (paperback)
1. Color in gardening. 2. Gardens—Design. 3. Plants, Ornamental. I. Title.
            SB454.3.C64Z54   1996
712' .2—dc20   95-33265
                                                      CIP

*Dedicated
to the memory of
my mother,
Catherine Patterson,
with love*

Contents

Foreword

GARDEN design is an art form and a science, and the best gardens are based on knowledge in both fields. But we are used to instant gratification, and we demand that we get everything right the first time. Few of us have the patience to wait and see, gardening by trial and error, moving plants around over several seasons until the plant associations are just right. Experience with a broad plant palette takes years to attain. *The Harmonious Garden* provides a short cut, through illustrations and discussions of successful plant combinations.

While written particularly for designers and experienced gardeners, this book will nonetheless be indispensable for those taking their first wobbly steps toward designing their own outdoor space. Even those with tiny gardens will benefit from the ideas presented here. Ms. Ziegler's photographs give ample examples of plant associations by flower and foliage color, in sun or shade, in damp or dry soils, and for large or limited spaces. Carefully and methodically she explains why certain plant associations work, while others, seemingly similar, do not. The positioning and numbers of plants required to provide a balanced picture are practical aspects of garden design seldom spelled out; the appendices are invaluable as quick reference tools.

Ms. Ziegler's years of design experience and teaching shine throughout this book. She does not try to blind you with high tech terms, but rather leads you step by step toward creating a beautiful, personal outdoor room. This is a book that you will return to again and again.

Ruth Rogers Clausen
Valhalla, New York

Acknowledgments

I WOULD especially like to thank the following people for their cheerful and encouraging assistance during the preparation of this book: Amy Harrington, Dawn Lombardi Orza, Elizabeth Spar, Jamie Weisberg, Bill Ziegler, Nancy Ziegler, Susan Ziegler, and my editor, Micheline Ronningen. I am also grateful to the Somerset Fire Brigade, England, for permission to use the photographs taken at Hestercombe; and Susan Ziegler and Dawn Lombardi Orza for the line drawings, Dency Kane for photographs 3, 48, and 147, and Jerry Pavia for photos 30, 33, 75, 92, 146, and 148. Finally, I would like to thank the creators of the outstanding public and private gardens who have, often without special recognition, given so much pleasure and contributed to this book.

Catherine Ziegler
Bedford, New York

Introduction

I STARTED my investigation into the principles of combining plants many years ago when first studying landscape design, as I was perplexed about why some of the customary beliefs about color associations produced such dull compositions. It was obvious that bloom color, form, leaf texture, and other plant attributes were enhanced by appropriate neighbors, but exactly which plants and why was a puzzle. Later, in teaching planting design, I worked with people just beginning to piece together the form, texture, colors, habit, and growth rate of the hundreds of plants common in design use. I decided to establish tools for these students' use that would allow them to choose and associate plants with confidence. Eventually I developed lists of pleasing associations of plants that flourish in similar conditions while integrating various factors, such as coincidental bloom time and harmony of color, texture, or form.

In preparing these lists, I read a great deal, created many designs, and observed a great many growing combinations. Over many years I have employed all the general principles for combining plants that are presented in this book. As I created four-dimensional compositions with ephemeral effects constantly altered by weather, moisture variation, animal foraging, or human blight, it became clear that while theories about color, scale, and other design factors must be thoroughly understood, in itself this is not enough. Theoretical knowledge can only be usefully employed when adapted for each particular situation and refined by the experience, taste, and careful observations of the designer and gardener.

There are a few basics to consider before creating plant compositions, and these are reflected in the information about each plant given in Part Two. Culturally, the designer must begin by knowing the conditions existing in the planting space: light and wind direction, richness or leanness and character of the soil, and the average amount of moisture available. Some plants will flourish in a wide range of conditions. Many of the plants seen in Part One thrive in average soil and moisture in sun, yet most plants can be encouraged to tolerate some variance from the ideal, perhaps slightly more shade or somewhat leaner soil.

Next, the composition must be of appropriate scale for the space involved, yet must satisfy the primary function of the planting—whether that is to draw attention to a particular area, delineate space, or create a vibrant or soothing mood. Then the plants of single or multiple compositions are selected and arranged to harmonize with each other, with their immediate neighbors, and with the themes and character of the environment. This final phase of selection and placement warrants a pronounced simplicity. Restraint in the number of different plants used and consistent attention to the correct scale, both in the individual plant group and in its place in the entire landscape, will produce the strongest design.

This book concentrates on associations among the smaller features of planting design, that is, herbaceous plants and small shrubs. This is the scale at which there is the greatest choice in color, form, and texture, and which often embraces the greatest design confusion.

Color, form, and texture are not equal in the attention they receive. One notices color before form and form before texture. In fact, when colors are strong and compelling, most people become blind to texture and vague about form. Since color is the most striking characteristic of plants it warrants first consideration.

In studying plant characteristics as they relate to color, I was frustrated by the commercially available color charts. None adequately illustrated the range of light and pale tints dominating flower colors. Eventually I created my own color chart to give me a simple, workable frame of reference. Many of the other puzzling and confusing aspects of color were eventually clarified by my readings. I found Penelope Hobhouse, Florence Robinson, Henry Gleitman, Louise Beebe Wilder, and Johannes Itten particularly illuminating. Eventually, after testing the standard color theories with color charts to hand and eye, I arrived at a number of conclusions and guidelines.

First, it is important to train one's eyes to detect *relative* differences in hue or tint. Color charts can be useful in this initial training, although they are not absolutely essential. One should be able to see, for instance, that the flowers of *Geranium* 'Johnson's Blue' are a light violet rather than the blue its name might imply. Their violet color is especially obvious when comparing flowers of *Brunnera macrophylla*, which are truly light blue. From such refined observations, one can speculate that this violet *Geranium* will associate more smoothly with the red-violet *Allium giganteum* than the blue *Brunnera* because of the amount of harmonizing violet in the geranium and allium.

It also seems expedient to consider flower color in terms of the sixteen-color wheel that follows, rather than the widely used six-color wheel. I find the more complex color wheel better suited to the needs of the garden or landscape designer. For one thing, it reflects the physiological basis of color vision, particularly the important connection between red/green and blue/yellow. It also illustrates significant intermediate hues, such as yellow-green and red-violet, so common in foliage and flowers. These two colors are seen far more often in plants than the orange and blue emphasized in the six-color wheel.

Looking at the sixteen-color wheel, a person can readily pick up some of the simpler recommendations for color harmony. Any two, three, or four colors *adjacent* on the sixteen-color wheel will combine well; all directly opposite colors, such as blue-violet and greenish yellow, red and green, or blue and yellow, will *complement* each other when combined. References to colors being *adjacent* or *complementary* stem from this placement on the color wheel. Furthermore, any color in one quadrant will harmonize and make a pleasing near-complementary association with any color in the opposite quadrant.

The marked predominance of certain colors and values among flowers also suggests certain guidelines for their associations. Most flower colors in temperate climates are tints, containing varying amounts of white that dilute the pure color. All tints therefore contain a unifying white presence. The white component gives pale colors a link, and pastel or very pale hued combinations are smooth and successful, if sometimes bland. For gardeners in temperate climates flower colors are overwhelmingly red, red-violet, violet, blue-violet, yellow, and yellow-green. It is relatively easy to meet success using these colors because of the abundant choice in different bloom forms, textures, and sizes in both tints and stronger, purer versions of these colors.

The remaining colors in the sixteen-color wheel are underrepresented among blooms. Blue-green, blue, and orange in particular are quite rare in both flowers and foliage. Consequently, it is more difficult to create engaging compositions using these colors as a base.

Few flowers bloom in pure, undiluted strong hues. Even fewer bloom in dark shades. However, when strong pure colors are used in planting design, careful balancing is required. Place such elements with companions of equal color strength, or compensate for differences by decreasing the quantity of the pure hue or increasing the quantity of tinted or shaded colors. Recommendations as to the quantities of each plant needed to achieve harmonious color or textural balance are given for each suggested plant grouping. The photo section also includes the approximate space requirement for a minimum arrangement for each association.

Considerations of flower color are always qualified by the context of foliage color. Natural foliage colors in temperate climates are typically shades of yellow-green. Rare exceptions involve pure green, yellow, blue-green, and dark shades of red, red-violet, and red-orange. The actual color of silvery foliage is generally very pale, grayed yellow-green. These pale gray foliages popularly combine with each other and with pale tints of other hues, again because the composition is unified by the white in each. Gray-leaved plants also associate well with blooms in violet, blue-violet, and blue, and are satisfactory with yellow. I find pale foliage disturbing when combined with intense warm colors such as pure red, red-orange, or orange.

After color, or when one color is used in a monochromatic design, form assumes design significance. Distinct flower forms include spires (*Liatris*), disks (*Cosmos*), or globular forms (*Allium*). Where flower form is less distinct or treated as a transient element, the overall plant form may make the principal design contribution. A number of plants develop pronounced vertical or horizontal growth that has a decisive and sometimes dramatic effect on design. Others weep or develop as indistinct masses, useful as textural foils against which to display the more pronounced forms of companions. Some variation in form is essential to interesting design and basic in enlivening monochromatic themes.

Textures of flowers and foliage may be simply described as broad, medium, or fine. On the small scale with which we are concerned here, texture in a garden is determined by such things as the character and distribution of leaves or flowers. However, one should be aware that texture changes with scale. An entire plant or plant massing may be needed to produce a contributing texture in a large-scale planting. The same planting may add a broad texture when viewed across a small space, yet contribute a fine or medium texture to a larger design scale.

Small-scale plants characterized as fine-textured have weak visual impact over viewing distances greater than 20 ft (6 m). Their fine texture characteristics dissolve to a subtlety beyond note. Medium- to large-scale plants displaying medium to broad texture are far more effective at such distances.

Their elemental vigor can withstand distancing. Foliage texture has a greater design impact than is often recognized. Keep in mind that even the longest blooming perennials seldom flower for more than eight weeks, many for only two or three weeks, which often leaves foliage as the focus of attention for many months.

General principles for associating colors, forms, and textures in the landscape are illustrated by the photographs in Part One. While the photographs generally present settings of excellent combinations, the photo texts go on to offer substitutes and extensions to expand their potential. Considerations of all three design elements—color, form, and texture—are further integrated into the lists of useful associations included in Part Two. Many classic plant associations, some popular for a century or more, are not presented among the photographs but are noted in Part Two.

Photographs are presented by ease of association. The simplest and most easily contrived plantings appear earliest. For example, those using only white blooms initiate the sequence. White blooms are the most common, existing in so many forms at so many different seasons that sheer choice permits the production of many excellent designs. Only slightly more difficult is the monochromatic planting. With herbaceous plants this usually involves a single color in different blooms or a single color with white. Next in difficulty are plantings combining adjacent warm colors, yellow, yellow-orange, orange, red-orange, and red, or adjacent cool colors, red-violet, violet, blue-violet, and blue.

Associations of complementary opposite hues are a little more complex because the color quantities require more delicate balancing. This section includes yellow and blue as well as yellow and violet, the easiest near-complementary association because of the numbers of available plants. It ends with blue-green and red-orange, one of the more difficult associations because of the rarity of plants of these hues. Part One concludes with examples of the more complex combinations of three colors. The methods of association suggested in the photo descriptions may be used to create innumerable combinations, many more than are specified in Part Two.

Appendix A gives bloom options according to preferred exposure, flowering season, and color. Use this appendix to select a floral association or create a new one. Look first under the exposure offered by the site—sun, shade, or part shade—then choose the preferred flowering season. Review the plants listed by color for that season and turn to the individual descriptions in Part Two to find recommendations for companion groupings. Appendix B highlights foliar qualities and is especially useful used with Appendix A to create new groupings from the flowering and foliage plants listed for that season and exposure. Appendix C cross references common names of plants with their botanical names.

Appreciation of color harmonies is not innate or even unchanging. Preferences in color associations, as well as favorite forms and textures, vary from culture to culture, and generation to generation. Current Western planting design has evolved from the requirements of cooler northern climates. Perhaps our design sense is limited by a Eurocentric bias. Many popular planting schemes, regardless of location, reflect a preference for the planting patterns and tranquil pale and cool hues of such temperate climates. Indiscriminate design adaptations from distant climates and cultures are frequently disappointing and inappropriate for their settings. Had the early exponents of planting design so admired by Western gardeners and designers lived in tropical or near-tropical zones, perhaps powerful, warm floral hues would be more evident in our planting schemes.

The Sixteen-Color Wheel

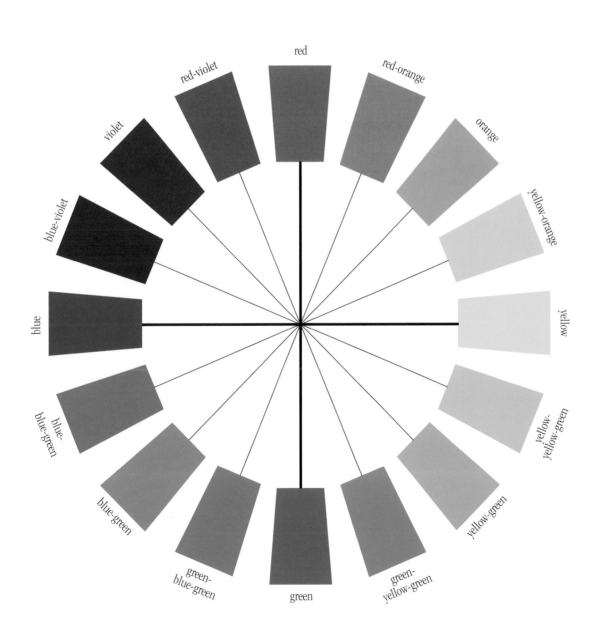

PART ONE

The Visual Statement

PHOTO 1. New York
Botanical Garden, New
York City, August.
ENVIRONMENT: sun or
part shade in soil of
average to poor fertility
and average moisture.
USDA Zones 4–9.
FEATURE: foliage
summer to fall; flower
late summer to fall.

ALTHOUGH associations of all-white blooms are among the easiest to create and are immensely pleasing, the subtlety of very pale green and white together is sometimes better suited to small-scale plantings. *Sedum* 'Autumn Joy' is an extremely useful plant, valued by gardeners and designers for its ease of culture, strong form, long season of interest, and the strength of its late-season color contribution. These qualities lead to its frequent use as the backbone of many fine compositions.

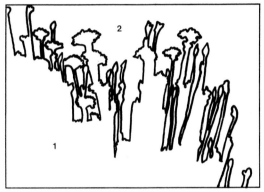

1. *Allium tuberosum*, two bulbs, 18–24 × 12 in
   (45–60 × 30 cm)
2. *Sedum* 'Autumn Joy', one plant, 18–24 × 24 in
   (45–60 × 60 cm)

Here the sedum is seen in its pale yellow-green stage, when it harmonizes beautifully with the white umbel of the ornamental allium. The sedum colors are very subdued at this stage. As the season progresses, its color changes to a warm light red; by fall it displays a dark red tending towards red-orange. The horizontal, rounded 'Autumn Joy' corymbs repeat the allium flower form, providing an added visual link.

While most alliums have meager foliage, declining early and requiring disguise, *Allium tuberosum*'s onion-scented foliage appears early in the growing season and persists well after flowering. In this situation, it is providing a grassy form which underplants and conceals the sometimes bare lower stems of the *Sedum*. This pair combines easily with other pale-flowering compositions and makes an excellent, low-maintenance mass planting as the foreground of shrubs.

This small-scale composition requires a minimum space of 2 × 3 ft (0.6 × 0.9 m), with a ratio of one *Sedum* in the background and two *Allium* in the foreground.

PHOTO 2. Ziegler Garden, Bedford, New York, June. ENVIRONMENT: sun in soil of average fertility and moisture. USDA Zones 3–7. FEATURE: foliage late spring to fall; flower late spring.

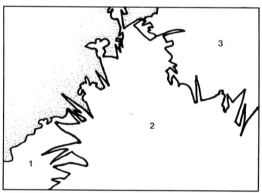

1. *Geranium sanguineum* 'Album', one plant, 12–24 × 24 in (30–60 × 60 cm)
2. *Iris sibirica* 'White Swirl', three plants, 18–36 × 9 in (45–90 × 25 cm)
3. *Paeonia lactiflora* 'Festiva Maxima', one plant, 30–36 × 36 in (75–90 × 90 cm)

THERE ARE many reasons why all-white compositions and all-white gardens are currently so popular. There are minimal decisions about balancing intensities and values or of harmonizing hues in combinations of all-white blooms. Also, a high percentage of cultivated plants produce white flowers from early spring until fall. A vast selection eases any garden design process. Another reason for their popularity is the stunning effect of a few white blooms against a large quantity of dark green foliage. This particular late spring grouping is only one of hundreds which may be composed for June displays in cool climates. This one contrasts distinctive flower and foliage forms. Leaf contrasts offer reason alone for this planting combination, setting aside the brief magnificence of the white blossoms.

The peonies provide shrubby background mounds of medium dark green foliage to accent the narrow ascending iris forms and the low, finely dissected and delicately textured lighter green geranium foliage. Yet flowering is decidedly brief, generally lasting for about a week to ten days in a cool spring or perhaps only five days with a hot spell. The geranium's blooms persist several weeks longer than its companions', showing advantageously against the attractive iris and peony foliage.

This medium-scale combination requires a minimum space of 3 × 5 ft (0.9 × 1.5 m), with one peony in the rear, three to four closely spaced irises in the midground, and one geranium in the foreground.

PHOTO 3. Peconic River Herb Farm, Calverton, New York, May.
ENVIRONMENT: part shade in average to rich soil with above average moisture. USDA Zones 4–7.
FEATURE: foliage mid spring to fall; flower mid spring to summer.

THE PAIRING of yellow-green with white is in many ways more engaging and only slightly more difficult to compose than an association which rigidly adheres to all-white blooms. *Hosta fortunei* 'Marginato-alba' supplies a dominant form with its broad mass of white-rimmed foliage. It also contributes a substantial contrast to the finely textured flowers and foliage of *Galium odoratum* and the intermediate size leaves of *Alchemilla mollis*.

Hostas can be considered dependable, backbone plants, which in one variety or another are used again and again in planting designs where exposure and moisture conditions are appropriate. It is one of the few plants offering the broad-textured leaf so essential to planting design. The hosta foliage is just beginning its spring expansion in this photo. Its foliage will later cover more space than is shown here, and it is important to space plants to allow for hosta growth.

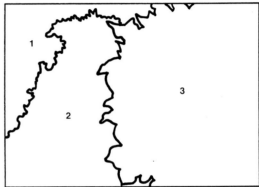

1. *Alchemilla mollis*, one plant, 12 × 18 in (30 × 45 cm)
2. *Galium odoratum*, five plants, 6–12 × 12 in (15–30 × 30 cm)
3. *Hosta fortunei* 'Marginato-alba', one plant, 12–18 × 24 in (30–45 × 60 cm)

Yellow-green *Alchemilla* flowers are just emerging and will briefly coincide with the lightly scented white-flowering *Galium*. The hosta's arresting light violet, spiked flowers emerge in summer, pale enough to attract notice in a lightly shaded area. This combination makes an excellent mass planting, weaving between shrub groups in lightly shaded woodlands and borders.

Used as a small group, a minimum space of 3 × 4 ft (0.9 × 1.2 m) will be needed with one *Hosta* in the rear, one *Alchemilla* in the middle, and a foreground grouping of five *Galium* to balance the mass developed by the *Hosta* and *Alchemilla*.

PHOTO 4. Stonecrop Gardens, Cold Spring, New York, May. ENVIRONMENT: part shade in soil of average fertility and average to greater moisture. USDA Zones 4–8. FEATURE: foliage late spring to fall; flower mid to late spring.

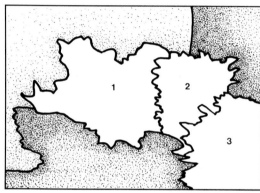

1. *Dicentra eximia* 'Alba', one plant, 12–18 × 12 in (30–45 × 30 cm)
2. *Polygonatum biflorum*, two plants, 12–24 × 12 in (30–60 × 30 cm)
3. *Adiantum pedatum*, one plant, 12 × 12 in (30 × 30 cm)

PLANTING design encompasses many different types of plant arrangements tailored to specific situations. Each situation is different. Many factors contribute to decisions about complexity, formality or informality, and focus, each influencing final plant organization. A planting design may be as simple and elegant as the small composition in this woodland scene. The location and this association hint at an indigenous composition appropriate to, but certainly not limited to, the lightly shaded woodland garden.

The finely textured low foliage mound of *Adiantum* harmonizes well with the similarly fine, but more feathery foliage of *Dicentra*. The firm, arching *Polygonatum* stems rise above and arch over the flowers and foliage of the plant's companions, offering a contrasting form and a broader texture. Substituting *Polygonatum odoratum* 'Variegatum' for *P. biflorum* would contribute a more ornamental composition, as its white leaf margins would repeat the color of the *Dicentra* blooms.

Polygonatum briefly produces tiny, pendulous, bell-like blooms in spring that are often partly concealed by its foliage. Planting the group in an elevated location, closer to eye level, as viewed in this photograph, allows their delicate details to be more visually accessible.

An area 2 × 2 ft (0.6 × 0.6 m) will accommodate all three plant types, with one *Adiantum* and one *Dicentra* in the foreground and two *Polygonatum* plants at the rear of the group.

PHOTO 5. Stapehill Gardens, Dorset, England, June. ENVIRONMENT: sun in soil of average to low fertility and average or less moisture. USDA Zones 7–9. FEATURE: foliage late spring to fall; flower mid to late summer.

GRAY FOLIAGE plants are often recommended as a harmonizing element between disparate colors, although I find them limited for this purpose. Although they blend well with all tints and pastel colors, since a certain whiteness is common to all, pale blooms harmonize easily with each other without assistance.

Gray foliage certainly combines beautifully with blue, blue-violet, and violet hues, and can minimize the minor discord which sometimes occurs between blue and violet blooms. Yet since gray foliage plants are seldom pleasing with pure yellows, oranges, or red-oranges, they are not helpful in making critical transitions between cool and warm colors. Considered on their own merits, groupings of silver or gray plants can be arresting and soothing, as seen in this large-scale arrangement. The planting is preserved from monotony by the few, rather startling, red *Potentilla* blooms. Substituting a flowering plant with white, blue-violet, or violet blooms would assure a soothing rather than a startling effect.

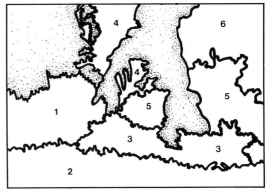

1. *Helichrysum angustifolium*, six plants, 12–18 × 12 in (30–45 × 30 cm)
2. *Stachys byzantina*, three plants, 12–15 × 12 in (30–40 × 30 cm)
3. *Convolvulus cneorum*, six plants, 12–24 × 18 in (30–60 × 45 cm)
4. *Onopordum acanthium*, two plants, 72 × 36 in (185 × 90 cm)
5. *Potentilla flamea*, three plants, 12 × 12 in (30 × 30 cm)
6. *Buddleja fallowiana* 'Lochinch', one plant, 4–6 × 5 ft (1.2–1.8 × 1.5 m)

Variations in the lightness and grayness of the underlying gray-green are clearly evident here—ranging from the near white grayness of *Stachys* to the much greener gray of this *Helichrysum*. Texture and form variations must be carefully selected for any largely monochromatic or foliar design. Both the selection and placement in this example are very skillful.

An area 9 × 12 ft (2.7 × 3.7 m) will fit one *Buddleja*, two *Onopordum* in the rear, and six *Convolvulus* in the midground, with three *Potentilla*, three *Stachys*, and six *Helichrysum* in the foreground.

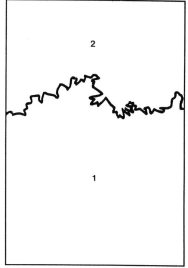

1. *Tiarella cordifolia*, two plants,
   8–12 × 12 in (20–30 × 30 cm)
2. *Dicentra spectabilis* 'Alba', one
   plant, 24–36 × 18 in (60–90 × 45
   cm)

PHOTO 6. Conservatory Garden, New York City, May. ENVIRONMENT: part shade to shade in soil of average to greater fertility and average or greater moisture. USDA Zones 3–8. FEATURE: foliage mid spring to summer; flower late spring.

MANY PLANT compositions look splendid in small groups, but for various reasons do not lend themselves to multiplication into larger quantities or for massed underplantings of trees and shrubs. Texture is one of the determining factors. This ornamental combination has such fine textures it will simply appear disorderly if massed over distances greater than about 75 ft (25 m) unless associated with broader textures and bolder forms. However, when placed in a smaller setting, within a highly structured framework of unobtrusive foliage, such as a sheared hedge, its textural detail will be focused and contained and the all-white blooms well displayed.

The medium-size, feathery *Dicentra* foliage contrasts strikingly with the small flower spires and foliage of *Tiarella*. Adding *Phalaris arundinacea* var. *picta*, a variegated ribbon grass, and *Lamium maculatum* 'White Nancy', a prostrate, easily grown, fine- to medium-textured plant, will enrich the scale, form, and texture of this pairing. However, *Phalaris* and *Lamium* are more aggressive plants than these companions and, especially where moisture is plentiful, would need careful supervision to keep them within appropriate bounds. If a large space is available, *Digitalis purpurea* 'Excelsior' hybrids would extend the composition and add tall spires in late spring to provide a welcome vertical contrast to the other four plant forms.

The inclusion of all five plants in a medium space 5 × 4 ft (1.5 × 1.2 m) allows one *Dicentra* and two *Digitalis purpurea* 'Excelsior' hybrids in the rear, one *Phalaris arundinacea* var. *picta* in the middle or rear ground, two *Tiarella* in the middle, and six *Lamium maculatum* 'White Nancy' in the front of the composition. The basic pairing in the photograph requires 2 × 4 ft (0.6 × 1.2 m).

PHOTO 7. Conservatory Garden, New York City, July.
ENVIRONMENT: part shade in soil of average fertility and moisture. USDA Zones 6–8.
FEATURE: foliage mid spring to fall; flower late spring to fall.

I N BLOOM, *Crambe cordifolia* is a large-scale, finely textured plant that may temporarily expand the vertical scale of a composition. When not in flower, the broad mass of foliage makes a bold contribution only near ground level. Any composition including *Crambe*, or plants with similar habit, must recognize this dramatic alteration in scale during flowering and non-flowering periods. One solution is to place associated groups in a larger space, large enough to readily accommodate a temporary change in scale.

For example, here, as the *Miscanthus* develops, it serves as a medium-scale transition between the tiny *Polygonatum* and the large *Crambe* in flower. When the *Crambe* has finished flowering, the *Miscanthus*

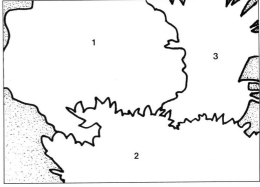

1. *Crambe cordifolia*, one plant, 4–7 × 4 ft (1.2–2.1 × 1.2 m)
2. *Polygonatum odoratum* 'Variegatum', five plants, 12–24 × 12 in (30–60 × 30 cm)
3. *Miscanthus sinensis* 'Zebrinus', one plant, 60–72 × 36 in (150–185 × 90 cm)

becomes the largest plant and re-determines the scale of the composition. This composition would be improved by the addition of a finely textured, medium-size plant, such as *Asteromoea mongolica*, providing a later season scale transition between the *Miscanthus* and the *Polygonatum*.

Notice that *Polygonatum* is used as a small-scale plant in this composition but is one of the larger plants in the composition in photo 4. This illustrates the design fundamental that a plant's scale and texture are always related to viewing distance and the sizes and textures of associated plants.

The minimum space required for this composition, to include two *Asteromoea mongolica*, is 5 × 6 ft (1.5 × 1.8 m), with one *Crambe* in the rear and one *Miscanthus* placed in front or to one side of the *Crambe*, with two *Asteromoea* in the midground behind five *Polygonatum*.

PHOTO 8. Stonecrop Gardens, Cold Spring, New York, May. ENVIRONMENT: part shade to sun in soil of average fertility and moisture. USDA Zones 5–8. FEATURE: foliage spring to fall; flower mid spring.

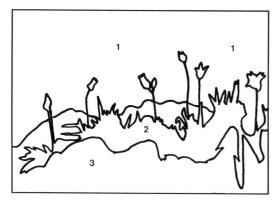

1. *Hedera helix*, 6 ft (1.8 m)
2. *Tulipa* 'White Triumphator', 18–24 × 6 in (45–60 × 15 cm)
3. *Epimedium* × *versicolor* 'Sulphureum', 12 × 12 in (30 × 30 cm)

THREE FREQUENTLY used planting design devices are employed in this simple planting of white tulips rising through the *Epimedium*, with both displayed against a dark background of *Hedera*. The most obvious device is the use of white and near-white combinations to illuminate darker sections of the garden and landscape. A second is the dramatic juxtaposition of light against dark or dark against light. The horticultural trick of allowing one plant to rise through or entwine in the foliage of another is a third.

The contrast of light against dark, provided by the white tulips scattered against a vertical backdrop of ivy, is a particularly important influence on the effectiveness of this composition. Furthermore, the irregular placement of the tulips gives an impression of informality which reflects the character of the larger landscape. Interplanting the bulbs with a groundcovering, such as *Epimedium*, spares one the potentially dismal sight of spindly tulip stems rising from bare soil. Planted in a low-growing groundcover, the tulip stems appear to burst from luxuriant foliage.

This combination does best when grown in a space that provides spring sunshine for the tulips and later season shade for the *Hedera* and *Epimedium*. After the tulips have flowered, the ivy and the medium-textured *Epimedium* leaves would provide an excellent framework for a further appearance from lilies, *Gladiolus callianthus*, or other summer-flowering bulbs.

This composition can be expanded to whatever space is available, with the extent of the vertical ivy wall determined by its context in the garden or landscape.

PHOTO 9. Stonecrop Gardens, Cold Spring, New York, May. ENVIRONMENT: sun to part shade in soil of average fertility and moisture. USDA Zones 3–6. FEATURE: foliage late spring to fall; flower mid to late spring.

YELLOW FLOWERS are produced with greater frequency than any other color except white. Given the abundant choice of yellow-flowering plants, a monochromatic yellow planting is easily accomplished and can be stunning. Most yellow blooms display a pure strong color, with relatively few plants developing flowers in pale or dark yellow. Pure yellow has the advantage that it is highly visible even in intense sunlight and, like other warm colors, its strength is only slightly diminished with distance.

Pale yellow is particularly effective in a lightly shaded garden or one that is frequented at dusk. It is a high-value hue and therefore highly visible, standing out in shaded areas more than any color except white. Since yellow-flowering plants are so abundant, they have been subject to use in a careless or accidental manner—in harsh and jarring color combinations or in associations too powerful or intense for the scale or character of the space. However, the above combination in strong yellow works at its larger scale by including *Trollius* in full flower with *Tulipa* underplanting a large yellow tree peony just in bud. Unless there is a particular desire to continue the yellow theme, annuals of any color may be planted in the space left by the passing of the tulip blooms.

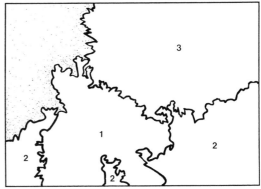

1. *Trollius europeus* 'Superbus', three plants, 12–24 × 12 in (30–60 × 30 cm)
2. *Tulipa* 'Golden Artist', nine bulbs, 14 × 6 in (35 × 15 cm)
3. *Paeonia suffruticosa*, one plant, 4–5 × 4 ft (1.2–1.5 × 1.2 m)

The tree peony requires quite a bit of space relative to its associates. To balance the *Paeonia* mass, one needs three *Trollius* interplanted with six to nine *Tulipa* in a space 4 × 5 ft (1.2 × 1.5 m).

PHOTO 10. Stonecrop Gardens, Cold Spring, New York, July. ENVIRONMENT: sun to part shade in soil of average fertility and moisture. USDA Zones 5–7. FEATURE: foliage mid spring to fall; flower late spring to late summer.

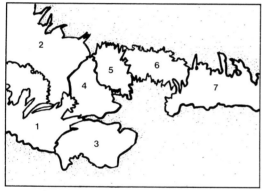

1. *Hemerocallis* 'Colonial Dame', two plants, 18 × 12 in (45 × 30 cm)
2. *Iris pseudacorus*, two plants, 24–36 × 18 in (60–90 × 45 cm)
3. *Alchemilla mollis*, four plants, 12 × 18 in (30 × 45 cm)
4. *Lysimachia punctata*, three plants, 18–30 × 24 in (45–75 × 60 cm)
5. *Phalaris arundinacea* var. *picta*, one plant, 18–36 × 18 in (45–90 × 45 cm)
6. *Lilium* 'French Vanilla', five bulbs, 36 × 12 in (90 × 30 cm)
7. *Verbascum chaixii*, two plants, 30–60 × 18 in (75–150 × 45 cm)

DESIGNING a harmonious herbaceous planting for a large garden space can be simplified by incorporating a dominant color theme. Careful attention must be given to variation in form and texture and to the provision of a clear focus, even if the focus changes every few weeks to avoid monotony. This composition, photographed in midsummer, focuses on the pale *Phalaris* wands and the similarly pale tall mass of lily blooms. Although other plants are flowering in more intense tones of yellow, they are few and subordinated to the dominant vertical clusters which carry attention towards the light and bright center of the composition. In late spring, the important and dominating plant in this composition is the tall yellow *Iris pseudacorus*.

The varied foliage forms and textures have extended ornamental interest, as vertical *Iris* and *Verbascum* spires contrast the lower mounds of *Alchemilla* and the strap-like foliage of *Hemerocallis*. *Verbascum* will rebloom in fall if cut down, but the true glory of this group occurs in midsummer.

An area 6 × 6 ft (1.8 × 1.8 m) will suit one *Phalaris*, two *Iris,* and five *Lilium* in the rear, three *Lysimachia* and two *Verbascum* in the midground, and four *Alchemilla* and two *Hemerocallis* in the foreground. When multiplying plant quantities in monochromatic schemes to fit larger spaces, increasing the quantity of one of the midground components will establish it as the dominant plant and enhance the larger composition.

PHOTO 11. New York Botanical Garden, New York City, August. ENVIRONMENT: sun in soil of average fertility and moisture. USDA Zones 4–8. FEATURE: foliage late spring to fall; flower summer to fall.

LARGE SPACES, particularly in strongly architectural settings, sometimes require boldly simple statements in planting design. A monochromatic scheme, using a single color with green, is one of the simplest and most frequently successful designs. The above setting focuses on two forms: the bold, very floriferous mound of yellow-orange daisies of *Rudbeckia* 'Goldsturm', in display against the plunging, fine-textured grassy foliage of *Miscanthus sinensis* 'Gracillimus'.

Silphium perfoliatum, commonly referred to as the cup plant, is a six or seven foot (about two meters) tall plant that develops yellow daisy-form flowers. It is also included in this composition,

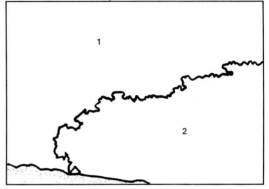

1. *Miscanthus sinensis* 'Gracillimus', one plant, 4–7 × 5 ft (1.2–2.1 × 1.5 m)
2. *Rudbeckia* 'Goldsturm', two plants, 18–24 × 18 in (45–60 × 45 cm)

though it is not visible in the photograph. *Silphium*, placed behind *Miscanthus*, establishes a strong vertical to stretch the scale of the composition while repeating the flower form and color of *Rudbeckia*. The intense orange-yellow *Rudbeckia* flowers persist for many weeks in summer. This characteristic makes it a very useful plant for large spaces, since its mass of advancing color can be counted on to carry boldly across spaces of 75 ft (25 m) or more.

The later, fall bloom of *Miscanthus* provides tall, pale plumes often reaching six or seven feet to extend the planting scale. This composition may be strident and probably too large scale in a space where the viewing distance is less than 20 ft (6 m). It is certainly unsuitable for inclusion in an intimate space where pastel hues and delicate flowering details are featured.

A minimum of 6 × 5 ft (1.8 × 1.5 m) would accommodate three *Silphium perfoliatum* plants behind one *Miscanthus* with two *Rudbeckia* in the foreground.

PHOTO 12. Stonecrop Gardens, Cold Spring, New York, August. ENVIRONMENT: sun to part shade in soil of average fertility and average or greater moisture. USDA Zones 7–8. FEATURE: foliage late spring to fall; flower summer.

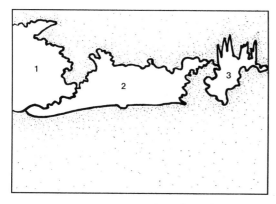

1. *Gunnera manicata*, one plant, 6–7 × 6 ft (1.9–2.1 × 1.9 m)
2. *Ligularia dentata* 'Desdemona', three plants, 36 × 24 in (90 × 60 cm)
3. *Ligularia stenocephala* 'The Rocket', five plants, 48–60 × 24 in (120–150 × 60 cm)

A BOLD, BROAD texture is a desirable contrast for the huge numbers of medium- and fine-textured plants used in garden and landscape design and is often essential to success. Unfortunately, bold, broad-textured plants are few in number. Most are tropical in origin and constrained by hardiness ranges, or they have such particular requirements of culture and exposure that their uses are limited. Broad-leaved plants, such as the enormous *Gunnera manicata* shown here, are especially valuable for highlighting a chosen point in the landscape.

Gunnera manicata is contrasted in this composition with the vertical yellow spires of *Ligularia stenocephala* 'The Rocket' and the mounded *L. dentata* 'Desdemona' with its yellowish orange daisy-like flowers. Both *Ligularia* cultivars develop foliage which in most other situations would be considered broad and bold. Here their leaves are dwarfed by the *Gunnera* and provide a medium range of texture and scale.

The effective period of this planting could be extended by adding the late spring-flowering yellow *Iris pseudacorus* to the group, siting them close to the water line. Yellow-flowering plants are an especially strong choice in relation to this undefined, dark wooded background and dark watery foreground, since the advancing yellow traces the limits of the large spaces in this composition throughout daylight.

A minimum space of 8 × 11 ft (2.4 × 3.4 m) would accommodate one *Gunnera*, five *Ligularia stenocephala* 'The Rocket', and three *L. dentata* 'Desdemona', with eight to nine *Iris pseudacorus* fronting the composition.

PHOTO 13. Henrietta
Lockwood Garden,
Bedford, New York, July.
ENVIRONMENT: sun in
soil of average fertility
and average or less
moisture.
USDA Zones 6–8.
FEATURE: foliage late
spring to fall; flower late
spring to late summer.

PARTLY BECAUSE yellow flowers can be in bloom from early spring to fall, yellow monochromatic plantings are a great temptation. Such plantings require close attention to hue variation, and distinct texture and form variations must be present to avoid monotony. A pleasing yellow and white arrangement is sometimes more effective and easier to create.

The relatively large scale of this yellow and white association is determined by *Heliopsis scabra*, a plant valuable for the length of its blooming period and the dense texture of its dark green foliage mass, against which one can display other blooms. The daisy form of its flowers contrasts with the narrow *Lysimachia* spires and bold *Oenothera* clusters. The variations in yellow tones and forms are emphasized by the unifying effect of the field of white and yellow tanacetum.

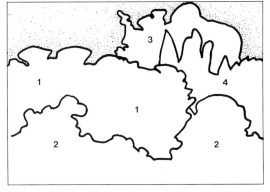

1. *Tanacetum parthenium*, three plants, 12–36 × 12 in (30–90 × 30 cm)
2. *Oenothera tetragona*, five plants, 18 × 12 in (45 × 30 cm)
3. *Heliopsis scabra*, one plant, 36–60 × 24 in (90–150 × 60 cm)
4. *Lysimachia punctata*, two plants, 18–30 × 24 in (45–75 × 60 cm)

The effectiveness of the tanacetum as a loose lacy field depends on its characteristic of abundant self-seeding. The composition may be most effective in its second year when the tanacetum has had the opportunity to self-seed among its companions. All the plants included here are of easy culture and can multiply to the point of invasiveness. They will all require careful watching and occasional judicious removal.

The group requires a minimum space 4 × 5 ft (1.2 × 1.5 m), with one *Heliopsis* in the background, two *Lysimachia* and three *Tanacetum* in the midground, and five *Oenothera* in the foreground.

PHOTO 14. Stonecrop Gardens, Cold Spring, New York, June. ENVIRONMENT: sun to part shade in soil of average fertility and moisture. USDA Zones 5–7. FEATURE: foliage late spring to fall; flower late spring to late summer.

1. *Argyranthemum frutescens*, three plants, 12–30 × 12 in (30–75 × 30 cm)
2. *Solidago* 'Cloth of Gold', two plants, 20 × 12 in (50 × 30 cm)
3. *Iris pseudacorus*, two plants, 24–36 × 18 in (60–90 × 45 cm)
4. *Aruncus dioicus*, one plant, 48–72 × 36 in (120–185 × 90 cm)
5. *Digitalis grandiflora*, three plants, 24–36 × 18 in (60–90 × 45 cm)
6. *Weigela florida* 'Variegata', one plant, 4–5 × 4 ft (1.2–1.5 × 1.2 m)

WHEN CONFRONTED by a space which is formed in part by the wall of a building or a high fence, it is often convenient to use large shrubs as part of a planting. Shrubbery can add a stable three-dimensional shift in scale from the large vertical wall or fence to the smaller horizontal scale of an herbaceous composition.

A background *Weigela* shrub, placed in front of a fence, expands the scale of this small herbaceous group to fit both the garden space and its tall perimeter. Its pale red-violet, late spring flowers do not quite harmonize with this yellow and white composition, but fortunately their blooming period is brief. For the balance of the growing season, its light-edged leaves brighten a dark corner and give a finely textured appearance to contrast nicely with the smooth ascending form of the large *Iris* leaves and the feathery *Aruncus* foliage. This yellow *Iris* usually flowers first, followed by *Aruncus* and pale yellow *Digitalis*. Summer-flowering *Argyranthemum* carries the group's flowering period well until frost, being joined in late summer by the dark yellow *Solidago* spikes. Adding a broader textured plant, such as a hosta or another iris, to the right and fronting the *Weigela* would strengthen the textural composition.

Eliminating the *Weigela*, an area 5 × 5 ft (1.5 × 1.5 m) is enough for a minimum arrangement of one *Aruncus* plant in the rear, with two *Iris*, two *Solidago*, and three *Digitalis* in the midground, and three *Argyranthemum* plants in the foreground. Including the *Weigela* requires another 5 × 5 ft (1.5 × 1.5 m) space to be added to this composition.

PHOTO 15. Barnsley House, near Cirencester, Gloucestershire, England, July. ENVIRONMENT: sun to part shade in soil of average fertility and moisture. USDA Zones 5–8. FEATURE: foliage mid spring to fall; flower mid spring to fall.

OFTEN IN garden and landscape design, one goal is the visual arrangement of formless spaces into shapes and proportions with which humans feel at ease. Periodic repetition of intense color is one of the simpler ways to define spaces visually. The yellow used here carries a viewer's interest throughout the entire space.

Corydalis lutea is the principal source of yellow in the background. The yellow-green *Alchemilla mollis* flowers are principal to the foreground. Yet the color theme is also evident in the shrubs' yellow leaf margins, as effective a design element as the yellow blossoms.

Because the scale of the chosen plants is small, the textures fine to medium, and the quantity of color presented by the various blooms and different foli-

1. *Argyranthemum frutescens*, 12–30 × 12 in (30–75 × 30 cm)
2. *Helichrysum petiolare*, 12–24 × 24 in (30–60 × 60 cm)
3. *Corydalis lutea*, 9–15 × 12 in (25–40 × 30 cm)
4. *Alchemilla mollis*, 12 × 18 in (30 × 45 cm)

ages rather small and scattered, these particular plants are most effective in a relatively limited space. This outdoor area is about 8 × 12 ft (2.5 × 3.7 m). In a larger space, the mass of color should be proportionately increased and much larger plants would be needed to create a similar visual effect.

The white-flowering *Argyranthemum* and the very pale, gray yellow-green *Helichrysum* in the portable containers contribute fresh forms and textures, as well as brightness, and preserve the design from any possibility of monotony. These plants could be combined together in the ground, but it is the partial elevation of some of them in containers which makes them so effective as space organizers. In the ground, where the maximum height would probably not exceed 24 in (60 cm) there would be a loss of visual influence.

PHOTO 16. Wave Hill, Bronx, New York, April. ENVIRONMENT: sun in soil of average fertility and average or less moisture. USDA Zones 3–7. FEATURE: foliage early spring to late summer; flower early to mid spring.

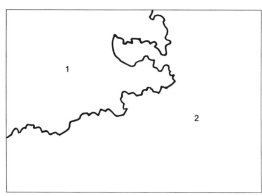

1. *Iberis sempervirens* 'Snowflake', two plants, 8–10 × 18 in (20–25 × 45 cm)
2. *Aurinia saxatilis*, two plants, 8–10 × 12 in (20–25 × 30 cm)

COMPOSITIONS in which all three dimensions are exploited to create depth are often the most compelling. Yet here is a situation which requires plants simply to clothe or decorate horizontally. This situation is typical with already clearly defined forms—mounds, slopes, geometric patterns, or horizontal structures such as walls and steps. Small-scale prostrate plants, such as *Aurinia saxatilis* and *Iberis sempervirens* shown here, are among many which are useful in these largely two-dimensional goals.

This very basic yellow and white combination for the early spring is often seen in rock gardens where rock defines shape. Pure yellow and white is a strong color association. It is visible over a great distance and may be used to restrain larger garden spaces and tie them together with powerful repetition. However, the intensity of these two colors may be too bold among the fragile forms and delicate hues of many early spring flowers. In a small space, or in association with delicate bloom colors, the pale lemon-yellow of *Alyssum saxatilis* 'Citrinum' may be a more pleasing associate for *Iberis*.

As *Iberis* is an evergreen prostrate woody shrub, its finely textured dark green foliage is valuable year-round. During the growing season it makes a striking light/dark contrast with the gray yellow-green *Aurinia* foliage.

Aurinia and *Iberis* may be planted in equal amounts with a minimum of two each for a decorative effect. An area 2 × 3 ft (0.6 × 0.9 m) is required for a minimal planting.

PHOTO 17. Caramoor Center for Music and the Arts, Katonah, New York, August. ENVIRONMENT: sun in soil of average fertility and moisture. USDA Zones 5–8. FEATURE: foliage late spring to fall; flower late spring to fall.

PALE YELLOW and pure white is a simple and pleasing color combination. The paler the yellow (that is, the greater the proportion of white in its color), the greater the easy harmony of the overall composition. Here this common color association makes a promising beginning with three easily grown annuals. All will continue to thrive in summer heat.

Marigolds (*Tagetes*) are justifiably popular, undemanding, strongly scented flowers, useful in many difficult situations. However, their somewhat pudgy, dense form implies a design demand for an ascending spire or contrast of lighter textures and looser forms to lessen their rather squat nature. *Cleome*, with its height and fine, airy texture contributes a much-needed contrast.

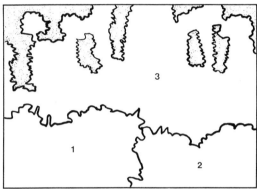

1. *Tagetes* 'Primrose Lady', one plant, 15 × 15 in (40 × 40 cm)
2. *Zinnia* 'Dreamland Ivory', two plants, 12–15 × 12 in (30–40 × 30 cm)
3. *Cleome spinosa* 'Helen Campbell', three plants, 24–60 × 12 in (60–150 × 30 cm)

One weakness in this composition is the similarity in both height and bloom size of the marigold and zinnia. The composition could be strengthened by substituting a taller, pale marigold such as *Tagetes* 'Snowbird'. Also, at this early summer stage the composition lacks the advantage of a bold leaf texture. An emerging group of fragrant *Gladiolus callianthus*, just visible at left, rising through and above the *Tagetes* and *Zinnia* will bring a desirable vertical form and foliage strength with its iris-like leaves. A single broad-leafed *Nicotiana sylvestris* at the rear would also add fragrance and improve the composition where space permits.

The extended composition requires a minimum space 3 × 3 ft (0.9 × 0.9 m), with three *Cleome* in the rear, five *Gladiolus callianthus* in the midground, and one *Tagetes* and two *Zinnia* in the foreground. Including the *Nicotiana sylvestris* in back with the *Cleome* requires an additional 1.5 × 2 ft (0.4 × 0.6 m).

PHOTO 18. Stonecrop Gardens, Cold Spring, New York, July. ENVIRONMENT: sun in soil of average fertility and average or less moisture. USDA Zones 5–9. FEATURE: foliage summer to fall; flower summer to fall.

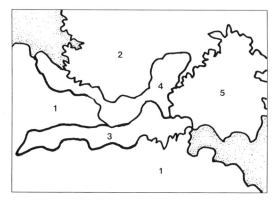

1. *Knautia macedonica*, three plants, 24 × 18 in (60 × 45 cm)
2. *Prunus* × *cistena*, one plant, 4–7 × 5 ft (1.2–2.1 × 1.5 m)
3. *Perilla frutescens*, three plants, 24–36 × 18 in (60–90 × 45 cm)
4. *Cosmos bipinnatus* 'Versailles Tetra', three plants, 36–48 × 18 in (90–120 × 45 cm)
5. *Rosa* 'Prospero', one plant, 30 × 30 in (75 × 75 cm)

CAREFULLY displayed dark red blooms can unobtrusively define space. The dark red color, although powerful, does not advance or dominate the landscape as much as a floral pure red. The deeper the red used to highlight the landscape, the greater will be the feeling of tranquillity. In sunny hot climates, the use of dark red oddly generates a soothing feeling of coolness. This is especially true of dark red and/or dark red-violet foliage, such as seen in the *Perilla* above.

In this particular example, adjacent warm and cool reds mingle together—an often hazardous association with pure bright hues. Such hazards have been minimized by the unifying blackness present in all these low-value dark or very dark reds and red-violets.

This tranquil grouping will have a long period of bloom in summer and late summer when *Cosmos*, *Knautia*, and *Rosa* bloom heavily. *Cosmos* flowers well into the fall, continuing to stand out against dark-foliaged companions when *Knautia* and *Rosa* have ceased blooming.

The large *Prunus* × *cistena* shrub determines the space required for this entire planting. An area 7 × 7 ft (2 × 2 m) will fit one *Prunus* in the background, one *Rosa* 'Prospero' and three *Cosmos* in the midground, with three *Knautia* and three *Perilla* in the foreground.

PHOTO 19. Clapton Court Gardens, Crewkerne, Somerset, England, July. ENVIRONMENT: part shade to sun in soil of average fertility and moisture. USDA Zones 5–8. FEATURE: foliage late spring to fall; flower late spring to summer.

THE DIFFERENCES between red and red-violet are difficult to judge in some plants, and often it is not necessary to make a precise distinction. Red-violet in flowers is sometimes not a clear hue, tilting towards red or toward violet even within the same plant. I have seen flowering plants identified as *Geranium* 'Wargrave Pink' which have a decidedly red-violet cast to their pale blossoms while others appear more purely pale red. Such ambiguity can be rather useful.

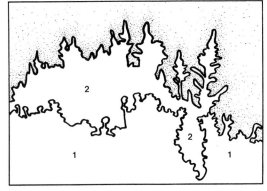

1. *Geranium endressii* 'Wargrave Pink', one plant, 12–24 × 24 in (30–60 × 60 cm)
2. *Astilbe × arendsii* 'Cattleya', two plants, 36 × 18 in (90 x 45 cm)

This geranium develops a large mound of graceful foliage and a sprinkling of pale flowers, mixing easily with its warm- and cool-hued neighbors. 'Wargrave Pink' connects especially well with flowering plants of equal pastel tinting. Associating *Geranium* 'Wargrave Pink' here with a stronger, cool pink *Astilbe* in light shade provides a soothing repetition of the same hue in appealingly different forms while neither plant dominates the setting.

It is easy to appreciate both the strong vertical form and more powerful color of the *Astilbe* and the airy restrained grace of the companionable *Geranium*. The geranium's pale flower color stands out eagerly in light shade, producing a strong three-dimensional quality in this simple composition. *Geranium* also thrives in sun, and another association with different soil and exposure conditions can be seen in photo 144.

This easy association will require a minimum space of 3 × 3 ft (0.9 × 0.9 m), with two *Astilbe* behind one *Geranium*.

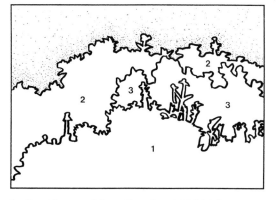

PHOTO 20.
Conservatory Garden,
New York City, August.
ENVIRONMENT: sun in
soil of average fertility
and moisture.
USDA Zones 5–8.
FEATURE: foliage
summer to fall; flower
summer to fall.

1. *Gomphrena globosa* 'Strawberry Fields', three plants, 12–24 × 12 in (30–60 × 30 cm)
2. *Zinnia elegans* 'Red Sun', one plant, 36 × 24 in (90 × 60 cm)
3. *Perilla frutescens*, two plants, 24–36 × 18 in (60–90 × 45 cm)

SEVERAL techniques can unify a monochromatic color design while preserving it from dullness. One is the repetition of a dominant form with only minor color variations, as seen with the tulips in photo 21. Another technique is the use of incremental tone variations, perhaps from the pure hue through several lighter tints or darker tones, as in photo 27. A third way is to use a single tone of one color but to vary the forms. This planting is a skillful example of that technique.

The reds used are not precisely the same, since *Gomphrena* blooms tends towards red-orange, but with minimal distancing the globose *Gomphrena* flowers appear the same red as the daisy-like blooms of *Zinnia elegans* 'Red Sun'. Variation in flower form is emphasized by contrasting the flowers against darker backgrounds or occasionally, although less effectively, against each other. *Gomphrena* blooms are highlighted by the darker-toned adjacent color of deep red-violet *Perilla* leaves while the *Zinnia* blooms enjoy a background of smooth dark green from the sheared hedge.

The sheared hedge is not an essential background for this combination, which could be freestanding, but the hedge certainly eliminates distractions and focuses attention entirely on the flower forms. The three basic plants could be fitted in a minimum space of 3 × 4 ft (0.9 × 1.2 m), with one *Zinnia* in the background, two *Perilla* in the midground, and three *Gomphrena* in the foreground.

PHOTO 21. Stonecrop Gardens, Cold Spring, New York, May. ENVIRONMENT: sun in soil of average fertility and moisture. USDA Zones 4–8. FEATURE: foliage late spring to fall; flower late spring.

THE PERCEPTION of color is moderated to some extent by adjacent hues. The red of *Tulipa* 'Red Shine' appears even more brilliant because of the darkness of the deep red-orange *Berberis* foliage. To a lesser extent its impact is heightened by the very deep red-violet of *Tulipa* 'Queen of Night'. These red tulips would add a pleasingly bright element against green foliage, as seen with the few tulip flowers poised against a tendril of vine on the background fence. However, as seen in photo 20, red blooms can appear brilliant against a smooth, very dark green background, such as a sheared yew hedge. This composition would be improved by placing the darker and smaller *Tulipa* 'Queen of Night' in the foreground so *T.* 'Red Shine' acts as a background, offering greater contrast than does the *Berberis*.

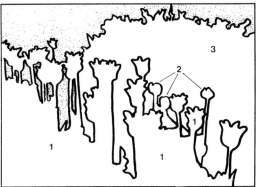

1. *Tulipa* 'Red Shine', eight bulbs, 24 × 6 in (60 × 15 cm)
2. *Tulipa* 'Queen of Night', twelve bulbs, 24 × 6 in (60 × 15 cm)
3. *Berberis thunbergii* 'Atropurpurea', one plant, 5 × 5 ft (1.5 × 1.5 m)

The *Berberis* shrub is an excellent, easily pruned, and frequently used background for many flowering compositions. Its foliage color ranges from deep red-violet to deep red-orange, although usually its color is concentrated in the warm hues. It harmonizes with all adjacent warm tones as well as the complementary bluish greens.

Using *Berberis thunbergii* 'Atropurpurea' increases the scale of this planting, and a minimum space of 5 × 6 ft (1.5 × 1.8 m) would permit one *Berberis*, eight *Tulipa* 'Red Shine' in the midground, and twelve *T.* 'Queen of Night' in the foreground. Appropriate groundcovers could be planted to share the space occupied by the tulips (see photo 8).

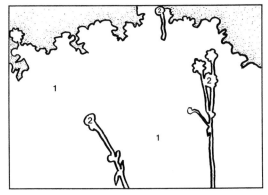

1. *Centranthus ruber*, three plants, 18–24 × 12 in (45–60 × 30)
2. *Knautia macedonica*, three plants, 24 x 18 in (60 × 45 cm)

WHEN FLOWER color is modified by graying, as opposed to lightening with white or darkening with black, the result is a reduction in color intensity. Graying is unusual in flowers although it occurs frequently in foliage. These less intense colors are excellent contrasts for more vivid companions in the same or adjacent hues. The blooms of some varieties of *Dicentra eximia*, *Echinops*, and many *Sedum*, as well as the *Centranthus ruber* used here, have this dusky, neutral quality. The flush of late spring *Centranthus* blooms is a fine foil for brilliant, intense dark reds, such as the long-blooming *Knautia* used here. *Centranthus* works equally well for such dark red annuals as *Antirrhinum majus* 'Frontier Crimson'. I would hesitate to recommend connecting this grayed bloom color with the bright pure reds, but slightly darker or slightly lighter reds contrast well.

Centranthus also combines well with bluish violet blooms, such as *Geranium* 'Johnson's Blue', various *Salvia × superba* cultivars, and *Lavandula*, since its own subdued hue allows their more saturated colors to gain force by contrast. This particular composition would be improved by adding significantly more dark red-flowering *Knautia* or adding a group of *Antirrhinum* 'Frontier Crimson'. The greater presence of a dark hue is needed to make a statement against the mass of *Centranthus* blooms.

A space 3 × 4 ft (0.9 × 1.2 m) would suit three *Centranthus* interplanted with four *Knautia*. Two *Antirrhinum majus* 'Frontier Crimson' could be sited to one side, increasing the space requirement to 3 × 5 ft (0.9 × 1.5 m).

PHOTO 23. Cloister Hotel, Sea Island, Georgia, May. ENVIRONMENT: sun in soil of average or less fertility with average or less moisture. USDA Zones 5–9. FEATURE: foliage mid spring to fall; flower mid spring to fall.

SMALLER-SCALE plants with intense red blooms abound among annuals. This *Celosia* 'New Look' is currently widely available. *Salvia splendens* 'Blaze of Fire' is another frequently used plant with similar coloring. Both are very attractive and their intense bloom colors and distinct form make strong statements in any garden or landscape. Associated plants must be chosen with care so the boldness of their coloring is employed to enhance the landscape rather than to unsettle the viewer or exhaust the eye. Since they will certainly be the focus in any composition, careful placement within that composition and within the larger landscape setting is essential.

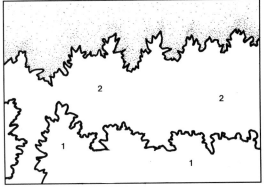

1. *Senecio cineraria* 'Silver Queen', one plant, 8 × 8 in (20 × 20 cm)
2. *Celosia plumosa* 'New Look', five plants, 12–15 × 12 in (30–40 × 30 cm)

Grading nearby colors to darker or lighter reds or to adjacent warm hues, such as red-orange, orange, and yellow-orange, or contrasting them with a complementary dark green will take best advantage of these powerful colors. Sudden shifts from bright red to white or to near-white silvery foliage are often jarring and visually tiring. White and red scream equally for attention in most situations. Such radical and ultimately boring shifts may be useful where the goal is to bring the viewer's attention to a certain point immediately and abruptly. I presume this is the reason such color combination are used so frequently in public spaces. I find designs that permit one hue to dominate while the other merely accents to be much more pleasing. A dash of red among silver-foliaged plants, as in photo 5, or a scattering of white to deftly lighten a predominantly red planting, as in photo 24, are usually more pleasing than rigid adherence to equal linear masses of each color.

For this composition five *Celosia* with one *Senecio* in a space 2 × 2 ft (0.6 × 0.6 m) would ensure a strong yet enticing statement.

PHOTO 24. Dorset, England, August. ENVIRONMENT: sun in soil of average or less fertility and average moisture. USDA Zones 7–8. FEATURE: foliage late spring to fall; flower late spring to late summer.

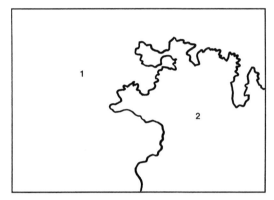

1. *Papaver rhoeas,* 12–24 × 12 in (30–60 × 30 cm)
2. *Leucanthemum vulgare,* 12–30 × 12 in (30–75 × 30 cm)

A SMALL AMOUNT of pure red goes a very long way in any scale of landscape. Red carries powerfully over distance and has almost as much impact on adjacent colors as white. In similar quantities, red and white attract attention more or less equally. Yet both red and white seem to drain the strength from associated hues and need to be used sparingly and thoughtfully with other colors and with each other.

A dominant red planting with a scattering of white, such as the naturally-occurring meadow association pictured here, is captivating. Its spirit can be translated to the planned garden or landscape setting in many ways. Red or white occurring in sparsely blooming plants, such as *Salvia* 'Lady in Red' or *Asteromoea mongolica,* or in billowy, cloudlike or diaphanous flowering forms, like *Gypsophila* or *Crambe cordifolia,* readily adapt to planting schemes.

Unfortunately, pure red blooms predominantly appear in dense and concentrated forms and rarely in a billowy manner. Sometimes combining red and white in markedly uneven quantities, intentionally making one plant the focus, improves their association.

I once saw a clever transition from a formally planted area to a pasture by means of a grassy bank of *Tanacetum parthenium* laced with self-seeded *Papaver rhoeas.* Similar airy-textured combinations of red and white blooms can be created by using the compact white *Cosmos bipinnatus* 'Sonata White' and *Salvia* 'Lady in Red' or *Cleome spinosa* 'Helen Campbell' and *Monarda didyma* 'Cambridge Scarlet'. See Part 2 for details on plant sizes for any of these associations.

PHOTO 25. Conservatory Garden, New York City, April.
ENVIRONMENT: sun to part shade in soil of average fertility and moisture.
USDA Zones 4–9.
FEATURE: foliage mid spring to late spring; flower mid spring.

PALE COLORS predominate in spring-flowering native plants in the northern regions, and nature's color theme is continued in this association of white with pink. Pink is simply red or red-violet lightened with white and it is the presence of white in both these bloom colors that lends unity to the composition. This harmony is further emphasized by the repetition of pendulous, bell-like forms in both flowers.

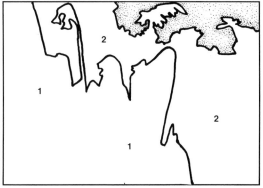

1. *Leucojum aestivum* 'Gravetye Giant', five plants, 24 × 4 in (60 × 10 cm)
2. *Dicentra spectabilis*, one plant, 24–36 × 18 in (60–90 × 45 cm)

The foliage of both these plants dies by early summer. The resultant void may or may not be significant depending on the location of the group. This pairing is often used to provide ephemeral spring display at the base of rhododendrons and other spring-flowering shrubs. It may not be significant that bare ground or mulch is visible past spring in such locations. Where foliage is required for the remainder of the growing season, later-emerging perennial plants with slowly expanding leaves, such as *Hosta* or *Brunnera macrophylla*, may be planted alongside *Dicentra* so their foliage will cover the bare spaces.

Ideally, the *Leucojum* stems, which have no basal foliage, should rise through a base of foliage provided by a companion plant. *Epimedium* × *versicolor* 'Sulphureum', *Lamium maculatum* cultivars, *Myosotis sylvatica,* or *Vinca minor* are perennials frequently used for this purpose. The basic pairing of *Dicentra* and *Leucojum* may be fitted into a space 2 × 2 ft (0.6 × 0.6 m), with a minimum of one *Dicentra* in the rear and five or six *Leucojum* bulbs in the foreground. See Part 2 for further information on the companion plants mentioned.

PHOTO 26. New York Botanical Garden, New York City, May. ENVIRONMENT: part shade in soil of average fertility and average to greater moisture. USDA Zones 5–7. FEATURE: foliage mid spring to fall; flower mid spring to fall.

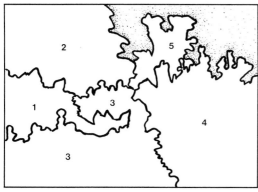

1. *Hosta fortunei* 'Marginato-alba', one plant, 12–18 × 24 in. (30–45 × 60 cm)
2. *Cimicifuga racemosa*, two plants, 36–60 × 24 in (90–150 × 60 cm)
3. *Dicentra eximia* 'Luxuriant', three plants, 12–18 × 12 in (30–45 × 30 cm)
4. *Aquilegia* (unknown) cultivar, five plants, 18–24 × 15 in (45–60 × 40 cm)
5. *Thalictrum aquilegifolium* 'Album', one plant, 36–48 × 36 in (90–120 × 90 cm)

ASSOCIATIONS of pink and white have none of the design hazards of red and white. Their many advantages, especially for light shade, include a large selection of plants to choose from with pink or pale red blooms, with white flowers, or with white-edged foliage, and with bloom times ranging from late spring until early fall.

Some, such as the *Dicentra* shown here, bloom almost continuously from spring to fall and associate easily with a succession of companions in the same hue. White blooms and foliage with white markings, such as the *Hosta* in this group, are clearly visible in shade and in all low-light situations. The white component of all pastel hues also allows them to shine in low light, and the paler the pink blooms selected for these combinations the more visible they will be in light shade.

The flowers of all these plants are light textured and freely scattered above their foliage, so that none is more dense and dominant than another. This group combines an easy color scheme with striking variation in foliage textures, sustaining the association's complex appeal when bloom is finished. The hosta's broad, variegated mass contrasts with the finely textured gray-green *Dicentra* and *Thalictrum* leaves and with the lighter green, medium-textured *Cimicifuga* foliage. *Aquilegia* 'Rose Queen' could substitute for this unknown cultivar.

This group will require a space 5 × 6 ft (1.5 × 1.8 m), with one *Thalictrum* and two *Cimicifuga* in the rear, five *Aquilegia* in the midground, and three *Dicentra* and one *Hosta* in the foreground.

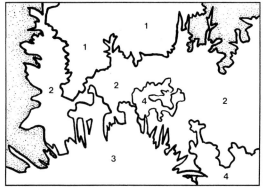

PHOTO 27. Henrietta Lockwood Garden, Bedford, New York, July. ENVIRONMENT: sun in soil of average fertility and moisture. USDA Zones 5–7. FEATURE: foliage late spring to fall; flower late spring to summer.

THE COMBINATIONS that may be made with various tints and shades of red-violet are almost unlimited. Numerous plants in cultivation flower or develop foliage in that color. Unlike some other hues, such as yellow, which is almost entirely seen in the pure and pale shades, red-violet flowers and foliage are available in practically every tint and shade. From the very palest to the very deepest, they lend themselves to all sorts of enticing experiments with flower form and juxtapositions of light and dark.

In this group there is a tonal range from the very pale umbels of *Allium senescens,* to the darker magenta tint of *A. cernuum,* to the dark red-violet *Clematis* flowers, and finally to the very deepest red of the annual *Atriplex hortensis* 'Cupreata' foliage. This long gradation of tints and shades within one hue readily succeeds in reds and red-violets and in foliar greens. Such an exercise is far more difficult in flowers of all the other hues because of the limited range of tints and shades.

1. *Clematis* (unknown) cultivar, one plant, 6–10 ft (1.8–3.0 m)
2. *Atriplex hortensis* 'Cupreata', one plant, 12–48 × 18 in (30–120 × 45 cm)
3. *Allium senescens*, three bulbs, 12–18 × 12 in (30–45 × 30 cm)
4. *Allium cernuum*, three bulbs, 12–18 × 12 in (30–45 × 30 cm)

A space 3 × 3 ft (0.9 × 0.9 m) will accommodate one *Clematis* on a fence or other support, with one *Atriplex* making a background for three *Allium cernuum* and three *A. senescens* in the foreground. *Clematis × jackmanii* could substitute for this unknown cultivar. *Perilla frutescens*, though not as tall, could substitute for *Atriplex*. *Perilla frutescens* generally reaches a height of just 24–36 in (60–90 cm) and has comparable space requirements.

PHOTO 28. Stonecrop Gardens, Cold Spring, New York, July. ENVIRONMENT: sun in soil of average moisture and fertility. USDA Zones 5–7. FEATURE: foliage late spring to fall; flower late spring to fall.

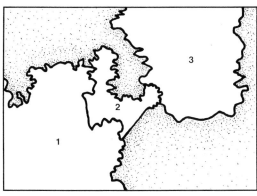

1. *Astrantia major*, one plant, 24–30 × 12–18 in (60–75 × 30–45 cm)
2. *Cleome spinosa* 'Pink Queen', three plants, 24–60 × 12 in (60–150 × 30 cm)
3. *Cosmos bipinnatus* 'Pinkie', two plants, 36–48 × 18 in (90–120 × 45 cm)

MANY GARDEN designers prefer to allot specific areas to the different flowering seasons. For example, spring-flowering bulbs will occupy one space, perhaps with an interplanting of ferns or other perennials to disguise the later decline of bulb bloom and foliage. Another area will offer late spring flowers, another midsummer blooms, and so on. The great merit of this scheme is that it permits a sensational concentration of bloom for that particular period.

However, limitations set by the size of the planted area and the time available to care for it often do not permit dedicating a special area to each season. If a fairly continuous display of bloom is desired in a limited space, it is best to choose long-blooming plants such as the cosmos and the lightly scented cleome used here. A simple color scheme of green foliage with blooms in a single color or in two adjacent or complementary colors will ensure color harmony with modest effort. The pale red and pale red-violet hues are an excellent choice for this purpose since so many plants flower in those hues.

Foliage forms are nebulous and indistinct. This hazy quality allows focus on the broad flower forms in cosmos and cleome. Adding another broader and larger flower form such as a tall *Lilium* 'Silver Elegance Strain' would bring even stronger focus to the composition.

This composition of two readily available annuals and the valuable, under-used perennial *Astrantia major*, may be placed alone or to strengthen other annual or perennial combinations and will provide a very long season of bloom with little effort. A few repetitions of this group can provide the backbone of a summer flowering scheme.

A space 3 × 3 ft (0.9 × 0.9 m) will accommodate two *Cosmos* and three *Cleome* mingled with one *Astrantia*. Adding one *Lilium* will increase space requirements to 3 × 4 ft (0.9 × 1.2 m).

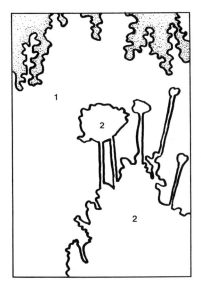

1. *Salvia sclarea*, one plant, 36–60
   × 36 in (90–150 × 90 cm)
2. *Papaver somniferum*, three
   plants, 30 × 12 in (75 × 30 cm)

PHOTO 29. Stourton House Garden, Wiltshire, England, July. ENVIRONMENT: sun in soil of average fertility and moisture. USDA Zones 8–9. FEATURE: foliage late spring to fall; flower summer.

A REDUCTION in color intensity by graying occurs in very few flowers, although it is often evident in foliage. The tinting or shading of individual colors is more important than color intensity in planting design and is more easily judged. Nevertheless, occasionally it is appropriate to observe relative variations in the intensity of flower color. The garden designer may wish to use this phenomenon in a design or perhaps compensate for dilution effects by increasing mass.

This lessening of color intensity and the addition of a certain grayed quality is very evident in this association of two plants of similarly softened hue. The foreground *Papaver* has a pale red-violet bloom. Yet its relative color intensity shows it to be not nearly as pale or as grayed as the tiny, diffuse *Salvia* blooms. The background *Salvia* allows the flower form of the slightly stronger-hued *Papaver* to shine.

Both the papavers and salvias display foliage in a soft gray-green color which harmonizes beautifully with pale red-violet blooms. Both foliages are also broad-textured, a comparatively rare quality that, contrasted with the hazy *Salvia* blooms, makes a valuable contribution to this composition. This grayed, restrained presentation of the much vilified magenta hue looks wonderful in large groups. A foreground grouping of *Lavandula angustifolia* 'Hidcote' will contribute basal mass to *Papaver* and *Salvia*. When associated with other colors, relatively large amounts of this pair may be needed to maintain pleasing color balance with other more brilliant hues. Transitions to other colors may also be handled by introducing gray-foliaged plants.

A minimal planting of one *Salvia* with three *Papaver* requires 3 × 4 ft (0.9 × 1.2 m). Including three *Lavandula angustifolia* 'Hidcote' in the foreground increases the space required to 3 × 5 ft (0.9 × 1.5 m).

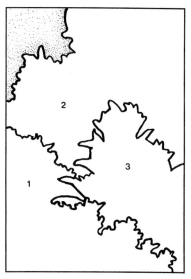

1. *Salvia officinalis* 'Purpurea',
   fifteen plants, 12–18 × 12 in
   (30–45 × 30 cm)
2. *Syringa microphylla* 'Superba',
   one plant, 4–6 × 6 ft (1.2–1.8 ×
   1.8 m)
3. *Symphytum officinale*, one plant,
   36 × 36 in (90 × 90 cm)

PHOTO 30. Denmans, West Sussex, England, April. ENVIRONMENT: sun to part shade in soil of average fertility and moisture. USDA Zones 5–7. FEATURE: foliage mid spring to fall; flower mid spring to summer.

BROAD-TEXTURED foliage is often used as a dominant design element and needs to be balanced by at least an equal mass of any finer-textured associates. The amount of *Syringa* bloom and *Salvia* foliage visible in the photograph is almost exactly right for the mass of the broad-leaved *Symphytum*. The *Salvia* is a well-chosen base planting since it also offers a dark hue to anchor the composition while nicely embracing the fragrant dwarf *Syringa* and the *Symphytum*.

Symphytum blooms are pendulous, diminutive drops of light and dark red-violet. These surprising blooms repeat the hue of the dwarf *Syringa* flowers and the *Salvia* foliage and make a very skillful association when their brief flowering periods coincide. Furthermore, the light yellowish green *Symphytum* foliage is complemented by its opposite color in the dark red-violet sage.

However, as *Symphytum* develops it will occupy a space twice that seen here in a spring photograph. By summer it will probably overgrow and obscure much of the purple sage foliage and throw this excellent composition out of balance. If more sage is added, this trio will offer a splendid association of foliage colors, forms, and textures until early fall. This dwarf *Syringa* often reaches 4–5 ft (1.2–1.5 m) in height and width and will appear at its best if balanced by an equally large foreground planting.

One *Syringa* in the background with one *Symphytum* in the midground and at least fifteen *Salvia* wrapping around the foreground will require a space 6 × 9 ft (1.8 × 2.7 m).

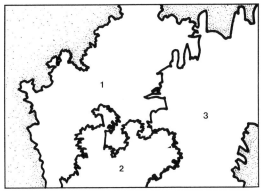

PHOTO 31. Henrietta Lockwood Garden, Bedford, New York, August.
ENVIRONMENT: sun in soil of average or less fertility and average or less moisture.
USDA Zones 4–7.
FEATURE: foliage late spring to fall; flower mid to late summer.

O UR PERCEPTIONS of space are affected by the colors used within that space. Distance is visually reduced and spaces made to seem smaller by warm colors in the landscape, especially red, red-orange, and yellow. Cool colors, such as blue, violet, and red-violet, may increase the sense of distance. Using cooler colors at the rear of other plantings will introduce a haziness which gives the illusion of expanded space.

Agastache foeniculum planted in large groups is one medium-scale plant whose hazy violet blooms can successfully create an expanded feeling of space. It combines well with its adjacent hues in the lighter red-violet and blue-violet blooms, as well as with silvery, gray-hued plants. This simple, easily grown association is of medium to large scale and could be the beginning of a long series of variations on themes of gray and cool-hued blooms.

1. *Malva moschata*, two plants, 24–36 × 18 in (60–90 × 45 cm)
2. *Eryngium giganteum*, one plant, 36–48 × 36 in (90–120 × 90 cm)
3. *Agastache foeniculum*, three plants, 24–60 × 18 in (60–150 × 45 cm)

The very light red-violet blooms contributed by *Malva* seem more sparkling for being associated with the gray of *Eryngium* and the grayed light violet of *Agastache*. The forms of these plants are significantly varied to assure interest—from the spiked *Agastache* contrasting the stiff, gray, thistlelike *Eryngium*, to the softer, flat, smaller-scale *Malva* blooms. This group needs to be grown in average to poor soil since too rich a soil and too much moisture or too little sun causes the plants to stretch too high and quickly flop down if they are not staked.

A space 4 × 5 ft (1.2 × 1.5 m) will accommodate one *Eryngium* in the background, three *Agastache* in the midground, and two *Malva* in the foreground.

PHOTO 32. Russian River, California, September. ENVIRONMENT: sun in soil of average fertility and moisture. USDA Zones 5–8. FEATURE: foliage late spring to late summer; flower late spring to late summer.

1. *Lobularia maritima* 'Carpet of Snow', one plant, 3 × 12 in (10 × 30 cm)
2. *Salvia splendens* (unknown) cultivar, three plants, 12 × 12 in (30 × 30 cm)
3. *Lobularia maritima* 'Royal Carpet', one plant, 3 × 12 in (10 × 30 cm)
4. *Petunia* 'Burgundy Madness', three plants, 9–12 × 12 in (25–30 × 30 cm)

WHEN BALANCING arrangements of powerful colors, the quality of isolation or quantity of color provided by each plant in bloom is an especially important consideration. Some plants, such as the *Lobularia* here, have numerous flower heads densely packed with color. Others, such as the *Salvia* in this group may provide highlight color scattered and isolated against foliage. These different flower forms affect color distribution and consequently color balance.

Note that the scale here is very small. The dominant red-violet hue would not have as much impact as in mid-size or large-scale plants with similarly intense colors, such as if *Liatris spicata* or *Echinacea purpurea* were used. Also, the strength of the hue is weakened as if it were tinted by the presence of a small amount of white in the *Salvia* blooms, in *Lobularia maritima* 'Royal Carpet', and in the white *Lobularia maritima* 'Carpet of Snow'. Notice how just a tiny amount of white has quite a significant effect in brightening the group and moderating the impact of the strong red-violet.

As with most annual associations, foliage texture is undistinguished, but a long bloom season allows focus on flower form and color. This same color scheme could be reproduced, perhaps rather monotonously, with four different varieties of *Petunia*. However, it is the differences among the forms—*Salvia* spires, prostrate *Lobularia* mats, and relatively large *Petunia* blooms—that makes this association so appealing. *Salvia splendens* 'Laser Purple' would work very nicely with this color scheme.

A minimum of three *Salvia*, two *Petunia*, and one of each *Lobularia* cultivar would need a space 3 × 3 ft (0.9 × 0.9 m).

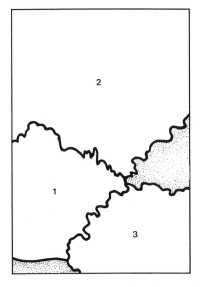

1. *Lavandula stoechas*, five plants,
   12–15 × 15 in (30–40 × 30 cm)
2. *Rosa* (unknown) cultivar, one
   plant, 36 × 36 in (90 × 90 cm)
3. *Erigeron karvinskianus*, three
   plants, 9–18 × 12 in (25–45 × 30
   cm)

SMALL violet-hued flowers can quickly recede to nothingness in the landscape if not given a light background to clarify their color and form. They are often best displayed against light blooms or light-colored materials such as painted or bleached wood, stucco walls, or pale weathered stone. Since color in structures, paving, walls, and ornaments must always be considered as part of a composition, one can often use existing pale structures to enhance plants flowering with the darker cool hues.

PHOTO 33. Santa Barbara, California, May. ENVIRONMENT: sun in soil of average fertility and moisture. USDA Zones 9–10. FEATURE: foliage mid spring to summer; flower late spring to summer.

Just how easily the small bracts, fine texture, and dark hue of *Lavandula stoechas* flowers can dissolve into the background, even over a very short distance, is readily apparent in the above composition. Where the lavender juxtaposes the background light red-violet roses and the very light red-violet *Erigeron* daisies, the form, texture, and color of *Lavandula* is strengthened. This allows *Lavandula* to make a far greater contribution to the planting composition.

As a general rule, dark against light combinations are easier to design in the same hue than in varying hues. Also, by using same-hue associations one can usually avoid a feeling of busyness or discord. When a design warrants the stronger contrasts provided by mixing lights and darks in different hues, such compositions will demand exacting balancing of the quantities of each hue in order to be entirely satisfactory.

Any light red to red-violet flowering rose such as *Rosa* 'Chaucer' would be a suitable background against which to display a minimum of five *Lavandula* combined with three *Erigeron*. Although options allow a lot of latitude in space requirements for the rose, a minimum for five *Lavandula* and three *Erigeron* is 3 × 4 ft (0.9 × 1.2 m).

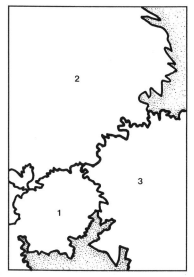

1. *Dicentra eximia* 'Luxuriant', one
   plant, 12–18 × 12 in (30–45 × 30 cm)
2. *Dicentra spectabilis* 'Alba', one plant,
   24–36 × 18 in (60–90 × 45 cm)
3. *Pulmonaria saccharata* 'Mrs. Moon',
   two plants, 10 × 15 in (25 × 40 cm)

PHOTO 34. Ziegler Garden, Bedford, New York, May. ENVIRONMENT: part shade in soil of average fertility and average to greater moisture. USDA Zones 3–7. FEATURE: foliage mid spring to fall; flower mid spring to fall.

REPETITIONS of even minor design elements between plants in a composition can effectively harmonize a grouping, as seen in the small color repetitions and duplicated foliage forms in the above photo.

Pulmonaria saccharata 'Mrs. Moon', seen in the lower right, is a gravely underused plant offering several valuable design elements. It develops startling blue flowers that emerge from pink buds in early spring and persist for many weeks, and broad dark green foliage with white speckles which is attractive until late summer.

This spring association takes advantage of all its design assets. For example, the white in the *Pulmonaria* foliage repeats in the overarching white blooms of *Dicentra spectabilis* 'Alba'. This association will persist for six weeks or more, effective long after *Pulmonaria* has finished blooming. The pink in the *Pulmonaria* buds briefly repeats in the red-violet blooms of *Dicentra eximia* 'Luxuriant', which continue to harmonize with the *Pulmonaria* flowers as they turn blue.

The two *Dicentra* cultivars will continue to flower together for many weeks after the *Pulmonaria* blooms fade. 'Luxuriant' will bloom throughout the entire growing season except in the very hottest weather. Cutting it back after the first flush of bloom will encourage fresh new leaves and flowering. Eventually 'Alba', the larger *Dicentra*, will yellow and die to the ground in late summer and cannot be sustained by pruning back. The two *Dicentra* foliages mirror each other's form at different scales for much of the season and both contrast nicely with the broad, speckled *Pulmonaria* leaves.

A space 2 × 3 ft (0.6 × 0.9 m) will easily accommodate one *Dicentra spectabilis* in the rear, one *D. eximia* in the midground, and two *Pulmonaria* in the foreground.

PHOTO 35. New York Botanical Garden, New York City, August. ENVIRONMENT: sun in soil of average fertility and moisture. USDA Zones 5–8. FEATURE: foliage summer to fall; flower summer to fall.

Preferences in flower color combinations are influenced by many variables, including culture, fashion, availability, childhood recollections, and so on. The regional light quality and the flower colors prevalent in native plants of a particular region may also prejudice choice. High-intensity, pure hues seem popularly accepted in regions closer to the equator where light is stronger and native plants flower in brilliant hot colors. Pastels, cool hues, and grayed tones, with warm-hued accents, are often favored in the mistier, grayer northern regions.

Variations on the restrained color association shown here, with its subdued light tints of red-violet contrasted against similar and adjacent hues in the foliage of the *Berberis* shrub, are common in the northern parts of the United States and in northern Europe. This composition reflects a late summer combination with a blooming sequence persisting eight weeks or more.

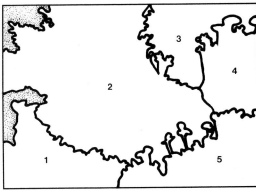

1. *Sedum* 'Vera Jameson', three plants, 10–15 × 12 in (25–40 × 30 cm)
2. *Anemone vitifolia* 'Robustissima', two plants, 36 × 18 in (90 × 45 cm)
3. *Berberis thunbergii* 'Atropurpurea', one plant, 5 × 5 ft (1.5 × 1.5 m)
4. *Allium tuberosum*, three bulbs, 18–24 × 12 in (45–60 × 30 cm)
5. *Gomphrena globosa* 'Lavender Lady', five plants, 18–24 × 18 in (45–60 × 45 cm)

The little, lavender *Gomphrena* umbels are effective from early summer through fall and contrast with the grayed reddish *Sedum* foliage and the dark red *Berberis* foliage. The *Gomphrena* flowers are joined in late summer by the distinctive, horizontal, white *Allium* umbels and the flat blooms of the very pale red-violet *Anemone* and grayish red-violet *Sedum*. The forms and foliages of each of these plants make significant contributions to this complex picture. In particular, beginning in late spring, the mass of dark green *Anemone* leaves provides an attractive background for all its companions.

A space 6 × 8 ft (1.8 × 2.4 m) will accommodate one *Berberis* in the background, with two *Anemone* and three *Allium* in the midground, and three *Sedum* and five *Gomphrena* in the foreground.

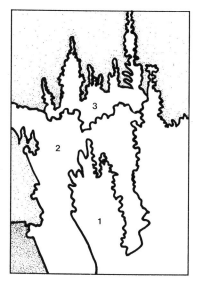

1. *Salvia sclarea*, one plant, 36–60
   × 36 in (90–150 × 90 cm)
2. *Verbena bonariensis*, six plants,
   36 × 12 in (90 × 30 cm)
3. *Alcea rosea* 'Single Mix' type,
   two plants, 72–84 × 24 in
   (180–210 × 60 cm)

PHOTO 36. Conservatory Garden, New York City, June. ENVIRONMENT: sun in soil of average fertility and moisture. USDA Zones 5–8. FEATURE: foliage mid to late summer; flower mid to late summer.

VERTICAL FORMS make excellent focal points in planting compositions, establishing focus and centers of interest whether alone or in combination. Verticals are so visually commanding they will engage our attention well before similarly scaled horizontal or weeping forms. *Alcea* provides the dominant and focal vertical in this combination.

The red-violet centers in the white blooms of *Alcea rosea* harmonize with red-violet *Verbena bonariensis* and the specks of red-violet in *Salvia sclarea*. The scattered *Verbena* flowers nicely anchor the midground between the spikes of *Alcea* and the fine-textured, foamy *Salvia* blooms in the foreground, and mute the often unsightly lower portions of the *Alcea*.

The diffuse *Verbena* foliage generally lacks the density required for a solitary planting. Its foliage more effectively associates in contrast with another plant displaying medium- or broad-textured foliage, as here. The flowering *Salvia* spikes are poorly defined against the diffuse texture of the *Verbena* blossoms; *Salvia* is mostly useful here for its broad, grayish yellow-green pubescent leaves.

This *Alcea* is about 6 ft (2 m) high and consequently needs to be balanced by a foreground planting equal in depth. A space 4 × 6 ft (1.2 x 1.8 m) is the minimum for this group, with two *Alcea* in the rear, a mass of six *Verbena* in the midground, and one *Salvia* in the foreground.

PHOTO 37. New York Botanical Garden, New York City, September. ENVIRONMENT: sun in soil of average fertility and moisture. USDA Zones 5–8. FEATURE: foliage summer to fall; flower summer to fall.

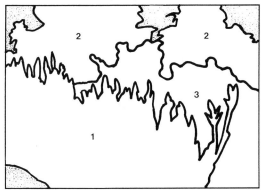

WHILE the foliage of many flowering annuals is undistinguished, contributing little to overall design, a long bloom season gives variation in annual flower forms greater design significance. The flower forms used here are excitingly different, while color repetition establishes compositional unity.

Red-violet and white associate easily, occurring in garden designs almost as frequently as yellow and white because of the large numbers of flowers produced in tints and shades of red-violet. Here the red-violet of *Celosia* and *Verbena* combine with white *Cleome*. The red-violet color repeats in two quite distinct flower forms: the hazy masses of *Verbena* and the spires of *Celosia* with their intense red-violet tips shading paler and paler to the base of the blooms. A white cluster is contributed by the tall, nebulous, fragrant *Cleome* blooms scattered among green foliage.

1. *Celosia elegans* 'Pink Tassles', three plants, 24–36 × 12–18 in (60–90 × 30–45 cm)
2. *Cleome spinosa* 'Helen Campbell', three plants, 24–60 × 12 in (60–150 × 30 cm)
3. *Verbena bonariensis*, six plants, 36 × 12 in (90 × 30 cm)

A couple of near-white *Zinnia elegans* 'Silver Sun' plants are also included here, adjacent to *Celosia*, although not visible in the photo. Their large daisy form contributes an eye-catching mass to the composition. Just a few of these broad-textured zinnias could be used, carefully placed to avoid unbalancing the entire composition.

The scale of the tall *Cleome* dictates the need for a space at least 3 × 5 ft (0.9 × 0.9 m), with three *Cleome* in the rear, six *Verbena* in the midground intermingled with two *Zinnia elegans* 'Silver Sun', and three *Celosia* in the foreground.

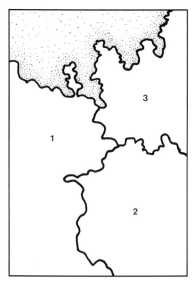

1. *Nepeta mussinii* 'White Wonder',
   one plant, 12–18 × 18 in (30–45 ×
   45 cm)
2. *Viola* 'Baby Lucia', five plants,
   4–6 × 9 in (10–15 × 25 cm)
3. *Geranium sylvaticum*
   'Mayflower', one plant, 24 × 24 in
   (60 × 60 cm)

PHOTO 38. Stonecrop Gardens, Cold Spring, New York, May. ENVIRONMENT: sun to part shade in soil of average fertility and moisture. USDA Zones 6–8. FEATURE: foliage mid spring to fall; flower mid to late spring.

THIS LONG-BLOOMING, rich association adds white to the pairing of adjacent harmonious tones of red-violet and violet and illustrates the drama of extreme light and dark contrasts. As its scale is small, it needs to be placed in an easily viewed location where its diminutive beauty can be appreciated without undue stooping or peering.

If *Geranium sylvaticum* 'Mayflower' is not available, *G. endressii* 'Wargrave Pink' will substitute, although some color intensity and the tiny yet delightful repetition of white will be lost. Dark violet *Viola* 'Baby Lucia' is used in the above setting, yet any small-flowered viola in the red-violet or violet color range may be substituted. For example, *Viola corsica* would do well and is particularly desirable for its long blooming season.

The textures and forms of the plants used in this grouping are very similar, with slight variation offered by the loose flowering spikes of the *Nepeta*. This lightly textured white bloom is important here because it repeats the white in the *Geranium* petals, yet brightens and emphasizes the darkness of the *Viola*.

This compact arrangement may be accommodated in an area 3 × 3 ft (0.9 × 0.9 m), with one *Geranium* in the rear, one *Nepeta* in the midground, and five *Viola* plants in the foreground.

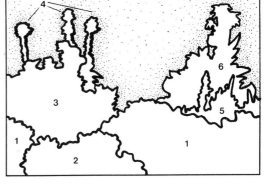

PHOTO 39. Caramoor
Center for Music and the
Arts, Katonah, New
York, August.
ENVIRONMENT: sun in
soil of average fertility
and moisture.
USDA Zones 5–8.
FEATURE: foliage late
spring to fall; flower late
spring to fall.

WHITE COMBINED with other colors is often more dynamic than white alone. The mere careful placement of a few plants of another color can frame and focus white groupings. In this association, found in a predominantly white garden, red-violet and pale blue-violet are sparingly associated with white. Taller, white-blooming plants are framed by background shadows.

Cleome spinosa 'Helen Campbell', *Argyranthemum frutescens*, and *Antirrhinum majus* provide the bulk of the white flowering. Pale blue-violet *Ageratum houstonianum* 'Southern Cross' anchors the foreground, while a red-violet *Cleome* 'Violet Queen' defines the background for the white blooms of the middle ground. A larger grouping of *Cleome* 'Violet Queen' would increase their design effectiveness. Using *Cleome* 'Pink Queen' as a substitute would create a lighter atmosphere.

A void left between *Cleome* and the broad-textured *Nicotiana* serves to focus attention on the shadowed spaces beyond and emphasizes the important horizontal layering of the planting composition. An unbroken rear planting of *Cleome* and *Nicotiana* would destroy the hint of depth and mystery. This arrangement at Caramoor was much appreciated at night, when the white blooms illuminated the space and emphasized shadowing, and the fragrance of the *Nicotiana* and *Cleome* was best appreciated.

A large space is necessary to accommodate all these plants, at least 5 × 5 ft (1.5 × 1.5 m), with five assorted *Cleome* and one *Nicotiana* in the background, two *Antirrhinum* and four *Argyranthemum* in the midground, and nine *Ageratum* in the foreground.

1. *Argyranthemum frutescens*, four plants, 12–30 × 12 in (30–75 × 30 cm)
2. *Ageratum houstonianum* 'Southern Cross', nine plants, 8–12 × 8 in (20–30 × 20 cm)
3. *Cleome spinosa* 'Helen Campbell', two plants, 24–60 × 12 in (60–150 × 30 cm)
4. *Cleome spinosa* 'Violet Queen', three plants, 24–60 × 12 in (60–150 × 30 cm)
5. *Antirrhinum majus* 'White Rocket', two plants, 30–36 × 12 in (75–90 × 30 cm)
6. *Nicotiana sylvestris*, one plant, 48–60 × 18 in (120–150 × 45 cm)

PHOTO 40. Cloister Hotel, Sea Island, Georgia, May. ENVIRONMENT: sun in soil of average fertility and moisture. USDA Zones 5–9. FEATURE: foliage early spring to fall; flower mid spring to fall.

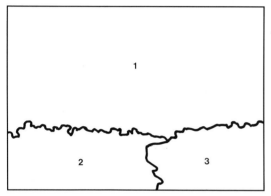

1. *Antirrhinum majus* 'Princess White with Purple Eye', five plants, 12–18 × 12 in (30–45 × 30 cm)
2. *Lobularia maritima* 'Easter Bonnet Deep Pink', three plants, 3 × 12 in (10 × 30 cm)
3. *Lobularia maritima* 'Carpet of Snow', three plants, 3 × 12 in (10 × 30 cm)

PLANT COMPOSITIONS of complex color, form, and texture often require frequent attention and adjustment if they are to excel. Where time and devotion are limited, a planting of annuals in pastel hues offers a satisfactory composition without onerous demands on the gardener. Tinted pastel colors harmonize easily, requiring little thought to balance color quantities. Another concession is the possibility of a long bloom display, as annuals frequently bloom from spring to frost. If the plants are correctly selected for the available cultural conditions, they will thrive, adjust, and need minimal care and attention.

This low-maintenance selection of plants, seen in the photograph squeezed into a square space, is perfect for filling in the formal, geometric beds of parterres and knot gardens. These annuals also lend themselves to far more informal arrangements and look well loosely clustered at the edges of terraces or spilling between paving stones. Where site character demands informality, take a few extra plants from an orderly association and plant them at random nearby. The apparently accidental placement of two or three wayward plants mimics the work of nature and makes the whole composition appear less studied. Often, in the following season, natural forces will continue the work with random seedlings of sweet alyssum (*Lobularia*) springing up wherever their preferred well-drained, warm conditions occur.

A beginning planting of five dominating *Antirrhinum* and three of each *Lobularia* cultivar will fit into an irregularly shaped space about 2 × 5 ft (0.6 × 1.5 m).

PHOTO 41. New York Botanical Garden, New York City, May. ENVIRONMENT: sun in soil of average fertility and moisture. USDA Zones 3–8. FEATURE: foliage mid spring to late summer; flower mid to late spring.

VIOLET AND blue-violet are harmonious colors, adjacent on the color wheel, and they can make many splendid associations. Especially when brightened with a scattering of white or very pale yellow blooms, violet and blue-violet will shine. However, as this particular photograph illustrates, a gulf can develop between the color values. The flowers of the very dark violet *Iris* and the very pale blue-violet *Amsonia* in the background create a tonal gap which needs to be filled. An attempt at linking these disparate values has been made with a white-flowering *Leucanthemum* and with violet *Aquilegia*. The association would further improve if more of the intermediate tints of violet or blue-violet were added to the group. Additional plants could, for example, be chosen from the light-tinted flowers of certain *Iris*, *Baptisia*, *Nepeta*, or *Tradescantia*. Additions could be used to fill the space between the *Iris* and *Amsonia* since they appear widely separated in a large border.

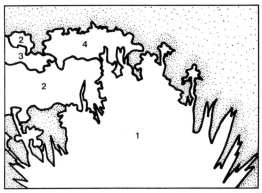

1. *Iris × germanica*, three plants, 18–24 × 12 in (45–60 × 30 cm)
2. *Aquilegia vulgaris*, three plants, 12–24 × 12 in (30–60 × 30 cm)
3. *Leucanthemum × superbum* 'Alaska', one plant, 24 × 18 in (60 × 45 cm)
4. *Amsonia tabernaemontana*, one plant, 24–36 × 24 in (60–90 × 60 cm)

A frequent weakness of very deep borders is inadequate vertical emphasis. This could be improved here by positioning the *Iris* and *Amsonia* closer together while including a visually terminating shrub at the rear. The shrub's height should approximate the depth of the border. Sloping a very deep border from back to front will also increase the vertical importance of the rear plantings.

This group could be arranged in a space 3 × 4 ft (0.9 × 1.2 m), with three *Iris* and one *Amsonia* in the rear, and one *Leucanthemum* and three *Aquilegia* in the foreground.

PHOTO 42. Ziegler Garden, Bedford, New York, July. ENVIRONMENT: sun in soil of average fertility and moisture. USDA Zones 5–8. FEATURE: foliage late spring to late summer; flower late spring to late summer.

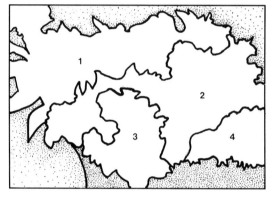

1. *Heliotropium* 'Marine', one plant, 12–18 × 12 in (30–45 × 30 cm)
2. *Nierembergia hippomanica* var. *violacea* 'Purple Robe', one plant, 6–8 × 6 in (15–20 × 15 cm)
3. *Ageratum houstonianum* 'Blue Puffs', two plants, 6–8 × 9 in (15–20 × 25 cm)
4. *Lobelia erinus* 'White Cascade', three plants, 4 × 6 in (10 × 15 cm)

THIS DIMINUTIVE group of long-blooming annuals works well as a container planting. With the quantities increased, the plants will nestle nicely among rocks or at the top of a wall, beside a patio, or in any well-drained, sunny, or lightly shaded area where the tiny scale and receding colors of this delicate grouping may be appreciated. Adding violet or white petunias will continue the color theme and enlarge the scale, fitting it for larger areas. However, such small-scale, predominantly fine-textured groupings are seldom effective over viewing distances greater than 40 to 50 ft (12 to 15 m).

The light to dark progression of hue—from white *Lobelia*, to pale violet *Ageratum*, to blue-violet and white *Nierembergia*, and finally to lightly scented violet *Heliotropium*—is compelling. *Lobelia erinus* 'White Cascade' offers precisely what its name suggests, a tiny cascade of white blooms. Since *Neirembergia* will also cascade, this combination is suitable also for hanging baskets.

Foliage contributes a dark yellow-green, while leaf textures play between the comparatively broad form of the *Heliotropium* leaves, the medium scale of the rounded *Ageratum* leaves, and the very fine, lance-shaped leaves of *Nierembergia*. Container color should be selected carefully to harmonize with the delicate hues found in the blooms. A solid white container would diminish the colors of the cascading plants, yet terracotta, dark green or dark gray would contain the plants modestly.

A space 2 × 2 ft (0.6 × 0.6 m) would accommodate an intermingled group of two *Ageratum*, one *Neirembergia*, and one *Heliotropium*, with three *Lobelia* plants lolling in the foreground.

PHOTO 43. Conservatory Garden, New York City, May.
ENVIRONMENT: part shade in soil of average fertility and moisture. USDA Zones 3–7.
FEATURE: foliage mid spring to fall; flower mid spring to summer.

S EVERAL contemporary garden writers have observed that blue, blue-violet, and violet should be separated. In my view, colors adjacent on the sixteen-color wheel harmonize very easily. I love to bring these hues together, particularly when they share a similar intensity and lightness of hue as they do here. Generally, the effect is harmonious if violet and blue-violet blooms dominate the composition while a much smaller quantity of blue flowers makes a minor contribution.

The *Brunnera* has tiny persistent flowers of pure blue in spring and late spring. Its diminutive blooms are here associating with an annual *Viola* that flowers until early summer in New York, or longer with adequate moisture in cooler regions. The *Hosta* cultivar is interplanted to provide late summer white and fragrant blooms.

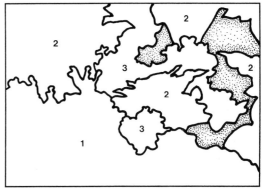

1. *Brunnera macrophylla*, two plants, 18 × 24 in (45 × 60 cm)
2. *Hosta plantaginea* 'Royal Standard', one plant, 24–36 × 24 in (60–90 × 60 cm)
3. *Viola × wittrockiana*, eight plants, 6–8 × 9 in (15–20 × 25 cm)

Both *Hosta* and *Brunnera* foliage will expand during the growing season, covering more space than is shown here, overtaking the space vacated by the declining pansies. Their broad foliage forms have different shapes which contrast nicely with each other and maintain textural interest until fall. Also, the dark green *Brunnera* foliage establishes color contrasts against the lighter yellow-green hosta leaves throughout the growing season. Grown here in the preferred light shade beneath deciduous trees and shrubs, this group will also perform well in full morning sun with afternoon shade.

Plant a minimum of one *Hosta* with two *Brunnera*, interplanted with about ten *Viola* in a space 4 × 4 ft (1.2 × 1.2 m).

PHOTO 44. Henrietta Lockwood Garden, Bedford, New York, August. ENVIRONMENT: sun in soil of average fertility and moisture. USDA Zones 3–8. FEATURE: foliage late spring to fall; flower mid to late summer.

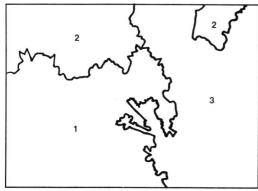

1. *Platycodon grandiflorus*, two plants, 18–24 x 12 in (45–60 × 30 cm)
2. *Eryngium amethystinum*, one plant, 24–30 × 18 in (60–75 × 45 cm)
3. *Physostegia virginiana* 'Summer Snow', two plants, 30–48 × 18 in (75–120 × 45 cm)

VIOLET AND white combinations which permit advancing white to dominate slightly over receding violet are more tranquil than the more frequently used red and white, a pairing that juxtaposes two equally dominating and advancing colors. Here white associates with light violet and grayed blue-violet rather than a pure strong violet or blue-violet. The relative pallor of these whitened, tinted hues allows them to blend easily with white and with each other.

Physostegia is an excellent summer-flowering plant valued for its loose spikes of small white flowers and its persistent, dark green, shining foliage. *Platycodon* offers comparatively large light violet to blue-violet bell-like blooms with similarly dark, lance-shaped foliage. The pale blue-violet *Eryngium* umbels strike an intermediate, transitional tone between the colors of the plant's companions. Spikey *Eryngium* foliage contrasts the lance-shaped forms of *Physostegia* and *Platycodon* leaves.

The relatively small scale and delicacy of these blooms, and the receding qualities of the violet and blue-violet colors, recommend this group for a small space close to the viewing point. In a larger space adding a strong adjacent color, such as light red-violet, would draw attention to the group, enliven it, and modify its tranquil character. *Liatris spicata* 'Kobold' could add the light red-violet flower color and contribute accent with its strong vertical form.

A space 3 × 4 ft (0.9 × 1.2 m) would be needed for the basic three plants pictured, with two *Physostegia* in the background, one *Eryngium* in the midground, and two *Platycodon* in the foreground. Including two *Liatris spicata* 'Kobold' increases space requirement to 3 × 5 ft (0.9 × 1.5 m).

PHOTO 45. New York Botanical Garden, New York City, June. ENVIRONMENT: sun in soil of average fertility and moisture. USDA Zones 4–7. FEATURE: foliage mid spring to fall; flower late spring to summer.

THE STALKY, light red-violet *Stachys* flowers are not particularly favored in contemporary planting design. The blooms appear awkward and intrusive in form and scale and are usually pruned out. The design aspects of the plant lie in its soft, tactile, silvery-looking leaves. The leaf color is actually a very light, very gray, yellow-green. The downy texture of the leaves (due to their matte woolly hairs) also adds to the whitish or silvery quality. This riveting pale gray color and prostrate form suggest its use in the foreground of primarily white and pastel plantings.

Stachys combines especially well with lighter tints in complementary red-violet, violet, and blue-violet

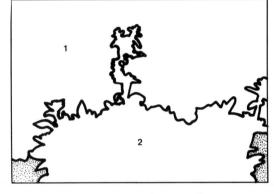

1. *Salvia* (unknown), one plant, 18–36 × 18 in (45–90 × 45 cm)
2. *Stachys byzantina*, three plants, 12–15 × 12 in (30–40 × 30 cm)

blooms, or with other gray-leaved plants. Here it is associated with blue-violet *Salvia* flowers, and its brilliant pallor brightens and strengthens the stunning hue of its companion.

Stachys combines equally well with many other plants. For example, *Geranium* 'Johnson's Blue' offers a flower color similar to *Salvia* and would be an excellent addition to this pair. The geranium choice also introduces a different yet compatible form and its fine foliage contrasts beautifully with *Stachys*. The trio makes a fine foreground planting for gray-leaved, blue-violet flowering *Buddleja* cultivars. It is important to plant *Stachys* in sufficient density to provide a complete covering of the soil. Otherwise the effect may be one of spotty individual clumps of gray foliage in indecisive isolation against brownish soil.

Salvia haematodes is an excellent choice to substitute for the unknown cultivar shown here. A minimum planting of one *Salvia* and three *Stachys* would occupy a space 2 × 3 ft (0.6 × 0.9 m). The *Geranium* 'Johnson's Blue' has a sprawling habit and a space requirement of 2 × 2 ft (0.6 × 0.6 m) per plant. To use all three in association would merit a space 3 × 4 ft (0.9 × 1.2 m), with one *Salvia* in the rear, four *Stachys* in the foreground, and one *Geranium* in the midground.

PHOTO 46. New York Botanical Garden, New York City, April. ENVIRONMENT: sun in soil of average fertility and average or less moisture. USDA Zones 4–7. FEATURE: foliage mid spring to summer; flower mid spring.

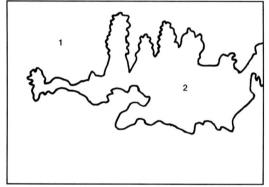

1. *Arabis caucasica*, one plant, 6–9 × 12 in (15–25 × 30 cm)
2. *Muscari armeniacum*, three bulbs, 6–8 × 4 in (15–20 × 10 cm)

THIS IS a fine example of interplanting in layers, with small bulbs rising through a groundcover.

This *Muscari* is a long-flowering spring bulb developing flower spikes of an exquisite light blue-violet that combine well with the fragrant white *Arabis* blooms. Although not shown in this photograph, two additions were made to this composition to increase subtlety and extend the period of bloom within the same color theme. Contributing greatly to the design intent, the two additions were the common violet, *Viola cucullata*, and *Narcissus* 'Thalia', a small, mid-season, fragrant daffodil with white flowers. This quartet makes an excellent foreground planting for spring-flowering shrubs. It looks especially poetic underplanting a *Magnolia stellata*. Common lilacs with dwarf *Rhododendron* 'Ramapo' or *R.* 'Purple Gem' are also fine companions since all bloom at roughly the same time and in adjacent colors, and all may be grown in very light shade or sun.

Arabis does not bloom profusely in light shade, yet lasts well. Scented white *Arabis* and *Viola* can interweave while fragrant *Muscari* and *Narcissus* 'Thalia' push through or stand behind their low-growing associates. As *Viola* leaves expand considerably once the plant has completed its flowering cycle, its leaf mass can then cover the area left after dieback from the bulbs. The foliar dieback is actually not wildly unsightly because the leaves of both *Muscari* and *Narcissus* 'Thalia' are fine textured. Note that *Viola cucullata* seeds easily and spreads rapidly and needs to be carefully managed. *Viola cornuta* or *V. odorata* could substitute for *V. cucullata* and may require less management.

One *Arabis* with three *Muscari* require a space only 1 × 1.5 ft (0.3 × 0.5 m). A minimum planting of all four plant types requires a space about 2 × 2 ft (0.6 × 0.6 m), with one *Arabis* and three *Viola cucullata* plants, five *Narcissus* 'Thalia' and three *Muscari* bulbs, intermixed.

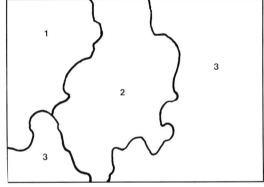

PHOTO 47. Edmondsham House Gardens, Dorset, England, June. ENVIRONMENT: sun to part shade in soil of average fertility and moisture. USDA Zones 3–7. FEATURE: foliage late spring to late summer; flower late spring to summer.

COMPOSITIONS featuring flowers of markedly similar form and size may appear weak and undistinguished even if colors vary. Where foliage forms and textures are also undifferentiated the design may be further diminished. Adding a single companion with a bolder leaf, plant, or flower shape may be sufficient to transform a weak group into a commanding association.

Nigella damescena 'Miss Jekyll' offers fine light blue to blue-violet flowers in late spring and summer. Here it is associated with white, delicate, but similarly formed *Malva moschata* flowers. This blue and white composition is modestly pleasing since the white *Malva* blooms dominate slightly. However, the calculated addition of greenish yellow *Alchemilla* blooms, complementing the blue-violet tints in *Nigella*, strengthens focus. Stronger foliage contrasts are also established by mingling finer *Nigella* and *Malva* textures with the broad *Alchemilla* leaves.

1. *Alchemilla mollis*, one plant, 12 × 18 in (30 × 45 cm)
2. *Nigella damescena* 'Miss Jekyll', three plants, 15–24 × 12 in (40–60 × 30 cm)
3. *Malva moschata* 'Alba', one plant, 24–36 × 18 in (60–90 × 45 cm)

Other useful companions might include a brightening red-violet spire of *Digitalis purpurea* or the broad-leaved blue-flowering annual *Borago officinalis* in the rear. A foreground planting of broad-leaved *Ajuga* or variegated *Lamium maculatum* 'White Nancy' would increase the design interest. *Nigella damescena* 'Miss Jekyll' is easily grown from seed and also self-seeds readily. Flowering continues for about six weeks and may be further prolonged by deadheading. If left to mature, the flowers evolve into conspicuous, ornamental, beige seed pods tinged with dark red, making a design contribution in the late summer and fall.

The basic trio occupies a space 2 × 4 ft (0.6 × 1.2 m), with one *Malva* in the rear, three *Nigella* in the midground, and one *Alchemilla* in the foreground.

PHOTO 48. Peconic Herb Farm, Calverton, New York, May. ENVIRONMENT: part shade in soil of average fertility and moisture. USDA Zones 4–8. FEATURE: foliage mid spring to summer; flower mid spring.

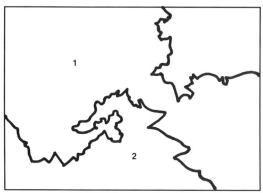

1. *Trillium grandiflorum*, one plant, 12–18 × 12 in (30–45 × 30 cm)
2. *Myosotis sylvatica*, six plants, 6–8 × 8 in (15–20 × 20 cm)

A THOROUGH appreciation of any plant design usually begins with an evaluation of the colors, whether of foliage or bloom, proceeds to a comparison of shapes and forms, and ends with an assessment of textural variations between the plants. When blooms are absent, distinctive forms may capture our attention before foliage colors. The *Trillium* and *Myosotis* pairing also illustrates the importance in composition of skillfully eliminating unwanted patches of bare earth. Correct plant spacing ensures leaves and flowers will eventually merge at the height of their season. Plants spaced too far apart come across as individuals isolated in a frame of soil and will not present a blended composition. *Trillium* contrasted against a field of blue *Myosotis* flower and foliage presents a far finer picture than would *Trillium* and *Myosotis* plants isolated against bare soil.

This simple composition for light shade uses soothing colors: light blue flowers in *Myosotis*, a color rare in cultivated flowers, and white, fading to purplish pink in *Trillium* blooms. The dark green, broad-textured *Trillium* foliage is an important part of this composition. Its leaves serve as a dark background for the intensely white blooms and also make broad-patterned masses which highlight the light blue *Myosotis* flowers. The *Trillium* may be one of North America's most exquisite native woodland plants. It is important to purchase any native plants from reputable nurseries where commercial propagation is guaranteed to ensure plants have not been plundered from the wild.

A minimum space of 2 × 2 ft (0.6 × 0.6 m) is needed to accommodate one *Trillium* framed by six *Myosotis*.

PHOTO 49. Conservatory Garden, New York City, May.
ENVIRONMENT: part shade in soil of average fertility and average to greater moisture.
USDA Zones 3–9.
FEATURE: foliage early to late spring; flower mid spring.

Planting schemes employing native plants in conditions duplicating or approximating their native habitats are being designed more widely and with greater frequency than ever before. Still, many people think of planting design only as the arrangement of color-filled masses in brilliant borders. Border planning and planting is immensely challenging and creative. Unfortunately it frequently leads to a great deal of work, expense, and elaborate contrivance to maintain what is often an artificial and/or exotic plant community. A more naturalized, subtle composition can equal or exceed the creativity of intricate hand-wrought borders and educate in the pleasures of simple, yet varied, planting associations.

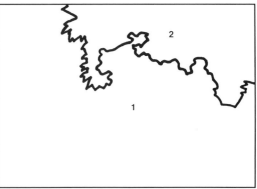

1. *Mertensia virginica*, three plants, 12–24 × 12 in (30–60 × 30 cm)
2. *Podophyllum peltatum*, five plants, 12–18 × 12 in (30–45 × 30 cm)

This pair of native plants is probably seldom arranged in nature as exquisitely as here on a tree-shaded bank in New York City. The brilliant blue *Mertensia* flowers gleam with the glossy companion foliage of *Podophyllum*. As this planting is elevated on a bank, bell-like white *Podophyllum* blooms are visible beneath its foliage. *Mertensia* dies to the ground in late spring and the space can be occupied by another spring-expanding native, such as *Hemerocallis* or *Dryopteris noveboracensis*.

An area 2 × 4 ft (0.6 × 1.2 m) will be large enough for a preliminary planting of three *Mertensia* mingled with five *Podophyllum*.

PHOTO 50. Conservatory Garden, New York City, April.
ENVIRONMENT: part shade to shade in soil of average fertility and average to greater moisture. USDA Zones 3–9.
FEATURE: foliage mid to late spring; flower mid to late spring.

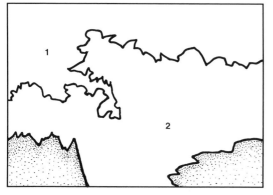

1. *Dicentra spectabilis* 'Alba', one plant, 24–36 × 18 in (60–90 × 45 cm)
2. *Mertensia virginica*, three plants, 12–24 × 12 in (30–60 × 30 cm)

THE NATIVE North American perennial *Mertensia virginica* is one of spring's treasures, with fragrant, pure blue flowers emerging from pink buds subtly raised above its gray-green foliage. It lends itself to mass planting in drifts in lightly shaded woodlands or individually in small garden compositions. It combines well with a large range of spring's pale flowers. Here it associates with *Dicentra spectabilis* 'Alba' and the foliage of Siberian irises and *Astilbe* emerging to the left and right of *Mertensia*. Choosing violet or blue-violet Siberian irises and a white-flowered *Astilbe*, such as *Astilbe × arendsii* 'Deutschland' or 'Bridal Veil', will extend the color theme into late spring.

Adding *Hosta fortunei* 'Marginato-alba' to this basic group would contribute a pleasing complexity, with the *Hosta*'s white leaf margins repeating the flower color of *Dicentra* and *Astilbe*. The hosta's broad foliage texture will also supplement the narrow vertical form contributed by the iris and the feathery astilbe leaves, and will sustain a compelling foliage composition until fall. The hosta would also add light violet flower spikes in summer to the basically foliar composition.

Furthermore, the expanding *Hosta* leaves resolve one of the difficulties of using *Mertensia* since they will cover the void left when *Mertensia* foliage declines in late spring. This is an outstanding combination for lightly shaded areas where white-edged leaves and blooms stand out.

A minimum space 3 × 4 ft (0.9 × 1.2 m) would accommodate one *Dicentra*, three *Mertensia*, three *Iris sibirica*, one *Astilbe × arendsii* 'Deutschland' or 'Bridal Veil', and one *Hosta fortunei*. If space permits, plant in drifts and increase quantities proportionately.

PHOTO 51. Conservatory Garden, New York City, May.
ENVIRONMENT: part shade in soil of average to greater fertility and average to greater moisture.
USDA Zones 3–8.
FEATURE: foliage mid spring to fall; flower early spring and summer.

GREEN or yellow-green combinations usually rely on foliage characteristics, and the challenge lies in harmonizing various leaf colors, textures, and forms. There is extensive variation within the greens, blue-greens, and yellow-greens of foliage hues, far more than is typical to specific flower hues. Foliage color values vary from pale to very deep tones, reflecting and affected by maturation and cultivation practices.

The intensity of these tints and shades ranges from slightly grayed, with partially diminished intensity, to very gray as seen in photo 5. Given such abundant choices, the number of foliar combinations is enormous. The primary design challenge of foliar compositions lies in juxtaposing light and dark tones and grayed and intense hues or, as in this case, shiny and matte surfaces, while contrasting sympathetic forms and textures.

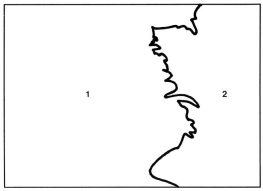

1. *Helleborus orientalis*, two plants, 12–24 × 24 in (30–60 × 60 cm)
2. *Hosta plantaginea* 'Royal Standard', one plant, 24–36 × 24 in (60–90 × 60 cm)

Yellow-green options are not confined to foliage. There are quite a few plants which bloom in this interesting color (see Appendix A), although often they are passed over in favor of the more brilliant, colorful, or showy. In this pairing, pale hellebore blooms are framed for a long season against the darker tones of their own shiny foliage and broad, smooth hosta leaves. Hellebore's outstanding foliage makes a fine display with later-blooming perennials such as the *Astilbe chinensis* 'Pumila' as seen in photo 105.

The minimum planting area for one *Hosta* with two *Helleborus* is 3 × 4 ft (0.9 × 1.2 m).

PHOTO 52. Conservatory Garden, New York City, May.
ENVIRONMENT: part shade in soil of average to greater fertility and average to greater moisture. USDA Zones 4–8.
FEATURE: foliage mid spring to fall; flower mid spring to late summer.

1. *Hosta fortunei*, one plant, 12–18 × 24 in (30–45 × 60 cm)
2. *Athyrium nipponicum* 'Pictum', three plants, 6–12 × 12 in (15–30 × 30 cm)
3. *Polygonatum odoratum* 'Variegatum', two plants, 12–24 × 12 in (30–60 × 30 cm)

THESE COMPANIONS offer subtle foliage textures and forms. The contrast of light and dark foliage clearly demonstrates that flowers and bright colors are not essential to fine planting design. Many of the most soothing and elegant plant compositions are created with only green and dark red foliage. Light shade is essential to many foliage compositions—to intensify the subtle colors, making their often slight hue variations more evident, and to promote the moisture level necessary for the best appearance of much foliage.

The dark red of the *Athyrium* stems subtly contrasts its pale foliage markings. Its pallor repeats in white-edged *Polygonatum* leaves and both contrast with the brighter green of the hosta foliage. Textures and scales vary from the finely dissected *Athyrium* fronds to the mid-sized *Polygonatum* leaves and the very broad, smooth *Hosta* leaves. *Ajuga reptans* would be a fine addition to the foreground of this group. Its light violet to blue-violet flower spikes appear in spring, at about the same time as *Polygonatum* blooms, and its leaves repeat the hint of dark red found in the fern stems. The fine texture, small scale, and subdued coloring of this group demand an easily viewed location.

A space as small as 3 × 3 ft (0.9 × 0.9 m) will suit one *Hosta* and two *Polygonatum* in the background, with three *Athyrium* and three *Ajuga reptans* in the foreground.

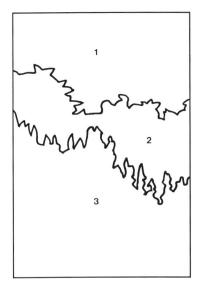

1. *Hydrangea quercifolia*, one
   plant, 6 × 6 ft (1.8 × 1.8 m)
2. *Lysimachia ciliata* 'Purpurea',
   three plants, 30–36 × 24 in
   (75–90 × 60 cm)
3. *Nepeta mussinii*, five plants,
   12–18 × 18 in (30–45 × 45 cm)

PHOTO 53. Conservatory Garden, New York City, June. ENVIRONMENT: sun to part shade in soil of average fertility and moisture. USDA Zones 5–8. FEATURE: foliage late spring to fall; flower late spring to summer.

ALTHOUGH color is usually the first thing noticed and appreciated in planting design, form is the second most important element and must not be ignored in the design process. The third element of planting design is the texture of flowers and/or foliage, and in some compositions this is of greater significance than either color or form. The several foliar compositions illustrated base their appeal on variations in the textures of the leaves, from broad to medium to fine.

Broad textures are often used at the rear of a composition to provide a strong background against which to display other textures. Occasionally, broad textures are used at the base or in the foreground of a composition to offer a solidly anchoring form from which finer textures may ascend. Placing fine textures in the foreground or at the top of the composition ensures quality of detail is not lost.

When associated with herbaceous plants, the coarse-textured *Hydrangea* demands dense-textured companions and careful transitions from its broad leaves to medium and then to fine textures. It would be a loss, for example, to plant a group of blue-violet *Aquilegia* at the base of this shrub since *Aquilegia* has neither the mass nor the textural density needed to compete with such a bold companion. The powerful, dark-colored *Lysimachia* foliage mass however, associates well and makes a smooth transition from the broad texture and large *Hydrangea* form to the fine texture and small scale of *Nepeta*. *Perilla frutescens* could be substituted for this *Lysimachia*, as its texture, form, and hue would provide similar contrasts.

A space 7 × 8 ft (2.1 × 2.4 m) would fit one *Hydrangea* at the rear with three *Lysimachia* in the midground and five *Nepeta* in the foreground. Substituting *Perilla frutescens* for the *Lysimachia* would not affect space requirements.

PHOTO 54. Stonecrop Gardens, Cold Spring, New York, July. ENVIRONMENT: part shade to shade in soil of average to greater fertility and moisture. USDA Zones 6–8. FEATURE: foliage early spring to late summer; flower early spring.

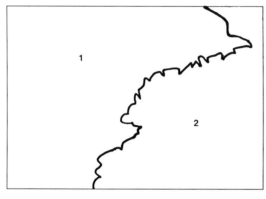

1. *Hakonechloa macra* 'Aureola', one plant, 12–18 × 15 in (30–45 × 40 cm)
2. *Sanguinaria canadensis*, two plants, 6–9 × 12 in (15–25 × 30 cm)

I USUALLY FIND it desirable to choose indigenous plants whenever possible. When their cultural requirements are met and some thought given to their arrangement the results can be as pleasing as in photo 49. Yet at times I mix native plants with exotics to achieve a particular design effect.

A spectacular effect is created in the above arrangement by contrasting a pale yellow and yellow-green grass with a North American native wildflower. *Hakonechloa* is a popular plant because its bright color and grassy form are rarely found in shade-loving plants. Although *Hakonechloa* is compact, it presents a relatively large quantity of bright, advancing color. Its brilliance and vigor stand out in shaded compositions and its unusual form may be stunningly contrasted with other spring and summer foliages of strong form. The broad *Sanguinaria* foliage seems especially dark, grayed, and elegant in contrast to the brilliance of its companion. Planted with foliage of a different color, perhaps dark English ivy or yew, *Sanguinaria* leaves would appear more brightly yellow-green. *Sanguinaria* produces emphemeral, single white blooms in very early spring as the leaves are unfolding. Leaves persist until late summer in moist climates and are larger and more lush in moist summers, disappearing rather rapidly when summers are dry.

One *Hakonechloa* planted with one *Sanguinaria* can fit a space about 1 × 3 ft (0.3 × 0.9 m). However, particularly in a designed shade garden, more will be better. Irregular repetitions of this compact pair may be used to shape and delineate a shaded space.

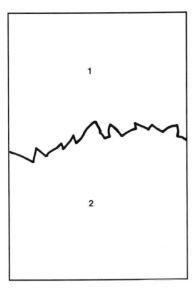

1. *Elymus arenarius*, two plants,
   18–24 × 15 in (45–60 × 40 cm)
2. *Hosta montana* 'Aureo-marginata',
   one plant, 24–36 × 36 in (60–90 ×
   90 cm)

THOUGHTFUL combinations of the various foliage hues and forms are for many people more appealing than exercises in the manipulation of flower color. As this spring photo illustrates, attention is arrested by the dramatic contrast of foliage forms as well as the unusual color association. The drama will continue uninterrupted as the hosta leaves unfurl to maturity.

PHOTO 55. Conservatory Garden, New York City, May. ENVIRONMENT: part shade in soil of average fertility and moisture. USDA Zones 3–8. FEATURE: foliage late spring to fall; flower summer.

Although commonly foliage is referred to as green, most foliage is yellow-green. Very rarely is it pure green and even more rarely is it blue-green. Most of our garden compositions use a tint or shade and frequently a grayed version of yellow-green. Plants described as blue-leaved are often revealed to be simply a very grayed yellow-green when examined closely. The blue tinge is normally imparted from a waxy or powdery surface coating of the leaves. These relative blue-green qualities may be usefully exaggerated when combined with purer yellow-green foliage.

The *Elymus* used here is one of the very few plants with truly blue-green foliage. Its unusual hue receives emphasis here by its association with the hosta's yellow-rimmed, dark gray-green leaves. The various yellow-greens and blue-greens are rather widely separated on the color wheel, and many people do not find this unusual association harmonious. A lessening of the yellow tinge, perhaps by substituting a white-rimmed hosta such as *Hosta fortunei* 'Marginato-alba', meets more general approval. *Elymus* is also pleasing with pale, gray-leaved plants, such as *Artemisia* 'Powis Castle' or *Stachys byzantina*.

Two *Elymus* with one *Hosta* will require a space 3 × 4 ft (0.9 × 1.2 m).

PHOTO 56. New York Botanical Garden, New York City, June. ENVIRONMENT: part shade in soil of average to greater fertility and average moisture. USDA Zones 3–8. FEATURE: foliage late spring to fall; flower late spring to summer.

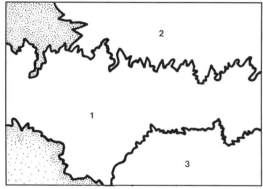

1. *Astilbe × arendsii* 'Deutschland', three plants, 18–24 × 18 in (45–60 × 45 cm)
2. *Hosta sieboldiana* 'Frances Williams', one plant, 30–36 × 36 in (75–90 × 90 cm)
3. *Athyrium nipponicum* 'Pictum', five plants, 6–12 × 12 in (15–30 × 30 cm)

VARIEGATED foliage needs to be used with some restraint. The temptation to create entirely variegated plantings is occasionally succumbed to, and usually results in a composition dominated by bewildering visual confusion. A successful application of the quality of variegation is seen here. Generally, it is more desirable to combine broader variegated textures with finer-textured plain foliages. The finer, variegated foliages in contrast mix well with broad, smooth plain leaves. Nearest companions should always be a consistent shade of green so the variegated leaf markings are readily appreciated.

The variations in leaf color of the *Athyrium* are separated from the yellow-green variegated leaves of the *Hosta* by the intermediate single-hued *Astilbe* foliage. Two differently variegated plants combined without an assertive separation can appear fragmented, like scattered paper scraps. Foliage and flower colors are deftly repeated. The color of the *Hosta*'s light yellowish green leaf margins repeat in the very pale cream *Astilbe* blooms. As the *Astilbe* flowers fully unfold and reveal their whiteness, they will more closely repeat the whitish gray markings on the fern leaves. Other hostas with white leaf margins, such as *Hosta fortunei* 'Marginato-alba', could substitute nicely as a paler hue would again repeat the whiteness of the fern markings.

This bold combination for light shade looks best in masses. If little space is available, it could be attempted in 4 × 5 ft (1.2 × 1.5 m), with one *Hosta* in the rear, two *Astilbe* in the midground, and five *Athyrium* in the foreground.

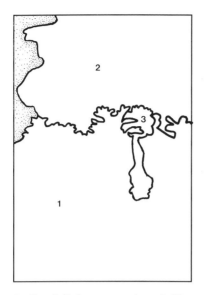

1. *Corydalis lutea*, one plant, 9–15 × 12 in (25–40 × 30 cm)
2. *Ruta graveolens*, one plant, 24–36 × 15 in (60–90 × 40 cm)
3. *Cosmos sulphureus* 'Sunny Red', two plants, 15–18 × 15 in (40–45 × 40 cm)

PHOTO 57. Ziegler Garden, Bedford, New York, August. ENVIRONMENT: sun or light shade in soil of average fertility and moisture. USDA Zones 5–7. FEATURE: foliage early spring to fall; flower early spring to fall.

SOME COMPLEMENTARY color associations, such as orange or red-orange with blue-green, are scarcely found in planting design although they offer wonderful opportunities for striking planting compositions. This scarcity is partly due to the rarity of true blue-green plants. There are a few plants, such as this *Ruta* and several of the hostas whose dark and very grayed green foliage has a bluish appearance, which associate quite well with red-orange.

Light orange and light red-orange flowers can be found in an increasing number of annuals and perennials. For example, the annual *Cosmos sulphureus* 'Sunny Red' used here develops bicolored blooms in bright, light-tinted warm colors scattered above its fine-textured foliage. *Cosmos* and *Ruta* harmonize satisfactorily with the near-adjacent light yellow of *Corydalis* and its foliage repeats the foliage texture of *Ruta*. A pleasing textural companionship is established which persists until frost.

For optimal color balance there should be three or four more *Cosmos* blooms visible and an appropriate balance may be achieved in a minimum space 2 × 3 ft (0.6 × 0.9 m), with one *Ruta* in the rear, two *Cosmos* in the midground, and one *Corydalis* in the foreground.

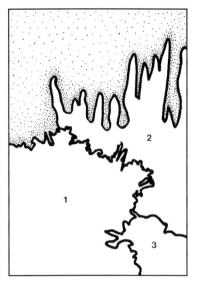

1. *Hemerocallis* 'Sammy Russell', two plants, 24–36 × 18 in (60–90 × 45 cm)
2. *Ligularia stenocephala* 'The Rocket', one plant, 48–60 × 24 in (120–150 × 60 cm)
3. *Dahlia* 'Ellen Houston', two plants, 36 × 24 in (90 × 60 cm)

PHOTO 58. Stonecrop Gardens, Cold Spring, New York, July. ENVIRONMENT: sun to part shade in soil of average fertility and moisture. USDA Zones 5–8. FEATURE: foliage late spring to fall; flower summer to fall.

INTENSE WARM colors dominate the summer season, often in large-scale blooms. The design challenge lies in associating these strong hues and forms sympathetically while avoiding the confusion or dissonance such mixtures often produce. These difficulties are well handled in this combination of intense colors in different forms. Broad, dense *Dahlia* globes nestle beneath *Ligularia* spires and horizontal, lily-like *Hemerocallis* flowers.

The vertical form of the bright yellow *Ligularia* contributes most dramatically since the plant's tall, ascending spire effects a sense of upward movement. Without the activity contributed by *Ligularia* the composition of the remaining plants would appear dull. The *Dahlia* provides a red daisy-like form in the foreground, and the midground is filled by the very deep red and red-orange tones of the *Hemerocallis* flowers. These near-adjacent bloom colors combine very harmoniously while the textures and colors of the foliages also offer considerable variety.

Often, such medium- to large-scale, strong-hued blooms are employed in larger settings, perhaps viewed over a distance greater than 30 ft (9 m), permitting appreciation of powerful colors without obtrusiveness. I have successfully used these colors in an intimate garden space however, placing them less than 15 ft (4.6 m) from the principal viewing point. The large plant form and intensity of these colors in close proximity may not please everyone and definitely restricts color choices for nearby plants.

To improve color balance there should be twice as much red and red-orange as yellow, so the *Dahlia* quantity should be increased slightly. A space 4 × 4 ft (1.2 × 1.2 m) would accommodate a minimum grouping of one *Ligularia* in the rear, two *Hemerocallis* in the midground, and two *Dahlia* in the foreground.

PHOTO 59. Ziegler Garden, Bedford, New York, July.
ENVIRONMENT: sun to part shade in soil of average fertility and moisture.
USDA Zones 5–9.
FEATURE: foliage late spring to fall; flower late spring to fall.

OFTEN DESIGNERS introduce a tiny amount of a warm color to energize a small garden space or simply to offer a compatible divergence for cool colors. Tinted, or pastel versions of warm colors serve this intention very well. Unfortunately the number of easily cultivated plants in these pale warm colors is fairly limited, although it is increasing through hybridizing efforts. Two such cultivars are combined in a container here, yet they are just as easily grown in a garden setting. A pale yellow is presented in the *Lonicera* blooms and the bright warm colors of the *Lantana* flowers are moderated by their mix and diminutive petals.

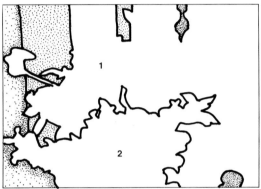

1. *Lonicera periclymenum* 'Graham Thomas', one plant, 12 ft (4 m)
2. *Lantana* 'Confetti', three plants, 12–15 × 15 in (30–40 × 40 cm)

The vigorous *Lonicera* vine blooms from spring until fall where summers are cooler and offers fragrant blossoms. Its pale blooms also modify the intensity of some of the colors appearing in the *Lantana*. This *Lantana* produces many different colors in its flat, smallish, fragrant flower heads, including pale yellow, yellow-orange, orange, and red. Although the colors are individually strong, the relative quantity of each color is rather minute. There is just enough warmth and variation to impart a mood of gaiety and lend the sense of energy often associated with warm colors.

Any of these colors could be repeated in other plants added to this pair. Orange or darker yellow daylilies, for example, would add a valuable foliage texture as well as a harmonious bloom color. The *Lonicera* vine, of course, must be trained over a fence, shrub, wall, or trellis, with its companions planted in front of it.

A minimum ground space of 2 × 3 ft (0.6 × 0.9 m) will be needed for the basic pairing. For a container planting similar to the one pictured, plants will need an 18 in × 18 in (45 × 45 cm) container.

PHOTO 60. New York Botanical Garden, New York City, August. ENVIRONMENT: sun in soil of average fertility and moisture. USDA Zones 5–8. FEATURE: foliage summer to fall; flower summer to fall.

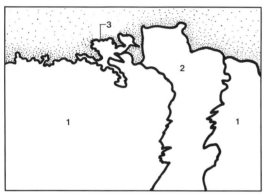

1. *Helenium autumnale* 'Brilliant', two plants, 36 × 18 in (90 × 45 cm)
2. *Helenium autumnale* 'Riverton', one plant, 36–48 × 18 in (90–120 × 45 cm)
3. *Zinnia elegans* 'Red Sun', two plants, 36 × 24 in (90 × 60 cm)

NATURE GENEROUSLY allows an abundance of warm, powerful, intense hues in late summer, and hybridizers have been quick to expand on the bounty. These hues combine easily with each other or with the near-complementary cool hues. Small daisy-like or composite flower forms also occur frequently among late-blooming perennials and can be useful as a unifying element between more striking forms and textures. Here several composite plants in adjacent hues cluster together with relative harmony.

Although the color blending is adequate, greater variation in flower form and size and greater attention to color balancing would improve the composition. The largest flower is the *Zinnia* and the remaining daisy-like blooms are all of very similar size. *Helenium autumnale* 'Riverton' (sometimes listed as 'Riverton Gem') develops a yellow and dark red flower. An unnamed yellow-flowered *Helenium autumnale* intermingles with the very dark red-orange *Helenium autumnale* 'Brilliant', but is not essential for this design. A few more zinnias in the composition would aid the color balance and increase the variation in flower size.

These lanky heleniums benefit from a foreground planting to disguise their lower stems. A densely foliaged plant 18–24 in (45–60 cm) tall, such as *Solidago* 'Crown of Rays', would accomplish this nicely and also bring a much-needed form variation to the composition.

The minimum grouping needed for color balance, including two *Solidago* 'Crown of Rays' in the foreground, requires a space 4 × 4 ft (1.2 × 1.2 m), with two *Zinnia* and one *Helenium autumnale* 'Riverton' in the rear and two *Helenium autumnale* 'Brilliant' in the midground.

PHOTO 61. Henrietta Lockwood Garden, Bedford, New York, July. ENVIRONMENT: sun in soil of average fertility and moisture. USDA Zones 4–8. FEATURE: foliage late spring to late summer; flower mid to late summer.

Novice designers often avoid the use of bold warm colors because they can seem strident and may war with neighboring hues. Yet the vibrancy and energy of intense warm colors is valuable whenever an energetic mood is needed. They are also particularly dramatic, and are often used, in sunny climates at latitudes yielding strong bright light and extreme contrasts of light and shade.

Keep in mind, however, that it is necessary to provide careful transitions from pure intense warm colors, such as those shown here, to lighter tints. The cool-hued pastels, such as pale blue or pale violet, do not readily combine with pure and intensely warm colors. Necessary color transitions are best handled by graduating first to paler tints of the warm colors, then to pale tints of cool hues, and finally on to stronger, purer cool hues if such range is necessary.

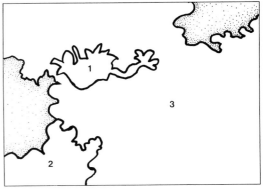

1. *Lilium* 'Enchantment', two plants, 24 × 12 in (60 × 30 cm)
2. *Tropaeolum majus* 'Alaska', two plants, 12 × 12 in (30 × 30 cm)
3. *Oenothera tetragona*, one plant, 18 × 12 in (45 × 30 cm)

This yellow-flowered *Oenothera* is one of the most easily grown summer-flowering plants and quickly spreads to all available space. Paired here with the dark orange 'Enchantment' lily and the orange, yellow-orange, and dark red of the *Tropaeolum*, a small-scale grouping of adjacent warm colors is developed. The variegated leaves of the *Tropaeolum* bring a lightness to the composition and command a special affinity with the yellow *Oenothera* bloom. Another *Tropaeolum* with similar bloom colors, such as *T.* 'Double Dwarf Jewel Series' or 'Gleam Series', could substitute nicely, although the small design advantage of variegated leaves would be sacrificed.

A relatively small space of 2 × 3 ft (0.6 × 0.9 m) is needed for a minimum quantity of two *Lilium* in the rear, one *Oenothera* in the midground, and two *Tropaeolum* in the foreground.

PHOTO 62. Stonecrop Gardens, Cold Spring, New York, July. ENVIRONMENT: sun in soil of lean to average fertility and moisture. USDA Zones 3–9. FEATURE: foliage late spring to late summer; flower summer.

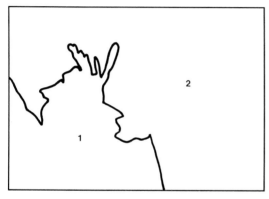

1. *Hemerocallis* 'Colonial Dame', two plants, 18 × 12 in (45 × 30 cm)
2. *Achillea millefolium* 'Weser River Sandstone', three plants, 18–36 × 18 in (45–90 × 45 cm)

THIS IS NOT a dramatic color combination, merely repeating a range of warm colors in two plants, yet it lends itself to use in small spaces where intense colors may be inappropriate. It is also a useful combination for effecting transitions from more intense warm colors to lighter cool colors and eventually to intense cool colors.

These *Achillea* are impressive, hardy plants, with aromatic leaves and are valuable for their unusual flower colors, long bloom, and tolerance of poor or lean soil conditions. They are so adapted to poor soil that too rich a soil causes their flower heads to flop. Any companions should be equally tolerant of lean soil conditions. These *Achillea* combine well with many other flower colors, including the abundant yellows and oranges of summer and the cool blue-greens and blue-violets which complement their warm red-orange and yellow-orange tints.

The yellow-orange and darker stripes of this *Hemerocallis* flower combine perfectly with similar hues in the *Achillea*. Any light or pale yellow-orange *Hemerocallis* in the 18–24 in (45–60 cm) range would fit as well. Overlapping bloom is here sustained for several weeks while *Achillea* continues to bloom sporadically for several months. The contrast of form and texture between ferny *Achillea* foliage and straplike *Hemerocallis* leaves is quite as interesting as the color harmony.

This pair fits into a 3 × 3 ft (0.9 × 0.9 m) space. Use three *Achillea* plants interplanted with two *Hemerocallis*.

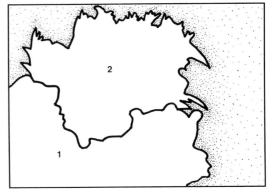

PHOTO 63. Stonecrop Gardens, Cold Spring, New York, July. ENVIRONMENT: sun in soil of average fertility and moisture. USDA Zones 5–8. FEATURE: foliage late spring to fall; flower late spring to summer.

ALTHOUGH bright warm colors are always bold and advancing in any composition, the size, quantity, and distribution of the bloom relative to the foliage significantly alters their impact. The flower of the annual *Zinnia* 'Old Mexico' has fine warm-color balance inherent in its blooms, which display a larger proportion of dark red over yellow. The small bloom scale allows a stronger design contribution from the foliage texture and color. The dominance of this dark red in its flowers also brings a rather subdued overall effect, enabling it to harmonize well with just the few dark orange 'Sombrero' daylilies.

1. *Zinnia* 'Old Mexico', three plants, 12–18 × 12 in (30–45 × 30 cm)
2. *Hemerocallis* 'Sombrero', one plant, 24–36 × 18 in (60–90 × 45 cm)

The warm zinnia hues stand out particularly well against the dark yellow-green, narrow, grasslike daylily foliage. Strong, warm colors harmonize easily with dark foliage, as most dark foliage is either dark yellow-green or dark red-orange and therefore shares a warm tone. Very few dark foliage colors are found in the cool shades of dark or deep red-violet.

If the *Zinnia* bloom contained more yellow and its blooms were larger, significantly more *Hemerocallis* would be needed to balance the strength of the yellow. The mood of the composition would become more cheerful. As it is, this composition has all the advantages of warm color with none of the usual stridencies. Its subtlety suits it to a small garden space where it is not always easy to place warm-hued combinations.

The minimum group will require an area 2 × 3 ft (0.6 × 0.9 m), with one *Hemerocallis* 'Sombrero' or similarly colored daylily in the rear and three to five *Zinnia* in the foreground.

PHOTO 64. Cloister Hotel, Sea Island, Georgia, May. ENVIRONMENT: sun in soil of average fertility and moisture. USDA Zones 5–8. FEATURE: foliage mid spring to fall; flower mid spring to fall.

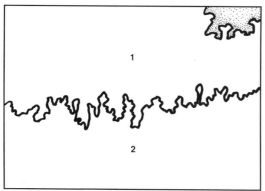

1. *Coreopsis* 'Sunray', one plant, 18–24 × 12 in (45–60 × 30 cm)
2. *Celosia cristata* 'Sparkler Mix', three plants, 9–12 × 12 in (25–30 × 30 cm)

MANY DESIGN situations benefit from the addition of brightly colored annuals that transplant almost instant color for several months. Variation in flower form may provide enough textural interest while variation in foliage is usually sadly absent in annual plantings of color spots. The warm color association of this perennial yellow-orange *Coreopsis* and annual multihued *Celosia* is frequently seen uniting large spaces in public gardens. Their repetition will fulfill the same function in the more compact spaces of private gardens in smaller quantities.

The flower forms are distinctly varied between the daisy of *Coreopsis* and the small spikes of *Celosia*. Inserting a third flower form, such as the globose, dark red-orange *Gomphrena globosa* 'Strawberry Fields', behind or interplanted with *Coreopsis*, would bring a welcome extension to form and improve the color balance.

Undistinguished foliage is a general characteristic of annuals. Here, the foliage of the perennial is also rather insignificant and very similar to the annual's scale and texture. Adding another background plant with a bolder foliage form, such as *Iris* or *Heliopsis scabra*, would provide textural structure.

These plants, including two *Gomphrena globosa* 'Strawberry Fields' in the rear, can be combined in an area 2 × 3 ft (0.6 × 0.9 m), with one *Coreopsis* and three *Celosia* in the foreground. These quantities approximate a more desirable color balance by maintaining a slightly larger quantity of red-orange than yellow-orange while subordinating foliar concerns.

PHOTO 65. Ziegler Garden, Bedford, New York, September. ENVIRONMENT: part shade to sun in soil of average to greater fertility and average moisture. USDA Zones 5–9. FEATURE: foliage mid spring to fall; flower late spring to fall.

SOMETIMES an individual plant is so visually or physically dominant and vigorous that its companions must be selected and placed with extra care to achieve harmony. In this grouping of adjacent warm colors, a harmonious balance of color would allow roughly twice as much red flower as yellow flower and slightly more orange than yellow. What is seen is a great deal of *Rudbeckia* yellow-orange.

Rudbeckia has been described as too coarse for most gardens and this may be a valid point. It is very bold and generally contributes more color than is needed, especially in small spaces. Too much yellow or yellow-orange is problematic in multihued designs. Blooms are typically dense and large in yellow-flowering plants and they also tend to be vigorous and spread easily, rapidly multiplying the yellow abundance. Confining them to maintain color harmony usually requires special effort, including occasionally removing perfect blooms to aid color proportions.

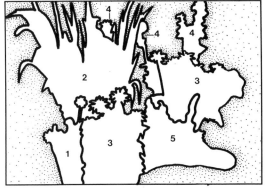

1. *Cosmos sulphureus* 'Sunny Red', three plants, 15–18 × 15 in (40–45 × 40 cm)
2. *Iris pseudacorus*, one plant, 24–36 × 18 in (60–90 × 45 cm)
3. *Rudbeckia* 'Goldsturm', one plant, 18–24 × 18 in (45–60 × 45 cm)
4. *Lobelia cardinalis*, three plants, 30–42 × 12 in (75–110 × 30 cm)
5. *Salvia* 'Lady in Red', three plants, 12–15 × 12 in (30–40 × 30 cm)

The flower forms featured in the above association make a valuable contribution to its success: the contrast between vertical *Iris* and *Lobelia* spires, and the daisy forms of *Cosmos* and *Rudbeckia* blooms establish the diversity and interest for this planting. Improved color proportion for this group would allow the combined efforts of pure red provided by *Lobelia* and *Salvia* to balance the yellow of the *Rudbeckia*.

To achieve a sense of color proportion requires a space 3 × 5 ft (0.9 × 1.5 m), with one *Iris* and two *Lobelia* in the rear, one *Rudbeckia* in the midground, and three *Salvia* and three *Cosmos* in the foreground.

PHOTO 66. Hadspen Garden, Sandra and Nori Pope, owners, Somerset, England, July. ENVIRONMENT: sun in soil of average fertility and moisture. USDA Zones 4–8. FEATURE: foliage late spring to late summer; flower late spring to summer.

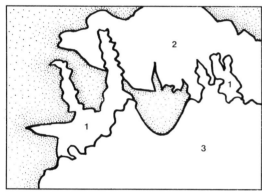

1. *Digitalis* × *mertonensis*, three plants, 30–48 × 18 in (75–120 × 45 cm)
2. *Achillea millefolium* 'Salmon Beauty', two plants, 18–36 × 18 in (45–90 × 45 cm)
3. *Potentilla* 'Tangerine', one plant, 36 × 36 in (90 × 90 cm)

THIS COMBINATION employs closely adjacent harmonious tints of light red, light orange, and light red-orange. The total effect is soothing and tranquil—due to both the pleasing repetition of pale red-orange tints in *Achillea* and *Digitalis* and the grayed, fine-textured foliage in *Achillea* and *Potentilla*. Compare this with the warm hues used in their intense pure forms in photo 65, where the effect is more decidedly dynamic and vibrant. Altering one of the light-valued hues in this combination, perhaps by substituting a pure orange or red *Potentilla*, would lessen the pastel harmony but enliven the composition.

Striking contrasts in flower form occur between the *Digitalis* spikes, the flat *Achillea* corymbs, and the small *Potentilla* blooms. Doubling the number of *Digitalis* would improve the balance between vertical and horizontal forms and strengthen the design.

The addition of one *Geranium endressii* 'Wargrave Pink' in the foreground would bring greater complexity to both flower and foliage textures and extend the composition's bloom time to late summer. *Achillea millefolium* 'Weser River Sandstone' will substitute satisfactorily for *Achillea millefolium* 'Salmon Beauty' in this association since its flowers display light yellow and light red accents that harmonize well with *Digitalis* × *mertonensis*.

Three *Digitalis* should be placed with two *Achillea* in the midground and one *Potentilla* in the foreground in an area 4 × 5 ft (1.2 × 1.5 m). Adding one *Geranium* in the foreground would increase space requirements to 5 × 5 ft (1.5 × 1.5 m).

PHOTO 67. New York Botanical Garden, New York City, July. ENVIRONMENT: sun in soil of average fertility and moisture. USDA Zones 5–9. FEATURE: foliage late spring to late summer; flower late spring to late summer.

VERY WARM colors reliably fulfill their design functions in spaces that are dramatically altered by changing light and shadow. They do not bleach out in strong light nor do they fade away in light shadow as cool colors do. Hot colors also carry well across large distances whereas cool colors weaken over distance. For this reason I use them often by combining red and yellow, an association I like particularly.

The intense, pure warm red of these *Crocosmia* and the strong dark yellow of *Achillea* are ideal companions because the blooms display near-equal color strength. Furthermore, the strongly ascending form of the *Crocosmia* foliage balances the pronounced

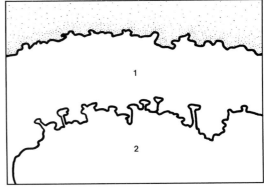

1. *Crocosmia* 'Lucifer', two plants, 24–48 × 12 in (60–120 × 30 cm)
2. *Achillea* 'Coronation Gold', one plant, 24–36 × 18 in (60–90 × 45 cm)

horizontal line created in the flat form of the *Achillea* flower heads. There is a strong feeling of movement in these contrasting shapes, emphasized by the swooping form of *Crocosmia*'s tilted blooms.

These plant forms bring energy to the composition and reinforce the vibrancy created by the color association. However, this dominant composition must be placed carefully. It can be a focal point in a large space, yet is not too overwhelming viewed across a space as small as 15 ft (5 m).

For best color balance one should have about twice as much *Crocosmia* flower as *Achillea* flower. Relatively small quantities of these two plants will produce a great effect, so in a space of 3 × 4 ft (0.9 × 1.2 m) one could place two *Crocosmia* and one *Achillea*.

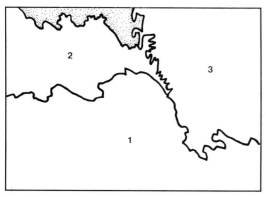

1. *Potentilla flamea*, two plants, 12 × 12 in (30 × 30 cm)
2. *Hemerocallis* (unknown) cultivar, two plants, 18–48 × 12 in (45–120 × 30 cm)
3. *Lilium lancifolium*, five bulbs, 24–48 × 12 in (60–120 × 30 cm)

COMBINATIONS of adjacent, pure warm colors require careful color proportioning and thoughtful siting in the landscape. Careful placement is essential with all warm-color compositions, especially where a pure, intense color is included, since it will easily dominate a small space and weaker-hued companions.

This summer association of adjacent warm colors is done at a relatively small scale and, at this stage, is superbly balanced in its red, yellow-orange, and orange hues. Generally there should be half as much yellow-orange and orange as there is red in such combinations. The yellow-orange used here is a lighter version of the pure, intense color. This slight tinting demands a modest increase in the quantity of yellow-orange to keep the color in balance with *Potentilla*'s pure undiluted red. When the orange lilies open, more orange is added to the composition and the color balance temporarily shifts.

This particular *Potentilla* is unusually compact. The *Hemerocallis* and *Lilium* need to be compact too, growing in the 18–30 in (45–80 cm) range, so their blooms are not visually separated from the *Potentilla* at their base. An Asiatic hybrid lily, such as *Lilium* 'Enchantment', will substitute for the *Lilium lancifolium*. *Potentilla atrosanguinea* 'Gibson's Scarlet' may be substituted for *P. flamea*. Daylilies whose reblooming characteristics would permit them to substitute for the unknown beauty shown here include *Hemerocallis* 'Stella d'Oro' or 'Mayan Gold'.

A space 3 × 3 ft (0.9 × 0.9 m) would allow five *Lilium* in the rear, with two *Hemerocallis* in the midground, and two *Potentilla* in the foreground.

PHOTO 69. Donald M.
Kendall Sculpture
Gardens, Pepsico's World
Headquarters, Purchase,
New York, June.
ENVIRONMENT: sun in
soil of average fertility
and moisture.
USDA Zones 4–7.
FEATURE: foliage late
spring to fall; flower late
spring.

THIS GROUPING of late spring-flowering plants illustrates some of the advantages of combining colors adjacent on the color wheel. These violet and light blue-violet blooms are pleasantly unified by the presence of violet in both. Also, the benefit of placing light colors against dark colors is evident: the paler color appears to brighten when placed against the darker violet *Salvia* background.

The similarity of form and texture, which in another context might be monotonous, is here acting as a unifying element. Sufficient variation occurs in the slight changes in hue and in the light/dark juxtaposition. However, a third contrasting form in the same or adjacent hues would provide a welcome

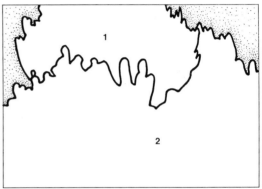

1. *Salvia* × *superba* 'May Night', three plants, 18 × 18 in (45 × 45 cm)
2. *Nepeta mussinii*, one plant, 12–18 × 18 in (30–45 × 45 cm)

focus for the group. The globes of red-violet *Allium giganteum* or the wands of blue-violet *Tradescantia* × *andersoniana* 'Blue Stone' would serve this purpose nicely.

Another color would also bring sparkle to the group. Pale yellow spires of *Digitalis grandiflora* would provide satisfying color contrast. Red *Centranthus ruber* or red-violet *Lychnis coronaria* would add adjacent but warmer colors and bring vibrancy at midday when the lighter violet hues may be drained of their color by strong light. These warmer red and red-violet colors would also brighten the group at dusk when violet colors recede significantly.

The basic pair requires a space 3 × 3 ft (0.9 × 0.9 m), with three *Salvia* in the rear and one *Nepeta* in the foreground. Adding two *Allium giganteum* would increase space requirement to 4 × 3 ft (1.2 × 0.9 m). Information on associate plants mentioned can be found in Part 2.

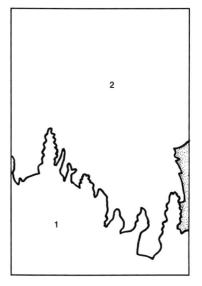

1. *Muscari armeniacum*, twelve
   bulbs, 6–8 × 4 in (15–20 × 10 cm)
2. *Tulipa* 'Pink Impression', six
   bulbs, 18–24 × 6 in (45–60 × 15
   cm)

PHOTO 70. Conservatory Garden, New York City, April. ENVIRONMENT: sun in soil of average fertility and moisture. USDA Zones 4–8. FEATURE: foliage mid to late spring; flower mid spring.

R ED-VIOLET and blue-violet blooms occur in large numbers of cultivated plants, especially in bulbs that can be found to flower from early spring until late summer. Red-violet and blue-violet are near-adjacent colors on the sixteen-color wheel and therefore harmonious, lending themselves easily to an enormous range of different combinations.

Tulips in particular, with their huge range of colors, tints, and shades, inspire dazzling spring experiments in combining warm and cool colors, adjacent colors, and complementary colors. Whatever the favorite color harmony and whatever the color theme of a spring planting, a tulip may be found to accommodate it. Despite this, one sees many bulb plantings in public gardens which appear to have been planted without even the modest amount of planning needed to ensure a harmonious color scheme.

The above early-spring bulb combination is not especially original, but it is very pleasing because the intensities of the two blooms involved are very closely matched and will continue to coordinate as the blooms open and fade. *Muscari* blooms in a rich light blue-violet and the tulip a slightly dark red-violet. Both flower types will lighten as they mature. After the tulip finishes blooming, the decline of its foliage needs to be masked by rising perennials or an interplanting of annuals. Some suggestions for masking are given with photo 78.

This pair looks wonderful planted in masses and drifts, or a tiny group at the base of a spring-flowering shrub is just as lovely. Plant six *Tulipa* behind twelve *Muscari* in a space about 2 × 2 ft (0.6 × 0.6 m).

PHOTO 71. Hidcote Manor Garden, National Trust property, Gloucestershire, England, July. ENVIRONMENT: part shade to sun in soil of average fertility and moisture. USDA Zones 5–8. FEATURE: foliage mid spring to fall; flower late spring to fall.

ONE OF the problems with container planting is that the plant grouping is often bunched at the top of the container and appears isolated from its context. Usually this difficulty is resolved by including trailing plants to creep down the sides of the container and link the contained planting to the surrounding space or base. Another solution is offered here. A former lead cistern, converted into a planter, has been given a permanent location and then surrounded by a perennial planting of sufficient height and mass to unite the ground with the contained composition. The plants in the planter and those in the earth surrounding it comprise one composition.

Light violet *Verbena* and the very gray yellow-green trailing *Helichrysum* in the planter are annuals in many places. The grape-leaved *Anemone*, contributing its pale red-violet blooms a bit later in the

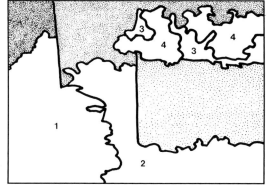

1. *Anemone hupehensis* 'September Charm', 24–36 × 24 in (60–90 × 60 cm)
2. *Campanula portenschlagiana*, 6–9 × 12 in (15–25 × 30 cm)
3. *Helichrysum petiolare*, 12–24 × 24 in (30–60 × 60 cm)
4. *Verbena* 'Amethyst', 12 × 12 in (30 × 30 cm)

season, and the spreading, very light violet *Campanula* are perennials which will permanently associate the planter to its setting even if the annuals in the container are changed.

This planting's subdued color scheme is executed in the harmonious adjacent hues of pale red-violet, light violet, and blue-violet. Combined with the complementary hue of very pale, gray yellow-green *Helichrysum*, all associate well with the lead-gray cistern. The four plant types would not be as effective if all were planted directly into the ground since *Anemone*'s bold form and scale would dwarf its three companions unless an intermediate-scale plant were added.

One *Anemone* and five *Campanula* require a space of 3 × 3 ft (0.9 × 0.9 m). The container used in this setting is about 26 in (65 cm) high.

PHOTO 72. Stonecrop Gardens, Cold Spring, New York, May. ENVIRONMENT: sun in soil of average fertility and moisture. USDA Zones 4-8. FEATURE: foliage mid spring; flower mid spring.

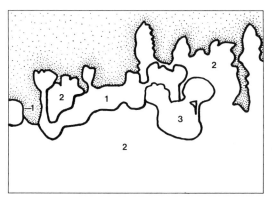

1. *Tulipa* 'Purple Rain', nine bulbs, 18–24 × 6 in (45–60 × 15 cm)
2. *Camassia quamash*, four bulbs, 18–24 × 6 in (45–60 × 15 cm)
3. *Allium aflatuense* 'Purple Sensation', two bulbs, 24–36 × 12 in (60–90 × 30 cm)

PLANTING design creates four-dimensional compositions which are constantly altered by factors over which the designer has limited or no control. Differences in topography and weather, especially available moisture and soil type, the presence of animal predators, and many other factors affect the extent to which specific design principles may be applied or deemed successful. Although general principles about color, scale, and other design considerations are given, they are raw materials. Each must be adapted for each situation and refined by the experience, taste, and observations of the designer.

All plant composition photos capture a particular stage of growth, and light and moisture conditions, all of which soon will change. It is this emphemeral, constantly changing aspect of planting design which is its delight and its great frustration. However, plant design does not aim to fix a composition at its necessarily fleeting moments of perfection, except perhaps on film. Change should be regarded as an element of consideration, not as a barrier.

This composition was photographed just past its peak of perfection and features some of the less commonly used bulbs in the near-adjacent colors red-violet and blue-violet. The *Allium* offers its medium-size, red-violet globes to play against the vertical light blue-violet *Camassia* spires and dark red-violet *Tulipa*.

There are several outstanding *Camassia* cultivars currently available, *Camassia* being an easily grown but rather neglected spring-flowering bulb. If *Tulipa* 'Purple Rain' is not available, substitute the widely available and similarly tinted *Tulipa* 'Negrita'. The primary association requires a companion plant to spread and cover the bare area left by the bulbs' departure, and suggestions are given with photo 78.

Two *Allium* behind four *Camassia* and nine *Tulipa* would make an excellent minimum group in a space 2 × 3 ft (0.6 × 0.9 m).

PHOTO 73. New York
Botanical Garden, New
York City, September.
ENVIRONMENT: sun in
soil of average fertility
and moisture.
USDA Zones 5–8.
FEATURE: foliage late
spring to fall; flower
summer to fall.

RED-VIOLET, violet, and yellow are the flower
colors which naturally dominate the fall bloom
season. Spring-flowering colors are usually pale, with
whites and pale yellows predominating. Late spring
brings stronger yellows, pinks, and blue-violet and
violets in abundance. Summer's hues are often powerful reds, yellows, and oranges. The color intensity
in flowers begins to fade and become subdued by
fall, although in some climates deciduous leaves
briefly lend similar intensity to the landscape.

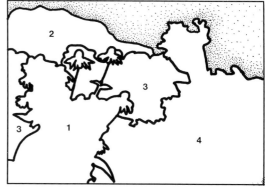

1. *Echinacea purpurea* 'Bright Star', one plant,
   24–36 × 18 in (60–90 × 45 cm)
2. *Aster frikartii* 'Mönch', two plants, 24–36 × 24 in
   (60–90 × 60 cm)
3. *Sedum* 'Autumn Joy', one plant, 18–24 × 24 in
   (45–60 × 60 cm)
4. *Anemone vitifolia* 'Robustissima', one plant, 36 ×
   18 in (90 × 45 cm)

Fall-flowering compositions require more thought
because there are fewer choices in varieties of highlight plants. It is harder to maintain a full, dense
planting in beds and borders as so many plants are
reaching the finish of their growing season and gaps
develop. Again, garden designers can rely on repetitions or slight variations of a single color theme or
plant form to establish viewer's interest in a defined
space and suggest fullness and cohesion.

The dominant color here is red-violet, available in many tints and shades in many
plants in many seasons. Light red-violet makes a powerful extended appearance in the
broad daisy form of *Echinacea*, which blooms from late summer into fall, and in the
pale *Anemone* blooms. Although the *Sedum* blooms are closer to red, they display the
same grayish quality typical of many sedums that is also reflected in the *Echinacea*
bloom. The light blue-violet *Aster* varies the color composition with a harmonious hue
in a smaller-scale daisy bloom.

This entire group, proportioned for color balance, will fit into a space 4 × 4 ft (1.2
× 1.2 m), with one *Sedum* in the foreground, one *Echinacea* in the midground, and
two *Aster frikartii* and one *Anemone* clustered around them in the rear.

PHOTO 74. Filoli, Woodside, California, June. ENVIRONMENT: sun in soil of average fertility and moisture. USDA Zone 8. FEATURE: foliage mid spring to fall; flower late spring to late summer.

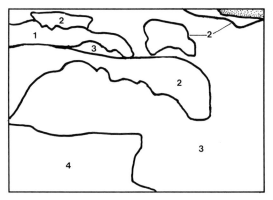

1. *Ballota pseudodictamnus*, one plant, 12–24 × 18 in (30–60 × 45 cm)
2. *Berberis thunbergii* 'Atropurpurea Nana', one plant, 18–24 × 30 in (45–60 × 75 cm)
3. *Lavandula angustifolia* 'Munstead', three plants, 12 × 12 in (30 × 30 cm)
4. *Teucrium chamaedrys*, two plants, 12–18 × 12–18 in (30–45 × 30–45 cm)

ALTHOUGH herbaceous plants are usually thought of as the chief source of garden color, color arrangements are also generated by using the foliage of shrubs and subshrubs. The color range is greatly qualified in such cases, but that very limitation often results in superior designs.

This knot garden depends heavily on the color triad of blue-violet in *Lavandula* blooms, red-orange in *Berberis* foliage, and complementary yellow-green in the dark foliage of *Lavandula* and *Teucrium*. Their relatively subdued and receding color qualities are rescued from dullness by the brilliance of the extremely pale *Ballota*. In a parterre or knot garden, where the plants are often clipped to maintain a strict pattern, the plants' individual forms and textures are less significant than their foliage color and ability to withstand shearing. When not used for such exacting design purposes, these plants will associate nicely without clipping and create a relaxed, finely-textured, natural-looking shrubby composition.

One *Berberis* in the rear, three *Lavandula*, two *Teucrium*, and one *Ballota* would make an effective group in any design where simplicity of form and subdued color is required. A minimum area of 3 × 4 ft (0.9 × 1.2 m) would be required. *Santolina chamaecyparissus* could substitute for *Ballota* without affecting space requirements.

1. *Allium aflatuense*, 24–36 × 12 in
   (60–90 × 30 cm)
2. *Tulipa* 'Greenland', 18–24 × 6 in
   (45–60 × 15 cm)
3. *Viola* × *wittrockiana*, 6–8 × 9 in
   (15–20 × 25 cm)

PHOTO 75. Monet's Garden, Giverny, France, May. ENVIRONMENT: sun in soil of average fertility and moisture. USDA Zones 4–8. FEATURE: foliage mid to late spring; flower mid to late spring.

ABSENCE of focus and lack of a distinctive plant form weakens many garden associations to the point of dullness. The striking vertical form and distinctive umbels of many alliums can give immediate focus to almost any planting composition and for this reason alone the plants merit inclusion at multiple scales of garden design.

Matched here by a similar tulip form, allium globes contrast each other and a textural bed of 'Maxim Marina'-type hybrid violas. The adjacent hues and similar delicate tints of these light red-violet tulips and alliums and predominantly light violet violas harmonize effortlessly. The violas are an essential base for *Allium* and *Tulipa* , whose stems rise from the bare ground amid very little foliage of their own. One of the limitations general to alliums is that their foliage dies rapidly, in some alliums while the flowers are still vibrant, and all benefit from a surrounding interplanting of annuals or perennials that will obscure any foliar deficits. These same disguising plants are particularly useful if they later expand their foliage and flower to fill the space left by the decline and disappearance of the tulips.

The technique illustrated here of intermingling plants and scattering bulbs at random contributes to a natural appearance. If the overall character of the site is rather formal, arranging tulips and alliums more or less symmetrically will reflect that quality. A dense planting that completely fills the space allotted is the best way to use these bulbs and annual combinations.

PHOTO 76.
Conservatory Garden,
New York City, May.
ENVIRONMENT: sun to
part shade in soil of
average fertility
and moisture.
USDA Zones 4–7.
FEATURE: foliage late
spring to fall; flower
late spring to summer.

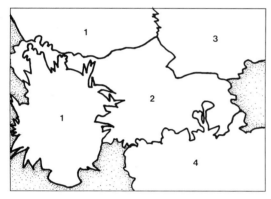

1. *Iris sibirica*, three plants, 18–36 × 9 in (45–90 ×
   25 cm)
2. *Geranium endressii* 'Wargrave Pink', one plant,
   12–24 × 24 in (30–60 × 60 cm)
3. *Amsonia tabernaemontana*, two plants, 24–36 ×
   24 in (60–90 × 60 cm)
4. *Brunnera macrophylla*, one plant, 18 × 24 in (45
   × 60 cm)

THIS *Amsonia* is a very graceful perennial with
some common design limitations: it blooms very
briefly, often for only a week in mid spring, and its
indistinct texture and pale recessive flower color create difficulties in locating companions that do not
overwhelm its fine texture and delicate color. This
fine composition overcomes these difficulties by
associating *Amsonia* with a series of plants with small
flowers in pastel hues.

All four flowering plants bloom in adjacent and
therefore harmonious hues of blue, blue-violet, violet, and red-violet or red. *Brunnera* is one of the best
companions for *Amsonia* since its blue flowers are
in a harmonious adjacent color and are also tiny and
relatively diffuse so they do not dominate. Its broad,
low, dark green leaves provide a striking contrast to
the finely textured *Amsonia* foliage and anchors it
solidly to the ground.

Because *Amsonia* flowers cluster at the top of long stems, they contribute an ascending quality to the design which is here repeated in the bold form of nearby *Iris* foliage
and flowers. *Geranium* foliage makes a solid visual line for the rising *Amsonia* stems
and leaves as its scattered, small, pale red to pale red-violet blooms complement the
airily delicate *Amsonia* flowers.

The large group shown here could be reduced to fit into a space 5 × 5 ft (1.5 × 1.5
m), with two *Amsonia* and three *Iris* in the rear and one *Geranium* and one *Brunnera*
in the foreground.

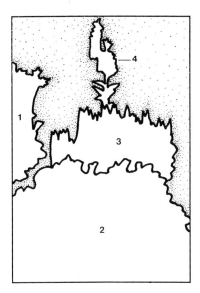

1. *Aquilegia alpina,* four plants, 12–24 × 12 in (30–60 × 30 cm)
2. *Geranium macrorrhizum,* one plant, 12–18 × 18 in (30–45 × 45 cm)
3. *Veronica latifolia* 'Crater Lake Blue', one plant, 18 × 12 in (45 × 30 cm)
4. *Digitalis purpurea* 'Excelsior', three plants, 36–60 × 18 in (90–150 × 45 cm)

PHOTO 77. Ziegler Garden, Bedford, New York, June. ENVIRONMENT: sun to part shade in soil of average fertility and moisture. USDA Zones 4–8. FEATURE: foliage late spring to late summer; flower late spring.

THIS overlapping combination has about a week of absolute glory in June. It combines intense pure violet, red-violet, and blue-violet with a few lighter tints of these colors occurring among the hybrid *Digitalis.* It is not a combination that appeals to everyone because of the strident intensity of the colors involved. I find it useful as an accent group and at times have used irregular repetitions of this group to outline briefly a small space lacking definition. Depending on the weather conditions, the group provides several weeks of gradual flowering before its week of peak expression.

Violet *Aquilegia* blooms first and is soon joined by light red-violet *Geranium,* blue-violet *Veronica,* and eventually the *Digitalis.* A hard crushing rain may smash down *Veronica,* so it needs to be supported. Avoid very light tints and pale pastels among the foreground *Geranium* and *Veronica* if this group is enlarged or joined. Pale colors will be diminished by these powerful red-violet and blue-violet hues and will simply look lost or abandoned. A stronger clump of *Digitalis* in the rear and a denser *Aquilegia* planting would strengthen the overall composition. Note that the *Geranium* is the only plant here to develop foliage that remains attractive and fragrant until fall.

A space about 3 × 5 ft (0.9 × 1.5 m) will accommodate an enlarged and stronger composition with three *Digitalis* in the rear, four *Aquilegia* in the midground, and one *Geranium* and one *Veronica* in the foreground.

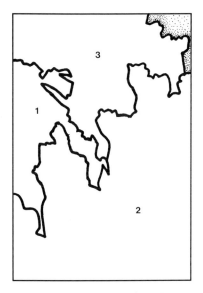

1. *Viola × wittrockiana*, five plants, 6–8 × 9 in (15–20 × 25 cm)
2. *Tulipa* 'Negrita', six bulbs, 18–24 × 6 in (45–60 × 15 cm)
3. *Tulipa* 'Arabian Mystery', six bulbs, 18–24 × 6 in (45–60 × 15 cm)

PHOTO 78. Conservatory Garden, New York City, May. ENVIRONMENT: sun in soil of average fertility and moisture. USDA Zones 5–8. FEATURE: foliage mid to late spring; flower mid spring.

THIS ASSOCIATION addresses a previously mentioned problem with bulbs, that of bare stems poking out of bare ground. The difficulty is resolved by planting a hybrid pansy in front of the tulip display in this garden. The richness of this color combination gives an idea of the great experimental possibilities in combining different *Tulipa* colors and *Viola*.

A *Viola* flowering in blue-violet has been chosen to harmonize with the deep red-violet bloom colors of the two tulip cultivars. It is planted solidly in front of dense symmetrical blocks of tulips, making a stiffer and more formal design than the loose, intermingled arrangement seen in photo 75. Many public and fewer private gardens solve the dilemma of covering the ground left bare by disappearing tulips and other spring-flowering bulbs simply by digging out the bulbs after flowering and replanting the resulting space with annuals. Another solution is to interplant the tulips with companion perennials which expand their foliage in late spring and eventually cover the bare space left by the decline of bulb flowers and foliage.

Campanula carpatica 'Blue Clips', *Myosotis sylvatica*, and various *Lamium* cultivars, including the white-flowering *Lamium maculatum* 'White Nancy', are often used as companion perennials for spring-flowering bulbs. *Brunnera macrophylla* is also a helpful foreground planting for tulips. It develops tiny, blue, spring flowers which combine readily with many tulip flower colors, and its dark, heart-shaped leaves continue to expand during the spring and quickly cover bare spaces.

A space as small as 2 × 3 ft (0.6 × 0.9 m) would accommodate six of each *Tulipa* with five *Viola* in the foreground. See Part 2 for further details on the specific companions mentioned for spring-flowering bulbs.

PHOTO 79.
Conservatory Garden,
New York City, May.
ENVIRONMENT: part
shade in soil of average
fertility and moisture.
USDA Zones 4–9.
FEATURE: foliage late
spring to late summer;
flower early to late
spring.

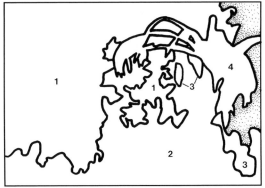

E VEN A VERY small amount of white is useful in a shaded space. It will stand out in the darkness and draw attention to a planting which may otherwise feature dim blue and violet hues. Although this group will flourish in a shaded site, light shade will permit the receding blue and violet colors to be seen more clearly. A position in front of shrubs under the canopy of very high or fine-foliaged deciduous trees would be ideal.

The flowering peak occurs in spring when the intense light violet to blue-violet *Ajuga* spikes bloom simultaneously with blue *Mertensia* and white *Ajuga*. *Hemerocallis* has been included to provide a later summer bloom and to partially cover the spaces left when *Mertensia* disappears into the ground in late spring. Any *Hemerocallis* may be selected for this composition and it could also serve as a link to an adjacent composition.

1. *Mertensia virginica*, two plants, 12–24 × 12 in (30–60 × 30 cm)
2. *Ajuga reptans* 'Atropurpurea', three plants, 6 × 12 in (15 × 30 cm)
3. *Ajuga reptans* 'Alba', three plants, 6 × 12 in (15 × 30 cm)
4. *Hemerocallis* (unknown) cultivar, two plants, 18–48 × 12 in (45–120 × 30 cm)

This is a long-lived, very low-maintenance association, requiring little care beyond deadheading the *Hemerocallis* after bloom. A space 3 × 3 ft (0.9 × 0.9 m) would accommodate a minimum planting of two *Mertensia*, two *Hemerocallis*, three *Ajuga reptans* 'Alba', and three *Ajuga reptans* 'Atropurpurea'. Arrange plants in long, thin, intertwined drifts so the emerging *Hemerocallis* plants disguise the decline of *Mertensia* foliage in late spring. If the group is planted with shrubs, ratios should be enlarged in proportion to the mass offered by the shrub grouping.

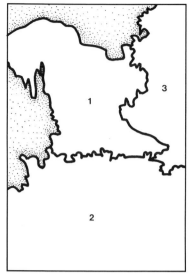

1. *Veronica latifolia* 'Crater Lake Blue', one plant, 18 × 12 in (45 × 30 cm)
2. *Dianthus* × *allwoodii* 'Essex Witch', two plants, 12–18 × 12 in (30–45 × 30 cm)
3. *Aquilegia* 'Heavenly Blue', two plants, 24–30 × 18 in (60–75 × 45 cm)

PHOTO 80. Donald M. Kendall Sculpture Gardens, Pepsico's World Headquarters, Purchase, New York, June. ENVIRONMENT: sun in soil of average fertility and moisture. USDA Zones 4–8. FEATURE: foliage mid spring to fall; flower mid spring to summer.

LIGHT AND pale tints weaken and diminish in bright sunlight. In climates where strong sunshine is common, intense pure colors are possibly more desirable in planting design. Most intense hues occur in the warm color range and a powerful, intense cool color, such as the blue-violet of this *Veronica*, is unusual and may be a useful focus.

Its intense flower hue and tiny reflective petals can drain color from nearby plants unless associates display equally powerful complementary colors, lighter versions of its own blue-violet, or harmonious colors of violet and red-violet. When the right situation with appropriate companions is found, the spectacular beauty of this plant radiates. I have also combined this veronica with white blooms from time to time, with moderately pleasing results.

Its floral companions here are a fragrant, red-violet centered *Dianthus* and a blue-violet and white *Aquilegia*. Any *Aquilegia* flowering in light violet or light blue-violet will associate well with the strong hue of this *Veronica*. Some further options in associating this uncommon saturated color are considered with photo 100.

A space 3 × 3 ft (0.9 × 0.9 m) will satisfy two *Aquilegia*, one *Veronica*, and two *Dianthus*.

PHOTO 81. Donald M. Kendall Sculpture Gardens, Pepsico's World Headquarters, Purchase, New York, August. ENVIRONMENT: sun in soil of average fertility and moisture. USDA Zones 3–9. FEATURE: foliage late spring to late summer; flower mid to late summer.

APPROXIMATELY 20% of commonly grown plants used in herbaceous borders flower in yellow and about 15% in violet. The sheer choice of flowers blooming in these colors allows many easily contrived associations. However, rather a large number of these blooms, particularly among the yellows, are in intense pure colors. In combination they may make a powerful, even strident, association. It is often worthwhile to seek out the plants which flower in tints (paler tones) or shades (darker tones) of yellow, and the smaller number with pale violet flowers.

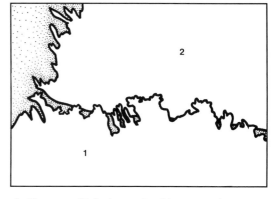

1. *Hemerocallis* (unknown) cultivar, two plants, 18–48 × 12 in (45–120 × 30 cm)
2. *Perovskia atriplicifolia*, three plants, 36 × 18 in (90 × 45 cm)

Here we see a softer connection in a light yellow *Hemerocallis* with pale violet *Perovskia* blooms. This pastel modification has tremendous advantages in a small space where more intense hues may dominate and create an unintended focal point. In a very large garden or landscape however, this informal association may project a limited design influence since the colors lack the strength to carry across a large space.

Diluted colors demand less care in proportioning and balancing since the whiteness present in all paler hues serves to unify. Light yellow is still the more advancing color of the two, especially in low light, and a balance of approximately two-thirds *Perovskia* and one-third *Hemerocallis* blooms is desirable. Although here they are arranged at the top and bottom of a retaining wall, they may be combined at the same level just as easily.

Use *Hemerocallis* 'Hyperion' or some of the pale yellow mid- to late-season hybrids in a minimum space of 3 × 4 ft (0.9 × 1.2 m), with three *Perovskia* behind two *Hemerocallis*.

PHOTO 82. Stonecrop Gardens, Cold Spring, New York, June. ENVIRONMENT: sun to part shade in soil of average fertility and moisture. USDA Zones 5–7. FEATURE: foliage late spring to fall; flower early spring to fall.

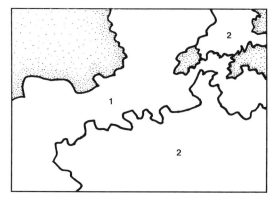

1. *Campanula portenschlagiana*, one plant, 6–9 × 12 in (15–25 × 30 cm)
2. *Corydalis lutea*, one plant, 9–15 × 12 in (25–40 × 30 cm)

THIS LATE spring or early summer flowering combination has strong color presence by combining light violet with a near-complementary light yellow bloom flushed with yellow-green. This compact grouping is ideal planted at the front of a border, cascading from walls or over rocks, or alongside a path. Both plants grow well in sun with protection from hot late afternoon sun, or in very light shade. When sited in a lightly shaded area, these light colors project well and effortlessly brighten a small space. The reserved qualities of each form balance nicely, with one not being too powerful for the other.

Campanula produces a dense flush of bloom, while faintly scented *Corydalis* flowers are always lightly scattered above its foliage. They provide a natural color proportioning when planted together, with more of the receding violet and less of the advancing warm yellow. After the *Campanula* flowers, its mats of foliage make an unobtrusive foil for the *Corydalis*, which continues to bloom until late fall. Both plants seed easily. This pair requires so little maintenance one may leave them almost entirely to themselves and simply enjoy the exhilarating summer combination. Complexity can be increased by adding another slightly larger plant with a different form that is suited to the same environment. *Alchemilla mollis* or a compact lavender, such as *Lavandula angustifolia* 'Munstead', would fit very nicely.

A preliminary grouping with one *Corydalis* placed behind one *Campanula* will fit a space 1 × 2 ft (0.3 × 0.6 m). See Part 2 for further description on the *Alchemilla* and *Lavandula* suggested.

PHOTO 83. Stonecrop Gardens, Cold Spring, New York, June. ENVIRONMENT: part shade in soil of average fertility and moisture. USDA Zones 5–8. FEATURE: foliage mid spring to fall; flower early spring to summer.

THIS LIGHT violet and yellow combination is a classic example of juxtaposing near-complementary colors while employing variety in texture and form. The color values, or qualities of lightness or darkness in each hue, are similarly light and enhance the harmony.

Light blue *Pulmonaria* blooms appear first in early spring, followed by yellow *Iris*, light violet to red-violet *Geranium*, and then pale yellow *Digitalis* in late spring. *Geranium*'s long blooming period allows it to combine with two different tones of yellow—in *Iris* and *Digitalis*, both yellow tones useful in brightening a darker space. The light violet flower color of *Geranium*, although of relatively high value, still is less visible than both yellows and is best visible in very light shade. All the plants in this group will thrive in sun with plenty of moisture, yet light shade is more ideal.

1. *Geranium* × *magnificum*, one plant, 18–24 × 24 in (45–60 × 60 cm)
2. *Iris pseudacorus*, one plant, 24–36 × 18 in (60–90 × 45 cm)
3. *Digitalis grandiflora*, three plants, 24–36 × 18 in (60–90 × 45 cm)
4. *Pulmonaria saccharata* 'Mrs. Moon', two plants, 10 × 15 in (25 × 40 cm)

Foliage form and texture is nicely varied and contributes significantly to the success of this combination: between linear swordlike *Iris* leaves, lance-shaped *Digitalis* leaves, small *Geranium* leaves, and the broad, smooth, white-speckled *Pulmonaria* foliage.

This medium-scale combination will need 4 × 4 ft (1.2 × 1.2 m), with one *Iris* and three *Digitalis* in the rear, one *Geranium* in the midground, and two *Pulmonaria* in the foreground. The more readily available *Geranium* 'Johnson's Blue' may be substituted for the *Geranium* × *magnificum* shown above.

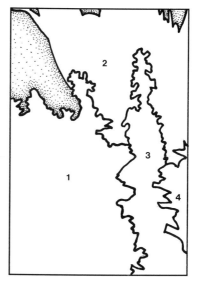

1. *Geranium* × *magnificum*, one plant,
   18–24 × 24 in (45–60 × 60 cm)
2. *Iris pseudacorus*, one plant, 24–36 ×
   18 in (60–90 × 45 cm)
3. *Digitalis grandiflora*, three plants,
   24–36 × 18 in (60–90 × 45 cm)
4. *Pulmonaria saccharata* 'Mrs. Moon',
   two plants, 10 × 15 in (25 × 40 cm)

PHOTO 84. Stonecrop Gardens, Cold Spring, New York, June. ENVIRONMENT: part shade in soil of average fertility and moisture. USDA Zones 5–8. FEATURE: foliage mid spring to fall; flower early spring to summer.

DIRECT complementary color associations are always combinations of a warm color and a cool color. Warm colors appear to advance and dominate while cool colors seem to weaken or diminish in association. This effect will be modified by the strength of the colors involved, by background color and texture, and by proximity to the viewer.

Bringing warm and cool colors into visual balance is one of the challenges of planting design. Often this balance is achieved by reducing the quantity of the warm hue and increasing the quantity of the cool hue. Providing 70% blue blooms to 30% yellow blooms for example, results in a color balance allowing equal appreciation of both flower colors. Another method of balancing color is to simply use lighter or tinted versions of the same color. This tinting effect somewhat reduces the drama evoked by a basic complementary color combination, but in some instances less drama is desirable.

The grouping in this photograph represents a slightly later phase of the combination shown in the previous photograph. Here however, the light violet *Geranium* blooms are paired not with a pure yellow, but with the pale yellow of *Digitalis* flowers and with a complementary hue in yellow-green foliage. The association of pale yellow with any tint or shade of violet is usually pleasing, and the placement of this pale color behind the *Geranium* enhances the violet form. A larger quantity of *Digitalis* than appears in the photo would strengthen this effect.

A 4 × 4 ft (1.2 × 1.2 m) area would allow one *Iris* and three *Digitalis* in the rear, one *Geranium* in the midground, and two *Pulmonaria* in the foreground.

PHOTO 85. Clapton Court
Gardens, Crewkerne,
Somerset, England, July.
ENVIRONMENT: sun in soil
of average fertility and
average or less moisture.
USDA Zones 5–9.
FEATURE: foliage late spring
to fall; flower late spring to
summer.

SIMPLE combinations are often the most successful. This one offers near-complementary and
opposite bloom tints in pale yellow *Coreopsis* and
light violet *Lavandula*. The flower forms are also varied nicely between the daisy-like *Coreopsis* and the
delicate, fragrant *Lavandula* spikes. The plants are
about the same height when in bloom, but the
brighter advancing color and daisy form of the *Coreopsis* flowers dominate.

Planting proportions should favor the lavender, or
its low-value violet spikes may be reduced to
insignificance by the brilliance of the coreopsis. A
near-perfect color proportioning is about two-thirds
Lavandula bloom to one-third *Coreopsis*.

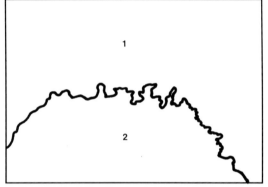

1. *Lavandula angustifolia* 'Hidcote', two plants, 18
   × 12 in (45 × 30 cm)
2. *Coreopsis verticillata* 'Moonbeam', one plant,
   15–24 × 24 in (40–60 × 60 cm)

The above setting includes some creamy white blooms of *Corydalis ochroleuca*,
which look nice, but the plant is often difficult to obtain. The complexity of the *Core-
opsis/Lavandula* association may be extended more easily by adding *Achillea* 'Moonshine', another pale yellow blooming plant with scented leaves frequently and delightfully combined with lavender. 'Moonshine' can add a contrasting horizontal flower form
and its attractive, deeply dissected gray-green foliage strengthens the finely textured
dark foliage of the basic association. Other yellow-flowering plants may be added to
the original pair, yet it is important to maintain the same relative proportion of yellow
to violet.

A minimum planting requires an area 2 × 3 ft (0.6 × 0.9 m) for one *Coreopsis* with
two *Lavandula*. Including one of the *Achillea* mentioned increases the planting area
to 3 × 4 ft (0.9 × 1.2 m); planting ratios would then be one *Coreopsis* and one *Achillea* to four *Lavandula*.

PHOTO 86. New York Botanical Garden, New York City, June. ENVIRONMENT: sun in soil of average fertility and moisture. USDA Zones 4–7. FEATURE: foliage late spring to late summer; flower late spring to late summer.

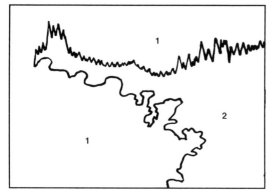

1. *Achillea* 'Coronation Gold', one plant, 24–36 × 18 in (60–90 × 45 cm)
2. *Salvia* × *superba* 'East Friesland', three plants, 15–18 × 18 in (40–45 × 45 cm)

VIOLET AND yellow is one of the most frequently used near-complementary color associations, chiefly because of the large number of yellow- and violet-blooming plants. Combining tinted or shaded versions of the pure colors modifies the intensity of any association. Since there are more choices of tinted and shaded blooms in yellow than in violet, it is usually easier to modify the warm component of the pair.

The flowers of *Achillea* 'Coronation Gold' are a dark yellow, thus the intensity of pure yellow is softened. They combine splendidly with the pure violet flowers of *Salvia* × *superba* 'East Friesland', with blooms associating for several weeks in late spring and early summer.

It is important to proportion correctly the amount of violet and yellow as even a slightly darkened yellow quickly overwhelms the receding violet. The balance for this darker shade of yellow is reached with about 30% yellow and 70% violet. Ideally they should be planted against a light background, or in an island bed or large border. If *Salvia* or any pure violet blooms are seen in front of a dark, fragmented background such as shrub foliage, the color recedes and effectively diminishes.

Where there is protection from late afternoon sun, the lightly fragrant *Corydalis lutea* in the foreground will add to the textural complexity and extend the composition's blooming season well into fall. The enlarged association requires the *Salvia* be cut down after first bloom to rebloom in late summer.

One *Achillea* combined with about three to four well-developed *Salvia* require a space about 3 × 3 ft (0.9 × 0.9 m). Including two *Corydalis lutea* in the foreground would certainly demand four *Salvia* and enlarge the area total to 3 × 4 ft (0.9 × 1.2 m).

PHOTO 87. New York Botanical Garden, New York City, September. ENVIRONMENT: sun in soil of average fertility and moisture. USDA Zones 5–8. FEATURE: foliage late summer to fall; flower late summer to fall.

THIS FALL association continues the frequently used near-complementary combination of yellow, yellow-green, and violet and is very useful for sustaining this color theme late in the growing season. It also echoes one of nature's common fall color schemes. The color intensities of yellow/violet are subdued in this planting, appropriate to a season in which many colors are fading and appealing to those who are uncomfortable with intense color combinations. The gentler, uncompetitive quality of these colors allows them to fit easily into a garden or border framework.

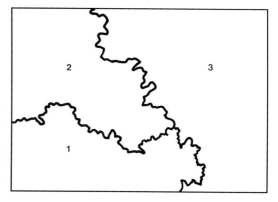

1. *Chrysanthemum pacificum*, one plant, 9–12 × 12 in (25–30 × 30 cm)
2. *Aster novae-angliae* 'Purple Dome', three plants, 12 × 12 in (30 × 30 cm)
3. *Solidago* 'Crown of Rays', one plant, 18–24 × 12 in (45–60 × 30 cm)

The *Aster* flowers offer a light violet color, while the *Solidago* contributes a dark greenish yellow, and both move away from the intensity of the pure hues. Here the *Aster* and the *Solidago* flowers are not yet fully opened, but when they are it will be apparent that a larger quantity of *Aster* is needed to fully compensate for the stronger advancing qualities of the yellow *Solidago* blooms. The association is joined by the light yellow daisy flowers of *Chrysanthemum* as the *Solidago* flowers begin to fade.

The contrast of form between the *Aster* and *Chrysanthemum* mounds and the spiked *Solidago* creates design interest before flowering begins. Foliage textures are also pleasingly varied between the broader, variegated *Chrysanthemum* leaves, the finely textured *Aster* mound, and the medium-textured, lance-shaped *Solidago* foliage.

To correctly balance bloom colors, this group should include at least one *Solidago* and three *Aster* with one *Chrysanthemum* in the foreground in a space 2 × 3 ft (0.6 × 0.9 m).

PHOTO 88. New York Botanical Garden, New York City, September. ENVIRONMENT: sun in soil of average fertility and moisture. USDA Zones 5–8. FEATURE: foliage late spring to fall; flower late spring to fall.

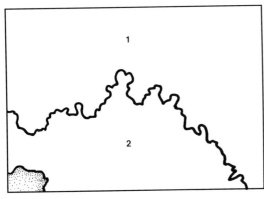

1. *Salvia farinacea* 'Victoria', three plants, 18–24 × 12 in (45–60 × 30 cm)
2. *Tagetes patula*, one plant, 10–12 × 12 in (25–30 × 30 cm)

THIS ASSOCIATION is very useful in the drier northern latitudes where summer sunlight drains color until all but the most intense hues fade significantly. In moist, cloudy climates, colors are strengthened by the moisture in the air rather than weakened by the brightness of the sun. This intensely colored association may be a bit strident for cloudier climes.

Salvia and *Tagetes* is a very easy association to contrive since it depends on two readily available annual plants which thrive in sun with adequate moisture. It is important to note that greater success is achieved by using a pure or light yellow or yellowish green flowering *Tagetes* in a small bloom size. While *Salvia farinacea* 'Victoria' is often combined with larger *Tagetes* blooms such as 'Inca Yellow', the greater quantity of yellow contributed by the larger dense blooms overwhelms the smaller flowers and receding color of violet *Salvia farinacea* and tilts the color composition out of balance.

The lighter textured marigold, *Tagetes signet* 'Lemon Gem' will substitute nicely for *T. patula*. Adding violet-flowered cultivars of *Heliotropium*, for a different form and fragrance and an increase in the quantity of violet bloom, would strengthen the complexity of the composition.

A minimum space of 2 × 2 ft (0.6 × 0.6 m) is needed for three *Salvia* in the rear and one *Tagetes* in the foreground. A larger grouping is definitely recommended. See Part 2 for a description of *Heliotropium* 'Marine'.

PHOTO 89. Conservatory Garden, New York City, July.
ENVIRONMENT: sun in soil of average fertility and moisture.
USDA Zones 4–8.
FEATURE: foliage late spring to fall; flower late spring to summer.

ALTHOUGH violet is frequently combined with yellow, blue-violet provides a closer complementary color and a softer alternative for landscape use. A large quantity of receding blue-violet is needed to achieve balance with any strong accompanying yellows. As the above photo shows, here there is insufficient blue-violet to balance all the yellow blooms.

The group will bloom successively for several months, with *Coreopsis* flowers providing a continuous link. The other players contribute their blooms at different times, beginning in late spring with *Heliopsis*, *Achillea*, and possibly *Hemerocallis*, depending on the cultivar selection. At this stage, the grouping may be regarded as a yellow monochromatic planting. *Coreopsis* flowers strengthen the yellow association in summer and are soon joined by *Veronica*'s complementary blue-violet blooms, which persist for several weeks.

The flower forms are interestingly varied—*Veronica* and *Lysimachia* spires play against the flat *Achillea* umbels and the daisy forms of *Coreopsis* and *Heliopsis*. The foliage textures add to design expression, especially the large, coarse, dark green *Heliopsis* leaves juxtaposed with gray-green, feathery, fragrant *Achillea* leaves and the finely textured *Coreopsis* foliage.

A space 5 × 6 ft (1.5 × 1.8 m) will be required for one *Heliopsis* in the rear, two *Achillea*, and seven *Veronica* in the midground, with one *Lysimachia*, one *Hemerocallis*, and two *Coreopsis* in the foreground.

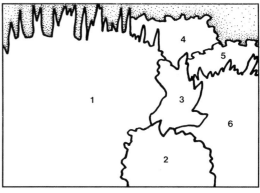

1. *Veronica spicata* 'Blue Charm', seven plants, 24–30 × 12 in (60–75 × 30 cm)
2. *Coreopsis verticillata* 'Moonbeam', two plants, 15–24 × 24 in (40–60 × 60 cm)
3. *Lysimachia punctata*, one plant, 18–30 × 24 in (45–75 × 60 cm)
4. *Heliopsis scabra*, one plant, 36–60 × 24 in (90–150 × 60 cm)
5. *Achillea* 'Coronation Gold', two plants, 24–36 × 18 in (60–90 × 45 cm)
6. *Hemerocallis* (unknown) cultivar, one plant, 18–48 × 18 in (45–120 × 30 cm)

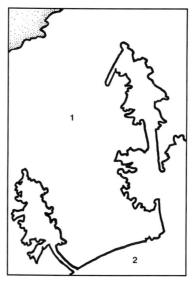

1. *Corydalis lutea*, one plant, 9–15
   × 12 in (25–40 × 30 cm)
2. *Hyacinthoides hispanica*, three
   bulbs, 15 × 6 in (40 × 15 cm)

PHOTO 90. Conservatory Garden, New York City, May. ENVIRONMENT: sun to part shade in soil of average fertility and moisture. USDA Zones 5–7. FEATURE: foliage early spring to fall; flower early spring to fall.

GARDEN and landscape design frequently employs simple, dependable combinations which adapt to many situations. A variety of exposure and moisture conditions on the same site may demand the unity provided by repeated use of a single association. Abrupt changes in scale may also be smoothed by massed plantings of one texture or hue combination. Often, it is also necessary for the same association to blend easily and unobtrusively with other plant groupings.

Corydalis lutea and *Hyacinthoides hispanica* combine to satisfy many design situations. Both thrive in sun or light shade and also contribute a delicate fragrance to their environment. They can be used extensively on tree-shaded banks and are also very suitable for mass planting near shrubs where large groupings may be effectively juxtaposed.

Corydalis lutea blooms from early spring to late fall, self seeds readily, and lends itself to many small-scale associations. Its distinctive, finely cut and textured foliage is easily contrasted with bolder textures and forms and suggests endless design experiments. Shown here growing in light shade with delicately fading blue-violet *Hyacinthoides* blooms, the pair offers an engaging complementary color combination in hues light enough to mix smoothly with paler or stronger tints.

There is sufficient contrast in plant forms as the finely textured yellow and yellow-green *Corydalis* mound juxtaposes the taller ascending *Hyacinthoides* flower spikes and broader straplike leaves. *Corydalis* also combines beautifully with smaller ferns, pale yellow-flowered dwarf *Hemerocallis*, *Brunnera*, and many other plants enjoying similar growing conditions. Near associates of this pair need a maximum height of 15–18 in (40–45 cm) so their small scale is not diminished or overly dominated.

In spaces of less than 6–10 sq ft (1.8–3.0 sq m) the two plants may be randomly intermingled. In larger spaces drift planting is recommended. A space only 1 × 1 ft (0.3 × 0.3 m) would accommodate one *Corydalis* and three intermingled *Hyacinthoides*.

PHOTO 91. Henrietta Lockwood Garden, Bedford, New York, July. ENVIRONMENT: sun in soil of average fertility and moisture. USDA Zones 6–7. FEATURE: foliage late spring to late summer; flower late spring to summer.

WHEN DARKER violet and blue-violet blooms are placed in shaded spaces or against dark backgrounds, color strength diminishes and the impact of any particular form and textural quality is greatly reduced. Enhancement occurs when they are displayed against a light background, such as a painted structure, or mingling with light tinted flowers or foliage.

This skillful association places a dark blue-violet *Delphinium* against a background of very pale pink climbing roses. The very pale, near-white, unopened *Achillea* corymbs and white *Tanacetum* blooms repeat the pallor of the rose, and the three plants harmonize the foreground, midground, and background spaces. When all *Achillea* blooms are open the intensity and quantity of yellow shifts the focus of the composition to the yellow *Achillea* and dark blue-

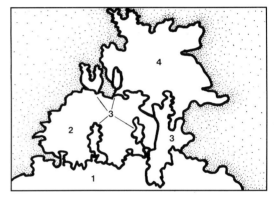

1. *Achillea* 'Coronation Gold', one plant, 24–36 × 18 in (60–90 × 45 cm)
2. *Tanacetum parthenium*, two plants, 12–36 × 12 in (30–90 × 30 cm)
3. *Delphinium belladona*, two plants, 36–48 × 36 in (90–120 × 90 cm)
4. *Rosa* (unknown) cultivar, one plant, 20 ft (6 m)

violet *Delphinium*. There is excellent contrast in flower forms between the horizontal *Achillea* corymbs, the vertical *Delphinium* spires, and the fragmented texture of the *Tanacetum*. In a large space such as this, when this group is not blooming, other earlier and later blooming associations may be tucked between the specified plants.

Rosa 'New Dawn' could substitute for the unknown cultivar pictured here. A minimum space of 5 × 5 ft (1.5 × 1.5 m) will accommodate one *Rosa* trained on a fence or trellis to provide background, two *Delphinium*, two *Tanacetum*, and one *Achillea*.

PHOTO 92. Sissinghurst Garden, Kent, England, May.
ENVIRONMENT: part shade in soil of average fertility and moisture.
USDA Zones 3–8.
FEATURE: foliage mid spring to fall; flower mid spring to summer.

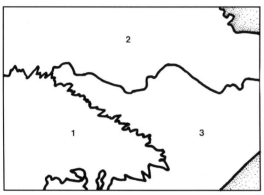

1. *Hosta fortunei* 'Aurea', five plants, 15–24 × 24 in (40–60 × 60 cm)
2. *Rhododendron* (unknown) cultivar, one plant, 5–7 × 5 ft (1.5–2.1 × 1.5 m)
3. *Hyacinthoides hispanica*, sixty bulbs, 15 × 6 in (40 × 15 cm)

MANY PEOPLE have observed that blue and blue-violet are more readily appreciated when associated with yellow. Using the sixteen-color wheel, the theoretical complement for blue-violet is a greenish yellow, and this large spring border provides plenty of evidence in support of complementary associations.

As this greenish yellow-leaved *Hosta* will not thrive in strong sunlight and needs to be in light shade during the late spring and summer, this situation matches the ideal for blue-violet *Hyacinthoides*. Any of the yellow-flowering *Rhododendron* Knaphill-Exbury deciduous hybrid azaleas, such as *R.* 'Golden Dream', will thrive in similar conditions and complete a fine composition with *Hosta* and *Hyacinthoides* at its base. For the planting bed to be properly proportioned, allow the depth of the bed to equal the height of the tallest plant. In this case, the height of the *Rhododendron* determines the bed depth. The bed must also burst with flower and foliage as shown in this setting. Fullness is essential in such a mass planting.

Hyacinthoides foliage is persistent, yet it eventually disappears in summer. It may become unsightly in the process, so this composition should be planted where bulb decline goes unnoticed or is otherwise disguised. An alternative is to plant the *Hyacinthoides* in long, narrow, irregular drifts, alternating with drifts of a later-blooming perennial, such as *Astilbe* or *Hemerocallis*, whose foliage and flower disguises the decline of the bulb foliage. *Hyacinthoides non-scriptus* will substitute for *Hyacinthoides hispanica*.

One mature Knaphill-Exbury *Rhododendron* hybrid will be balanced by a base planting of approximately five *Hosta* and sixty *Hyacinthoides*, and together will occupy a space about 7 × 10 ft (2.1 × 3.0 m).

PHOTO 93. Henrietta Lockwood Garden, Bedford, New York, July. ENVIRONMENT: sun in soil of average fertility and moisture. USDA Zones 4–7. FEATURE: foliage late spring to fall; flower late spring to summer.

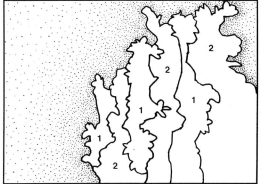

HIGH-INTENSITY color combinations of near-complementary colors are often stunningly dramatic. Such combinations provide an immediate focus for a garden or landscape, something which is often lacking in designs populated entirely by pastel hues.

This particular pair also provides excellent contrast of flower form, between spikes of *Delphinium* and low clusters of *Oenothera* blooms. *Delphinium*'s dark violet-blue flowers are a near complement to those of *Oenothera* and are particularly satisfying since the strength of the two colors is equal. Adding other plants with different flower forms will increase the complexity and interest of the composition and alter its dramatic effect.

1. *Delphinium grandiflorum* 'Blue Butterfly', three plants, 24 × 12 in (60 × 30 cm)
2. *Oenothera tetragona*, one plant, 18 × 12 in (45 × 30 cm)

Repeating either hue in a paler tone will soften the color intensity and facilitate transitions to neighboring groupings. Light blue-violet *Nepeta* 'Six Hills Giant' blooms and a pale yellow-flowering yarrow, such as *Achillea* 'Moonshine', are design possibilities. *Oenothera* and *Achillea* 'Moonshine' contribute yellow tints at different heights and, though bloom does not fully coincide, the effective period for the color theme will be lengthened. Also, cutting *Delphinium* and *Achillea* stalks after bloom encourages rebloom in late summer. Since the foliage texture and form for this group is not especially strong, between blooming periods attention may be diverted elsewhere.

The basic pair will need an area 2 × 2 ft (0.6 × 0.6 m). A ratio of three *Delphinium* to one *Oenothera* will establish a desirable color balance of about 70% blue-violet and 30% yellow. To expand the basic pairing while maintaining color harmony add one *Achillea* to one *Oenothera* with four *Delphinium* in the rear. Alternatively, use one *Nepeta* in the midground, one *Oenothera* in the foreground, and three *Delphinium* at the rear. Both of the more complex associations will need a minimum area of about 3

PHOTO 94. New York Botanical Garden, New York City, September. ENVIRONMENT: sun in soil of average fertility and moisture. USDA Zones 5–8. FEATURE: foliage summer to fall; flower late summer to fall.

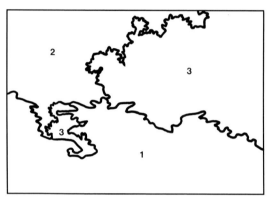

1. *Solidago* 'Crown of Rays', one plant, 18–24 × 12 in (45–60 × 30 cm)
2. *Perilla frutescens*, one plant, 24–36 × 18 in (60–90 × 45 cm)
3. *Aster frikartii* 'Mönch', two plants, 24–36 × 24 in (60–90 × 60 cm)

REPETITION of form or color in planting design helps unify a composition at any scale. Only occasionally will too rigid an application of this principle lead to monotony. Quite small and subtle repetitions can be surprisingly effective, as seen here in the sparing repetition of the dark greenish yellow present in both *Solidago* and in the center of the rayed *Aster* disks.

There are two other factors making this particular composition satisfying. First, there is a stimulating contrast in form between the horizontally spiked *Solidago* and daisy-like *Aster* blooms. Second, compositional interest is heightened by the light-against-dark contrast created by the placement of pale, fading *Aster* blooms against the very deep red-violet *Perilla* leaves. This color association of greenish yellow and complementary blue-violet and red-violet is a very pleasing color triad and seen surprisingly infrequently considering the great choice of plants developing in these hues. It is given particularly subtle expression here by the subdued tints and tones and the light-against-dark contrasts. It also closely approximates one of nature's brilliant late-season associations in northern climates when yellow goldenrod blooms with New England asters.

A minimum space of 3 × 4 ft (0.9 × 1.2 m) will accommodate one *Perilla* in background, two *Aster* in the midground, and one *Solidago* in the foreground.

PHOTO 95. Hestercombe
Gardens, Somerset,
England, July.
ENVIRONMENT: sun in
soil of average fertility
and moisture.
USDA Zones 7–8.
FEATURE: foliage late
spring to fall; flower late
spring to late summer.

O NE OF the challenges of planting design is
understanding the scale appropriate to the
planting area. This establishes the sizes, quantities,
and number of varieties of plants to be used. A larger
space is usually best filled by expanding individual
plants in a basic combination into groupings or drifts,
usually done while still approximating the same proportions of plants. If new plants are added, they
should continue a color, form, or textural theme
already established by the basic composition.
Furthermore, quantity increases may be limited by
the sizes and textures of plants in the original group,
relative to a greatly increased viewing distance. See
comments in the introduction and under photos 7
and 42.

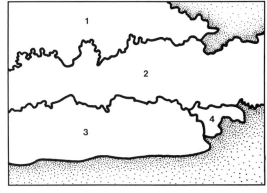

1. *Jasminum officinale*, one plant, to 40 ft (12 m)
2. *Echinops* 'Taplow Blue', one plant, 24–48 × 24 in
   (60–120 × 60 cm)
3. *Lavandula angustifolia* 'Hidcote', two plants, 18
   × 12 in (45 × 30 cm)
4. *Achillea* 'Moonshine', one plant, 12–24 × 12 in
   (30–60 × 30 cm)

The minimum space for this combination is 3 × 4
ft (1 × 1.2 m) and one *Jasminum*, one *Echinops*, one
Achillea, and two *Lavandula* are used. When the space is enlarged to 7 × 5 ft (2.0 ×
1.5 m) the quantities are increased to three *Achillea*, six *Lavandula*, and three *Echinops*,
with one *Jasminum* still sufficient background. This proportion is adjusted to take into
consideration the mature size of each plant and the contribution of bloom color.

Perhaps in a larger space it is more critical that the arrangement of the groups avoids
rigid ranks of smaller, medium, and larger plants, attending one behind the other. One
modification may allow the *Lavandula* to spill to the foreground between two groups
of this small *Achillea*. The addition of a taller, yellow *Achillea*, such as *A.* 'Coronation
Gold', placed between the *Lavandula* and *Echinops*, will repeat form and color,
strengthen the composition, and compensate for the receding qualities of the violet
blooms against the *Jasminum* foliage. Any addition should maintain the balance of
color, which requires about 25% yellow and 75% violet and blue-violet blooms. Fragrance in *Jasminum* and *Lavandula* blooms and *Achillea* foliage enhances this setting.

PHOTO 96. Conservatory Garden, New York City, April.
ENVIRONMENT: sun in soil of average fertility and average or less moisture. USDA Zones 4–8.
FEATURE: foliage mid to late spring; flower mid to late spring.

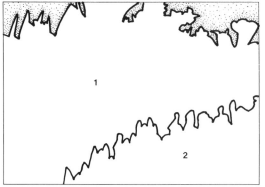

1. *Narcissus* 'Trevithian', six bulbs, 12–18 × 6 in (30–45 × 15 cm)
2. *Muscari armeniacum*, twelve bulbs, 6–8 × 4 in (15–20 × 10 cm)

NARCISSUS and *Muscari* are one of the easiest spring bulb combinations. Both develop fragrant flowers and are dependable, long-lived bulbs, reappearing year after year and easily combining with other bulbs and spring perennials which coincide with their long flowering season.

The choice of *Narcissus* color and the color's strength affect the mood created. Purer stronger yellows and oranges offer more dramatic contrasts and suggest energy and vigor. Paler tints of these hues suggest tranquillity. Since *Muscari* flowers are blue-violet, they combine most delightfully with colors in its near-complementary opposites of yellow, greenish yellow, and yellow-orange. Unfortunately, yellow-orange, and particularly pale yellow-orange, occurs infrequently in flowers, and in foliage this color indicates disease or deficiency. Pure yellow, particularly when the quantity of color is not carefully proportioned, easily overwhelms the more delicate blue-violet of *Muscari*.

Many may still consider this *Narcissus* and *Muscari* a rather intense color association, even though a degree of tinting exists in both flowers. The colors seem strong especially when compared to the paler tones of yellow and blue-violet seen in photo 97. This is also partly the result of the concentration of yellow blooms in this example and the scattering apparent in photo 97. The color balance of the group shown here would be improved by increasing the quantity of *Muscari* to two-thirds and reducing the *Narcissus* to about one-third. Mingling a few very pale yellow-flowering *Narcissus* cultivars with these light yellow *Narcissus* would improve the color balance by diluting the yellow component with the whiteness evident in all pale hues.

A space 2 × 2 ft (0.6 × 0.6 m) would require six *Narcissus* planted behind twelve *Muscari* to display an acceptable color balance.

PHOTO 97. Conservatory Garden, New York City, April.
ENVIRONMENT: sun to part shade in soil of average fertility and moisture. USDA Zones 4–9.
FEATURE: foliage early to late spring; flower early to late spring.

THE SUBTLETY of the complementary color use in this early spring association for light shade produces a sublime combination. The predominantly pale and light yellow bi-colored *Narcissus* with light violet to blue-violet *Ajuga* spikes and light blue *Mertensia* blooms mirror the pale hues of nature's spring plantings. The color intensity present in many contrived early spring combinations is here wonderfully absent. The nearly equal tinting of these complementary and near-complementary colors allows them to blend in a serene statement.

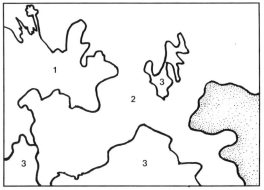

1. *Narcissus* 'Clare', eight bulbs, 12–18 × 6 in (30–45 × 15 cm)
2. *Mertensia virginica*, three plants, 12–24 × 12 in (30–60 × 30 cm)
3. *Ajuga reptans*, five plants, 6 × 12 in (15 × 30 cm)

The foliage offers splendid color contrasts and textures from the broad leaves of *Mertensia*, grassy *Narcissus*, and the prostrate foliage of *Ajuga*. The *Ajuga* foliage at this stage in spring is tiny, although it too expands into a broader form as spring advances. In late spring or early summer, the foliage of both *Narcissus* and *Mertensia* decline and leaves bare ground which must be covered if attention continues to focus on this area. *Brunnera*, *Hosta*, or *Hemerocallis* may be planted near or behind this group so their expanding leaves fill such voids.

The delicacy of the tints make precise color balance less of an imperative in the floral distribution of violet *Ajuga*, pale yellow *Narcissus*, and blue *Mertensia*. The proportion used here, roughly one-third yellow and two-thirds violet and blue, is satisfactory but would be improved by scattering more *Narcissus*.

A minimum space of 3 × 3 ft (0.9 × 0.9 m) is needed for three *Mertensia* and five *Ajuga* in the foreground and eight *Narcissus* scattered between.

PHOTO 98. New York
Botanical Garden, New
York City, June.
ENVIRONMENT: sun to part
shade in soil of average
fertility and moisture.
USDA Zones 5–8.
FEATURE: foliage mid
spring to late summer;
flower early to late spring.

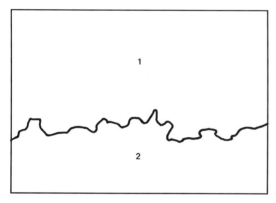

1. *Iris pseudacorus*, one plant, 24–36 × 18 in (60–90
   × 45 cm)
2. *Myosotis sylvatica*, ten plants, 6–8 × 8 in (15–20 ×
   20 cm)

PLEASING quantitative balance of warm and cool colors is a desirable design objective. Often, however, recollections of the color strength and quantity of color presented by individual plants may be imprecise. When an association finally blooms the resulting color balance may be imperfect. Such oversights are seldom disastrous if the color pairing is based on an adjacent or complementary color theme.

Myosotis flowers develop into a beautiful light tint of blue, a trait I particularly appreciate since it is quite rare and disarming in flowers. However, its tiny blooms often fade considerably by the time *Iris pseudacorus* flowers appear, so it is difficult to provide the mass of true blue necessary to balance the strength of its complementary yellows.

Still, this association employs one of the most pleasing design uses for *Myosotis* as a hazy base through which *Iris*, or other spring-flowering plants, may emerge and contrast its nebulous blooms. Since *Myosotis* makes splendid bedding for tulips and is frequently seen with them, a fine complementary balancing is achieved when a very few pale yellow or pale yellow-orange tulip blooms, such as *Tulipa* 'Apricot Beauty', are scattered and rise on slender stems through a dense bed of *Myosotis*.

The color balance in this association can be improved by reducing the quantity of yellow *Iris* so they do not overwhelm the faded *Myosotis* quite so much. A minimum space 3 × 3 ft (0.9 × 0.9 m) will accommodate one *Iris* surrounded by ten *Myosotis* in more pleasing color balance.

PHOTO 99.
Conservatory Garden,
New York City, May.
ENVIRONMENT: sun to
part shade in soil of
average fertility and
average to greater
moisture.
USDA Zones 5–7.
FEATURE: foliage early
spring to fall; flower
early spring to fall.

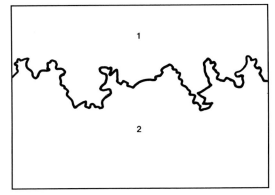

1. *Corydalis lutea*, one plant, 9–15 × 12 in (25–40 × 30 cm)
2. *Brunnera macrophylla*, two plants, 18 × 24 in (45 × 60 cm)

MOST NATURALIZED plants of temperate regions growing in light shade flower in spring in quite pale hues and with relatively small blooms. This *Corydalis* and *Brunnera* mimic the scale and color theme of some of nature's spring combinations.

This is not a dramatic combination but a delicate one, as both plants produce rather small flowers lightly scattered above the foliage. This light distribution of bloom offers an advantage since both plants associate gently without dominating. They will do nicely in morning sun or light shade and are a fine example of the complementary combination of blue and yellow. This pair also offers outstanding foliage: *Corydalis* develops light yellow-green, small-scale, finely dissected leaves which contrast well with the dark, broad, heart-shaped *Brunnera* leaves.

Furthermore, the invaluable, delicately fragrant *Cordyalis* blooms from early spring until fall. It easily combines with later blooming plants, such as *Linum perenne* in sun, or *Geranium* 'Johnson's Blue' in light shade, evolving comfortably into a light violet and yellow association. Other *Corydalis* associations are shown in photos 82 and 90. The balance of color needs to be carefully orchestrated with roughly 30% *Corydalis* bloom for 70% *Brunnera* bloom—a different proportion than shown in this photograph.

As a minimum, plant one *Corydalis* with two *Brunnera* in a space 2 × 3 ft (0.6 × 0.9 m) to allow more careful color balance.

PHOTO 100. Leeds Castle, Kent, England, June. ENVIRONMENT: sun in soil of average fertility and moisture. USDA Zones 3–8. FEATURE: foliage mid spring to summer; flower late spring.

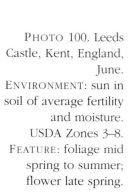

1. *Veronica latifolia* 'Crater Lake Blue', two plants, 18 × 12 in (45 × 30 cm)
2. *Allium moly*, five bulbs, 12 × 6 in (30 × 15 cm)

THE MAJORITY of yellow-blooming plants are suited to full sun and open situations. Often these yellows are strong, clear, powerful hues which are visible from a distance, a design advantage in larger spaces. In more intimate settings, fine-textured yellow blooms or those in pale tints or small scale are desirable. Here a strong yellow hue in compact *Allium* blooms associates with a near-complementary intense blue-violet *Veronica*.

This *Veronica* needs careful association since its intense flower hue tends to completely overpower pastel blooms. It is a fairly unusual color since most blue-violet blooms are light tinted. (Another example of this color can be seen in the *Delphinium* in photo 143.) Nor does the intensity of this *Veronica* fade as flowers decline, making even white blooms appear poor when associated with its brilliance.

When such a blue is joined with equally intense colors, either in adjacent hues of blue, violet, and red-violet, or with an opposite intense yellow or yellow-orange, the result is a powerful or perhaps overly intrusive combination. Even at the small scale of this pair, such a color combination compels attention and demands isolation amid a soothing mass of foliage.

The distinctive *Allium* umbels contrast well with the somewhat formless *Veronica* clusters, which lack the definite spiked form found in many veronicas. This *Allium* foliage is slower to decline than most, yet its departure is completely masked by the floppy *Veronica* foliage.

An arresting association can be made with just two *Veronica* and five *Allium* in a space 1 × 3 ft (0.3 × 0.9 m).

PHOTO 101. Conservatory Garden, New York City, May.
ENVIRONMENT: sun to part shade in soil of average fertility and moisture. USDA Zones 4–7.
FEATURE: foliage mid spring to fall; flower mid spring to summer.

V*ALUE* and *intensity* of color are often confused. *Value* refers only to the shading and tinting of a color, its darkness or lightness. Many herbaceous blooms are light tinted and therefore are regarded as having high value. The less common low value, darker hues occur mostly in the warm colors—red, red-orange, and orange. *Intensity* refers to the strength of color. An intensely colored flower is a floral color undiluted by gray. Few flowers have the intensity of their colors weakened by gray, but an example is the *Sedum* 'Vera Jameson' in photo 120. However, a graying effect and therefore a dilution of color intensity always occurs when plants are placed in shadow.

1. *Hemerocallis* (unknown) cultivar, one plant, 18–48 × 12 in (45–120 × 30 cm)
2. *Brunnera macrophylla*, two plants, 18 × 24 in (45 × 60 cm)
3. *Euphorbia polychroma*, one plant, 12–18 × 18 in (30–45 × 45 cm)

One of the ways a designer can sometimes modify difficult colors, such as the intensely yellow *Euphorbia* bracts, is to site them in partly or lightly shaded locations. Partially opened *Euphorbia* bracts, shown here at an early stage of flowering, display only a moderate amount of their intense yellow and easily harmonize with the light blue *Brunnera* flowers. Later, the effects of the partially shaded location will moderate any tendency to clash. The *Hemerocallis* selected needs a height of about 24–36 in (60–90 cm) in flower. The species daylily *Hemerocallis lilio-asphodelus* could be used in a light shade setting due to its suitable height and fragrant, pale yellow blooms.

After the summer *Hemerocallis* blooming, the contrast in this trio's foliage colors and forms attains prominence. The horizontal, dark, heart-shaped *Brunnera* leaves, the tiny, round, yellow-green *Euphorbia* leaves, and the drooping *Hemerocallis* leaves remain modestly attractive for the entire growing season.

To provide color and textural balance plant one *Euphorbia* in the rear with one *Hemerocallis* and two *Brunnera* in the foreground in a minimum space of 3 × 4 ft (0.9 × 1.2 m).

PHOTO 102.
Conservatory Garden,
New York City, July.
ENVIRONMENT: sun in
soil of average fertility
and moisture.
USDA Zones 5–7.
FEATURE: foliage late
spring to fall; flower mid
spring and summer.

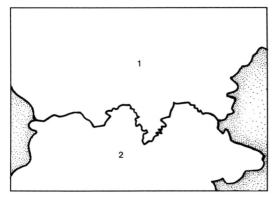

1. *Achillea taygetea*, one plant, 12–24 × 18 in
   (30–60 × 45 cm)
2. *Brunnera macrophylla*, one plant, 18 × 24 in (45
   × 60 cm)

IN REGIONS with cool moist summers, such as England, western Europe, and the northwestern United States, certain perennials may be expected to bloom together for many weeks and even months and can provide the backbone of a flowering composition. However, hot dry summers, as usual in much of the United States and lower latitudes, shorten perennial flowering. Design then may depend much more on successive bloom, foliage texture, and plant form.

Here is an example of a thoughtful textural composition which also offers successive flowering. First, in spring, *Brunnera* offers tiny, delicate light blue flowers clustered above its dark, heart-shaped foliage. During this blooming period, pale *Achillea* is just emerging and gradually expands to offer the foliage contrast evident here. Since *Brunnera* flowering does not coincide with *Achillea*, the *Achillea* variety can be chosen less for flower color harmony than for scale. The *Achillea* needs to be small enough at maturity to maintain proportion to the small size of *Brunnera*.

The composition could be enhanced by a third plant with an intermediate blooming period and a different form and texture. *Veronica spicata* 'Blue Fox', for example, placed between the *Achillea* and *Brunnera*, would offer a vertical form, a medium-textured, yellow-green leaf, and light blue-violet summer blooms.

A space 3 × 3 ft (0.9 × 0.9 m) would suit one *Achillea* in the rear, adding two *Veronica spicata* 'Blue Fox' in the midground and one *Brunnera* in the foreground. The basic pairing may be accomplished with a minimal space of 2 × 3 ft (0.6 × 0.9 m).

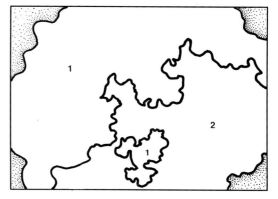

PHOTO 103. New York Botanical Garden, New York City, August. ENVIRONMENT: sun to part shade in soil of average fertility and moisture.
USDA Zones 4–7.
FEATURE: foliage late spring to fall; flower late spring and fall.

1. *Sedum* 'Rosy Glow', one plant, 6–12 × 15 in (15–30 × 40 cm)
2. *Alchemilla mollis*, one plant, 12 × 18 in (30 × 45 cm)

WHEN A dependable, attractive, low-maintenance plant is available, garden designers are quick to experiment with its usage. *Alchemilla mollis* is highly regarded as one of perhaps ten extremely dependable and useful garden plants. It has a long viable season and this late summer combination illustrates that the *Alchemilla* foliage is still just as enormously attractive in late summer as in spring (see photo 120). Its yellow-green foliage grays and darkens by late summer and combines with the buds and newly opening dark red to red-violet *Sedum* blooms.

This *Sedum* is also a very dependable, easily grown plant, providing a long season of interest. Its finely textured blooms provide an elegant contrast for the medium-textured *Alchemilla* foliage. Both plants evolve into fairly prostrate foliage forms, as the early spring mounding of *Alchemilla* blooms subsides with the season.

This is a small-scale combination for sun or very light shade and would be best used at the front of a border, alongside a walk, in a sloping rock garden, or on top of a retaining wall where its diminutive perfection can be better appreciated. This pair may be planted in larger groups than shown here, but the two forms appear similar at a distance and this combination may appear dull when planted in drifts or large masses. It is better used as a small accent or as a counterpoint to other plant groups with contrasting forms and textures.

One *Alchemilla* and one *Sedum* will occupy 2 × 2 ft (0.6 × 0.6 m).

PHOTO 104. Stonecrop
Gardens, Cold Spring,
New York, August.
ENVIRONMENT: very
light shade or morning
sun with afternoon
shade in soil of average
fertility and moisture.
USDA Zones 4–9.
FEATURE: foliage late
spring to fall; flower
summer to fall.

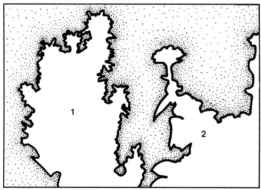

1. *Lobelia cardinalis*, one plant, 30–42 × 12 in
   (75–105 × 30 cm)
2. *Zinnia elegans* 'Red Sun', two plants, 36 × 24 in
   (90 × 60 cm)

COMPLEMENTARY associations of red and green make simple, arresting, and easily contrived focal points. As with white flowers, a very small amount of red bloom goes a long way in garden design.

Red is one of the most powerful and advancing colors and is visible over a considerable distance. However, under shady conditions its color strength declines more than in some other hues. For example, yellow and white continue to be highly visible in very low light situations. In bright light or light shade the strength of red is not diminished and a small amount can be used to great effect.

The simple pairing of the vertical *Lobelia* and the daisy form of the *Zinnia* flowers makes a striking combination against a dark foliage background. A background of matte dark green foliage is desirable for the best display of these pure red blooms, yet any dark background, a dark green fence for example, will allow these red blooms to stand out spectacularly. A background of too light a green or composed of leaves which are small, reflective, or shiny, presents a fragmented appearance against which the individual *Lobelia* blooms lose substance. This *Lobelia* is native to moist, shady places in eastern and central areas of the United States, but will thrive in average moisture and sun as long as it receives afternoon shade.

This pair may be associated in equal quantities with a minimum of one *Lobelia* and two *Zinnia* requiring a space 3 × 3 ft (0.9 × 0.9 m) in front of a dark green backdrop.

PHOTO 105.
Conservatory Garden,
New York City, August.
ENVIRONMENT: part
shade in soil of average
fertility and moisture.
USDA Zones 4–8.
FEATURE: foliage early
spring to fall; flower
early spring and late
summer.

RED AND GREEN orchestrations are frequently and effortlessly made in the lighter and paler tints because pinks are less startling or intrusive. Tints combine more easily with lighter as well as darker foliages than do the purer stronger reds. Associations of pinks and greens are used so often that the effort risks banality unless care is taken to select striking forms and textures.

The compact astilbe used here blooms much later than most astilbes, in a pale red to red-violet hue. Contrasted with the broad, glossy, segmented *Helleborus* leaves, the *Astilbe* foliage and flower seem to be of a particularly fine soft texture. The combination of textures seen here contributes as much to the

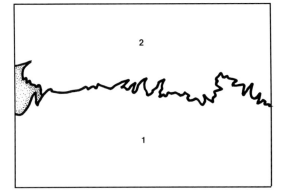

1. *Astilbe chinensis* 'Pumila', two plants, 12–18 × 12 in (30–45 × 30 cm)
2. *Helleborus orientalis*, one plant, 12–24 × 24 in (30–60 × 60 cm)

success of the design as the complementary color association. This is an excellent underplanting for shrubs or small trees in light shade, offering early flowers in *Helleborus*, late flowers in *Astilbe*, and excellent foliage in between. This pair is particularly effective when sited under a small *Magnolia soulangeana*. The hellebore blooms at the same time as the magnolia, in late winter or early spring, and offers red-violet and yellow-green flowers to repeat and complement the magnolia blossoms' pale hue.

A minimum space of 2 × 3 ft (0.6 × 0.9 m) would accommodate one *Helleborus* and two *Astilbe*. When used as an underplanting, much larger quantities are needed to balance the mass of the selected trees or shrubs.

PHOTO 106. Conservatory Garden, New York City, July. ENVIRONMENT: sun to part shade in soil of average fertility and moisture. USDA Zones 5–8. FEATURE: foliage late spring to late summer; flower late spring to late summer.

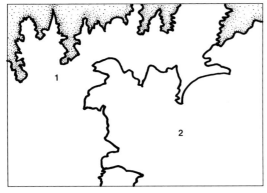

1. *Antirrhinum majus* 'Frontier Crimson', two plants, 24 × 12 in (60 × 30 cm)
2. *Beta vulgaris* subsp. *cicla*, one plant, 15 × 12 in (40 × 30 cm)

DIFFERENT tints and tones of red with green generate quite specific moods in the landscape. For example, baskets of bright red *Pelargonium* blossoms hung against a wall of English ivy generates a sense of activity as attention is diverted from one bright red point to the next. A similar energetic mood is created by twining red *Tropaeolum speciosum* through dark *Taxus* hedges.

The specific placement of dark red blossoms against a background of green foliage, on the other hand, is rarely seen in flowering displays and can offer a feeling of elegance and serenity. The association is particularly striking when the green foliage offers a broad, smooth texture to display velvety qualities of blossoms like those of *Antirrhinum*. In this pairing, dark red is also repeated in the stems and veining of the broad, lustrous, *Beta* leaves.

Transitions to other colors and plantings should be handled with care to avoid an abrupt or jarring change in mood or color. Introducing slightly higher value, lighter reds, and then gradually moving to other strong warm colors would brighten the mood. Association with dark red-violet and violet blooms would enhance the decorous effect. Both the *Antirrhinum* and the *Beta* are usually treated as annuals.

A small space of 1 × 3 ft (0.3 × 0.9 m) will accommodate two *Antirrhinum* and one *Beta*.

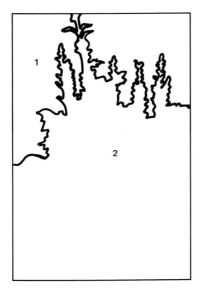

1. *Hosta plantaginea* 'Royal Standard', one plant, 24–36 × 24 in (60–90 × 60 cm)
2. *Astilbe* × *arendsii* 'Fanal', three plants, 24 × 18 in (60 × 45 cm)

PHOTO 107. New York Botanical Garden, New York City, June. ENVIRONMENT: part shade in soil of average to greater fertility and average moisture. USDA Zones 4–8. FEATURE: foliage mid spring to fall; flower mid and late summer.

DESIGNERS are often required to clothe large ground areas with mass plantings of simple associations. Design for commercial installations often demands a simple treatment and plantings with modest maintenance needs. Associations which succeed at the larger commercial scale can often be adapted for use in the domestic setting where minimal maintenance and simplicity is also frequently an objective.

Hostas and astilbes establish one of many associations useful for covering large, lightly-shaded areas under deciduous trees. Their late blooming recommends including them with some of the earlier spring-flowering shade associations which decline and disappear by early summer. The composition shown in photo 50 of *Mertensia* and *Dicentra* could precede this *Hosta* and *Astilbe* in flowering time, with groups arranged in alternating drifts of long, thin, plant groups. Declining foliage would be superseded by the expansion of the *Hosta* and *Astilbe* which occurs towards the end of the effective period for *Mertensia* and *Dicentra*.

The striking red *Astilbe* blooms make a powerful association with the complementary green contributed by the smooth large mass of the *Hosta* foliage. A darker green hosta leaf would be even more effective, but this hosta was selected more for its white, fragrant, late summer blooms than for leaf color.

Substituting a white-blooming *Astilbe*, such as *Astilbe* × *arendsii* 'Deutschland', would change the character of the composition from an arresting vibrancy of red and green to a tranquil association of white and green. It would also continue the color themes of the spring-blooming, white *Dicentra* if these associations are paired. This combination requires almost no attention beyond ensuring an ample supply of water for the *Astilbe*.

A minimum of one *Hosta* and three *Astilbe* would occupy a space 3 × 4 ft (0.9 × 1.2 m).

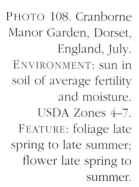

PHOTO 108. Cranborne Manor Garden, Dorset, England, July. ENVIRONMENT: sun in soil of average fertility and moisture. USDA Zones 4–7. FEATURE: foliage late spring to late summer; flower late spring to summer.

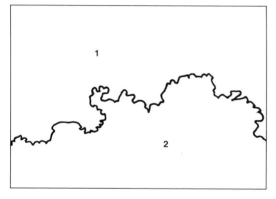

1. *Penstemon barbatus* (unknown) cultivar, two plants, 18 × 12 in (45 × 30 cm)
2. *Alchemilla mollis*, one plant, 12 × 18 in (30 × 45 cm)

THE CREATION of flowering compositions which are appealing over the entire growing season is another of the garden designer's challenges. The inherent difficulties can be minimized by employing, as a basis for serial designs, perennial plants which present excellent appearance for several months. Harmonious companions flowering at different times may then be juxtaposed to offer design continuity without great contrivance. *Alchemilla mollis* is one of several such basic plants; *Achillea millefolium* 'Weser River Sandstone', *Brunnera macrophylla*, *Coreopsis verticillata* 'Moonbeam', *Corydalis lutea*, *Sedum* 'Autumn Joy', *Veronica* 'Sunny Border Blue', and several *Hosta* cultivars are others.

Alchemilla mollis is indispensable in planting composition because its excellent foliage color and form and early arrival and late departure from the garden allow it to combine with many other plants over a very long season. Its delicate panicles of yellow-green flowers and grayed, yellow-green leaves harmonize particularly well with the complementary and near-complementary colors of red, red-violet, or violet which occur in a large percentage of frequently grown herbaceous plants.

Penstemon 'Rose Elf' is similar to the unknown cultivar shown here and is generally available. Its flower hue, somewhere between light red and light red-violet, combines well with yellow-green, resulting in the sort of dynamic color composition achieved only in complementary associations.

The *Alchemilla* blossoms may seem a bit too intensely yellow at this stage, rather than yellow-green. As that intensity fades, and it will, the hues blend more gently. After bloom, the modified yellow-green *Alchemilla* foliage makes a near-perfect color and form association with the longer-blooming *Penstemon*. Adding red-violet blooming *Geranium* × *magnificum* or violet *Geranium* 'Johnson's Blue' would increase the complexity of the color composition and contribute a finely textured foliage.

The basic combination fits into a space 2 × 2 ft (0.6 × 0.6 m). Allow about 40% yellow-green and about 60% red or red-violet to maintain color proportion. This could be achieved with one *Alchemilla* in the foreground and two *Penstemon* in the rear. Including either of the two *Geranium* mentioned increases space needs to 3 × 3 ft (0.9 × 0.9 m), siting one alongside the *Penstemon*.

PHOTO 109. Henrietta Lockwood Garden, Bedford, New York, July. ENVIRONMENT: sun in soil of average fertility and moisture. USDA Zones 4–7. FEATURE: foliage late spring to fall; flower late spring to late summer.

B ECAUSE red-violet and yellow-green are abundantly available in so many different plants with such varied forms, textures, and overlapping flowering periods, it is one of the easiest complementary color combinations to attempt. Although the scale of this composition is small, the strength of the colors and the broader foliage textures employed suggest its suitability for a larger space.

Transitions to other colors of similar intensity need to be graded carefully, using large quantities of adjacent colors such as violet and blue-violet. Hot colors, such as orange and red-orange, would be best avoided anywhere near these red-violet and yellow-green combinations.

The medium-sized *Allium senescens* umbels bloom over a long period and, as with all *Allium*, I find the distinctive form arresting and very valuable in composition. Its foliage continues to be important for some time after flowering. *Allium cernuum* offers a smaller, slightly different flower head, and both species combine subtly with the dark yellow-green *Alchemilla* foliage and more zestfully with its bright yellow-green flowers. Deep red *Atriplex* foliage offers a near-complementary color and a dark background for the intense hues of its companions.

A space 3×5 ft (0.9×1.5 m) will accommodate two *Atriplex* in the rear, a group of three *Allium senescens* and two *Allium cernuum* in the midground, and two *Alchemilla* as a foreground base.

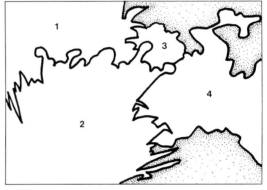

1. *Atriplex hortensis* 'Cupreata', two plants, 12–48 × 18 in (30–120 × 45 cm)
2. *Allium senescens*, three bulbs, 12–18 × 12 in (30–45 × 30 cm)
3. *Allium cernuum*, two bulbs, 12–18 × 12 in (30–45 × 30 cm)
4. *Alchemilla mollis*, two plants, 12 x 18 in (30 × 45 cm)

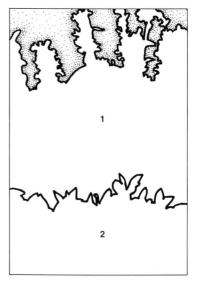

1. *Salvia officinalis* 'Purpurea', one plant, 12–18 × 12 in (30–45 × 30 cm)
2. *Salvia officinalis* 'Aurea', one plant, 12–18 × 12 in (30–45 × 30 cm)

PHOTO 110. Hadspen Garden, Sandra and Nori Pope, owners, Somerset, England, July. ENVIRONMENT: sun in soil of average fertility and moisture. USDA Zones 6–8. FEATURE: foliage late spring to fall; flower summer.

SIMPLE light/dark combinations are less complicated and involve fewer hazards than the attempt to establish color mixes. Often such a simple association of light and dark introduces just the right degree of complexity and could certainly be employed more often in planting design.

This combination of two *Salvia* cultivars employs lighter and darker tints and tones of the same plant type while repeating texture and general form. The complementary colors red-violet and yellow-green further the composition's elegant simplicity.

The light/dark contrast can be extended by adding *Heuchera* 'Palace Purple', another dark red, broad-leaved plant valued chiefly for its foliage. The flowering season can be lengthened and the scale enlarged by including the slightly taller *Veronica spicata* 'Blue Charm', offering a spiked blue-violet flower and a long bloom season. This enlarged grouping adds greater complexity of forms and textures to the basic *Salvia*.

The extended group can be accommodated in a space 2 × 3 ft (0.6 × 0.9 m), with one *Veronica spicata* 'Blue Charm' in the rear, one *Salvia officinalis* 'Purpurea' in the midground, and one *Salvia officinalis* 'Aurea' and one *Heuchera* 'Palace Purple' together in the foreground. The basic *Salvia* pairing requires a basic 1 × 2 ft (0.3 × 0.6 m) for one of each.

PHOTO 111. Conservatory
Garden, New York City,
August.
ENVIRONMENT: sun in soil
of average fertility and
moisture.
USDA Zones 4–8.
FEATURE: foliage late
spring to fall; flower
summer to fall.

LAYERING plants is often successful as layering is
founded on one of nature's own principals.
Stachys is one of the many groundcovers that may
be successfully interplanted with tiny contrasting
forms, such as small alliums or the *Gomphrena*
shown here. The tiny, delicate-toned blooms of this
compact *Gomphrena* rise through the *Stachys* foliage
and contrast its relatively broad, silvery-looking
leaves. More accurately the *Stachys* leaf color is a
pale gray yellow-green, suitable for association with
pale-hued complementary red-violet *Gomphrena*
blooms and many other pastel flowers.

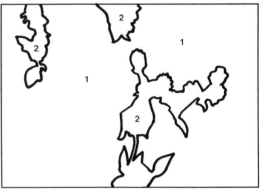

1. *Stachys byzantina*, three plants, 12–15 × 12 in
(30–40 × 30 cm)
2. *Gomphrena globosa* 'Rosy', three plants, 8–12 ×
12 in (20–30 × 30 cm)

Once a particular theme in color and form is established in a planting, further design extensions are
most effectively achieved by continuing with repetitions or slight variations on the original theme. For example, starting from the flower form, *Gomphrena* umbels could be
emphasized and repeated either in larger forms of *Gomphrena* or with various summer-flowering *Allium*. Or from a general starting point of the silvery foliage of *Stachys*,
one might add a slightly larger, differently textured grayed foliage plant, such as
Artemisia schmidtiana 'Silver Mound'. Continuing this point, for placement behind the
Artemisia, select a taller plant having slightly grayed leaves and umbel form in its
blooms, such as *Echinops* 'Taplow Blue' or *Eryngium amethystinum*.

It would be inappropriate to surround this delicate composition with a jarring, inharmonious bloom color, particularly any of the strong warm hues of yellow-orange or
red-orange. Far better to continue with pale tinted flowers or gradually intensifying yellow-green and red-violet blooms.

The preliminary association needs a space no larger than 2 × 3 ft (0.6 × 0.9 m), with
three *Stachys* interplanted with three *Gomphrena*.

PHOTO 112.
Conservatory Garden,
New York City, August.
ENVIRONMENT: sun in
soil of average fertility
and moisture.
USDA Zones 5–8.
FEATURE: foliage
summer to fall; flower
summer to fall.

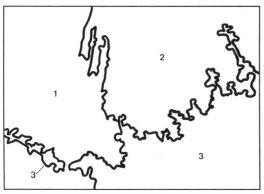

1. *Salvia farinacea* 'Victoria', three plants, 18–24 × 12 in (45–60 × 30 cm)
2. *Gomphrena globosa* 'Lavender Lady', two plants, 18–24 × 18 in (45–60 × 45 cm)
3. *Helichrysum petiolare*, one plant, 12–24 × 24 in (30–60 × 60 cm)

A N INDICATION of the receding nature of pure violet blooms and the advantages of giving them light backgrounds is evident in this planting. Here *Gomphrena* provides a light red-violet background for the violet *Salvia* flowers, violet being a receding color advanced only by a lighter-toned backdrop. Had the positions been reversed, with the recessive violet *Salvia* further away and minus a light background, *Salvia* quantities would need to be increased to bring the color composition into balance.

Generally violet and light red-violet hues of near-equal intensity should be present in near-equal quantities for harmonious balance. As a test, cover the extreme right side of the photo to reduce the total amount of *Gomphrena* and *Helichrysum* and note how the remaining composition appears more balanced. Using photos in this way often uncovers weaknesses that actual experience may obscure.

Helichrysum offers a wonderful contrasting texture and prostrate form for its companions and a startling near-white brightness which must be carefully managed so it does not disrupt the total composition. As with most apparently gray-leaved plants, the color is actually a white tinted grayed yellow-green. This underlying yellow-green allows it to harmonize with other foliage and with the complementary light red-violet offered here in the *Gomphrena* blooms.

This group thrives in 3 × 4 ft (0.9 × 1.2 m), with three *Salvia* in the background, two *Gomphrena* in the midground, and one *Helichrysum* in the foreground.

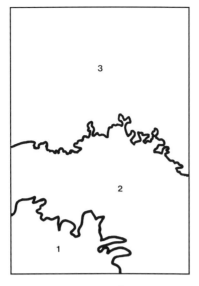

1. *Veronica spicata* subsp. *incana*, two plants, 6–12 × 12 in (15–30 × 30 cm)
2. *Penstemon hirsutus* 'Pygmaeus', two plants, 9 × 12 in (25 × 30 cm)
3. *Allium schoenoprasum*, one bulb, 12–15 × 12 in (30–40 × 30 cm)

PHOTO 113. Ziegler Garden, Bedford, New York, June. ENVIRONMENT: sun in soil of average fertility and average or less moisture. USDA Zones 4–7. FEATURE: foliage late spring to late summer; flower late spring.

DIMINUTIVE associations need to be placed very carefully so the delicacy of their form is not overwhelmed by nearby plantings of larger scale or stronger hues. Additionally, one can compensate for the tiny scale by planting in movable containers or growing them in a raised bed, on top of a wall, or in any location that brings the composition closer to eye level.

This group associates adjacent colors of violet and blue-violet blooms with various forms and textures of gray foliage. Pale violet *Allium* and dwarf *Penstemon* combine with the blue-violet spires of tiny *Veronica spicata* subsp. *incana. Veronica*'s striking foliage color, a very pale gray yellow-green, matches the pallor of the very pale violet tips of *Penstemon*'s corolla tubes.

The color association is continued in the plants not visible in the photograph, *Cerastium tomentosum* and *Artemisia* 'Powis Castle'. Both offer pale gray yellow-green foliage in different forms and textures. *Cerastium* is prostrate and provides slightly earlier small white flowers which also harmonize with *Penstemon* blooms. *Artemisia*'s feathery foliage provides a substantial background color and texture against which to display its smaller companions.

All five plants will fit a space 3 × 4 ft (0.9 × 1.2 m), with one *Artemisia* in the background, one *Allium* in the midground, and two *Penstemon*, two *Veronica*, and one *Cerastium* in the foreground. *Cerastium* spreads easily in some situations and may need careful supervision. The basic trio will accommodate an area 2 × 3 ft (0.6 × 0.9 m). All plantings do well in containers.

PHOTO 114. Longwood Gardens, Kennett Square, Pennsylvania, June. ENVIRONMENT: sun in soil of average fertility and average or less moisture. USDA Zones 4–8. FEATURE: foliage late spring to fall; flower late spring to fall.

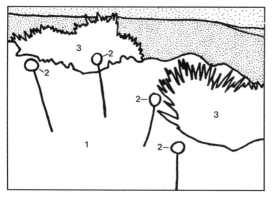

1. *Sedum* 'Autumn Joy', four plants, 18–24 × 24 in (45–60 × 60 cm)
2. *Allium giganteum*, five bulbs, 30–60 × 12 in (75–150 × 30 cm)
3. *Yucca filamentosa*, one plant, 36–60 × 36 in (90–150 × 90 cm)

GARDEN and landscape design students are usually advised early and perhaps more often than they care for, that all elements in the landscape contribute to a design. It is essential to consider what each element or factor contributes to the total, harmonizing or not with each other element and with the overall character of the entire space.

Some plant forms lend a strong architectural quality or impact. *Yucca* has an unusual form, making it a useful focal point, and its stiff, sword-shaped leaves can contrast well with the distinct, tall *Allium* umbels. All these unique forms and textures need to be appraised and then anchored and unified by a visually solid, yet noncompetitive, groundcover. This will enhance the architectural qualities of distinctive plant shapes, harmonizing their elemental contribution.

Sedum 'Autumn Joy' is used for that purpose here. At the newly emerging stage shown here, its yellow-green foliage contrasts well with the red-violet *Allium* umbels. Much later in the growing season, after the decline of the *Allium* flowers and the dramatic summer appearance of the creamy white (very pale yellow) *Yucca* spires, this *Sedum* fills the space with its horizontal, pale, yellow-green flower heads, which gradually deepen to red and deep red. There is something of a contemporary and architectonic character to this series of solo performers, and their drama is best displayed near hard materials, alongside a paved area, walls, or steps.

One *Yucca* and five *Allium* interplanted with five *Sedum* will create interest in an area 5 × 6 ft (1.5 × 1.8 m).

PHOTO 115. Hillside Gardens, Norfolk, Connecticut, June. ENVIRONMENT: sun to part shade in soil of average fertility and moisture. USDA Zones 4–8. FEATURE: foliage late spring to fall; flower mid spring to summer.

CHOICE of flower color in planting design often depends on personal preferences, but it should also be influenced by the location of the planting and the contribution it is expected to make to the surrounding landscape. Plant choices and their final positioning should be based, in part, on an assessment of the color strength and form best suited to the location, or the location should be chosen to best display a particular grouping. For instance, a large spiked form in a bold advancing color would focus attention over a long distance. Such boldness would not suit a small space designed to foster a tranquil mood, where softer pastels in diffuse forms may be more appropriate.

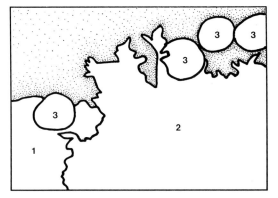

1. *Geranium sanguineum* var. *striatum*, one plant, 12 × 18 in (30 × 45 cm)
2. *Astilbe × arendsii* 'Bridal Veil', one plant, 18–30 × 18 in (45–75 × 45 cm)
3. *Allium christophii*, four bulbs, 12–18 × 12 in (30–45 × 30 cm)

This fine composition is well suited to its lightly shaded space where its pale blossoms gleam against shadows and are effectively viewed at close quarters. This little group would be lost if tucked into a large-scale border featuring intense colors.

Although this *Allium* species is quite short relative to others, its spherical umbels are among the largest of all *Allium*. Even long after the bloom color has faded and receded, the starry spheres maintain their arresting form well into late summer. Here, the fading *Allium* blooms take company with those of *Geranium*. The tiny geranium flowers repeat and extend the pale red-violet coloring for a long period in late spring and summer, with scattered repeat blooms throughout the cooler months.

The *Allium* and *Geranium* together will grow well in sun with average moisture, but since they are combined with a white-blooming, moisture-loving *Astilbe*, regular watering and a position with light afternoon shade are essential for this group. The *Astilbe* spires, *Allium* umbels, and prostrate, fine-textured *Geranium* mound make a fine composition of contrasted forms.

The slightly shorter *Astilbe* 'Deutschland' may be substituted for 'Bridal Veil', although its more intense and floriferous whiteness will not be quite as satisfactory as the soft creamy white blooms of 'Bridal Veil'. Any declining *Allium* foliage will be easily concealed amid the *Astilbe* and *Geranium* foliage.

A space 3 × 3 ft (0.9 × 0.9 m) will accommodate one *Astilbe* in the rear with four *Allium* in the midground and one *Geranium* in the foreground.

PHOTO 116. Caramoor Center for Music and the Arts, Katonah, New York, August. ENVIRONMENT: sun to part shade in soil of average fertility and moisture. USDA Zones 4–8. FEATURE: foliage summer to fall; flower summer to fall.

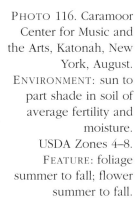

1. *Sedum* 'Autumn Joy', one plant, 18–24 × 24 in (45–60 × 60 cm)
2. *Monarda didyma* 'Violet Queen', four plants, 24–36 × 15 in (60–90 × 40 cm)

MOST FOLIAGE perceived as "green" is not true green but, particularly in temperate regions, contains tints and shades and grayed variations of yellow-green, the complementary color of red-violet. Nature provides more flowering plants in red-violet than in any other colors except yellow and white. This opens the possibilities for many varied, striking, and visually satisfying compositions using just one or two red-violet flowering plants in combination. Many present different foliage textures, especially invaluable for use as a summer contrast when red-violet blooms are most common.

The concept of red-violet being complementary to yellow-green is demonstrated here at its simplest with two easily grown plants. The *Monarda* bloom in an intense red-violet pairs perfectly with this *Sedum* at its light yellow-green stage. Texturally, the broad horizontal forms of *Sedum* heads stand out against the fine texture of the red-violet *Monarda* mass. After the *Monarda* finishes blooming this *Sedum* changes color, to pink developing to dark red, and lends itself to further association with later-blooming plants of distinctly contrasting form. To balance the color composition there should be about 60% red-violet to 40% yellow-green. Since *Monarda* also contributes a certain amount of darker yellow-green in its fragrant foliage, one needs to plant more *Monarda* than *Sedum* to achieve such balance.

This pair can be accommodated in a space 3 × 4 ft (0.9 x1.2 m), with four *Monarda* behind one *Sedum*.

PHOTO 117. Ziegler Garden, Bedford, New York, August. ENVIRONMENT: sun in soil of average fertility and moisture. USDA Zones 5–8. FEATURE: foliage summer to fall; flower late summer to fall.

GRASSES CAN offer late-season, distinctive soft foliage and an unusual drooping or descending form that associates well with many late summer and fall perennials. However, ornamental grasses generally require more cultural attention than is realized. Some grasses are quick to spread and seed themselves easily, others require regular back-breaking division.

In practice, such cultural issues may be far outweighed by the beauty and utility of the texture and form of their foliage and flower panicles. Although there are exceptions, I like to see plants spaced closely enough to permit the forms and textures to mingle as they are clearly doing here. This is particularly important where flower color is pale, quantity of bloom is sparse, and/or form is delicate.

These few, pale red-violet blooms of the native *Monarda* would disappear without the close backdrop of the grassy *Pennisetum* foliage and its translucent panicles. The drooping blooms of the native *Artemisia* are similarly delicate and need to be planted in great masses or combined, as here, in a delicately toned supporting composition.

Without the *Sedum* just developing in the foreground, this group has the airy lightness and informality of a meadow planting. The *Sedum* provides a stolid horizontal form and smooth texture to anchor the group firmly in a garden bed.

The minimum space required would be 6 × 7 ft (1.8 × 2.1 m), with one *Pennisetum* and three *Artemisia* in the background, three *Monarda* in the midground, and two *Sedum* in the foreground.

1. *Pennisetum alopecuroides*, one plant, 36 × 60 in (90 × 150 cm)
2. *Sedum* 'Autumn Joy', two plants, 18–24 × 24 in (45–60 × 60 cm)
3. *Monarda fistulosa*, three plants, 36–48 × 18 in (90–120 × 45 cm)
4. *Artemisia lactiflora*, three plants, 36–48 × 24 in (90–120 × 60 cm)

PHOTO 118. Ziegler Garden, Bedford, New York, October. ENVIRONMENT: sun in soil of average fertility and moisture. USDA Zones 4–8. FEATURE: foliage summer to fall; flower summer to fall.

1. *Sedum* 'Autumn Joy', two plants, 18–24 × 24 in (45–60 × 60 cm)
2. *Pennisetum alopecuroides*, one plant, 36 × 60 in (90 × 150 cm)

FOLIAR COLOR modifications as leaves mature are common to many plants, and in a few, such as *Sedum* 'Autumn Joy', flower color also changes. Although generally flower color fades and weakens, in this sedum it strengthens and darkens. Designers frequently attempt to fashion fresh compositions to accommodate or enhance evolving color alterations.

This particular late-flowering association is effective from late summer to late fall. It includes the same plants photographed in August in photo 117. By October the *Monarda* and *Artemisia* have been cut back and the *Sedum* has grown to its full height. *Pennisetum*'s long-lasting flower panicles mirror the color development in *Sedum*—both begin as a pale yellow-green with tinges of red-violet that gradually deepens to dark red. Such very dark colors are relatively rare in commonly used garden plants, and then almost exclusively are in the red, red-orange, and orange hues.

There is considerable disparity between the color intensities of the two plants at this stage, resulting in a dramatic, light/dark contrast between the deep red *Sedum* heads and pale gray-green *Pennisetum* foliage. The difference in intensity between the diluted foliage colors and the more intense flower colors allows the blooms greater significance. One can often see these intense dark hues isolated in nature in just this way, surrounded by a sea of grayed yellow-green. Associating this pair with some of the many *Rhododendron* and *Berberis* cultivars which develop this same deep red fall hue would enhance their effectiveness and link them effortlessly to a larger landscape composition.

Pennisetum is especially effective when backlighted by the rising or setting sun, and its pendulous leaves and flowers moderate the almost stolid form of the *Sedum* flower heads. The outstanding form contrast between the horizontal *Sedum* and drooping *Pennisetum* contributes much to the success of this association. *Sedum* benefits from an early season foreground planting to disguise its bare stems as they emerge from the soil and *Stachys byzantina* can do the job nicely.

A space 6 × 6 ft (1.8 × 1.8 m) will suit one *Pennisetum* with two *Sedum*. Including six *Stachys byzantina* will increase total space to 7 × 6 ft (2.1 × 1.8 m).

PHOTO 119. Stonecrop Garden, Cold Spring, New York, May. ENVIRONMENT: light shade in soil of average fertility and moisture. USDA Zones 3–8. FEATURE: foliage mid spring to fall; flower mid to late spring.

STRUCTURAL color, such as from walls, fences, and paths, forms a part of any landscape, necessitating that flower and foliage colors be selected to harmonize. In general, dark or neutral colors which do not wildly influence the planting color schemes provide the most appealing background. In specific instances, special color themes in plants can be continued in associated structures. Here, the weathered gray background fence is very important to this composition, adding a neutral color and smooth texture to highlight distinct *Hosta* and *Tulipa* forms and textures.

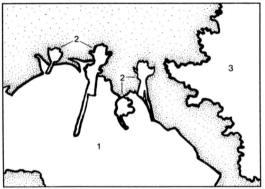

1. *Hosta sieboldiana*, two plants, 30 × 30 in (75 × 75 cm)
2. *Tulipa* 'Queen of Night', ten bulbs, 24 × 6 in (60 × 15 cm)
3. *Berberis thunbergii* 'Atropurpurea', one plant, 5 × 5 ft (1.5 × 1.5 m)

This particular *Hosta* is deservedly popular, its design value generated by the size of its broad-veined leaves and their unusual bluish tone. The blue-green quality suggests a pairing with blooms in a complementary light red-orange and this is indeed a successful association. But closer inspection reveals foliage color to be actually a very grayed yellow-green whose complement is red-violet. *Tulipa* 'Queen of Night' provides just the unusual deep red-violet hue to take this association from successful to brilliant.

Tulips interplanted with the hosta clearly display their striking form and dark hue against the light-colored, smooth, broad hosta foliage. Light red-violet tulips, such as *Tulipa* 'Pink Impression', would also associate well with this hosta, but it is the mystery of the dark red hue and the drama of dark against light which makes this association so compelling. The color composition is stretched and strengthened by the placement of the *Berberis* shrub against the paler fence. The berberis seems also to mirror the dark red-violet of the tulips, although in many situations its variable leaves seem more nearly red-orange.

For the above composition one *Berberis* behind two *Hosta*, interplanted with eight to ten *Tulipa* will occupy a space about 5 × 7 ft (1.5 × 2.1 m).

1. *Phlox paniculata* 'Bright Eyes',
   three plants, 24 × 18 in (60 × 45
   cm)
2. *Anemone vitifolia* 'Robustissima',
   two plants, 36 × 18 in (90 × 45
   cm)
3. *Miscanthus sinensis* 'Gracillimus',
   one plant, 4–7 × 5 ft (1.2–2.1 ×
   1.5 m)

PHOTO 120. Conservatory Garden, New York City, August. ENVIRONMENT: sun to part shade in soil of average fertility and moisture. USDA Zones 4–8. FEATURE: foliage late spring to fall; flower summer to fall.

LARGE-SCALE planting spaces often lack a clearly defined backdrop against which to display flowering compositions of differing scale. A backdrop can be introduced with fences or by planting hedges, or more simply by adding one or more large herbaceous plant.

Here the backdrop for this late-summer grouping is the maiden grass, *Miscanthus sinensis* 'Gracillimus', which also determines the scale of the composition. Its 6 ft (2 m) feathery plumes demand at least an equal depth of foreground planting. Here, in late summer, the finely textured arching foliage is not quite at maturity and its weeping form and excellent light gray yellow-green color establish a fine background for other plant colors and forms.

Red-violet is the complement of yellow-green and two different forms of late-season red-violet blooms benefit from this grassy backdrop. The *Phlox* develops arresting clusters of pale red-violet flowers with darker red-violet centers. *Anemone* adds to the late summer bounty by producing pale red-violet flowers, shown here in bud. Although the *Phlox* has texturally undistinguished foliage, its companion *Anemone* contributes dense foliage from late spring until fall in a valuable lustrous dark green and striking form.

The complexity of this red-violet/yellow-green complementary association can be increased by introducing *Thalictrum rochebrunianum* (see Part 2 for plant detail) between the *Anemone* and *Miscanthus*, where its light violet puffs of bloom can provide a diaphanous visual connection.

A large sunny space 6 × 8 ft (1.8 × 2.4 m) will accommodate one *Miscanthus* in the rear, two *Thalictrum rochebrunianum* and two *Anemone* in the midground, and three to four *Phlox* in the foreground. The basic trio requires at least 6 × 6 ft (1.8 × 1.8 m) to visually balance the height of the *Miscanthus*.

PHOTO 121.
Conservatory Garden,
New York City, August.
ENVIRONMENT: sun in
soil of average fertility
and average or less
moisture.
USDA Zones 6–8.
FEATURE: foliage late
spring to fall; flower late
summer to fall.

SOME DESIGNERS dislike combining pale gray foliage with pale blue-green foliage. I find these associations pleasant, since the combinations are harmonized by the large proportion of white present. This is easily seen in the pale blue-green foliage of such commonly used plants as *Elymus arenarius* (photo 130) and *Helictotrichon sempervirens* (blue oat grass) and in all the pale, grayed foliage plants. I am less happy combining pale gray foliage with pure yellow-green flowers or foliage. This often produces a sickly combination lacking any essential light-tinted unity.

The gray-foliaged *Artemisia* and gray budded *Sedum* used above also harmonize well with violet, blue-violet, and red-violet flowers. One can also associate any blooms whose color intensity is diluted

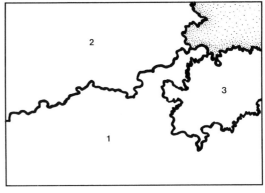

1. *Sedum* 'Ruby Glow', two plants, 6–12 × 15 in (15–30 × 40 cm)
2. *Perilla frutescens*, two plants, 24–36 × 18 in (60–90 × 45 cm)
3. *Artemisia* 'Powis Castle', one plant, 18–36 × 24 in (45–90 × 60 cm)

by gray, such as those of *Centranthus ruber* and many of the sedums. Such additions are useful too for introducing light/dark contrasts into a planting scheme. The dark red-violet *Perilla* used here also complements the *Artemisia* leaves' underlying pale yellow-green hue, and both harmonize with the subdued reddish tones in the *Sedum*. Adding dark red-violet umbels of *Allium sphaerocephalon* would introduce form variation and slightly intensify the dark/light contrasts.

I am very fond of this *Artemisia*. It has a wonderful pale gray yellow-green color, a fine foliage texture, and wonderful fragrance when leaves are rubbed. It is not winter hardy in my region, some miles north of New York City, and so I have to treat it as an annual.

A minimum planting in this subdued color scheme would require a space 3 × 4 ft (0.9 × 1.2 m), with two *Perilla* in the rear, one *Artemisia* in the midground, and two *Sedum* in the foreground. Adding four or five *Allium sphaerocephalon* in front of the *Artemisia* would increase the space requirement to 4 × 4 ft (1.2 × 1.2 m). See Part 2 for detail on further possibilities using *Allium sphaerocephalon* or *Centranthus ruber*.

PHOTO 122. New York Botanical Garden, New York City, September. ENVIRONMENT: sun in soil of average fertility and moisture. USDA Zones 5–8. FEATURE: foliage late spring to fall; flower late spring to fall.

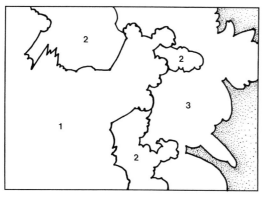

1. *Allium senescens* 'Glaucum', five bulbs, 12 × 12 in (30 × 30 cm)
2. *Sedum* 'Vera Jameson', one plant, 10–15 × 12 in (25–40 × 30 cm)
3. *Verbascum chaixii*, two plants, 30–60 × 18 in (75–150 × 45 cm)

A HANDFUL of newly flowering perennial plants, such as *Solidago* and *Aster*, offer bright color in fall, but in general subtle hues prevail. Fall is the season of modified yellows, violets, and red-violets, as many flower and foliage colors lose intensity and gray with age. This general reduction in color intensity may be exploited to highlight bright new blooms in fall-flowering plants against their less brilliant companions. Or deft compositions may emphasize the subtle tones of fall.

Allium senescens 'Glaucum' is unusual among alliums for its persistent foliage and for the slightly spiralled leaves inherited from *Allium senescens*. Its fading umbels are light red-violet and therefore associate harmoniously with the unusual grayish red-violet blooms of this *Sedum*. Both plants are associating with the complementary yellow-green *Verbascum* leaves just before its repeat bloom. Earlier in the growing season the stronger colors of red-violet *Allium* and *Sedum* blooms were at their most intense. Earliest to show were the pale yellow *Verbascum* spikes, which develop in late spring and early summer. This *Verbascum* will rebloom in late summer or early fall if cut back after this first bloom.

These small-scale plants, with their relatively delicate coloring and scattered bloom, are easily dominated by plants of larger scale, bolder texture, or more intense color. This group needs to be placed with plants of similar scale and hue with a gradual transition established to any bolder elements. Immediate transition possibilities can be gleaned from photos 131 or 140.

A space 3 × 4 ft (0.9 × 1.2 m) will accommodate a planting with two *Verbascum* in the rear, five *Allium* in the midground, and one *Sedum* in the foreground.

PHOTO 123.
Conservatory Garden,
New York City, June.
ENVIRONMENT: sun in
soil of average fertility
and moisture.
USDA Zones 5–8.
FEATURE: foliage late
spring to fall; flower late
spring to fall.

ASSOCIATIONS of equally tinted complementary colors in strikingly different forms practically guarantee success. Here, for example, *Verbena* contributes light violet and *Lythrum salicaria* 'Morden Pink' light red-violet, while *Miscanthus* provides their complement in light gray yellow-green. All of these colors establish a harmony by being more or less equally tinted or lightened versions of pure colors.

Red-violet is one of the colors occurring most often in commonly used garden plants. About half the time it is represented in the benign light red-violet shown here, where the stridency of the pure hue is modified by tinting.

An arresting tension is also created when ascending and descending forms are juxtaposed. This premise is confirmed in this composition by the vertical *Lythrum* spires and scattered *Verbena* blossoms contrasting with the loose, pendulous, grassy *Miscanthus*.

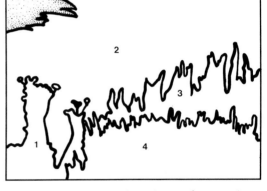

1. *Verbena bonariensis*, four plants, 36 × 12 in (90 × 30 cm)
2. *Miscanthus sinensis* 'Gracillimus', one plant, 4–7 × 5 ft (1.2–2.1 × 1.5 m)
3. *Lythrum salicaria* 'Morden Pink', two plants, 24–36 × 24 in (60–90 × 60 cm)
4. *Asteromoea mongolica*, two plants, 24–36 × 24 in (60–90 × 60 cm)

As *Verbena* continues flowering until frost, it pairs in late summer and fall with the white daisy-type *Asteromoea* blooms of the foreground. *Lythrum* has a shorter bloom season, and is considered destructively invasive in some areas. If local conditions restrict its use, the shorter *Liatris spicata* can offer similar color and form. *Veronica spicata* 'Blue Fox' also combines nicely with this group and adds harmonious light blue-violet spires.

Miscanthus always requires a rather large space, and supplying a balancing proportion of red-violet and violet color in the remaining plants extends this planting area quite a bit. To accommodate one *Miscanthus* in the background, two *Lythrum*, four *Verbena* in the midground, and two *Asteromoea* in the foreground requires an area of 6 × 6 ft (1.8 × 1.8 m). See Part 2 for detail on *Veronica spicata* 'Blue Fox' possibilities.

PHOTO 124. Stonecrop Gardens, Cold Spring, New York, June. ENVIRONMENT: part shade in soil of average to greater fertility and average to greater moisture. USDA Zones 3–8. FEATURE: foliage late spring to fall; flower late spring.

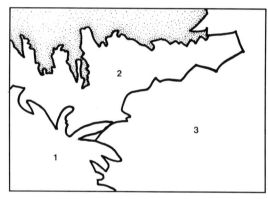

1. *Athyrium filix-femina*, two plants, 12–24 × 24 in (30–60 × 60 cm)
2. *Aquilegia* 'Olympia', four plants, 12–15 × 12 in (30–40 × 30 cm)
3. *Hosta sieboldiana*, one plant, 30 × 30 in (75 × 75 cm)

IN THE ABSENCE of direct practical experience of plant form, color, and habit, it is easy to miscalculate the plant quantities necessary to balance hues and textures in a grouping. Here, for instance, there is a theoretically sound color choice of violet bloom in *Aquilegia* and complementary, grayed yellow-green in the foliage of *Hosta* and *Athyrium*. However, the *Aquilegia* blooms contributing the violet color are small and delicate compared with the broad *Hosta* foliage mass. Greater familiarity with the *Aquilegia* form might have suggested massing that plant in association with *Hosta* to approximate an ideal color balance of about two-thirds violet and one-third yellow-green and to improve foliage texture distribution. Such oversights are easily adjusted for the next growing season.

Hosta is a highly prized plant in cooler climates, offering a range of foliage sizes and shades of yellow-green with minor textural or floral variations. Their durability and easy vigor inspire *Hosta* enthusiasts to ever greater collections. However, design differences within *Hosta* remain slight. A mass planting of *Hosta*, even of different types, can be monotonous unless contrasted with quite different forms and textures such as with the *Aquilegia* and *Athyrium* used here.

The late spring perfection of *Aquilegia* blooms persists for several weeks and then its fine foliage accents the medium-textured *Athyrium* foliage and the broad *Hosta* mass. The hosta also develops dainty flowers; pale violet, late spring blooms which barely rise above its leaves. *Hosta fortunei* has slightly smaller leaves and could substitute for *H. sieboldiana*. *Aquilegia* 'Black Star' has unusual, very dark red-violet blooms and would be a dramatic alternative to the *Aquilegia* used here.

A more ideal grouping of these plants would include more *Aquilegia* than shown above, and a minimum space of 4 × 5 ft (1.2 × 1.5 m) would place one *Hosta* in the rear, four to five *Aquilegia* in the midground, and two *Athyrium* in the foreground. The *Hosta* and *Aquilegia* alternatives suggested would not affect space needs.

PHOTO 125.
Conservatory Garden,
New York City, June.
ENVIRONMENT: part
shade in soil of average
fertility and moisture.
USDA Zones 4–7.
FEATURE: foliage mid
spring to fall; flower mid
to late spring.

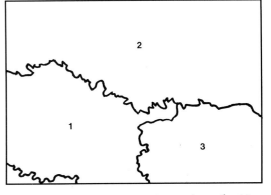

1. *Ajuga reptans* 'Atropurpurea', two plants, 6 × 12 in (15 × 30 cm)
2. *Polygonatum odoratum* 'Variegatum', three plants, 12–24 × 12 in (30–60 × 30 cm)
3. *Alchemilla mollis*, two plants, 12 × 18 in (30 × 45 cm)

ARCHING FORMS are used at times to guide attention downwards or to the center of a composition. They are relatively uncommon among the most frequently used herbaceous garden plants. *Aruncus dioicus*, *Leucojum aestivum*, *Lysimachia clethroides*, several grasses, and the *Polygonatum* shown here are among those developing arching forms.

Here, yellow-green *Polygonatum* and *Alchemilla* foliage associates easily and inoffensively with a complementary deep red to very deep red-violet shade in *Ajuga* foliage. These spiky, light violet to blue-violet *Ajuga* blossoms are followed in mid spring by yellow-green *Alchemilla* flowers, and later by very pale yellow, almost white, bell-like *Polygonatum* flowers arching over them both. The splendid and varied foliages of this group persist in an interesting composition of yellow-green touched by cream and very deep red for the balance of the growing season.

I have seen this diminutive group associated with *Aruncus dioicus* whose feathery foliage makes a perfect backdrop to this smaller composition. Although *Aruncus* is much taller than the other plants, perhaps disproportionately tall from a design viewpoint, when grown in light shade it can complete an especially lovely picture by also arching forward over other plants. It will also add its own buff-colored flowers in late spring.

The basic grouping requires 3 × 3 ft (0.9 × 0.9 m), with three *Polygonatum* in the middle and two *Alchemilla* and two *Ajuga* plants in the foreground. If one *Aruncus dioicus* is added in the rear, space should be increased to 4 × 4 ft (1.2 × 1.2 m).

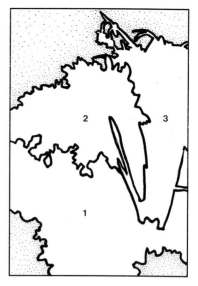

1. *Vinca minor*, five plants, 6 × 12 in (15 × 30 cm)
2. *Helleborus foetidus*, one plant, 18–24 × 18 in (45–60 × 45 cm)
3. *Leucojum aestivum* 'Gravetye Giant', six bulbs, 24 × 4 in (60 × 10 cm)

PHOTO 126. Ziegler Garden, Bedford, New York, May. ENVIRONMENT: light shade in soil of average fertility and moisture. USDA Zones 6–8. FEATURE: foliage mid spring to fall; flower early to late spring.

ONE OF THE best uses for spring herbaceous associations is as an underplanting for the many shrubs and trees with coincidental flowering time. Fragrant, white-flowering *Viburnum carlesii* or *V. carlecephalum* added to the association shown here, for example, would greatly expand the scale of this little group and produce a captivating three-dimensional spring composition.

Hellebores are exciting plants, producing unusual flower form and color in late winter or early spring, with some types maintaining their outstanding foliage year-round. The unusual light yellow-green blooms of this *Helleborus* appear in late winter and persist until late spring. Since these blooms are essentially the same color as the foliage, their appearance is not showy relative to most other spring-blooming bulbs and perennials. Their merit lies mainly in their unique blooms, attractive foliage, and ease of culture.

This simple association for light shade joins the yellowish green *Helleborus* bloom with its complementary blue-violet in the *Vinca* flowers, adding brightness with the white-flowering *Leucojum*. Actually the tips of the *Leucojum* flowers contain a small, yet unifying repetition of the light yellow-green of the *Helleborus* blooms. Form variety is established with the prostrate, scattered *Vinca* blooms, the drooping clusters of *Helleborus* flowers, and the vertical *Leucojum* form terminating in tiny, overarching, bell-like blooms.

Adding later bulbs, such as *Tulipa* 'Spring Green', to the *Vinca* planting will lengthen the flowering period and extend the pale green and white color theme.

Leucojum visually disappears in late spring, but the deeply divided *Helleborus* foliage contrasts the small shiny *Vinca* leaves and contributes to a fine, long-season foliage composition.

A minimum space 3 × 3 ft (0.9 × 0.9 m) will accommodate one *Helleborus* and six *Leucojum* surrounded by five *Vinca*. See Part 2 for plant details on the *Tulipa* 'Spring Green' bulb mentioned.

PHOTO 127.
Edmondsham House
Gardens, Dorset,
England, June.
ENVIRONMENT: sun in
soil of average or less
fertility and average or
less moisture.
USDA Zones 3–8.
FEATURE: foliage mid
spring to late summer;
flower mid spring to
summer.

COLOR associations of close-complementary blue or blue-violet and yellow-orange are among my favorites but are relatively rare. This scarcity results from the dearth of easily-grown flowers blooming in the light and pale yellow-orange hues which associate so well with the large numbers of predominantly light and pale blue-violet flower hues. Blue or blue-violet and yellow-orange occur more often in plants preferring dry, sandy, mild conditions, such as *Achillea*, *Eschscholzia*, *Lavandula*, *Nepeta*, *Osteospermum*, *Verbena*, and so on.

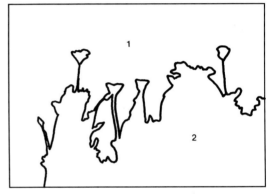

1. *Nepeta mussinii*, two plants, 12–18 × 18 in
   (30–45 × 45 cm)
2. *Eschscholzia californica*, seven plants, 8–18 × 12
   in (20–45 × 30 cm)

Since success with planting and design increases with the selection of indigenous species, this particular pairing may be inappropriate for those gardening in moist, cooler climates because it is ideal for hot, dry conditions. Still, many plants can be encouraged to stretch their limits of tolerance, and this pair was thriving nicely in a garden in southern England, admittedly during a rather dry summer. I have seen it doing just as well in New York gardens in late spring and early summer.

Nepeta, if cut back after bloom, will sprout fresh foliage and rebloom in late summer when its fragrance may be associated with the paler warm-hued achilleas, such as *Achillea millefolium* 'Weser River Sandstone', also with scented foliage. *Eschscholzia* ceases blooming by late summer and will usually scatter enough seed to provide new plants for the following year if the soil is well-drained.

Two *Nepeta* with six or eight of these delicate *Eschscholzia* will need a minimum space of 3 × 4 ft (0.9 × 1.2 m).

PHOTO 128. Conservatory Garden, New York City, April.
ENVIRONMENT: sun in soil of average fertility and average or less moisture. USDA Zones 6–8.
FEATURE: foliage mid spring; flower mid spring.

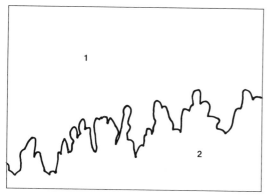

1. *Narcissus* 'Geranium', three plants, 12–18 × 6 in (30–45 × 15 cm)
2. *Muscari armeniacum*, six bulbs, 6–8 × 4 in (15–20 × 10 cm)

MANY EARLY spring plants in the northern latitudes are small-scale and develop flowers in receding violet blues or weak pastels whose effectiveness dwindles with distance. In very large landscapes, one must use strong, advancing warm colors in spring plantings or concentrate weaker colors in larger masses for adequate visual impact.

All plantings connected to trees and shrubs should be proportioned to the larger scale, and this usually means extensive planting areas. Such large-scale planting often requires considerable expenditure. Frequently the expenditure falls sadly short of the design intention, resulting in distracting splashes of color. Furthermore, early spring plants should not be used in large mixed borders unless massed and related to the foliage of adjacent plants. Otherwise the resulting composition will again be spotty and weak.

Early spring-flowering plants are often most effective in small, clearly defined spaces such as the compact urban garden where plant groupings of 4–5 sq ft (about 1.2–1.5 sq m) can have substance and impact. The association of fragrant bulbs shown here is common to either large or small spring designs.

This particular combination joins violet-blue *Muscari* with a bi-colored *Narcissus*, demonstrating the harmony of the rarely executed near-complementary color association of blue-violet, pale yellow, and yellow-orange. This spring planting would be very effective viewed over a distance up to about 50 ft (15 m) as long as the quantities are proportioned to the scale. Include about two-thirds *Muscari* to one-third *Narcissus*.

PHOTO 129. Stapehill Gardens, Dorset, England, June.
ENVIRONMENT: sun in soil of average fertility and moisture.
USDA Zones 5–7.
FEATURE: foliage mid spring to summer; flower late spring to summer.

THE ASSOCIATION of violet and yellow-orange includes two hues which have no special color wheel linkage since they are not opposite, adjacent, or closely complementary. The mass of yellow-green foliage, complementary to the violet *Salvia*, modifies the possibly strident effects of combining violet with yellow-orange. It is not as pleasing to me as the closer complement of the pairing in photo 127, but it has advantages. For one thing, this is a much easier association to contrive in moist, cool climates since both plants are readily available and of easy culture. The perennial *Salvia × superba* and its cultivars are available by mail order or from local nurseries. The annual *Calendula* can be started from seed or bought as transplants from most nurseries.

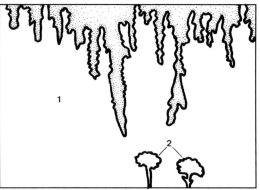

1. *Salvia × superba*, two plants, 18–36 × 18 in (45–90 × 45 cm)
2. *Calendula officinalis*, two plants, 12–24 × 12 in (30–60 × 30 cm)

The difference in flower form is very pronounced, the *Calendula* making a distinct and shapely daisy contrast against the dark *Salvia* spires. Foliage is slightly broader in *Calendula*. The precise flower color of this *Salvia* varies and in some strains is a lighter tint of violet. The quantity of this rather powerful statement in yellow-orange needs to be carefully controlled so it does not overwhelm the dark, receding violet. A general proportion of two-thirds violet bloom to one-third orange bloom is the aim.

A minimum planting of two *Salvia* plants behind two *Calendula* should provide the required color distribution and will occupy a space about 2 × 3 ft (0.6 × 0.9 m).

PHOTO 130. New York Botanical Garden, New York City, May. ENVIRONMENT: sun in soil of average fertility and moisture. USDA Zones 4–8. FEATURE: foliage mid spring to fall; flower insignificant.

1. *Elymus arenarius*, one plant, 18–24 × 15 in (45–60 × 40 cm)
2. *Berberis thunbergii* 'Atropurpurea Nana', one plant, 18–24 × 30 in (45–60 × 75 cm)

ANOTHER of the very rare color associations in planting design is blue-green paired with red-orange. This rarity results primarily from the shortage of true blue-green plants. I have seen this color only in the foliage of a few plants. There are quite a few plants whose foliage has a waxy or pubescent surface which gives a blue-green impression, but the color is actually a coated gray yellow-green. When paired with red-orange they do not offer quite the same sublime results as true blue-green foliage. Still, they are often a very pleasing substitute.

The pallor of *Elymus* foliage fits it for association with similar pastel hues in flowers, with gray-leaved plants, or with a scattering of white blooms. Dense white flower clusters would tend to drain color from the *Elymus*. Stunning associations of these unusual colors are made with light and pale red-orange or orange blooms, such as those occurring in *Achillea millefolium* 'Weser River Sandstone' and *Osteospermum* 'Salmon Queen'.

Contrasting pale *Elymus* with a very dark red-orange foliage had never occurred to me until I saw it planted in the ground with *Berberis thunbergii* 'Atropurpurea Nana' in a clever association of two quite different foliage forms. This idea could be continued by adding *Heuchera* 'Palace Purple', which would provide another foliage in a dark red hue. *Elymus* is a notoriously vigorous plant which spreads easily. The less vigorous *Helictotrichon sempervirens* could substitute.

One *Elymus* or one *Helictotrichon* with one *Berberis* will occupy a space 3 × 3 ft (0.9 × 0.9 m).

PHOTO 131. Donald M. Kendall Sculpture Gardens, Pepsico's World Headquarters, Purchase, New York, September. ENVIRONMENT: sun in soil of average fertility and average or less moisture. USDA Zones 4–8. FEATURE: foliage late spring to fall; flower late spring to fall.

COMPACT associations with long useful seasons are plentiful in temperate climates. This one is especially valuable to me because it approximates my favorite complementary color association—blue-green with red-orange. The harmony is particularly good here since *Dianthus* foliage has rather a grayed, greenish blue-green appearance and *Sedum* a dark red with a hint of orange.

This *Dianthus*, which is probably 'Essex Witch', offers small, pale red-violet, fragrant blooms with dark red-violet markings first appearing in June and continuing their show for several weeks. It easily associates with other June-blooming flowers as seen in photo 80. If the *Dianthus* foliage is cut back along with its fading blooms, it puts out a fresh crop of leaves with foliage color gradually developing in complexity. The fresh foliage color deepens as the prostrate *Sedum* starts to flower in late summer and fall. This spectacular association lasts about a month. Both plants are of very easy culture and easily join other pairings of similar hue, such as *Elymus arenarius*, one of the truly blue-green foliaged plants, and *Dicentra eximia* 'Luxuriant'.

The basic pair would need a space 2 × 3 ft (0.6 × 0.9 m), with two *Dianthus* beside one *Sedum*.

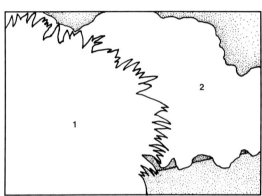

1. *Dianthus × allwoodii*, two plants, 12–18 × 12 in (30–45 × 30 cm)
2. *Sedum* 'Ruby Glow', one plant, 6–12 × 15 in (15–30 × 40 cm)

PHOTO 132.
Sissinghurst Garden,
Kent, England, June.
ENVIRONMENT: sun in
soil of low fertility and
average moisture.
USDA Zones 7–8.
FEATURE: foliage late
spring to late summer;
flower late spring to
late summer.

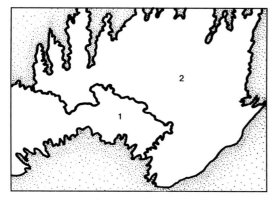

1. *Alstroemeria* Ligtu Hybrids, six plants, 24–48 × 18 in (60–120 × 45 cm)
2. *Macleaya microcarpa*, one plant, 5–8 × 4 ft (1.5–2.4 × 1.2 m)

DELIBERATE and thoughtful associations of orange and red-orange are very uncommon, although they bring a gorgeous warmth and startling brilliance to any space they inhabit. It is a color pairing generally suggestive of autumn and its employment can yield a sometimes unnatural sense that the flowering season is ending. Then too, often these colors typify marigolds. The dense and difficult marigold form and its careless overuse have lent the color association a banal summertime image.

In theory, lighter tinted or grayed orange blooms are much easier to place without offense, but they are uncommon in flowers. *Macleaya microcarpa* or especially *M. cordata* 'Coral Plume' has just such a valuable flower color and makes a fine, large-scale display in early summer. Similar colors are visible in the flowers of the *Alstroemeria* hybrids planted here. A fern, *Polystichum setiferum* 'Divisilobum', disguises the bare area left when *Alstroemeria* plants go dormant after flowering.

Both plant types are very loose and gracefully respond to any breeze. The broad, gray-green *Macleaya* leaves turn easily, revealing their light underside and adding a valuable sense of movement and liveliness to a garden or landscape. It should be placed where its fine foliage is not concealed.

Adding *Elymus arenarius* to the foreground of this basic light red-orange composition would be an excellent beginning for a more ambitious red-orange and blue-green association. This *Macleaya* is invasive and needs restraint to control its running roots. *Elymus* also has an invasive character and using sandy or lean soil will help inhibit both.

One *Macleaya* with six *Alstroemeria* and two *Polystichum setiferum* will need a space 5 × 6 ft (1.5 x1.8 m). Adding three *Elymus arenarius* to the front increases space to 5 × 7 ft (1.5 × 2.1 m).

PHOTO 133. Stonecrop Gardens, Cold Spring, New York, July. ENVIRONMENT: sun to part shade in soil of average fertility and moisture. USDA Zones 4–8. FEATURE: foliage mid spring to fall; flower summer.

THERE ARE only a few large, dark red foliage plants that can provide background to establish dark/light contrasts. These valuable few can also be used to display brighter and lighter tints in adjacent and complementary color blooms and foliage. As seen in the above planting, the dark red foliage of *Berberis* makes a unique contribution.

This *Berberis* is very hardy, of easy culture, and can be employed in many ways. An example of using its dark red coloration with red and dark red-violet in spring tulips can be seen in photo 21. Here is a summer pairing with a flowering dark red-orange *Hemerocallis*, which could also include spring-flowering tulips. Daylily foliage is about 10 in (25 cm) high at tulip bloom and can serve as a useful base planting at that time.

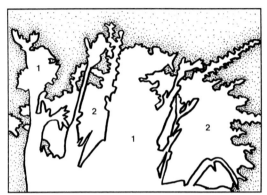

1. *Hemerocallis* 'Ed Murray', four plants, 24–36 × 18 in (60–90 × 45 cm)
2. *Berberis thunbergii* 'Atropurpurea', one plant, 5 × 5 ft (1.5 × 1.5 m)

There are many suitable daylily varieties. Choose from the red-orange to orange flowering range which grow to at least 24 in (60 cm) tall for this grouping. Note that hue variations in the *Hemerocallis* flowers will affect perception of the *Berberis* color— brighter red-orange flowers, for example, will make the *Berberis* foliage appear more dark red-violet. Adding a complementary blue-green foliaged plant, such as *Hosta sieboldiana* in a light shade setting or *Elymus arenarius* in sun, would make a striking addition to the simple combination of *Berberis* and *Hemerocallis*.

Planting at least four daylilies with the *Berberis* would allow sufficient quantities of bloom against the larger scale of the shrub. Including both requires a space 6 × 6 ft (1.8 × 1.8 m). Adding one *Hosta sieboldiana* or one *Elymus arenarius* would increase these space requirements to 6 × 7 ft (1.8 × 2.1 m).

PHOTO 134. Stonecrop Gardens, Cold Spring, New York, August. ENVIRONMENT: sun to part shade in soil of average fertility and moisture. USDA Zones 5–8. FEATURE: foliage late spring to late summer; flower mid to late summer.

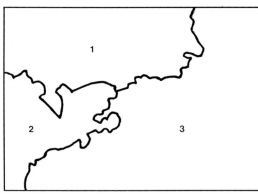

1. *Callistephus chinensis* 'Deep Red', one plant, 18–30 × 15 in (45–75 × 40 cm)
2. *Achillea millefolium* 'Paprika', two plants, 15–21 × 18 in (40–55 × 45 cm)
3. *Impatiens* 'Tempo Hybrid Red', two plants, 8–12 × 12 in (20–30 × 30 cm)

BLENDING warm and cool reds often results in a potent color association which some find disturbing, especially if all the colors are intense, pure hues. The greater the tilt in component blooms away from optimal red, towards red-violet or red-orange, the greater may be the sense of disharmony. The pure hues are easier to combine when softened by tinting towards pastels or shading towards deep colors. But pure bold colors—colors unaltered by lightening, darkening, or graying—when carefully handled, result in boldly spirited designs.

This example of a pleasing association of warm and cool reds with different values evidences a happy mix. Very dark red, found here in the *Callistephus*, introduces a somber, almost meditative mood to the composition. It makes an excellent, subdued focal point in the landscape. As with most dark red colors, careful repetitions of this hue gently define the limits of an outdoor space. A brighter, slightly cooler red is introduced in the *Impatiens*, while *Achillea* offers warm red and red-orange.

Callistephus chinensis 'Emperor Carmine' is a slightly taller annual China aster (36 in/90 cm) and may be substituted for *C. c.* 'Deep Red', but almost any red, annual China aster will work. The same can be said for almost any warm or cool red *Impatiens*.

This group will fit a space 3 × 3 ft (0.9 × 0.9 m) when planted in the ratio of one *Callistephus* in the rear with two *Achillea* in the midground and two *Impatiens* in the foreground.

A S DISCUSSED in the previous example, associations of warm reds and cool reds need to be handled with some care. Some people will always find them offensive and jarring, but they may offer a focusing brilliance which can be very useful in the landscape or garden. Most difficulties develop when the warm and cool reds are of similar intensity and purity. If only one of the hues is a powerful, undiluted color, the others being tinted or shaded or slightly grayed, then only that one intensely colored plant will dominate and the associated colors will be subordinated.

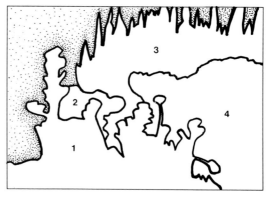

1. *Centranthus ruber*, three plants, 18–24 × 12 in (45–60 × 30 cm)
2. *Salvia guaranitica*, five plants, 36–60 × 24 in (90–150 × 60 cm)
3. *Lythrum salicaria* 'Morden Pink', three plants, 24–36 × 24 in (60–90 × 60 cm)
4. *Asteromoea mongolica*, two plants, 24–36 × 24 in (60–90 × 60 cm)

Here, the intense cool red-violet *Lythrum* spires are associated with the warm red *Centranthus* blooms. The intensity of the *Centranthus* hue is grayed as well as lightened. It is this muting of the pure color that permits it to associate calmly with more intense hues. The presence of the near-adjacent, but dark, blue-violet *Salvia* also has a pacifying effect. The calming element would be more pronounced if there were much more *Salvia* included.

The small white *Asteromoea* flowers emerge as the *Lythrum* and *Centranthus* flowers begin to fade. The *Asteromoea* continues to bloom into fall with the *Salvia*, altering the color association of the plant grouping and its value as a warm-hued focal point. The foliages of this group are unremarkable together, but the flower forms provide excellent variation.

More *Salvia* would improve the composition, and in a space 6 × 7 ft (1.8 × 2.1 m) place five *Salvia* in the rear, three *Lythrum* in the midground, and two *Asteromoea* and three *Centranthus* in the foreground.

PHOTO 136. Hadspen Garden, Sandra and Nori Pope, owners, Somerset, England, July. ENVIRONMENT: sun in soil of average fertility and moisture. USDA Zones 5–8. FEATURE: foliage late spring to fall; flower mid to late summer.

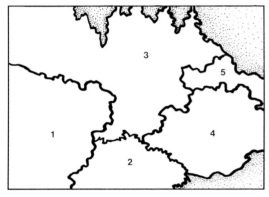

1. *Geranium psilostemon*, one plant, 24–48 × 24 in (60–120 × 60 cm)
2. *Salvia officinalis* 'Purpurea', two plants, 12–18 × 12 in (30–45 × 30 cm)
3. *Malva sylvestris* 'Mauritiana', one plant, 36–72 × 24 in (90–185 × 60 cm)
4. *Knautia macedonica*, two plants, 24 × 18 in (60 × 45 cm)
5. *Rosa* (unknown) cultivar, one plant, 30 × 30 in (75 × 75 cm)

CONTINUING with the challenging activity of combining intense warm reds with intense cool reds, note that another moderating tool available to designers is alteration in color value. Where very light tints (pinks) are used, discordancies are minimized by the strong presence of white in the pale colors. Or, as in this example, if very dark reds and very dark red-violets are used, potential discordancies are masked by the presence of black. Dark red hues bring a particular mood to their space, variously experienced as mournful or somber, or elegant and refined.

In this composition, warm and cool reds play among the red-violet flowers of *Geranium*, dark red *Knautia*, dark red 'Prospero' type *Rosa*, and very deep red-violet *Malva* flowers and *Salvia* foliage. Forms introduce reasonable variety and range from the tall *Malva* spires to the tiny red flower heads of *Knautia*. The textures of both flower and foliage are undistinguished and the addition of a broad-leaved plant, such as Swiss chard (*Beta vulgaris* subsp. *cicla*), in the foreground would improve the textural composition.

This group requires an area of about 5 × 5 ft (1.5 × 1.5 m) to include three *Beta vulgaris* subsp. *cicla* with two *Salvia* in the foreground, one *Malva* in the rear, and one floribunda or English *Rosa*, such as *Rosa* 'Prospero', one *Geranium*, and two *Knautia* in the midground.

PHOTO 137. New York Botanical Garden, New York City, September. ENVIRONMENT: sun in soil of average fertility and moisture. USDA Zones 5–8. FEATURE: foliage summer to fall; flower late spring to fall.

GARDEN designers are sometimes justifiably reluctant to include strong warm colors. Such colors associate competitively and it is easy to produce inharmonious compositions, especially while also juggling the other basic planting design elements of texture and form. This composition nicely obviates some color competition by introducing strong form contrasts—the floral-covered mounds of *Melampodium* juxtaposed with the vertical *Celosia* spires. However, the color association detracts from the intended strength of the form composition.

The difficulty in this planting lies not in the basic colors selected, but in differences in strength and value of those colors. *Melampodium* flowers offer

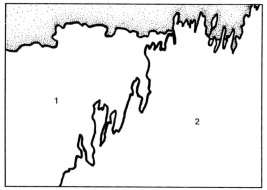

1. *Melampodium paludosum* 'Medallion', 12–18 x 15 in (30–45 × 40 cm)
2. *Celosia elegans* 'Pink Tassles', 24–36 × 12–18 in (60–90 × 30–45 cm)

such a pure, intense yellow-orange they overwhelm the predominantly pale and receding red-violet of *Celosia*. These unequal intensities and values make further adjustments difficult. To correct plant proportions for color balance would require an enormous and possibly boring mass of *Celosia*.

A pale yellow-orange bloom, to match the pallor of this *Celosia*, may be introduced by adding some of the *Hemerocallis* or the *Achillea millefolium* hybrids. Photo 37 shows *Celosia* combined more successfully with another red-violet in *Verbena bonariensis*, near-white *Zinnia elegans* 'Silver Sun', and the white *Cleome spinosa* 'Helen Campbell'. Red-violets and yellow-oranges are not especially harmonious, but can combine quite well when color strengths are matched and color proportions are balanced. See photo 147.

Photo 138. Mapperton House Gardens, Dorset, England, July. Environment: sun in soil of average fertility and moisture. USDA Zone 8. Feature: foliage late spring to late summer; flower mid to late summer.

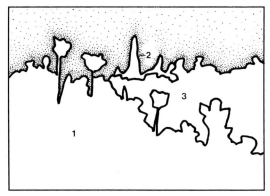

1. *Papaver somniferum*, five plants, 30 × 12 in (75 × 30 cm)
2. *Kniphofia* 'Atlanta', two plants, 36 × 18 in (90 × 45 cm)
3. *Geranium psilostemon*, one plant, 24–48 × 24 in (60–120 × 60 cm)

IT IS FAR more of a juggling challenge to balance three or four colors harmoniously than two. When one observes a natural or spontaneous composition including several flower colors, seldom are colors seen distributed in equal quantities. There are usually one or two reigning plants whose flower or foliage color dominate the landscape. Other simultaneously flowering plants occur in much smaller, subordinated colonies or even as isolated individuals. In our own multihued planting schemes it is an excellent idea to adopt nature's guideline and allow one or two plants to dominate.

The dominant color scheme here is the complementary red-violet in *Papaver* and *Geranium* blooms and the grayish yellow-green *Papaver* foliage. A recessive theme, employing hues which are equally strong and closely adjacent on the color wheel, plays out in red-orange *Kniphofia* and red-violet *Geranium* blooms. Yellow contributes relatively small accents. The proportioning of dominant and secondary colors allows this association to be a comfortable presence.

Another pleasing design factor here is the varied plant forms. The flowering *Kniphofia* spires rising behind a foliage mound contrast the small *Geranium* blossoms and broad, silky *Papaver* blooms, establishing interest through variety. Furthermore, the distinctive gray-green *Papaver* foliage makes a broad contrast for the finely dissected *Geranium* leaves.

A space 3 × 5 ft (0.9 × 1.5 m) will accommodate two *Kniphofia* behind one *Geranium* and five *Papaver*.

PHOTO 139.
Conservatory Garden,
New York City, July.
ENVIRONMENT: part
shade to sun in soil of
average fertility and
moisture.
USDA Zones 4–7.
FEATURE: foliage mid
spring to fall; flower late
spring to fall.

THE ULTIMATE design success of any association depends to a great extent on the attention
devoted to variation in plant form and texture. Texture as a design element is defined by entire plants
or, in the larger landscape, plant groups. At closer
quarters, in the small scale of the typical urban garden, textural quality is governed by such things as
leaf size, light-reflecting qualities, and shape, or the
spacing of blooms on a plant. Perception of leaf texture can also be affected by variations in foliage
color. For example, white-edged *Polygonatum odoratum* 'Variegatum' leaves present an apparently finer
and busier texture than does the foliage of the similar, but non-variegated *Polygonatum biflorum* seen
in photo 4.

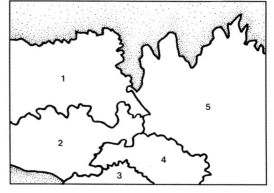

1. *Polygonatum odoratum* 'Variegatum', two plants,
   12–24 × 12 in (30–60 × 30 cm)
2. *Alchemilla mollis*, one plant, 12 × 18 in (30 × 45
   cm)
3. *Salvia officinalis* 'Aurea', one plant, 12–18 × 12 in
   (30–45 × 30 cm)
4. *Heuchera* 'Palace Purple', two plants, 12–24 × 12
   in (30–60 × 30 cm)
5. *Nicotiana langsdorffii*, two plants, 36–48 × 18 in
   (90–120 × 45 cm)

This particular composition is suitable for a small
garden space. Textural variation in foliage and flower
from the light-tinted diffuse cloud of *Nicotiana langsdorffii* blooms to the broader textured foliage in
Heuchera and *Alchemilla* are readily appreciated in an intimate setting. Subtle color contrasts ranging between the lighter tints of yellow-green, yellow, and darker blue-violet also
necessitate close viewing.

Color balance could be improved. Dark blue-violet *Salvia guaranitica* is present yet
barely visible in this photo view. Nevertheless it should be visible in large quantities to balance and contrast both the ambiguous deep red-violet to red-orange *Heuchera* foliage and
the brighter yellow-green in *Nicotiana*, *Alchemilla*, and *Salvia officinalis*. Adding another
Heuchera and more *Salvia guaranitica* would facilitate a more perfect color balance.

This group would require a space of 4 × 5 ft (1.2 x 1.5 m) for color balance. Use three
Salvia guaranitica in the rear, two *Nicotiana* and two *Polygonatum* in the midground, and
one *Alchemilla*, two *Heuchera*, and one *Salvia officinalis* 'Aurea' in the foreground.

PHOTO 140.
Conservatory Garden,
New York City,
September.
ENVIRONMENT: sun in
soil of average fertility
and moisture.
USDA Zones 5–8.
FEATURE: foliage
summer to fall; flower
late spring to fall.

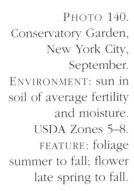

1. *Gomphrena globosa* 'Lavender Lady', three plants,
   18–24 × 18 in (45–60 × 45 cm)
2. *Gomphrena globosa* 'Rosy', two plants, 8–12 × 12
   in (20–30 × 30 cm)
3. *Nicotiana alata* 'Nicki Pink', three plants, 15–18 ×
   12 in (40–45 × 30 cm)
4. *Nicotiana alata* 'Lime Green', three plants, 18–30
   × 12 in (45–75 × 30 cm)
5. *Salvia farinacea* 'Victoria', five plants, 18–24 × 12
   in (45–60 × 30 cm)

OFTEN the simplest way to control color, texture, and reliable flowering over a long season is to concentrate on annuals. This group will flower dependably in temperate climates from late spring to fall. It offers a bold color floral quartet—using yellow-green Nicotiana with its complementary red-violet in the *Gomphrena* cultivars and two near-complementary colors, violet *Salvia* and light red (pink) *Nicotiana*. The color proportioning here is excellent. Just a small amount of advancing yellow-green in the *Nicotiana alata* 'Lime Green' is balanced by larger quantities of violet *Salvia* and light red-violet and light red in *Gomphrena* and *Nicotiana alata* 'Nicki Pink'.

The flower forms satisfy interest with globose *Gomphrena* flowers contrasting spiked *Salvia* and fragrant, funnel-shaped *Nicotiana* blooms. The foliage is typically less distinguished in annual plantings, displaying only a modest variation between fine, medium, and broad leaves. Since these annuals flower more or less continuously until frost, foliage form and texture are subsidiary.

Annuals have modest space needs and all of these will easily fit into 4 × 5 ft (1.2 × 1.5 m). Site three *Nicotiana alata* 'Lime Green' to mingle with five *Salvia* in the rear, three *Nicotiana alata* 'Nicki Pink' with three *Gomphrena globosa* 'Lavender Lady' in the midground, and two *G. g.* ' Rosy' in the foreground. As these plants grow through each other in a loose, appealing fashion, precise placement is not essential.

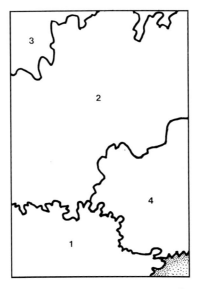

1. *Alchemilla alpina*, two plants, 6 × 12 in (15 × 30 cm)
2. *Ruta graveolens*, one plant, 24–36 × 15 in (60–90 × 40 cm)
3. *Astilbe × arendsii* 'Fanal', one plant, 24 × 18 in (60 × 45 cm)
4. *Campanula poscharskyana*, two plants, 6–12 × 12 in (15–30 × 30 cm)

PHOTO 141. Henrietta Lockwood Garden, Bedford, New York, July. ENVIRONMENT: sun to part shade in soil of average fertility and moisture. USDA Zones 4–7. FEATURE: foliage late spring to fall; flower late spring to late summer.

THIS RATHER unorthodox composition is successful for several reasons. For one thing, the tiny, delicate, diffuse flowers dilute the impact of the rather intense red, yellow, and violet color combination that is so disconcerting in photo 142 yet so inoffensive here. Also, the color offered by the few blooms is dispersed among large amounts of neutralizing green foliage.

Ruta foliage is a dark, gray yellow-green which, as it matures, appears bluish compared with the neighboring *Alchemilla* foliage. The *Ruta* foliage provides an excellent background for the light violet *Campanula* blossoms. The lower part of the planting, combining *Alchemilla*, *Campanula*, and *Ruta*, offers one pleasing composition, and the upper part, where *Ruta* flowers and foliage contrast with red *Astilbe* flowers, another.

The intense hot red of *Astilbe* blossoms dominates this little group and remains visible over a large distance. This high visibility may be used to define and unite a garden space by periodically repeating the plant in the same or different combinations. The viewer's eye will first track the progress of this powerful color before considering other colors in the designed space. Acceptable alternatives are *Alchemilla mollis* for *A. alpina* and *Campanula carpatica* 'Blue Clips' for *C. poscharskyana*.

A space 2 × 4 ft (0.6 × 1.2 m) will accommodate one *Astilbe* in the rear, one *Ruta* in the midground, and two *Alchemilla* and two *Campanula* in the foreground.

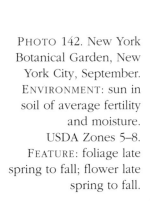

PHOTO 142. New York Botanical Garden, New York City, September. ENVIRONMENT: sun in soil of average fertility and moisture. USDA Zones 5–8. FEATURE: foliage late spring to fall; flower late spring to fall.

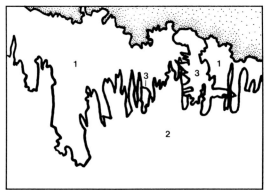

1. *Tagetes* 'Primrose Lady', 15 × 15 in (40 × 40 cm)
2. *Salvia farinacea* 'Victoria', 18–24 × 12 in (45–60 × 30 cm)
3. *Zinnia elegans* 'Red Sun', 36 × 24 in (90 × 60 cm)

RED, YELLOW, and blue together form a primary color triad frequently used in plant composition. Some garden writers and designers find it pleasing while others find it abhorrent. Certainly the greater the number of colors used in any design the more difficult to establish harmony.

For many, three colors presents a lot of difficulty. This particular planting attempts to overcome these difficulties but does not succeed. Failure is partly due to the pure violet of *Salvia* substituting for blue. Although violet nearly complements the pale greenish yellow flowers of *Tagetes* and harmonizes with the near-adjacent bright red *Zinnia*, the three colors together do not establish a promising relationship. If flower colors were all equally tinted, with pale yellow marigolds joined by pale violet and pale red (pink), the white present in all three tints would smooth out any color disharmonies. The strong, even somewhat jarring character would become one of delight and harmony.

Failure is also due to the plant forms and especially textures adding little to the composition. Although the vertical *Salvia* spires are useful in almost any design, association with the dense, solid textures of the large *Zinnia* and *Tagetes* flower heads forces an uninteresting trio. The *Zinnia* and *Tagetes* flowers present dominating blocks of color that unbalance the composition. They would benefit from the company of loosely textured, airy plants with smaller-scale blooms. Such color blocks also improve by positioning against smooth, dark, uncompetitive backgrounds, such as sheared hedges, where their striking color and solidly modeled forms can be seen to best advantage.

1. *Lychnis chalcedonica*, three plants, 24–36 × 18 in (60–90 × 45 cm)
2. *Delphinium* 'Charles Gregory Broan', two plants, 60–84 × 36 in (150–215 × 90 cm)
3. *Buphthalmum speciosum*, one plant, 36–72 × 36 in (90–185 × 90 cm)

PHOTO 143. Packwood House Gardens, a property of The National Trust, Warwickshire, England, July. ENVIRONMENT: sun in soil of average fertility and moisture. USDA Zones 3–7. FEATURE: foliage mid to late summer; flower summer.

RED, YELLOW, and blue flower compositions are *attempted* frequently, especially in municipal plantings, where bright colors excite interest. One seldom sees a true blue flower used in these large municipal plantings. This is chiefly because blue flowers are rare, often occurring in small-scale plants with tiny flowers such as *Lobelia erinus*, *Cynoglossum amabile*, or *Linum perenne*. Small flowers and small stature have little impact on large-scale mass plantings. Frequently violet is substituted for blue in these associations intended for a mass scale. Blue-violet, being closer to the desired blue, is usually a more successful choice.

Also, all three colors need be of similar value and intensity to be really effective and proportioned so there is about 30% red, 50% blue or blue-violet and only 20% yellow. Often one sees either equal amounts of each color or a very large quantity of yellow.

The dramatic association shown above almost succeeds in its color proportioning since the enormous dark blue-violet *Delphinium* spike offers such a mass of color. It dominates, as it should, the lesser quantity of yellow in *Buphthalmum* and red in *Lychnis*. These breathtaking colors should be used in a space suited to such flamboyance since together they outshine nearby compositions of weaker form and color intensity.

This particular grouping is sited on a mound, but in a flat space positions would be reversed to accommodate mature plant heights. A flat area 5 × 7 ft (1.5 × 2.1 m) will accommodate two *Delphinium* placed at the rear, one *Buphthalmum* in the midground, and three *Lychnis* in the foreground.

PHOTO 144. Wave Hill, Bronx, New York, June. ENVIRONMENT: sun to part shade in soil of average fertility and moisture. USDA Zones 4–7. FEATURE: foliage mid spring to late summer; flower late spring to summer.

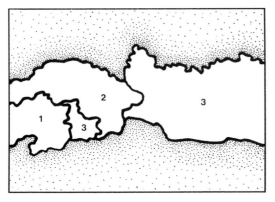

1. *Alchemilla mollis*, two plants, 12 × 18 (30 × 45 cm)
2. *Geranium endressii* 'Wargrave Pink', one plant, 12–24 × 24 in (30–60 × 60 cm)
3. *Campanula glomerata* 'Joan Elliot', five plants, 18 × 12 in (45 × 30 cm)

WHEN DIRECT complementary colors are mingled with near-complementaries, a stronger design impact is generated by adjoining the direct complementaries. Here, direct complementary hues in yellow-green *Alchemilla* and violet *Campanula* are separated by the light red *Geranium* bloom. Siting *Alchemilla* directly in front of *Campanula* would intensify the color composition.

The vertical form of *Campanula* and its globose flower heads contrast well with the beautiful mound forms of *Geranium* and *Alchemilla* in flower. The *Campanula* is used primarily for its flowering qualities. Its form and foliage are not especially interesting after bloom. Fortunately this is easily disregarded since *Geranium* and *Alchemilla* foliage are both wonderful. Also, if the *Geranium* and *Alchemilla* are cut back after flowering they will generate a crop of attractive new leaves. All plant types are adaptable to sun and part shade, and may be further enhanced by adding compatible plants.

In sun or part shade, *Aquilegia* 'McKana Giants' strain or *Aquilegia vulgaris* would continue and enhance the red-violet/violet color theme and add a tall, airy, flowering form for several weeks. Also happy with sun or part shade, *Geranium* 'Johnson's Blue' would strengthen the mass of recessive violet blooms, balancing the stronger advancing pink of the *Geranium* flowers and intense yellow-green of *Alchemilla* blooms.

A space about 3 × 4 ft (0.9 × 1.2 m) would be needed for the basic combination of five *Campanula* plants with two *Alchemilla* and one *Geranium* in the foreground. Adding one *Geranium* 'Johnson's Blue' in the rear and three to four *Aquilegia* between the *Alchemilla* and *Campanula* would increase space needs to 4 × 5 ft (1.2 x 1.5 m).

PHOTO 145. Cloister Hotel, Sea Island, Georgia, May. ENVIRONMENT: sun in soil of average fertility and moisture. USDA Zones 5–8. FEATURE: foliage late spring to late summer; flower late spring to late summer.

WHEN COMBINING violet to red-violet hues with yellow to yellow-orange hues, it is appropriate to have twice as much of the violets present as the yellows. In the above setting, both colors are pure and intense and balancing the hues is especially important. Yet balance is threatened because yellow blooms dominate. The composition could be improved by adjusting *Coreopsis* and *Verbena* quantities to approximate a 1:2 color proportion.

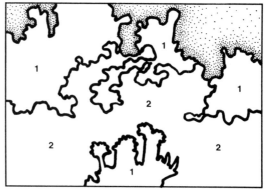

1. *Coreopsis* 'Sunray', one plant, 18–24 × 12 in (45–60 × 30 cm)
2. *Verbena canadensis* 'Homestead Purple', three plants, 10 × 10 in (25 × 25 cm)

This photo was taken in early spring and the plants are spaced far enough apart to permit a full season's growth. The bare ground visible here will be completely covered with foliage by late spring. The similarly sized and shaped flowers will be isolated amid a mass of gray-green foliage. It is this isolation, focusing the brilliance of the balanced complementary colors against foliage, which makes an eyecatching, cheerful spectacle in a large space. To make a more complex composition, add a distinctly vertical or horizontal form such as *Salvia farinacea* 'Victoria' or a *Heliotropium*, which could also strengthen the violet hue.

For the basic composition, providing twice as much red-violet as yellow, in a minimum space of 2 × 2 ft (0.6 × 0.6 m) intermingle one *Coreopsis* with three *Verbena*. See Part 2 for details on the plants suggested to add more complexity.

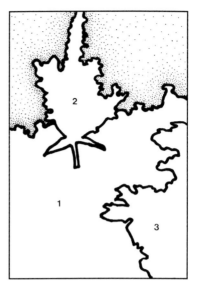

1. *Geranium* 'Ann Folkard', two
   plants, 18–24 × 24 in (45–60 × 60
   cm)
2. *Lysimachia punctata*, one plant,
   18–30 × 24 in (45–75 × 60 cm)
3. *Achillea taygetea*, two plants,
   12–24 × 18 in (30–60 × 45 cm)

PHOTO 146. Private garden, Seattle, Washington, July. ENVIRONMENT: sun to part shade in soil of average fertility and moisture. USDA Zones 5–8. FEATURE: foliage mid spring to fall; flower late spring to summer.

MATCHING nuances of form and texture in a color triad planting can challenge landscape designers to distraction. When such attempts succeed, however, the brilliance of their showing rewards the effort. Yellow-green forms a basic color triad with red-violet and yellow and the triad is seen frequently in spaces where bolder colors are appropriate. I find it particularly pleasing and here it is employed to perfection in matching contrasting bloom forms and leaf textures.

The *Lysimachia* spikes contrast with the horizontal *Achillea* heads and flowery *Geranium* mound. Foliage textures vary between the lance-shaped leaves of *Lysimachia*, the finely dissected *Geranium* foliage, and the grayish green, medium-textured, *Achillea* leaves. Colors are bold and dramatically juxtaposed and display an utter disregard for any notion of the general rule of using equal amounts of green and red-violet with only a touch of yellow. Color balance would appear even better had the photo been taken during a period of slightly more foliage and more *Geranium* bloom. The variation in tint and shading of the hues is very skillfully presented, particularly in using this *Geranium*, whose dark red-violet flower centers impart a darkness to the entire bloom and dramatize the contrast with *Achillea*. The small amount of pure yellow offered by *Lysimachia* strengthens the composition while not overpowering its lighter and darker companions.

A space 4 × 4 ft (1.2 × 1.2 m) will suit one *Lysimachia* in the rear with two *Geranium* and two *Achillea* in the foreground.

PHOTO 147. New York Botanical Garden, New York City, July. ENVIRONMENT: sun in soil of average fertility and moisture. USDA Zones 3–8. FEATURE: foliage late spring to fall; flower mid to late summer.

Y ELLOW-GREEN with yellow and red-violet is a common color triad. Because all three colors are seen frequently in small-scale garden plants and design, they represent a color association that develops both intentionally and unintentionally. Visual balancing effects will be affected by the advancing nature of yellow, the receding quality of red-violet, and the self-effacing grayness of most foliage colors. The general aim is to have about twice as much each of red-violet and green as yellow, or a 2:2:1 ratio. A small yellow accent is often sufficient. Still, there are many occasions when this general aim is disregarded, in photo 146 for example, and the consequences are not necessarily disturbing. Gradual

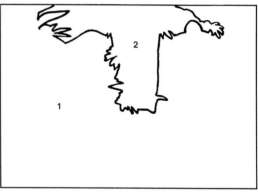

1. *Echinacea purpurea* 'Bright Star', one plant, 24–36 × 18 in (60–90 × 45 cm)
2. *Rudbeckia* 'Goldsturm', three plants, 18–24 × 18 in (45–60 × 45 cm)

adjustments of these color quantities will allow one to determine what yellow, yellow-green, and red-violet proportions are most personally pleasing.

A careful balancing of colors is clearly seen in this planting of *Echinacea* and *Rudbeckia*. The flower color of neither plant dominates, engaging attention almost equally. A significantly larger quantity of the pure yellow-orange *Rudbeckia* would eclipse the lighter red-violet of *Echinacea*. With a larger *Echinacea* element the presence of *Rudbeckia* would seem almost accidental.

This popular, long-blooming association is at its best in late summer and repeats a basic daisy-form bloom of almost equal size. The plant foliage is also similar, although broader leaves develop on the *Echinacea*. Since many composite daisy-form flowers appear in late summer and too many together can be monotonous, any additions to this pair will ideally be selected from distinctly vertical or horizontal flowering forms.

A basic planting will require a space 3 × 3 ft (0.9 × 0.9 m), intermingling three *Echinacea* and one *Rudbeckia*.

PHOTO 148. Manito Park, Spokane, Washington, July. ENVIRONMENT: sun in soil of average fertility and moisture. USDA Zones 3–9. FEATURE: foliage mid spring to fall; flower late spring to summer.

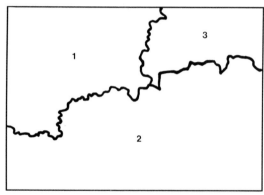

1. *Achillea* 'Coronation Gold', three plants, 24–36 × 18 in (60–90 × 45 cm)
2. *Catananche caerulea*, nine plants, 18–30 × 12 in (45–75 × 30 cm),
3. *Lythrum salicaria* 'Dropmore Purple' four plants, 24–36 × 24 in (60–90 × 60 cm)

CONTINUING with the exploration into balancing the common colors red-violet and yellow, it is obvious that problems lessen when the colors involved are not the pure intense hues seen in photo 145. The grouping above uses tinted or shaded colors to modify the strength of a pure color. As flower color lightens from a pure hue towards a pale pastel, all colors associate more easily since they are unified by the increasing amounts of white present in their tinting. Simply massing flower and foliage colors alters color perception and colors appear slightly lighter than when viewed individually.

Flowers of this *Lythrum* are a light red-violet, the *Catananche* a very light violet to blue-violet, while the *Achillea* blooms in dark yellow. All of these floral colors are modified here to some extent.

The complexity of this pleasant composition is increased by its varied flower forms, including *Lythrum* spires, horizontal *Achillea* heads, and diffuse, daisy-form *Catananche*. Even the slight light-dark contrast within the *Catananche* blooms contributes a positive note to the complexity of the composition.

This group will be ineffective in too small a quantity. I would suggest a minimum planting of four *Lythrum* behind three *Achillea* and eight or nine *Catananche* in the foreground in an area of 5 × 6 ft (1.5 × 1.8 m).

PHOTO 149. Private garden, Pierremont, New York, July.
ENVIRONMENT: sun in soil of average fertility and moisture.
USDA Zones 4–7.
FEATURE: foliage late spring to summer; flower late spring to summer.

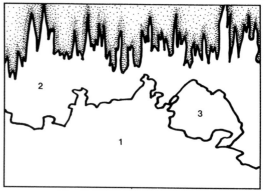

1. *Achillea filipendulina* 'Gold Plate', one plant, 36–48 × 18 in (90–120 × 45 cm)
2. *Lythrum salicaria* 'Morden Pink', two plants, 24–36 × 24 in (60–90 × 60 cm)
3. *Salvia × superba* 'East Friesland', three plants, 15–18 × 18 in (40–45 × 45 cm)

S PIRES, sword-shaped leaves, and other strongly vertical forms generally capture attention before weeping, horizontal, or mounded forms of comparable size. Their careful placement in the landscape, even as occasional accents, can provide the repetition necessary to unify a design and give it structure. They also may be used, as here, to define a strong visual line against a largely undefined landscape, or a watery expanse.

A relatively small number of vertical forms will balance a large group of horizontal forms because their visual impact far exceeds their mass. Emphasis on contrasting vertical and horizontal forms, often in the same hue, is one of the simpler ways of creating a captivating design. Especially in determinedly monochromatic compositions, form variation helps avoid possible monotony.

Vertical forms may also add a welcome additional dimension to any composition since they are so useful for extending interest upward and widening the limits of the composition. Even quite small flower spikes or wands, such as in this *Salvia*, are visually effective as a vertical form. A variety of plant forms or shapes can serve to maintain visual interest long after bloom color has faded. *Liatris spicata* 'Kobold', although a smaller plant, may be substituted for *Lythrum* and will provide similar color and vertical form.

For a minimum planting in a space 4 × 5 ft (1.2 × 1.5 m) use two *Lythrum* in the rear, one *Achillea* in the midground, and three *Salvia* in the foreground. If substituting two *Liatris spicata* 'Kobold' for the *Lythrum*, place *Achillea* to the rear and set the *Liatris* in the midground.

THIS SECTION is intended to extend one's range of associations beyond those given in the photo descriptions. Information specific to each plant mentioned in Part One, such as cultural and design detail, allows further experimentation. Additionally, all references made to a particular plant will be given, as well as further discussion regarding associations.

Plant details include botanical name and any synonyms or common names, and whether the plant is an annual, biennial, or perennial. Bulbs, ferns, grasses, shrubs, or vines are distinguished from the more typical majority of herbaceous perennials. "Bulb" is used in its most general sense. Mature size is given with spacing requirements. Note that fragrance, flower color and season, and foliage color and season are given primarily to highlight design considerations. Seasons given are the prime seasons for design use.

The general cultural requirements include plant needs as to soil type, moisture, exposure, and hardiness as reflected in the USDA Zone range. Specifics on cutting back to encourage re-bloom, or the significant trait of some plants to invade and conquer some situations are noted. Photo examples of the plant and text references from Part One conclude the beginning paragraph.

The "Associations" discussion reflects a complete listing of associated plants pictured or recommended in Part One, listed alphabetically by botanical name. Any extended suggestions for further plant associations include design points and conclude the plant's description.

Ratios are used to indicate number of plants in that particular association or planting composition. The first number always reflects the primary plant under discussion. For example, under *Achillea* 'Coronation Gold', the last paragraph recommends *Coreopsis* 'Sunray', *Iris kaempferi*, and *Leucanthemum × superbum* 'Alaska' as associates. The ratio given is 1:2:3:1. This means use one *Achillea* 'Coronation Gold', two *Coreopsis* 'Sunray', three *Iris kaempferi*, and one *Leucanthemum × superbum* 'Alaska' to establish compositional balance of color, form, and texture. Ratios also provide the information needed to multiply plantings.

PART TWO

Plant Details and Associations

Achillea 'Coronation Gold'

Herbaceous perennial, 24–36 × 18 in (60–90 × 45 cm), blooms dark yellow, late spring, foliage fragrant, very deep gray yellow-green, late spring to late summer. Plant in average to poor soil with dry to average conditions in sun. USDA Zones 3–9. Photos 67, 86, 89, 91, 148. See also discussions under *Achillea filipendulina* 'Gold Plate' and *Potentilla* 'Tangerine'.

ASSOCIATIONS: *Catananche caerulea*, photo 148; *Coreopsis verticillata* 'Moonbeam', photo 89; *Corydalis lutea*, photo 86; *Crocosmia* 'Lucifer', photo 67; *Delphinium belladona*, photo 91; *Heliopsis scabra*, photo 89; *Hemerocallis* cultivars, photo 89; *Lysimachia punctata*, photo 89; *Lythrum salicaria* 'Dropmore Purple', photo 148; *Rosa* 'New Dawn', photo 91; *Salvia × superba* 'East Friesland', photo 86; *Tanacetum parthenium*, photo 91; *Veronica spicata* 'Blue Charm', photo 89.

This plant with *Coreopsis* 'Sunray', *Iris kaempferi*, and *Leucanthemum × superbum* 'Alaska' (1:2:3:1) completes a predominantly yellow, yellow-orange, and white combination overlapping for several weeks in late spring and summer. These plants flower best in full sun. When selecting the iris, keep in mind the combination will be enlivened by a pure, intense, near-complementary violet or softened by a very pale blue-violet variety. Foliage will make a moderately interesting composition when blooming highlights are past.

Achillea filipendulina 'Gold Plate'

Herbaceous perennial, 36–48 × 18 in (90–120 × 45 cm), blooms dark yellow, summer, foliage fragrant, very deep gray yellow-green, late spring to summer. Performs well with average to poor soil, dry to average conditions, and sun. USDA Zones 3–9. Photo 149.

ASSOCIATIONS: *Lythrum salicaria* 'Morden Pink' and *Salvia × superba* 'East Friesland', photo 149.

Use with three *Achillea* 'Coronation Gold' in front of one *Miscanthus sinensis* 'Variegatus' (3:3:1). The dark, gray yellow-green foliage of

Achillea 'Coronation Gold' combines well with the pale foliage stripes of *Miscanthus*. The added height, ferny leaves, and later bloom of 'Gold Plate' extend interest as the season advances and the *Miscanthus* develops height.

Limonium latifolium and *Monarda didyma* 'Bluestocking' can also be used in a trio (2:3:2) to combine the near-complementary colors yellow and violet in a successively flowering scheme. Yellow *Achillea* blooms first, followed by the light violet hues in tall *Monarda* and shorter *Limonium*. Colors and textures are harmonious and stimulating when flowering overlaps.

Achillea millefolium 'Appleblossom'

Herbaceous perennial, 15–21 × 18 in (40–55 × 45 cm), blooms very pale red-violet, summer, foliage fragrant, deep gray yellow-green spring to late summer. Requires average to poor soil, dry to average conditions, and sun. USDA Zones 3–9.

ASSOCIATIONS: 'Appleblossom' is usually considered a medium-scale element, its flowers horizontal and broad-textured, its foliage fine-textured, contributing an indistinct mass. Pair with the medium- to large-scale *Veronica spicata* 'Blue Charm' (1:1). The pale and light floral hues of near-adjacent red-violet and blue-violet blend perfectly and over a long season. Spires of *Veronica* contrast the flat horizontal blooms of *Achillea*. This pair fits easily into a pastel or cool-hued scheme. Contrasting with broader foliaged plants enhances this pair's nebulous foliage. Can be enlivened with stronger hued additions, particularly from plants which bloom in pure red-violet.

Achillea millefolium 'Paprika'

Herbaceous perennial, 15–21 × 18 in (40–55 × 45 cm), blooms light red, summer, foliage fragrant, very dark gray yellow-green, mid spring to late summer. Plant in average to poor soil, maintain dry to average conditions in sun. USDA Zones 3–9. Photo 134.

ASSOCIATIONS: *Callistephus chinensis* 'Deep Red' and *Impatiens* 'Tempo Hybrid Red', photo 134.

To create a small-scale, warm-hued association using this perennial and two annuals, I would suggest *Cosmos sulphureus* 'Sunny Red' and *Tropaeolum majus* 'Gleam Series' (1:1:2) to feature pure, bright, strong colors. Flower forms vary between the flat, disk-like blooms of *Cosmos* and *Achillea*'s horizontal umbels. Foliage textures range from fine *Cosmos* to broad, edible nasturtium (*Tropaeolum*) leaves. *Tropaeolum* foliage serves as a broad, dense foreground for airy *Cosmos* foliage and flowers.

Achillea millefolium 'Salmon Beauty'

Herbaceous perennial, 18–36 × 18 in (45–90 × 45 cm), blooms light red-orange, summer, foliage fragrant, very dark gray yellow-green spring to late summer. Requires only average to poor soil, dry to average conditions, and sun. USDA Zones 3–9. Photo 66.

ASSOCIATIONS: *Digitalis × mertonensis*, *Geranium endressii* 'Wargrave Pink', and *Potentilla* 'Tangerine', photo 66.

Achillea millefolium 'Weser River Sandstone'

Herbaceous perennial, 18–36 × 18 in (45–90 × 45 cm), blooms light red and light orange to yellow-orange and very pale yellow-orange, summer, foliage fragrant, very dark gray yellow-green, mid spring to late summer. Requires average to poor soil with dry to average conditions, and sun. USDA Zones 3–9. Photo 62. See also discussions under *Osteospermum* 'Salmon Queen' and photos 127 and 130.

ASSOCIATIONS: *Berberis thunbergii* 'Atropurpurea Nana', photo 130; *Elymus arenarius*, photo 130; *Eschscholzia californica*, photo 127; *Hemerocallis* 'Colonial Dame', photo 62; *Nepeta mussinii*, photo 127.

Various warm tints in this *Achillea* suggest its association with plants flowering in complementary cool hues. *Platycodon grandiflorus* brings bell-like form and *Veronica spicata* 'Blue Fox' has spires, both in light blue-violet, to contrast with the flat *Achillea* umbels (1:1:2). Light yellow and yellow-orange tints in *Achillea* intensify the blue and blue-violet colors in *Platycodon* and *Veronica* blooms.

Achillea millefolium 'White Beauty'

Herbaceous perennial, 18–21 × 15 in (45–55 × 40 cm), blooms white, summer, foliage fragrant, very dark gray yellow-green, mid spring to late summer. Requires average to poor soil with dry to average conditions, and sun. USDA Zones 3–9.

ASSOCIATIONS: As a design element, 'White Beauty' can be treated as a medium-scale plant developing medium-textured, horizontal flowers. Its foliage is fine-textured, providing an indistinct mass even over short viewing distances. One 'White Beauty' will combine effortlessly with one *Leucanthemum × superbum* 'Alaska', two *Physostegia virginiana* 'Summer Snow', one *Tradescantia × andersoniana* 'Innocence', and two *Verbascum chaixii* (1:1:2:1:2). This white combination, with touches of pale yellow in *Verbascum* and *Chrysanthemum*, offers successive blooming over several weeks in summer with some repeat bloom from *Chrysanthemum* and *Achillea* in late summer or early fall. If desiring to add more color to this composition, pastel hues will blend easily.

Achillea 'Moonshine'

Herbaceous perennial, 12–24 × 12 in (30–60 × 30 cm), blooms pale yellow, late spring, foliage fragrant, dark gray yellow-green spring to fall. Requires average to poor soil with dry to average conditions, and sun. USDA Zones 3–8. Cut back after first flowering to encourage a later summer bloom. Photo 95. See also discussions under *Cynoglossum amabile*, *Geranium endressii* 'Wargrave Pink', *Salvia × superba* 'East Friesland', and photos 85 and 93.

ASSOCIATIONS: *Coreopsis verticillata* 'Moonbeam', photo 85; *Delphinium grandiflorum* 'Blue Butterfly', photo 93; *Echinops* 'Taplow Blue', photo 95; *Jasminum officinale*, photo 95; *Lavandula angustifolia* 'Hidcote', photos 85, 95; *Nepeta mussinii* 'Six Hills Giant', photo 93; *Oenothera tetragona*, photo 93.

The pale yellow in the flowers of *Achillea* 'Moonshine' and *Coreopsis verticillata* 'Moonbeam' present different forms and combine beautifully with *Lavandula angustifolia* 'Hidcote' (1:1:3) in a common association. *Coreopsis* will continue to bloom long after its partners have ceased flowering. The small scale and delicate hues of this composition are well suited to the confined and clearly defined spaces of a small enclosed garden.

A bolder, long-blooming composition could include annual *Salvia farinacea* 'Victoria' and *Verbascum chaixii* (1:3:1). Bloom overlaps, with the major effect gained in late spring and early summer. *Salvia* continues blooming until frost, and *Achillea* flowers again in late summer or early fall if cut back when it begins to fade. *Salvia farinacea* 'Victoria' expands until eventually its mass fills the visual gaps left by the late decline of *Verbascum* flowers. Herbaceous perennial *Salvia* × *superba* 'May Night' may be substituted to make an all-perennial association, but overall bloom season will be reduced.

Achillea taygetea

Herbaceous perennial, 12–24 × 18 in (30–60 × 45 cm), blooms pale yellow, summer, fragrant foliage, very dark yellow-green, mid spring to late summer. Requires average to poor soil with dry to average conditions, and sun. USDA Zones 5–8. Photos 102, 146. See also discussion under *Delphinium* 'Connecticut Yankee' and *Tradescantia* × *andersoniana* 'Blue Stone'.

ASSOCIATIONS: *Brunnera macrophylla*, photo 102; *Geranium* 'Anne Folkard', photo 146; *Lysimachia punctata*, photo 146; *Veronica spicata* 'Blue Fox', photo 102.

Acidanthera bicolor
See *Gladiolus callianthus*

Aconitum napellus,
common monkshood, helmet flower

Herbaceous perennial, 36 × 12 in (90 × 30 cm), blooms dark violet, mid to late summer, dark, gray yellow-green foliage, late spring to fall. Plant in average to rich soil, supply average moisture, and grow in sun or part shade. USDA Zones 3–8. All plant parts poisonous.

ASSOCIATIONS: Common monkshood contributes a large scale and medium textures. Flowers develop on tall spires above the rather scant and indistinct foliage. A striking summer association of strong cool and warm colors is achieved by combining its dark violet flowers with the doubled orange of late-blooming *Hemerocallis fulva* 'Kwanso Flore Plena' and dark orange *Lilium lancifolium* blooms (3:1:2). *Aconitum* should dominate to keep the violet/orange proportion in balance. Flower forms are distinctive, but plants are not particularly impressive after flowering.

Adiantum pedatum, maidenhair fern

Fern, 12 × 12 in (30 × 30 cm), flowers absent, foliage gray yellow-green, spring to late summer. Plant in average to rich soil with average to greater moisture in part or full shade. USDA Zones 3–8. Photo 4. See also discussions under *Primula japonica* and *Tulipa* 'Queen of Night'.

ASSOCIATIONS: *Dicentra eximia* 'Alba' and *Polygonatum biflorum*, photo 4.

Agapanthus orientalis
See *A. praecox*

Agapanthus praecox (*A. orientalis*),
blue African lily

Perennial or half-hardy annual, 20–36 × 15 in (50–90 × 40 cm), blooms light blue-violet, late spring to late summer, foliage dark yellow-green, mid-spring to fall. Plant in average soil, requires average moisture and sun. USDA Zones 8–10.

ASSOCIATIONS: May be considered for design use as a medium to large element with broad-textured, umbellate flowers. Its foliage is medium-textured, straplike, and weeping. See discussions under *Miscanthus sinensis* 'Variegatus' and *Salvia sclarea* for design connections with grayish green and pale red-violet.

Agastache anethiodora

See *A. foeniculum*

Agastache foeniculum (*A. anethiodora*), Mexican giant hyssop

Herbaceous perennial, 24–60 × 18 in (60–150 × 45 cm), blooms light violet, summer to fall, foliage very dark yellow-green, mid spring to fall. Needs only average to poor soil, dry to average conditions, and sun. USDA Zones 3–9. Photo 31.

ASSOCIATIONS: *Eryngium giganteum* and *Malva moschata*, photo 31.

This hyssop's light violet floral hues blend effortlessly with the pale, near-adjacent hues found in *Allium senescens*, *Echinops* 'Taplow Blue', and *Limonium latifolium* (1:2:2:1). This fairly large-scale grouping would have one *Agastache* in the rear, two *Echinops* in the midground, and two *Limonium* and one *Allium* in the foreground. Suited to a pastel or cool-hued mixed border.

Mingled with *Asteromoea mongolica* (1:1) its receding violet spires are brightened and its vertical form accented by the profusion of *Asteromoea*'s tiny daisy-like blooms.

Ageratum houstonianum 'Blue Horizon'

Generally grown as an annual in all zones, 18 × 15 in (45 × 40 cm), blooms pale blue-violet, late spring to fall, dark yellow-green foliage, late spring to fall. Needs average to rich soil, average to damp conditions, and sun. See also discussions under *Gomphrena* 'Lavender Lady' and *Helichrysum petiolare*.

ASSOCIATIONS: Use to provide a small- to medium-scale element in the garden landscape. Although both flower clusters and foliage are medium-textured, the ageratum's foliage form creates an indistinct mass. Its light blue-violet blooms find harmonious adjacent colors in the violet-flowered annual *Salvia farinacea* 'Victoria' and red-violet *Sedum* 'Vera Jameson' (1:2:1). Flowering in the two annuals continues for many weeks. Dusky *Sedum* hues mute the color intensity of its companions and the general effect is subdued. Plant form variety is established by the spiked *Salvia*, tufted *Ageratum* clusters, and flat, dusky *Sedum* heads.

Ageratum houstonianum 'Blue Puffs'

Generally grown as an annual in all zones, 6–8 × 9 in (15–20 × 25 cm), blooms pale blue-violet, late spring to late summer, foliage dark yellow-green, spring to fall. Plant in average to rich soil, supply average to damp conditions, and a sunny location. Photo 42.

ASSOCIATIONS: *Heliotropium* 'Marine', *Lobelia erinus* 'White Cascade', *Nierembergia hippomanica* var. *violacea* 'Purple Robe', photo 42.

Two of these will mingle easily with the other pastel hues and varied flower forms of one *Amsonia tabernaemontana*, two *Aquilegia* 'Rose Queen', one *Dianthus plumarius*, and two *Gomphrena globosa* 'Pomponette White' (2:1:2:1:2). Flowering effect is concentrated in late spring, although *Ageratum* and *Gomphrena* continue flowering into late summer. This small-scale white, pink, and blue-violet association is quite effective fronting a dark shrub or shady background.

Ageratum houstonianum 'Southern Cross'

Generally grown as an annual in all zones, 8–12 × 8 in (20–30 × 20 cm), blooms pale blue-violet and white, late spring to fall, dark yellow-green foliage, mid spring to fall. Plant in average to rich soil, supply average to damp conditions, and a sunny location. Photo 39.

ASSOCIATIONS: *Antirrhinum* 'White Rocket', *Argyranthemum frutescens*, *Cleome spinosa* 'Helen Campbell', *Cleome spinosa* 'Violet Queen', *Nicotiana sylvestris*, photo 39.

Two of these will associate well with the very

grayed yellow-green foliage of one *Artemisia* 'Powis Castle' and two *Stachys byzantina*, as both companions complement the brightness of blue-violet and white in this plant. Include the dark violet-flowered *Heliotropium* 'Marine' (2:1:2:2) for dramatic contrast. *Ageratum* and *Heliotropium* provide a very long bloom season and *Stachys* and *Artemisia* foliages are decorative until frost.

Ajuga reptans, common bugle weed

Herbaceous perennial, 6 × 12 in (15 × 30 cm), blooms light violet to blue-violet, mid to late spring, foliage dark yellow-green with very deep red-violet tones, mid spring to fall. Prefers sandy to average soil, average moisture, and part shade or sun. USDA Zones 4–9. *Ajuga reptans* is frequently considered a weed, as its common name implies, and it may be invasive. However, it has so many excellent qualities—including easy culture, excellent foliage form and color, and charming spring blooms—that it is well worth the extra supervision needed to curb its wandering tendencies. Photo 97. See also discussions under *Hyacinthoides hispanica, Tiarella cordifolia*, and photo 52.

ASSOCIATIONS: *Athyrium nipponicum*, photo 52; *Hosta fortunei*, photo 52; *Mertensia virginica*, photo 97; *Narcissus* 'Clare', photo 97; *Polygonatum odoratum* 'Variegatum', photo 52.

An easily grown trio can be developed using *Alchemilla mollis* and *Salvia officinalis* 'Aurea' (5:1:1). This combination exploits the pleasing red-violet foliage tints and violet bloom in *Ajuga* by associating it with the various complementary yellow-greens found in *Salvia* and *Alchemilla* foliage and bloom. Grown in a sunny location, the trio makes a compact, beautifully varied foliage composition for many months. Especially useful as a groundcover for shrubs or under deciduous trees offering very light shade.

Ajuga reptans 'Alba'

Herbaceous perennial, 6 × 12 in (15 × 30 cm), blooms white, mid to late spring, dark reddish green foliage, mid spring to fall. Needs sandy to average soil, average moisture, and part shade or sun. USDA Zones 4–9. Photo 79. Self-sows. Requires some effort towards population control. See also discussion under *Leucojum aestivum* 'Gravetye Giant'.

ASSOCIATIONS: *Ajuga reptans* 'Atropurpurea', *Hemerocallis* cultivars, *Mertensia virginica*, photo 79.

Combines particularly well with the compact *Lamium maculatum* 'Shell Pink' in areas of partial shade (1:1). This pairing will also thrive in full sun if plenty of moisture is provided. *Ajuga* flowers continue to appear sporadically in mid to late spring when *Lamium* produces minute, delicate, very pale red-violet (pink) flowers. They make an excellent carpet beneath small trees and shrubs, and a fine base for bulbs such as *Leucojum aestivum* 'Gravetye Giant' (3:3:3) or *Tulipa* (3:3:6).

Ajuga reptans 'Atropurpurea'

Herbaceous perennial, 6 × 12 in (15 × 30 cm), blooms light violet to blue-violet, mid to late spring, foliage very deep red-violet to dark yellow-green, mid spring to fall. Prefers lean to average soil, average moisture, and part shade or sun. USDA Zones 4–9. Photos 79, 125. See also discussions under *Camassia quamash, Iris* × *germanica* 'Sultan's Beauty', *Polygonatum biflorum*, and *Viola* 'Bowles Black'.

ASSOCIATIONS: *Ajuga reptans* 'Alba', photo 79; *Alchemilla mollis*, photo 125; *Aruncus dioicus*, photo 125; *Hemerocallis* cultivars, photo 79; *Mertensia virginica*, photo 79; *Polygonatum odoratum* 'Variegatum', photo 125.

This plant's deep red-violet, broad leaves, and light violet blooms show to advantage against the finely-textured, grayed yellow-green *Nepeta mussinii* foliage and light blue-violet blossoms (3:1). Full sun or light shade and drier conditions will allow both plants to flourish. *Nepeta* should be sheared back after blooming to encourage refreshed foliage and more flowers to extend compositional presence. Vigorous growth traits make this association ideal for carpeting a large space quickly.

Alcea rosea **'Single Mix'**

Biennial, 72–84 × 24 in (180–210 × 60 cm), blooms in varying shades of red-violet, mid to late summer, yellow-green foliage, mid spring to fall. Suitable for rich to average soil, average to moist conditions, and sun. USDA Zones 3–9. Photo 36.

ASSOCIATIONS: *Salvia sclarea* and *Verbena bonariensis*, photo 36.

Use two of these in a wonderfully large complex grouping with three *Asteromoea mongolica*, two *Lythrum salicaria* 'Morden Pink', one *Salvia sclarea*, two *Thalictrum rochebrunianum*, and four *Veronica spicata* 'Blue Charm' (2:3:2:1:2:4). Light tinted blue-violet and red-violet blooms are fairly powerful and eyecatching scattered among the small white *Asteromoea* floral disks. Distinctive forms include spires of *Alcea*, *Veronica*, and *Lythrum* mingling among the fine-textured hazy masses of *Asteromoea* and *Thalictrum*. Fits easily into a cool-hued mixed border, growing best in a sunny or very lightly shaded space.

Alchemilla alpina, alpine lady's mantle

Herbaceous perennial, 6 × 12 in (15 × 30 cm), blooms light to pale yellow-green, late spring, foliage dark yellow-green, mid spring to fall. Does well in average soil, moist to average conditions, and part shade or sun. USDA Zones 3–8. Photo 141.

ASSOCIATIONS: *Astilbe × arendsii* 'Fanal', *Campanula poscharkyana*, *Ruta graveolens*, photo 141.

Alchemilla mollis, lady's mantle

Herbaceous perennial, 12 × 18 in (30 × 45 cm), blooms light to pale yellow-green, late spring to summer, foliage dark yellow-green, mid spring to fall. Plant in average to rich soil, allow moist to average conditions, and part shade or sun. USDA Zones 4–8. Photos 3, 10, 15, 47, 103, 108, 109, 125, 139, 144. See also discussions under *Ajuga reptans*, *Allium moly*, *Centranthus ruber*, *Dryopteris noveboracensis*, *Kirengeshoma palmata*, *Ligular-*

ia stenocephala 'The Rocket', *Rodgersia aesculifolia*, *Salvia* 'Lady in Red', *Salvia officinalis* 'Aurea', *Salvia × superba* 'May Night', and text of photo 82.

ASSOCIATIONS: *Ajuga reptans* 'Atropurpurea', photo 125; *Allium cernuum*, photo 109; *Allium senescens*, photo 109; *Aquilegia* 'McKana Giants', photo 144; *Argyranthemum frutescens*, photo 15; *Aruncus dioicus*, photo 125; *Atriplex hortensis* 'Cupreata', photo 109; *Campanula glomerata* 'Joan Elliot', photo 144; *Campanula portenschlagiana*, photo 82; *Corydalis lutea*, photos 15, 82; *Galium odoratum*, photo 3; *Geranium endressii*, 'Wargrave Pink', photo 144; *Geranium* 'Johnson's Blue', photos 108, 144; *Geranium × magnificum*, photo 108; *Helichrysum petiolare*, photo 15; *Hemerocallis* 'Colonial Dame', photo 10; *Heuchera* 'Palace Purple', photo 139; *Hosta fortunei* 'Marginato-alba', photo 3; *Iris pseudacorus*, photo 10; *Lavandula angustifolia* 'Munstead', photo 82; *Lilium* 'French Vanilla', photo 10; *Lysimachia punctata*, photo 10; *Malva moschata* 'Alba', photo 47; *Nicotiana langsdorffii*, photo 139; *Nigella damescena* 'Miss Jekyll', photo 47; *Penstemon* 'Rose Elf', photo 108; *Phalaris arundinacea* var. *picta*, photo 10; *Polygonatum odoratum* 'Variegatum', photos 125, 139; *Salvia guaranitica*, photo 139; *Salvia officinalis* 'Aurea', photo 139; *Sedum* 'Rosy Glow', photo 103; *Verbascum chaixii*, photo 10.

Use with *Campanula portenschlagiana* and *Corydalis lutea* (1:2:1) to create a small-scale group for a sunny or lightly shaded location. Useful for fronting a border, underplanting shrubs, or edging a patio. They combine compact form and excellent foliage with a long flowering season in complementary yellow-green and light violet.

For a relatively effortless groundcover composition, plant along with *Geranium sanguineum* and *Geranium sanguineum* var. *striatum* (2:1:1). All three will thrive in sun or very light shade. Similarity of leaf and plant forms is emphasized, but there is also a lively complementary contrast between the yellow-green *Alchemilla* and red-violet *Geranium* blooms to avoid monotony. Scattered *Geranium sanguineum* var. *striatum* blooms occur throughout the cooler months. The low mounds of attractive foliage are presentable for the entire growing season, with *Geranium* foliage turning dark red in the fall.

Allium aflatuense, Persian onion

Bulb, 24–36 × 12 in (60–90 × 30 cm), blooms very light red-violet, late spring, dark yellow-green foliage, late spring. Does well in average soil with dry to average conditions in sun. USDA Zones 4–7. Photo 75.

ASSOCIATIONS: *Tulipa* 'Greenland' and *Viola wittrockiana*, photo 75.

Allium aflatuense 'Purple Sensation'

Bulb, 24–36 × 12 in (60–90 × 30 cm), blooms light red-violet, late spring, dark yellow-green foliage, late spring. Does well in average soil with dry to average conditions in sun. USDA Zones 4–7. Photo 72.

ASSOCIATIONS: *Camassia quamash* and *Tulipa* 'Purple Rain', photo 72.

Allium cernuum, nodding onion

Bulb, 12–18 × 12 in (30–45 × 30 cm), blooms pale red-violet, mid to late summer, dark yellow-green foliage, late spring to fall. Does well in average soil with average to dry conditions in sun. USDA Zones 2–7. Photos 27, 109. See also discussion under *Festuca glauca.*

ASSOCIATIONS: *Alchemilla mollis*, photo 109; *Allium senescens*, photos 27, 109; *Atriplex hortensis* 'Cupreata', photos 27, 109; *Clematis × jackmanii*, photo 27.

Allium christophii, downy onion

Bulb, 12–18 × 12 in (30–45 × 30 cm), blooms very pale red-violet, late spring to summer, dark yellow-green foliage, late spring to summer. Does well in average soil with dry to average conditions in sun. USDA Zones 4–8. Photo 115.

ASSOCIATIONS: *Astilbe × arendsii* 'Bridal Veil' and *Geranium sanguineum* var. *striatum*, photo 115.

The form of three specimens of this *Allium* will stand out well against the diffuse textures of one *Artemisia* 'Powis Castle', one *Aster frickartii* 'Mönch', one each of *Malva alcea* 'Fastigiata' and *Malva moschata* 'Alba', and two *Stachys byzantina* (3:1:1:1:1:2). Such a complex, medium-scale composition for sun contrasts tints of red-violet and light blue-violet with grayed yellow-green. A touch of white in *Malva moschata* 'Alba' brightens the association in summer. Successive flowering occurs from late spring to fall.

Allium giganteum, giant onion

Bulb, 30–60 × 12 in (75–150 × 30 cm), blooms red-violet, mid to late spring, dark yellow green foliage, mid spring. Does well in average soil with dry to average conditions in sun. USDA Zones 4–8. Photo 114. See also discussion under photo 69.

ASSOCIATIONS: *Nepeta mussinii*, photo 69; *Salvia × superba* 'May Night', photo 69; *Sedum* 'Autumn Joy', photo 114; *Yucca filamentosa*, photo 114.

Associates well with *Artemisia* 'Powis Castle' and *Foeniculum vulgare* 'Purpureum (3:2:1). The grayed, fine-textured *Foeniculum* and *Artemisia* foliages contrast arrestingly with the brilliant red-violet *Allium* globes in late spring. *Artemisia* also masks aging and yellowing *Allium* foliage. Dark red tints in the *Foeniculum* foliage continue to contrast with the *Artemisia* for the balance of season after the *Allium*'s decline.

Allium karataviense, Turkistan onion

Bulb, 8–10 × 8 in (20–25 × 20 cm), blooms very pale violet, mid to late spring, dark yellow-green foliage, mid to late spring. Does well in average soil with dry to average conditions in sun or part shade. USDA Zones 4–8.

ASSOCIATIONS: This ornamental onion is of small scale and broad textures. Its flowers cluster in a globular form on a single stem held well above the straplike leaves. See discussion under *Geranium* 'Johnson's Blue' for details on a large association of violet hues.

Compact *Phlox* 'Chattahoochee' has light blue-violet blooms with a red-violet center which harmonize with the heads of this *Allium* and can contrast brightly with silvery *Stachys byzantina* foliage in late spring (1:2:2). Bold *Allium* foliage repeats a similar leaf form in the smaller, silvery, *Stachys* leaves. This small-scale trio is at its best in late spring. Suited to a rock planting or fronting a pastel-hued border.

Allium moly, golden onion

Bulb, 12 × 6 in (30 × 15 cm), blooms yellow, late spring, dark yellow-green foliage, mid spring to summer. Does well in average soil with dry to average conditions in sun or very light shade. USDA Zones 4–8. Photo 100. See also discussion under *Alchemilla mollis*.

ASSOCIATIONS: *Veronica latifolia* 'Crater Lake Blue', photo 100.

Combine with *Alchemilla mollis, Iris pseudacorus*, and *Lysimachia clethroides* (5:1:1:2) to form a successive yellow-green, yellow, and white-flowering combination that can thrive in part shade, or sun with adequate moisture. Contrasting mounds, spikes, and umbels sustain the composition from spring to summer. Clustering the *Allium* between *Alchemilla* and *Lysimachia* will disguise the bulb's dieback. *Lysimachia's* fine, dark yellow-green foliage fills the visual gap between low *Alchemilla* and high *Iris* while providing an excellent background for *Allium*.

Allium ostrowskianum, Ostrowsky onion

Bulb, 8–12 × 8 in (20–30 × 20 cm), blooms pale red-violet, late spring to summer, foliage, very dark yellow-green, late spring to late summer. Requires only average soil, dry to average conditions and sun or very light shade. USDA Zones 4–8.

ASSOCIATIONS: Ostrowsky onion is a small-scale element with medium-textured flowers and fine-textured foliage. Flowers are globe-shaped rising above the straplike foliage. The outstanding groundcover qualities for light shade in *Vinca minor* are enhanced by adding these compact alliums. Use a ratio of 5:10. The alliums bloom much later than the vinca, piercing its foliage with their little globes. The effect is subtle, but persuasive and very useful when later season ornament is needed. Substituting the bright yellow flowers of *Allium moly* for the palish pink of *Allium ostrowskianum* gives a bolder effect. Suited to shrub underplanting and patio planting.

Allium schoenoprasum, garden chives

Bulb, 12–15 × 12 in (30–40 × 30 cm), blooms pale violet, late spring, foliage fragrant, dark yellow-green, mid spring to fall. Does well in average soil with dry to average conditions in sun or part shade. USDA Zones 3–9. Photo 113.

ASSOCIATIONS: *Artemisia* 'Powis Castle', *Cerastium tomentosum, Penstemon hirsutus* 'Pygmaeus', *Veronica spicata* subsp. *incana*, photo 113.

Allium senescens, ornamental onion

Bulb, 12–18 × 12 in (30–45 × 30 cm), blooms very light red-violet, summer to fall, dark yellow-green foliage, late spring to fall. Does well in average soil with dry to average conditions, in sun or part shade. USDA Zones 4–9. Photos 27, 109. See also discussions under *Agastache foeniculum* and *Allium tuberosum*.

ASSOCIATIONS: *Alchemilla mollis*, photo 109; *Allium cernuum*, photos 27, 109; *Atriplex hortensis* 'Cupreata', photos 27, 109; *Clematis* × *jackmanii*, photo 27.

The light red violet flowers of this *Allium* associate smoothly with pale red *Monarda didyma* 'Croftway Pink' blooms. Both are enhanced and connected by inserting the lightly textured, small, white-flowering *Tanacetum parthenium* (2:3:2). Simultaneous bloom lasts a few weeks. Foliage composition is rather weak, although *Allium's* excellent foliage anchors the group's foreground.

This medium-scale association blends easily into pastel-hued designs.

Allium senescens 'Glaucum'

Bulb, 12 × 12 in (30 × 30 cm), blooms very light red-violet, summer to fall, dark yellow-green foliage, late spring to fall. Does well in average soil with dry to average conditions, in sun or part shade. USDA Zones 4–9. Photo 122.

ASSOCIATIONS: *Sedum* 'Vera Jameson' and *Verbascum chaixii*, photo 122.

Allium sphaerocephalon, drumstick onion

Bulb, 18–30 × 12 in (45–80 × 30 cm), blooms very dark red-violet, mid to late summer, dark yellow-green foliage, late spring to summer. Does well in average soil with dry to average conditions, in sun or part shade. USDA Zones 5–8. See also comments under photo 121.

ASSOCIATIONS: *Allium sphaerocephalon* is usually employed as a medium-scale element developing spherical, medium-textured blooms, and fine-textured, straplike foliage. See text of photo 121 for connecting with *Artemisia* 'Powis Castle', *Perilla frutescens*, and *Sedum* 'Ruby Glow'.

Use eight of these with one *Alcea rosea* 'Single Mix', one *Echinacea purpurea* 'Bright Star', two *Lythrum salicaria* 'Morden Pink', and two *Phlox paniculata* 'Bright Eyes' (8:1:1:2:2) for a dramatic color and form composition. The dark red-violet spheres of this ornamental onion are highlighted in the midst of the pale red trusses of *Phlox* and light red-violet floral colors of *Lythrum* and *Echinacea*. *Alcea* continues the established color theme. *Alcea rosea* 'Nigra', flowering in a very dark red, would be a good alternative to 'Single Mix', repeating the dramatic shade of the *Allium* flowers. This large-scale group is striking in the mixed border.

Allium tuberosum, Chinese chives

Bulb, 18–24 × 12 in (45–60 × 30 cm), blooms white, late summer, foliage fragrant, dark yellow-green, late spring to fall. Does well in average soil with dry to average conditions, in sun or part shade. USDA Zones 4–9. Photos 1, 35.

ASSOCIATIONS: *Anemone vitifolia* 'Robustissima', photo 35; *Berberis thunbergii* 'Atropurpurea', photo 35; *Gomphrena globosa* 'Lavender Lady', photo 35; *Sedum* 'Autumn Joy', photo 1; *Sedum* 'Vera Jameson', photo 35.

A bright and ornamental effect of mirroring flower forms is created by clustering three of these with two *Allium senescens*, two *Gomphrena globosa* 'Lavender Lady', and three *Gomphrena globosa* 'Pomponette White'. This effect is especially marked if they are juxtaposed against the dark foliage of one *Anemone vitifolia* 'Robustissima (3:2:2:3:1). Red-violet and white globes in the alliums and annual gomphrenas also repeat the hues in the anemone's pale red-violet blooms.

Alstroemeria Ligtu Hybrids

Herbaceous perennial, 24–48 × 18 in (60–120 × 45 cm), blooms light red orange to light orange, late spring to summer, dark yellow-green foliage, late spring to summer. Performs well in average soil and moisture in sun or part shade. USDA Zones 7–10. Goes dormant after flowering. Self-sows. Photo 132. See also discussion under *Potentilla* 'Tangerine'.

ASSOCIATIONS: *Elymus arenarius*, *Maclayea microcarpa*, *Polystichum setiferum* 'Divisilobum', photo 132.

Alyssum saxatile
See *Aurinia saxatilis*

Alyssum saxatile 'Citrinum'
See *Aurinia saxatilis* 'Citrina'

Amsonia tabernaemontana, blue star

Herbaceous perennial, 24–36 × 24 in (60–90 × 60 cm), blooms very pale blue-violet, late spring, yellow-green foliage, late spring to fall. Plant in average to rich soil, supply moist to average conditions and site in part shade or sun. USDA Zones 3–9. Photos 41, 76. See also discussions under *Ageratum houstonianum* 'Blue Puffs' and *Viola corsica*.

ASSOCIATIONS: *Aquilegia vulgaris*, photo 41; *Brunnera macrophylla*, photo 76; *Geranium endressii* 'Wargrave Pink', photo 76; *Iris × germanica*, photo 41; *Iris sibirica*, photo 76; *Leucanthemum × superbum* 'Alaska', photo 41; *Nepeta mussinii*, photo 41; *Tradescantia × andersoniana* 'Blue Stone', photo 41.

Anaphalis margaritacea (*A. yedoensis*), common pearly everlasting

Herbaceous perennial, 12–36 × 12 in (30–90 × 30 cm), blooms white with yellow center, late summer to fall, grayish dark yellow-green foliage, summer to fall. Does well in average soil and moisture in sun or part shade. USDA Zones 3–8.

ASSOCIATIONS: This plant is considered a medium to large element of medium texture with flowers clustered above a nebulous foliage mass. An enrapturing, long-blooming group for a sunny area can be gained by adding one *Echinops* 'Taplow Blue', two *Nepeta mussinii*, one *Sedum* 'Autumn Joy', and three *Stachys byzantina* (2:1:2:1:3). Blue-violet in the blooms of *Nepeta* and *Echinops* contrasts with complementary yellow-green in *Sedum* heads and the grayed foliage in *Stachys* and *Anaphalis*. Striking *Sedum* and *Echinops* forms stand out amid the finer textures contributed by *Anaphalis* and *Nepeta*.

Anaphalis triplinervis 'Summer Snow'

Herbaceous perennial, 18–24 × 12 in (45–60 × 30 cm), blooms white, mid to late summer, whitish gray yellow-green foliage, summer to fall. Does well in average soil and moisture in sun or part shade. USDA Zones 3–8

ASSOCIATIONS: *Anaphalis triplinervis* is smaller than *Anaphalis margaritacea*, with pure white flower clusters and whitish gray foliage. Siting with *Artemisia* 'Powis Castle', *Caryopteris × clandonen-sis* 'Heavenly Blue', and *Elymus arenarius* (2:1:1:1) offers an association of predominantly pale, grayed, finely-textured foliage. The pronounced gray tint in the foliage relates to similar hues in *Artemisia* and *Caryopteris*. It also harmonizes with the pallor of near-adjacent, pale blue-green in the graceful *Elymus* leaves. White *Anaphalis* flowers and pale blue-violet *Caryopteris* blooms brighten the group periodically during the summer and fall.

Anaphalis yedoensis

See *A. margaritacea*

Anchusa myosotidiflora

See *Brunnera macrophylla*

Anemone 'Honorine Jobert'

Herbaceous perennial, 36–48 × 24 in (90–120 × 60 cm), blooms white, late summer to fall, very dark yellow-green foliage, mid spring to fall. Plant in average to rich soil, give average to greater moisture, and site in part shade or sun. USDA Zones 4–8. See discussions under *Anemone vitifolia* 'Robustissima' and *Caryopteris × clandonensis* 'Heavenly Blue' for connections to red-violet and blue-violet.

ASSOCIATIONS: This is a large-scale element of medium textures with flowers clustered well above the mostly basal exuberance of leaves.

The brightness of this anemone's white blooms against its dark foliage is an effect worth reinforcing by associating it with whiteness in other plants. Join one with two *Asteromoea mongolica* and add the white-striped foliage of one *Phalaris arundinacea* var. *picta* for a significant long-season impact. Continue by adding one *Caryopteris × clandonensis* 'Heavenly Blue' to reinforce the late-summer flowering show. *Asteromoea* and *Phalaris* will dominate this group until the *Anemone* flowering coincides with the *Caryopteris*. The color effect of this medium- to large-scale association is quite subtle and occurs rather late in the season. Varied foliage textures can carry the group's presence from late spring. A ratio of 1:2:1:1 permits the tiny flowers and fine foliage of *Asteromoea* to make a visual contribution.

Anemone hupehensis 'September Charm'

Herbaceous perennial, 24–36 × 24 in (60–90 × 60 cm), blooms very light red-violet, late summer to fall, dark yellow-green foliage, late spring to fall. Plant in average to rich soil, under average to moist conditions with part shade or sun. USDA Zones 4–8. Photo 71.

ASSOCIATIONS: *Campanula portenschlagiana*, *Helichrysum petiolare*, *Verbena* 'Amethyst', photo 71.

Overlapping blooms occur from late summer to fall when this plant is linked with *Eupatorium coelestinum* and *Hosta plantaginea* 'Royal Standard' (1:2:1). White *Hosta* spikes initially contrast with the flat *Anemone* blooms, which later overlap the hazy blue-violet *Eupatorium* clusters. Foliage association is outstanding, combining very broad with medium and finer leaves.

Anemone vitifolia 'Robustissima'

Herbaceous perennial, 36 × 24 in (90 × 60 cm), blooms pale red-violet, late summer to fall, very dark yellow-green foliage, mid spring to fall. Needs average to rich soil with average to greater moisture, and part shade or sun. USDA Zones 3–8. Prefers afternoon shade. Photos 35, 73, 120. See also discussions under *Allium tuberosum* and *Imperata cylindrica* 'Red Baron'.

ASSOCIATIONS: *Allium tuberosum*, photo 35; *Aster frikartii* 'Mönch', photo 73; *Berberis thunbergii* 'Atropurpurea', photo 35; *Echinacea purpurea* 'Bright Star', photo 73; *Gomphrena globosa* 'Lavender Lady', photo 35; *Miscanthus sinensis* 'Gracillimus', photo 120; *Phlox paniculata* 'Bright Eyes', photo 120; *Sedum* 'Autumn Joy', photo 73; *Sedum* 'Vera Jameson', photo 35; *Thalictrum rochebrunianum*, photo 120.

Join with *Hosta* 'Krossa Regal' and *Thalictrum rochebrunianum* in light shade in a ratio of 1:1:1 and enjoy the splendid contrast between their broad, fine, and medium foliage textures. Subtle variations in foliage hue are apparent from *Anemone*'s dark green to *Hosta*'s and *Thalictrum*'s slightly bluish tints. The light violet *Hosta* and *Thalictrum* blooms often develop simultaneously and further knit the composition.

A shorter, brighter, late season of bloom results from relating this anemone with *Anemone* 'Honorine Jobert', *Chelone lyonii*, and *Echinacea purpurea* 'Bright Star' (1:1:2:1). Red-violet and white are the flower hues employed in this larger-scale association. It suits very light shade with rich soil. *Chelone lyonii*, an excellent yet underused plant, has a fine color affinity with the hybrid anemones and also with *Echinacea* when bloom overlaps. Although flowering is late, the rich dark foliage of these plants is useful from late spring or early summer.

Antirrhinum 'Frontier Crimson'

Herbaceous perennial, usually grown as an annual, 24 × 12 in (60 × 30 cm), blooms very dark red, late spring to late summer, foliage very dark yellow-green, late spring to late summer. Requires average to rich soil with average moisture in sun or part shade. USDA Zones 8–10. Photo 106. See also discussions under *Celosia plumosa* 'New Look' and photo 22.

ASSOCIATIONS: *Beta vulgaris* subsp. *cicla*, photo 106; *Centranthus ruber*, and *Knautia macedonica*, photo 22.

Antirrhinum majus 'Princess White with Purple Eye'

Herbaceous perennial, usually grown as an annual, 12–18 x 12 in (30–45 × 30 cm), blooms white with red-violet, mid spring to summer, dark yellow-green foliage, mid spring to late summer. Does well in average soil and moisture in sun or part shade. USDA Zones 8–10. Photo 40. See also discussion under *Antirrhinum majus* 'White Rocket'.

ASSOCIATIONS: *Lobularia maritima* 'Carpet of Snow' and *L. m.* 'Easter Bonnet Deep Pink', photo 40.

Antirrhinum majus 'White Rocket'

Herbaceous perennial, usually grown as an annual, 30–36 × 12 in (75–90 × 30 cm), blooms white, late spring to late summer, very dark yellow-green foliage, late spring to late summer. Does well with average to rich soil with average moisture in sun or part shade. USDA Zones 8–10. Photo 39.

ASSOCIATIONS: *Ageratum houstonianum* 'Southern Cross', *Argyranthemum frutescens*, *Cleome spinosa* 'Helen Campbell', *Cleome spinosa* 'Violet Queen', *Nicotiana sylvestris*, photo 39.

An easily contrived annual combination associates two of these with three *Antirrhinum majus* 'Princess White with Purple Eye', three *Lobelia erinus* 'White Cascade', three *Petunia* 'Burgundy Madness', three *Verbena* 'Amethyst', and one *Zinnia elegans* 'Silver Sun' (2:3:3:3:3:1). This violet and white association can stand alone or enhance shrub plantings. Harmonizes particularly well with the red-violet blooms and white-edged leaves of *Weigela florida* 'Variegata'.

Aquilegia alpina, alpine columbine

Herbaceous perennial, 12–24 × 12 in (30–60 × 30 cm), blooms violet, mid to late spring, foliage very dark yellow-green, mid spring to fall. Suitable for rich to average soil with average to moist conditions in sun or part shade. USDA Zones 3–8. Photo 77.

ASSOCIATIONS: *Digitalis purpurea* 'Excelsior', *Geranium macrorrhizum*, *Veronica latifolia* 'Crater Lake Blue', photo 77.

The violet flowers of this columbine link nicely with cool tinted blue-violet, red-violet, and red. Use four columbines with one *Baptisia australis*, two *Dianthus plumarius*, one *Geranium endressii* 'Wargrave Pink', and two pale blue-violet *Iris × germanica*. This combination (4:1:2:1:2) produces an effect allowing its delicate form and receding hue to feature. This exhuberant association for full sun is at its best in June. Flower forms and leaf textures are varied and sustain the composition after its relatively brief flowering period.

Aquilegia 'Black Star'

Herbaceous perennial, 24–36 × 18 in (60–90 × 45 cm), blooms very dark red-violet, mid to late spring, dark yellow-green foliage, mid spring to fall. Suitable for rich to average soil with average to moist conditions in part shade or sun. USDA Zones 3–8. See also discussion under photo 124.

ASSOCIATIONS: *Athyrium filix-femina* and *Hosta sieboldiana*, photo 124. Considered a medium to large element of medium texture with flowers clustered above a nebulous foliage mass.

Dark red-blooming plants making striking focal points in small spaces with light backgrounds. Use four 'Black Star' with nine *Tulipa* 'Queen of Night' and combine their complementary yellow-green with that of the smooth broad leaves of two *Hosta plantaginea* 'Royal Standard'. Place this trio against a background of one *Prunus × cistena* to enlarge the scale and effect. Plant in a ratio of 4:9:2:1 so the hosta's broad mass does not eclipse its companions. *Aquilegia* and *Hosta* foliage persists in a pleasing combination until late summer.

Aquilegia 'Heavenly Blue'

Herbaceous perennial, 24–30 × 18 in (60–75 × 45 cm), blooms light blue-violet and white, mid to late spring, dark yellow-green foliage, mid spring to fall. Suitable for rich to average soil with average to greater moisture and part shade or sun. USDA Zones: 3–8. Photo 80.

ASSOCIATIONS: *Dianthus × allwoodii* 'Essex Witch' and *Veronica latifolia* 'Crater Lake Blue', photo 80.

Aquilegia 'McKana Giants'

Herbaceous perennial, 30–36 × 18 in (75–90 × 45 cm), blooms white, pale yellow, light red-violet, and very light violet, mid to late spring, dark yellow-green foliage, mid spring to fall. Suitable for rich to average soil in average to moist conditions and part shade or sun. USDA Zones 3–8. See also discussion under photo 144.

ASSOCIATIONS: In the context of garden design this

plant may be considered a medium to large element of medium texture with flowers clustered above a nebulous foliage mass. *Alchemilla mollis, Campanula glomerata* 'Joan Elliot', *Geranium endressii* 'Wargrave Pink', *Geranium* 'Johnson's Blue', photo 144.

Aquilegia 'Olympia'

Herbaceous perennial, 12–15 × 12 in (30–40 × 30 cm), blooms white and very light violet, mid to late spring, dark yellow-green foliage, mid spring to fall. Suitable for rich to average soil with average to moist conditions and part shade or sun. USDA Zones 3–8. Photo 124. See also discussion under *Lamium maculatum* 'White Nancy'.

ASSOCIATIONS: *Athyrium filix-femina* and *Hosta sieboldiana*, photo 124.

The rather delicate coloring of this columbine suits it for association with other white-flowering plants in light shade. Group three with one *Cimicifuga racemosa*, five *Galium odoratum*, and two *Polygonatum biflorum* (3:1:5:2) to achieve a delicate and successive bloom over a long period. Strong and varied foliage forms sustain the association's charm for several months.

Aquilegia 'Rose Queen'

Herbaceous perennial, 18–24 × 15 in (45–60 × 40 cm), blooms very light red and white, mid to late spring, very dark yellow-green foliage, mid spring to fall. Does well in average soil with average to greater moisture in sun or part shade. USDA Zones 3–9. Photo 26. See also discussion under *Ageratum houstonianum* 'Blue Puffs'.

ASSOCIATIONS: *Cimicifuga racemosa, Dicentra eximia* 'Luxuriant', *Hosta fortunei* 'Marginato-alba', *Thalictrum aquilegifolium* 'Album', photo 26.

Aquilegia vulgaris,
garden columbine, granny's bonnets

Herbaceous perennial, 12–24 × 12 in (30–60 × 30 cm), blooms light violet, light red-violet, and white, late spring, dark yellow-green foliage, mid spring to fall. Does well in average soil and moisture in part shade or sun. USDA Zones 3–10. Photo 41. See also discussions under *Myosotis sylvatica, Veronica spicata* subsp. *incana*, and *Viola corsica*.

ASSOCIATIONS: *Amsonia tabernaemontana, Iris × germanica, Leucanthemum × superbum* 'Alaska', *Nepeta mussinii, Tradescantia × andersoniana* 'Blue Stone', photo 41.

A pleasing near-complementary composition places garden columbine's violet blooms with the pale yellow blooms of *Corydalis lutea* and *Lamiastrum galeobdolon* 'Herman's Pride' (3:1:1). This makes an excellent underplanting for yellow azaleas or can be used as a groundcover for lightly shaded woodlands and rock plantings.

A softer effect is achieved by using cool, adjacent hues, such as in pale blue-violet *Camassia quamash* and red-violet *Dicentra eximia* 'Luxuriant' (2:3:1). *Camassia* spires contrast the nodding *Aquilegia* clusters and mound of *Dicentra* foliage and flowers. These delicate textures and receding colors are best viewed at close quarters in small borders or patio plantings.

Arabis albida
See *A. caucasica*

Arabis caucasica (*A. albida*), rockcress

Herbaceous perennial, 6–9 × 12 in (15–25 × 30 cm), blooms fragrant, white, mid spring, dark gray yellow-green foliage, mid spring to fall. Does well in average soil with average to dry conditions and sun. USDA Zones 4–7. Photo 46. See also discussion under *Phlox subulata*.

ASSOCIATIONS: *Muscari armeniacum, Narcissus* 'Thalia', *Viola cucullata*, photo 46.

Linking this with *Aurinia saxatilis* (1:1) produces a vibrant, bright yellow and white vision. This cheerful and frequently employed early-spring association is often used to carpet sunny, well-drained spaces. It also combines well with daffodil (*Narcissus*) plantings. The grayed foliages of this

Arabis and *Aurinia* are of fairly similar texture and are unobtrusive, even dull, after the flowering highlight.

Argyranthemum frutescens (*Chrysanthemum frutescens*), Marguerite daisy

Herbaceous perennial, usually treated as an annual, 12–30 × 12 in (30–75 × 30 cm), bloom color varies, white, yellow, or pink, late spring to fall, dark yellow-green foliage, spring to fall. Does well in average soil in average to dry conditions in sun or part shade. USDA Zones 9–10. Photos 14, 15, 39.

ASSOCIATIONS: *Ageratum houstonianum* 'Southern Cross', photo 39; *Alchemilla mollis*, photo 15; *Antirrhinum majus* 'White Rocket', photo 39; *Aruncus dioicus*, photo 14; *Cleome spinosa* 'Helen Campbell', photo 39; *Cleome spinosa* 'Violet Queen', photo 39; *Corydalis lutea*, photo 15; *Digitalis grandiflora*, photo 14; *Helichrysum petiolare*, photo 15; *Iris pseudacorus*, photo 14; *Nicotiana sylvestris*, photo 39; *Solidago* 'Cloth of Gold', photo 14; *Weigela florida* 'Variegata', photo 14.

To highlight the white or yellow components of its daisy-like blooms, associate with pale yellow *Hemerocallis lilioasphodelus* and pale yellow *Verbascum chaixii* spires (3:1:2). *Hemerocallis* contributes a weeping form to the modest foliage grouping. *Verbascum* may rebloom with *Argyranthemum* in fall.

Argyranthemum 'Mary Wootton' (*Chrysanthemum frutescens* 'Mary Wootton')

Herbaceous perennial, often treated as an annual, 30–36 × 24 in (75–90 × 60 cm), blooms pale red-violet, summer, dark yellow-green foliage, late spring to fall. Requires average to rich soil, average moisture, and sun. USDA Zones 9–10.

ASSOCIATIONS: 'Mary Wootton' is of medium scale and texture. Use with *Helichrysum petiolare* and *Stachys macrantha* 'Robusta' to make a non-intrusive association (2:1:1). Its pale and light red-violet blooms are echoed in those of *Stachys* and balance the brightness of grayed yellow-green *Helichrysum*. The summer bloom persists for several weeks and combines subtly varied forms in both flowers and foliage. Nearby groups should make gradual transitions from or continue this cool, pale color theme as these weak tints are easily eclipsed by stronger hues.

Artemisia lactiflora, white mugwort

Herbaceous perennial, 36–48 × 24 in (90–120 × 60 cm), blooms very pale yellow, late summer, dark yellow-green foliage, summer to fall. Does well in average soil with moist to average conditions in sun or part shade. USDA Zones 5–8. Photo 117.

ASSOCIATIONS: *Monarda fistulosa*, *Pennisetum alopecuroides*, *Sedum* 'Autumn Joy', photo 117.

Artemisia 'Powis Castle'

Herbaceous perennial, 18–36 × 24 in (45–90 × 60 cm), flowers absent or insignificant, fragrant foliage, pale, very gray yellow-green, late spring to fall. Does well in average soil with dry to average conditions in sun. USDA Zones 6–8. Photo 121. See also discussions under *Ageratum houstonianum* 'Southern Cross', *Allium christophii*, *Allium giganteum*, *Anaphalis triplinervis* 'Summer Snow', *Cotinus coggygria* 'Royal Purple', *Limonium latifolium*, *Salvia officinalis* 'Purpurea', *Sedum* 'Vera Jameson', *Verbena bonariensis*, and photo 113.

ASSOCIATIONS: *Allium schoenoprasum*, photo 113; *Allium sphaerocephalon*, photo 121; *Cerastium tomentosum*, photo 113; *Penstemon hirsutus* 'Pygmaeus', photo 113; *Perilla frutescens* and *Sedum* 'Ruby Glow', photo 121; *Veronica spicata* subsp. *incana*, photo 113.

This artemisia's striking feathery form and very pale hue delicately enhance bolder forms and darker hues. Group with *Aster frikartii* 'Mönch', *Echinops* 'Taplow Blue', and *Helictotrichon sempervirens* (1:1:1:1). The pale, stiff, blue-green *Helictotrichon* and blue-violet *Echinops* umbels are outstanding in late spring. Cut *Echinops* back for a second, late summer to early fall bloom, when it will appear with the light blue-violet *Aster* flowers.

On a slightly smaller scale, a more delicate, detailed effect is created by placing this artemisia with the annual *Gomphrena globosa* 'Lavender Lady' and *Sedum* 'Autumn Joy' (1:4:1). Small, pale red-violet *Gomphrena* umbels contrast in midsummer with the yellow-green horizontal *Sedum* heads and the grayed yellow-green *Artemisia*. This subtle, pleasing composition persists until fall when the grayed *Artemisia* contrasts with the deepening red of the *Sedum*.

My passion for blue and gray combinations was fully satisfied when I came upon an association which linked an artemisia similar to 'Powis Castle' with *Borago officinalis* (2:1) at Sissinghurst Garden, England. Stunning, light grayed foliage and pure blue borage blooms are outstanding in summer. Borage leaves are broad and contrast the fine texture of some artemisias, although borage may be considered rather coarse for the formal border.

Artemisia schmidtiana '**Silver Mound**'

Herbaceous perennial, 12 × 18 in (30 × 45 cm), flowers absent or insignificant, foliage very pale, very gray yellow-green, late spring to fall. Does well in average soil with dry to average conditions in sun. USDA Zones 3–7. See also discussions under *Campanula portenschlagiana*, *Convolvulus cneorum*, *Cotinus coggygria* 'Royal Purple', and *Heliotropium* 'Marine'.

ASSOCIATIONS: This is a perfect small-scale artemisia to contribute a silvery brilliance in a feathery mounded mass. Combines beautifully with the foliage and violet blooms of *Lavandula angustifolia* 'Munstead', the pale, blue flowers of *Lobelia erinus* 'Cambridge Blue', and the similarly silvery, broad-textured foliage of *Stachys byzantina* (1:2:3:1). Although small-scale, its brilliant foliage is determinedly eye-catching. Site with this consideration in mind.

Aruncus dioicus (*A. sylvester*, *Spiraea aruncus*), goat's-beard

Herbaceous perennial, 48–72 × 36 in (120–185 × 90 cm), blooms very pale yellow-orange, late spring to summer, dark yellow-green foliage, late spring to fall. Plant in average to rich soil, supply average to greater moisture, and site in part shade or morning sun. USDA Zones 3–7. Photo 14. See also discussions under *Macleaya microcarpa*, *Matteuccia struthiopteris*, *Phalaris arundinacea* var. *picta*, and photo 125.

ASSOCIATIONS: *Ajuga reptans* 'Atropurpurea', photo 125; *Alchemilla mollis*, photo 125; *Argyranthemum frutescens*, photo 14; *Digitalis grandiflora*, photo 14; *Iris pseudacorus*, photo 14; *Polygonatum odoratum* 'Variegatum', photo 125; *Solidago* 'Cloth of Gold', photo 14; *Weigela florida* 'Variegata', photo 14.

Thrives with *Hosta* with which it is often associated to contrast texture and form. Almost any *Hosta* variety would suit. Use one goat's-beard with two hostas, adding one each of *Phalaris arundinacea* var. *picta* and *Rodgersia aesculifolia* (1:2:1:1) as intermediate-scale plants to link the differing heights in *Hosta* and *Aruncus*. *Rodgersia* and *Phalaris* also bring varied leaf forms, and the composition is brightened by pale *Rodgersia* bloom and *Phalaris* leaf variegation.

Aruncus sylvester
See *A. dioicus*

Asclepias tuberosa '**Gay Butterflies**'

Herbaceous perennial, 12–30 × 18 in (30–75 × 45 cm), blooms yellow to orange to light orange, summer, dark yellow-green foliage, summer to fall. Needs only average to poor soil, average to dry conditions in sun. USDA Zones 4–9. See also discussions under *Gaillardia* × *grandiflora* 'Goblin' and *Zinnia* 'Old Mexico'.

ASSOCIATIONS: This plant provides a medium-scale element offering horizontal emphasis in its broad-textured flowers and vertical emphasis in fine-textured foliage. Its varied warm floral colors suggest combining it with other warm colors to contrast strong, cool colors. A bold, large-scale composition is contrived by associating it with yellow-orange *Heliopsis scabra* and *Rudbeckia* 'Goldsturm', and violet *Salvia farinacea* 'Victoria' (2:1:1:9). *Salvia* needs to be massed to compete effectively with the strong advancing colors and bold forms of its companions.

Asperula odorata

See *Galium odoratum*

Aster frickartii 'Mönch'

Herbaceous perennial, 24–36 × 24 in (60–90 × 60 cm), blooms very light blue-violet, late summer to fall, dark gray yellow-green foliage, late summer to fall. Does well in average soil and moisture in sun. USDA Zones 5–8. Photos 73, 94. See also discussions under *Allium christophii*, *Artemisia* 'Powis Castle', *Asteromoea mongolica*, and *Eupatorium coelestinum*.

ASSOCIATIONS: *Anemone vitifolia* 'Robustissima', photo 73; *Echinacea purpurea* 'Bright Star', photo 73; *Perilla frutescens*, photo 94; *Sedum* 'Autumn Joy', photo 73; *Solidago* 'Crown of Rays', photo 94.

Two of these asters will associate easily with other late-blooming plants with light blue-violet blooms in different forms, such as *Caryopteris × clandonensis* 'Heavenly Blue' and *Eupatorium coelestinum*. These in turn benefit by being contrasted with pale yellow-green to pink tinting, such as that displayed in the horizontal flower heads provided by *Sedum* 'Autumn Joy' (2:1:2:1). *Sedum*'s solid, bold form also contrasts nicely with the finer textures of its companions.

Aster novae-angliae 'Alma Potschke'

Herbaceous perennial, 24–36 × 24 in (60–90 × 60 cm), blooms light red-violet, late summer to fall, dark yellow-green foliage, late summer to fall. Does well in average soil and moisture in sun. USDA Zones 4–8.

ASSOCIATIONS: This aster can function in the landscape as a medium- to large-scale, fine-textured element. See discussions under *Aster novae-angliae* 'Purple Dome' and *Caryopteris × clandonensis* 'Heavenly Blue'.

Aster novae-angliae 'Purple Dome'

Herbaceous perennial, 12 × 12 in (30 × 30 cm), blooms light violet, late summer to fall, dark yellow-green foliage, late summer to fall. Does well in average soil and moisture in sun. USDA Zones 4–8. Photo 87.

ASSOCIATIONS: *Chrysanthemum pacificum* and *Solidago* 'Crown of Rays', photo 87.

A striking successive composition of brighter red-violet with violet hues combines two 'Purple Dome' asters with one *Aster novae-angliae* 'Alma Potschke', one *Chelone lyonii*, three *Cleome spinosa* 'Violet Queen', and three *Verbena bonariensis* (2:1:1:3:3). The annual cleome and verbena threaded between the perennial aster and chelone will be the first to flower in summer and all will bloom into fall.

Asteromoea mongolica (*Boltonia indica*)

Herbaceous perennial, 24–36 × 24 in (60–90 × 60 cm), blooms white, late summer to fall, dark yellow-green foliage, summer to fall. Does well in average soil and moisture in sun. USDA Zones 5–8. Photos 123, 135. See also discussions under *Agastache foeniculum*, *Alcea rosea* 'Single Mix', *Anemone* 'Honorine Jobert', and photo 7.

ASSOCIATIONS: *Centranthus ruber*, photo 135; *Crambe cordifolia*, photo 7; *Lythrum salicaria* 'Morden Pink', photos 123, 135; *Miscanthus sinensis* 'Gracillimus', photo 123; *Miscanthus sinensis* 'Zebrinus', photo 7; *Polygonatum odoratum* 'Variegatum', photo 7; *Salvia guaranitica*, photo 135; *Verbena bonariensis*, photo 123; *Veronica spicata* 'Blue Fox', photo 123.

Perilla frutescens can provide a fine dark foliage background to display *Asteromoea mongolica*'s daisy-type blooms, which are small yet abundant.

A larger daisy or disk form could be introduced by using light blue-violet *Aster frikartii* 'Mönch' (3:2:1). An excellent fall association.

Astilbe chinensis 'Pumila'

Herbaceous perennial, 12–18 × 12 in (30–45 × 30 cm), blooms light to pale red-violet, mid to late summer, dark yellow-green foliage, late spring to fall. Plant in average to rich soil, ensure average to moist conditions, and site in part shade or morning sun. USDA Zones 3–8. Photo 105. See also discussions under *Astrantia major* and *Ruta graveolens*.

ASSOCIATIONS: *Helleborus orientalis*, photo 105.

Abundant choice of other pale red-violet blooms makes for easy associations. Attention focuses on its small scale and vertical form when combined with *Dicentra eximia* 'Luxuriant' and *Sedum* 'Rosy Glow' (1:1:1). All will enjoy light shade or some sun with adequate moisture. *Dicentra*'s red-violet tinted blooms pierce its grayish foliage from spring to fall, with the flowering display enhanced in late summer by *Astilbe* and *Sedum* blooms. All tints are relatively subdued and plant forms and foliage vary subtly.

Astilbe × *arendsii* 'Bridal Veil'

Herbaceous perennial, 18–30 × 18 in (45–75 × 45 cm), blooms white, fading to very pale yellow, late spring to summer, dark yellow-green foliage, late spring to fall. Plant in average to rich soil, ensure average to moist conditions, and site in part shade or morning sun. USDA Zones 4–9. Photo 115. See also discussion under photo 50.

ASSOCIATIONS: *Allium christophii* and *Geranium sanguineum* var. *striatum*, photo 115.

Astilbe × *arendsii* 'Cattleya'

Herbaceous perennial, 36 × 18 in (90 × 45 cm), blooms pale red, late spring to summer, dark yellow-green foliage, late spring to fall. Plant in average to rich soil, supply average to moist conditions in part shade or morning sun. USDA Zones 4–9. Photo 19. See also discussions under *Geranium psilostemon* and *Hosta* 'Krossa Regal'.

ASSOCIATIONS: *Geranium endressii* 'Wargrave Pink', photo 19.

Astilbe × *arendsii* 'Deutschland'

Herbaceous perennial, 18–24 × 18 in (45–60 × 45 cm), blooms very pale yellow, late spring to summer, dark yellow-green foliage, late spring to fall. Plant in average to rich soil, ensure average to moist conditions, and site in part shade or morning sun. USDA Zones 4–9. Photo 56. See also discussions under *Geranium macrorrhizum*, *Hemerocallis* 'Hyperion', *Hosta fortunei* 'Marginato-alba', *Hosta* 'Krossa Regal', *Ligularia stenocephala* 'The Rocket', *Phalaris arundinacea* var. *picta*, *Rodgersia aesculifolia*, and photo 50.

ASSOCIATIONS: *Athyrium nipponicum* 'Pictum', photo 56; *Dicentra spectabilis* 'Alba', photo 50; *Hosta fortunei* 'Marginato-alba', photo 50; *Hosta sieboldiana* 'Frances Williams', photo 56; *Iris sibirica*, photo 50; *Mertensia virginica*, photo 50.

In locations with morning sun and afternoon shade, associate with the strikingly bold form of the large-scale *Ligularia stenocephala* 'The Rocket' and smaller *Alchemilla mollis* and *Phalaris arundinacea* var. *picta* (2:1:3:1). This astilbe's white blooms and the variegated *Phalaris* foliage form a fairly conventional combination, yet this grouping is enlivened in late spring or early summer by yellow-green *Alchemilla* blooms and in summer by the dark yellow *Ligularia* spires.

Astilbe × *arendsii* 'Fanal'

Herbaceous perennial, 24 × 18 in (60 × 45 cm), blooms red, late spring to summer, very dark yellow-green foliage, late spring to fall. Plant in average to rich soil, ensure average to moist conditions and site in part shade or morning sun. USDA Zones 4–9. Photos 107, 141.

ASSOCIATIONS: *Alchemilla alpina* and *Campanula poscharkyana*, photo 141; *Hosta plantaginea*

'Royal Standard', photo 107; *Ruta graveolens*, photo 141.

Astrantia major, masterwort

Herbaceous perennial, 24–30 × 12–18 in (60–75 × 30–45 cm), blooms white with very pale red flecks, mid to late summer, dark yellow-green foliage, late spring to fall. Suitable for rich to average soil with moist to average conditions and part shade or sun. USDA Zones 4–7. Photo 28.

ASSOCIATIONS: *Cleome spinosa* 'Pink Queen' and *Cosmos bipinnatus* 'Pinkie', photo 28.

Associate with plumed *Astilbe chinensis* 'Pumila' (1:1) to enhance the pale red tints and fine texture of the masterwort's blooms. Summer bloom in both plants is preceded by a foliage composition which I find pleasing despite textural similarity. This duo is excellent for underplanting small flowering trees or to carpet lightly shaded spaces.

Athyrium filix-femina, lady fern

Fern, 12–24 × 24 in (30–60 × 60 cm), flowers absent, foliage gray yellow-green, late spring to fall. Suitable for rich to average soil with average to greater moisture and part shade. USDA Zones 3–8. Photo 124. See also discussions under *Hyacinthoides hispanica* and *Polygonatum biflorum*.

ASSOCIATIONS: *Aquilegia* 'Olympia' and *Hosta sieboldiana*, photo 124.

Athyrium goeringianum 'Pictum'

See *A. nipponicum* 'Pictum'

Athyrium nipponicum 'Pictum' (*A. goeringianum* 'Pictum'), Japanese painted fern

Fern, 6–12 × 12 in (15–30 × 30 cm), flowers absent, foliage very gray yellow-green with dark red-violet markings, late spring to fall. Suitable for rich to average soil with average to greater moisture and part shade. USDA Zones 3–8. Photos 52, 56. See also discussion under *Viola* 'Bowles Black'.

ASSOCIATIONS: *Ajuga reptans*, photo 52; *Astilbe ×*
arendsii 'Deutschland', photo 56; *Hosta fortunei*, photo 52; *Hosta sieboldiana* 'Frances Williams', photo 56; *Polygonatum odoratum* 'Variegatum', photo 52.

Interplant this fern with *Primula japonica* (3:2) in light shade to produce a refined spring underplanting for shrubs. Clusters of red-violet *Primula* blooms rise above *Athyrium* in spring and repeat the dark reddish tones in its fronds and stems. Shrubs with red-violet, gray foliage or very dark green leaves associate well. Avoid shrubs with yellow or orange spring bloom.

Atriplex hortensis 'Cupreata'

Generally grown as an annual in all zones, 12–48 × 18 in (30–120 × 45 cm), flowers insignificant, foliage very deep red, summer to fall. Does well in average soil, average or less moisture, and sun. Photos 27, 109. See also discussion under *Verbena bonariensis*.

ASSOCIATIONS: *Alchemilla mollis*, photo 109; *Allium cernuum*, photos 27, 109; *Allium senescens*, photos 27, 109; *Clematis × jackmanii*, photo 27.

Aurinia saxatilis (*Alyssum saxatile*), basket-of-gold

Herbaceous perennial, 8–10 × 12 in (20–25 × 30 cm), blooms yellow, early to mid spring, dark gray yellow-green foliage, early spring to late summer. Plant in average to poor soil with dry to average conditions and site in sun. USDA Zones 3–7. Foliage will persist through the summer if sited with good drainage. Photo 16. See also discussion under *Arabis caucasica*.

ASSOCIATIONS: *Iberis sempervirens* 'Snowflake', photo 16;

Planting this with *Geum × borisii* (1:2) takes bold advantage of the strong, adjacent yellow and red-orange hues. Red-orange *Geum* blooms are scattered above the yellow mat of *Aurinia* flowers. Colors are stronger and more compelling than in many spring-flowering plants. Careful siting is essential so the association does not clash with neighboring bright red-violet hues and does not overwhelm pastel blooms.

Aurinia saxatilis 'Citrina' (*Alyssum saxatile* 'Citrinum')

Herbaceous perennial, 8–10 × 12 in (20–25 × 30 cm), blooms very pale yellow, early to mid spring, dark gray yellow-green foliage, early spring to late summer. Plant in average to poor soil, ensure dry to average conditions in sun. USDA Zones 3–7.

ASSOCIATIONS: This plant can be considered a small-scale element of fine textures and horizontal emphasis. For a delicate, small-scale floral association of complementary pale yellow and light blue, plant with *Myosotis sylvatica* (1:6). *Myosotis* needs to be massed to balance the advancing qualities of *Aurinia*'s pale yellow blooms and spreading habit. Sun, good drainage, and a location close to the viewing site will suit this pair and their hosts.

Ballota pseudodictamnus

Perennial, 12–24 × 18 in (30–60 × 45 cm), flowers insignificant, foliage very pale, very gray yellow-green, mid spring to fall. Does well in average soil with dry conditions and sun. USDA Zones 8–10. Photo 74.

ASSOCIATIONS: *Berberis thunbergii* 'Atropurpurea Nana', *Lavandula angustifolia* 'Munstead', *Santolina chamaecyparissus*, *Teucrium chamaedrys*, photo 74.

Baptisia australis,
blue wild indigo, blue false indigo

Herbaceous perennial, 36–48 × 36 in (90–120 × 90 cm), blooms very light blue-violet, mid to late spring, dark gray yellow-green foliage, mid spring to fall. Suitable for rich to average soil and moisture in sun or part shade. USDA Zones 3–9. See also discussions under *Aquilegia alpina*, *Digitalis grandiflora*, *Geranium* 'Johnson's Blue', and *Heliotropium* 'Marine'.

ASSOCIATIONS: Blue false indigo can be used to in-troduce a large-scale, mixed textural element to the garden landscape. A complex grouping of adjacent, light-tinted blue-violet, violet, and pale red in floral colors can be made by adding one *Geranium* 'Johnson's Blue', two *Centranthus ruber*, two *Digitalis × mertonensis*, three *Iris sibirica*, and three *Stachys byzantina* (1:1:2:2:3:3). Flowering continues for several weeks in late spring and early summer. All will thrive in sun to very light shade. Flower shapes are distinctive and contrasting foliage forms persist in a sustained composition throughout the summer.

Berberis thunbergii 'Atropurpurea',
red-leaf Japanese barberry

Shrub, 5 × 5 ft (1.5 × 1.5 m), pale yellow blooms rather insignificant, mid spring, foliage deep red or red-orange, often changing to red-violet, early spring to fall. Does well in average soil and moisture in sun or part shade. USDA Zones 4–8. Photos 21, 35, 119, 133.

ASSOCIATIONS: *Allium tuberosum*, photo 35; *Anemone vitifolia* 'Robustissima', photo 35; *Elymus arenarius*, photo 133; *Gomphrena globosa* 'Lavender Lady', photo 35; *Hemerocallis* 'Ed Murray', photo 133; *Hosta sieboldiana*, photos 119, 133; *Sedum* 'Vera Jameson', photo 35; *Tulipa* 'Queen of Night', photos 21, 119; *Tulipa* 'Red Shine', photo 21.

Berberis thunbergii 'Atropurpurea Nana',
(*B.t.* 'Crimson Pygmy'), dwarf red-leaf barberry

Shrub, 18–24 × 30 in (45–60 × 75 cm), blooms insignificant, very pale yellow, spring, foliage deep red or red-orange, often changing to red-violet, early spring to fall. Does well in average soil and moisture in sun or part shade. USDA Zones 4–8. Photos 74, 130.

ASSOCIATIONS: *Ballota pseudodictamnus*, photo 74; *Elymus arenarius*, photo 130; *Helictotrichon sempervirens*, photo 130; *Heuchera* 'Palace Purple', photo 130; *Lavandula angustifolia* 'Munstead', photo 74; *Santolina chamaecyparissus*, photo 74; *Teucrium chamaedrys*, photo 74.

Berberis thunbergii '**Crimson Pygmy**'

See *B. t.* 'Atropurpurea Nana'

Beta vulgaris **subsp.** *cicla*, Swiss chard

Biennial, grown as an annual, 15 × 12 in (40 × 30 cm), foliage edible, dark red and dark yellow-green, late spring to late summer. Since flowers are produced in the second year they are not a design consideration when grown as an annual. Plant in average to rich soil with average to greater moisture in sun or part shade. USDA Zones 3–10. Removing outer leaves will encourage new foliage. Photo 106. See also discussion under photo 136.

ASSOCIATIONS: *Antirrhinum* 'Frontier Crimson', photo 106; *Geranium psilostemon, Knautia macedonica, Malva sylvestris* 'Mauritiana', *Rosa*, and *Salvia officinalis* 'Purpurea', photo 136.

Boltonia asteroides '**Snowbank**'

Herbaceous perennial, 48 × 24 in (120 × 60 cm), blooms white with yellow center, fall, dark gray yellow-green foliage, summer to fall. Does well in average soil and moisture in sun or part shade. USDA Zones 3–10. May need staking when sited in light shade.

ASSOCIATIONS: 'Snowbank' lends a large-scale indistinct mass to the garden with its fine-textured foliage. Flowers are medium-textured with an aster-like form. See also discussion under *Caryopteris* × *clandonensis* 'Heavenly Blue'.

Boltonia indica

See *Asteromoea mongolica*

Borago officinalis, borage

Herbaceous perennial or half-hardy annual, 18–24 × 24 in (45–60 × 60 cm), blooms blue, late spring to summer, foliage edible, dark gray yellow-green, late spring to fall. Plant in average to lean, well-drained soil and sun. USDA Zones 8–10. May self-sow. See also discussion under *Artemisia* 'Powis Castle'.

ASSOCIATIONS: This is a medium-scale plant with fine-textured flower clusters and broad-textured foliage presenting an indistinct form. Plant with *Hemerocallis lilioasphodelus*, which develops blooms in pale yellow, for a nearly perfect complementary color scheme in two varied flower forms (2:1). Sun or very light shade is required. Fits well in a delicately hued informal border or patio planting.

Brunnera macrophylla (*Anchusa myosotidiflora*), Siberian bugloss

Herbaceous perennial, 18 × 24 in (45 × 60 cm), blooms very light blue, mid to late spring, dark yellow-green foliage, spring to fall. Does well in average soil with moist to average conditions in sun or part shade. USDA Zones 3–7. Photos 43, 76, 99, 101, 102. See also discussions under *Doronicum cordatum* 'Magnificum', *Erythronium* 'Pagoda', *Iberis sempervirens* 'Snowflake', *Narcissus* 'Trevithian', *Tulipa* 'West Point', and photo 90.

ASSOCIATIONS: *Achillea taygetea*, photo 102; *Amsonia tabernaemontana*, photo 76; *Corydalis lutea*, photo 99; *Euphorbia polychroma*, photo 101; *Geranium endressii* 'Wargrave Pink', photo 76; *Hemerocallis* cultivars, photo 101; *Hosta plantaginea* 'Royal Standard', photo 43; *Iris sibirica*, photo 76; *Veronica spicata* 'Blue Fox', photo 102; *Viola* × *wittrockiana*, photo 43.

An easily grown blue and white association can be made with *Dicentra spectabilis* 'Alba' and *Polygonatum biflorum* (2:1:3). The subdued effect of white and blue blooms is reinforced by association with the distinctive plant form and tiny white *Polygonatum* blooms. Substitute *Polygonatum odoratum* 'Variegatum' for a bolder, more dramatic foliage effect.

Matching flowers of a *Brunnera* with the stronger, advancing light red-violet of *Dicentra spectabilis* and another light blue provided by two *Mertensia virginica* makes a dramatic floral group for light shade. Add a bluish leaved *Hosta* × *tardiana* 'Halcyon' to provide late-summer bloom and a fine foliage companion after *Dicentra*'s and

Mertensia's disappearance in summer. Plant in a ratio of 1:1:2:1.

Buddleja fallowiana 'Lochinch'

Shrub, 4–6 × 5 ft (1.2–1.8 × 1.5 m), blooms light blue-violet, late summer, very gray yellow-green foliage, late spring to fall. Plant in average to poor soil, supply average or less moisture, and site in sun. USDA Zones 7–9. Cut back hard in spring. Photo 5. The smaller *Buddleja davidii* var. *nanhoensis* 'Nanho Blue' could substitute for *Buddleja fallowiana* 'Lochinch'. See also discussion under *Convolvulus cneorum*.

ASSOCIATIONS: *Convolvulus cneorum, Helichrysum angustifolium, Onopordum acanthium, Potentilla flamea, Stachys byzantina*, photo 5.

Buphthalmum speciosum (*Telekia speciosa*), ox-eye daisy

Herbaceous perennial, 36–72 × 36 in (90–185 × 90 cm), blooms yellow, summer, dark yellow-green foliage, summer to fall. Does well in average soil and moisture in sun. USDA Zones 3–9. Quite vigorous. Photo 143.

ASSOCIATIONS: *Delphinium* 'Charles Gregory Broan' and *Lychnis chalcedonica*, photo 143.

Calendula officinalis, pot marigold

Generally grown as an annual in all zones, 12–24 × 12 in (30–60 × 30 cm), blooms typically in yellow-orange, orange, and red-orange, late spring to summer, aromatic foliage, dark yellow-green, mid spring to summer. Does well in average soil and moisture in sun or part shade. Pinch faded flowers to extend bloom time. Photo 129.

ASSOCIATIONS: *Salvia × superba*, photo 129.

Callistephus chinensis 'Deep Red'

Generally grown as an annual in all zones, 18–30 × 15 in (45–75 × 40 cm), blooms very dark red, mid to late summer, dark yellow-green foliage, late summer to fall. Does well in average soil and moisture in sun. Photo 134.

ASSOCIATIONS: *Achillea millefolium* 'Paprika' and *Impatiens* 'Tempo Hybrid Red', photo 134.

Camassia esculenta

See *C. quamash*

Camassia quamash (*C. esculenta*), quamash

Bulb, 18–24 × 6 in (45–60 × 15 cm), blooms very pale blue-violet, mid to late spring, dark yellow-green foliage, mid spring. Does best in moist and rich soils, but will grow adequately in average soil and moisture. Plant in sun or part shade. USDA Zones 4–8. There is some confusion in the trade between *Camassia quamash* and *C. leichtlinii*, the latter appears to be taller with darker hued flowers, but they are interchangeable in these combinations. Photo 72. See also discussions under *Aquilegia vulgaris*, *Heuchera* 'Palace Purple', and *Viola corsica*.

ASSOCIATIONS: *Allium aflatuense* 'Purple Sensation' and *Tulipa* 'Purple Rain', photo 72.

Camassia flowers seem to assume the tones of nearby companions. Seen with *Amsonia* they look pale, with *Allium aflatuense* 'Purple Sensation' they take on red-violet. Associate three with the blue violet in *Ajuga reptans* 'Atropurpurea' and *Centaurea montana* (3:3:2), and they appear more nearly pure blue-violet. Dependable *Centaurea* will flower beautifully with *Camassia* and then may be cut back for later rebloom. *Ajuga* provides its own tiny, light violet spikes and an excellent foliage base, blushed with harmonious red-violet, out of which its companions will rise.

Campanula carpatica 'Blue Clips'

Herbaceous perennial, 6–9 × 9 in (15–25 × 25 cm), blooms light violet, late spring to late summer, dark yellow-green foliage, late spring to fall. Does well in average soil and moisture in sun or part shade. USDA Zones 3–8. See also discussion under *Cosmos sulphureus* 'Sunset'.

ASSOCIATIONS: 'Blue Clips' is most often employed as a small-scale element contributing bell-like flowers and horizontal foliage in medium textures. Its bloom color often prompts association with the pale yellow in *Coreopsis verticillata* 'Moonbeam' and other light violet or blue violet flowers such as *Perovskia atriplicifolia* (2:1:1). This medium-scale, soft-hued trio provides a long season of bloom in relatively varied forms. Prostrate *Campanula* and *Coreopsis* bloom longest, joined in midsummer by the diffuse *Perovskia* spires.

A slightly bolder, medium-scale color scheme is produced with *Coreopsis verticillata* 'Moonbeam', *Nicotiana alata* 'Nicki Pink', and *Veronica spicata* 'Blue Charm' (2:1:2:2). Adding the pale red in *Nicotiana* flowers makes this a more arresting three-colored association. The lengthy bloom period, light-tinted hues, and relatively compact size permit this association to fit easily into many garden designs.

Campanula glomerata 'Joan Elliot'

Herbaceous perennial, 18 × 12 in (45 × 30 cm), blooms violet, late spring to summer, dark yellow-green foliage, late spring to late summer. Does well in average soil and moisture in sun or part shade. USDA Zones 3–8. Photo 144. See also discussions under *Clematis* × *jackmanii* and *Dryopteris noveboracensis*.

ASSOCIATIONS: *Alchemilla mollis, Aquilegia* 'McKana Giants', *Geranium* 'Johnson's Blue', *Geranium endressii* 'Wargrave Pink', photo 144.

Campanula portenschlagiana,
Dalmatian bellflower

Herbaceous perennial, 6–9 × 12 in (15–25 × 30 cm), blooms very light violet, late spring to summer, foliage very dark yellow-green, late spring to late summer. Does well in average soil with average to dry conditions in sun or part shade. USDA Zones 4–8. Photos 71, 82.

ASSOCIATIONS: *Alchemilla mollis*, photo 82; *Anemone hupehensis* 'September Charm', photo 71;

Corydalis lutea, photo 82; *Helichrysum petiolare*, photo 71; *Lavandula angustifolia* 'Munstead', photo 82; *Verbena* 'Amethyst', photo 71.

The affinity of light violet with pale gray foliage can be exploited by associating this bellflower with *Artemisia schmidtiana* 'Silver Mound'. The rather receding violet component of the composition can be strengthened by adding the taller *Lavandula angustifolia* 'Munstead' (2:1:2). This small-scale composition needs full sun.

Campanula poscharkyana, Serbian bellflower

Herbaceous perennial, 6–12 × 12 in (15–30 × 30 cm), blooms very light violet, late spring to summer, very dark yellow-green foliage, late spring to late summer. Does well in average soil with average or less moisture in sun or part shade. USDA Zones 3–9. Photo 141.

ASSOCIATIONS: *Alchemilla alpina, Astilbe* × *arendsii* 'Fanal', *Ruta graveolens*, photo 141.

Caryopteris × clandonensis 'Heavenly Blue'

Shrub, 36–60 × 36 in (90–150 × 90 cm), blooms very light blue-violet, late summer to fall, dark gray yellow-green foliage, summer to fall. Does well in average soil with average or less moisture and sun. USDA Zones 5–9. See also discussions under *Anaphalis triplinervis* 'Summer Snow', *Anemone* 'Honorine Jobert', *Aster frikartii* 'Mönch', *Liatris spicata* 'Kobold', and *Sedum* 'Vera Jameson'.

ASSOCIATIONS: This is a large-scale, fine-textured landscape element. One *Caryopteris* × *clandonensis* 'Heavenly Blue' is often planted with three *Eupatorium coelestinum* to echo the light blue-violet evident in its bloom and embolden the color association. One *Anemone* 'Honorine Jobert' is often included with this pairing because the subtle, coincident white bloom is so captivating. However, the composition can be more dynamic if the dazzling red-violet flowers of one *Aster novae-angliae* 'Alma Potschke' make up a quartet of plants. A ratio of 1:3:1:1 will balance the differing values of these adjacent hues.

A strong fall connection is made between indistinct textures when the plant is combined with a strong grouping of *Aster novae-angliae* 'Alma Potschke' intermingled with the similar daisy form of *Boltonia asteroides* 'Snowbank' (1:2:1). The striking red-violet and dense clustering of aster blooms provides an outstanding background for the blue-violet hue of scattered *Caryopteris* blooms. *Boltonia's* white daisies soften the intensity of the aster blooms.

Catananche caerulea, cupid's dart

Herbaceous perennial, 18–30 × 12 in (45–75 × 30 cm), blooms very light violet, late spring to summer, dark yellow-green foliage, late spring to fall. Does well in average soil with dry to average conditions and sun. USDA Zones 3–9. Remove faded flowers to extend bloom time. Photo 148.

ASSOCIATIONS: *Achillea* 'Coronation Gold' and *Lythrum salicaria* 'Dropmore Purple', photo 148.

Celosia cristata 'Sparkler Mix'

Generally grown as an annual in all zones, 9–12 × 12 in (25–30 × 30 cm), blooms yellow, orange, red-orange and red, late spring to fall, dark yellow-green foliage, mid spring to fall. Does well in average soil and moisture in sun. Photo 64.

ASSOCIATIONS: *Coreopsis* 'Sunray' and *Gomphrena* 'Strawberry Fields', photo 64.

Celosia elegans 'Pink Tassles'

Generally grown as an annual in all zones, 24–36 × 12–18 in (60–90 × 30–45 cm), blooms very pale red-violet, mid spring to fall, dark yellow-green foliage, late summer to fall. Plant in average to rich soil, supply average moisture and site in full sun. Photos 37, 137.

ASSOCIATIONS: *Cleome spinosa* 'Helen Campbell', photo 37; *Melampodium paludosum* 'Medallion', photo 137; *Verbena bonariensis*, photo 37; *Zinnia elegans* 'Silver Sun', photo 37.

Associate two of these with three each of the similarly pastel pink-flowered annuals *Cleome spinosa* 'Pink Queen' and *Nicotiana alata* 'Nicki Pink'. All will display to even better advantage against the harmonizing dark red-violet fronds of grassy *Pennisetum* 'Burgundy Giant' (2:3:3:2). Although long-blooming, this association is at its best in late summer and fall when *Pennisetum* fully develops.

Celosia plumosa 'New Look'

Generally grown as an annual in all zones, 12–15 × 12 in (30–40 × 30 cm), blooms red, mid spring to fall, dark red foliage, late summer to fall. Does well in average soil and moisture and sun. Photo 23.

ASSOCIATIONS: *Senecio cineraria* 'Silver Queen', photo 23.

This plant's bright red plumes associate well with the similar hue in spiky *Antirrhinum majus* 'Frontier Crimson' blooms. The pair glistens when fronting dark green *Paeonia* foliage. To further the floral harmony, one could select a dark red-blooming herbaceous peony or *Paeonia lactiflora* 'Festiva Maxima', which develops white flowers with a crimson center (3:2:1).

Centaurea montana, perennial cornflower

Herbaceous perennial, 18–24 × 12 in (45–60 × 30 cm), blooms light blue-violet with light violet centers, mid spring to fall, foliage dark, gray yellow-green, late spring to fall. Does well in average soil with average to dry conditions in sun or part shade. USDA Zones 3–8. Cut back after spring flowering to encourage re-bloom. May self-sow. See also discussions under *Camassia quamash*, *Centranthus ruber*, and *Iris sibirica*.

ASSOCIATIONS: *Centaurea montana* is a medium-scale plant of medium textures and vertical form developing daisy-type flowers. A nearly effortless association is a pairing of this plant with *Dicentra eximia* 'Luxuriant' (2:1). The adjacent floral hues of light blue violet in *Centaurea* and light red violet in *Dicentra* create a very polished duo. *Cen-*

taurea can be cut back after spring bloom to re-bloom with *Dicentra*, which flowers through all but the hottest months. Flower forms and leaf textures are varied. This could make a useful underplanting for spring shrubs flowering in red-violet, such as *Rhododendron* 'Roseum Elegans'.

A fine blue-violet and white association can be contrived by planting with *Dicentra spectabilis* 'Alba', *Geranium sanguineum* 'Album', and *Tradescantia* × *andersoniana* 'Blue Stone' (2:1:1:1). Bloom is stunning and lasts from early to late spring. The scattered distribution of flowers on all four plants creates a delicate effect suitable for fairly close viewing. *Tradescantia* can also be cut down after flowering to encourage later re-bloom.

Centranthus ruber, red valerian

Herbaceous perennial, 18–24 × 12 in (45–60 × 30 cm), blooms very light red, late spring to summer, foliage very dark yellow-green, mid spring to fall. Requires only poor to average soil with average to dry conditions in sun or part shade. USDA Zones 5–8. Remove faded blooms. Self-sows freely. Photos 22, 135. See also discussions under *Baptisia australis, Geranium sanguineum*, and photos 69 and 121.

ASSOCIATIONS: *Antirrhinum majus* 'Frontier Crimson', photo 22; *Artemisia* 'Powis Castle', photo 121; *Asteromoea mongolica*, photo 135; *Knautia macedonica*, photo 22; *Lythrum salicaria* 'Morden Pink', photo 135; *Nepeta mussinii*, photo 69; *Salvia guaranitica*, photo 135; *Salvia* × *superba* 'May Night', photo 69; *Sedum* 'Ruby Glow', photo 121.

Red valerian harmonizes easily with the various light tints of violet and red-violet found in *Geranium* 'Johnson's Blue', *Lythrum salicaria* 'Morden Pink', and *Salvia* × *superba* 'East Friesland' (2:1:2:3). This medium-scale group features dynamic flower forms, varying between spires, clusters, and mounds, which bring a desirable complexity to a compelling color scheme. Flowering occurs for several weeks in late spring and summer.

A near complementary association of red blooms

is created by using palmate, yellow-green *Alchemilla mollis* foliage. Both continue to harmonize smoothly with the blue-violet blooms and grayed green foliage of *Centaurea montana* (1:1:2). *Centaurea* may be cut back after flowering to encourage later re-bloom for a fresh composition with broad *Alchemilla* foliage.

Cerastium tomentosum, snow-in-summer

Herbaceous perennial, 6–9 × 12 in (15–25 × 30 cm), blooms white, mid to late spring, foliage very light, very gray yellow-green, mid spring to fall. Suited to average to sandy soil with dry to average conditions in sun. USDA Zones 2–7. Shear after flowering. May spread to the point of invasiveness. See also discussion under photo 113.

ASSOCIATIONS: Snow-in-summer is a small-scale perennial of fine textures and a prostrate horizontal habit. See text of photo 113 for association with *Allium schoenoprasum, Artemisia* 'Powis Castle', *Penstemon hirsutus* 'Pygmaeus', and *Veronica spicata* subsp. *incana*.

Associations are generally with gray-foliaged plants and cool-hued blooms. Any association with white, red-violet, and blue-violet flowers serves to brighten *Cerastium tomentosum*'s grayed foliage. Use three specimens with one each of *Geranium sylvaticum* 'Mayflower', *Eryngium amethystinum*, and *Malva moschata* 'Alba', and two *Stachys byzantina* (3:1:1:1:2) to gain appropriate hues and link this tiny plant to a medium-scale composition. The group is easily extended, and L. Beebe Wilder suggests adding *Lavandula* and pink hollyhock (*Alcea*). This would emphasize the violet and red-violet hues and considerably enlarge the scale, requiring at least a doubling of the plant ratio to accommodate two *Lavandula* and one *Alcea*.

Ceratostigma plumbaginoides (*Plumbago larpentiae*), leadwort

Herbaceous perennial, 12–15 × 12 in (30–35 × 30 cm), blooms light blue-violet, late summer to fall, foliage dark yellow-green, reddening, late spring to fall. Does well in average soil with average to less moisture in sun or part shade. USDA Zones 5–9.

ASSOCIATIONS: Leadwort is usually used as a small-scale groundcover of medium textures and indistinct form. It can bring an irresistible light blue-violet bloom to contrast the complementary yellow in *Corydalis lutea* and *Kirengeshoma palmata* flowers (4:1:1) in late summer. *Kirengeshoma*'s shrubby form and bell-like blooms make a clearly structured background for its smaller companions. Light shade suits this entire group.

A sunny, long-blooming floral association develops with two of these plants combined with one each of the orange and near-complementary yellow *Cosmos sulphureus* 'Sunny Red' and *Tagetes* 'Primrose Lady'. Both annuals begin blooming months before *Ceratostigma*'s flowers emerge. The blue-violet element can be sustained from late spring to fall by including two *Veronica* 'Sunny Border Blue' (2:1:1:2).

Chelone lyonii, pink turtlehead

Herbaceous perennial, 24–48 × 18 in (60–120 × 45 cm), blooms light red to light red-violet, late summer to fall, dark yellow-green foliage, summer to fall. Does well in average to rich soil with average to greater moisture and part shade or morning sun. USDA Zones 3–8. See also discussions under *Anemone vitifolia* 'Robustissima' and *Aster novae-angliae* 'Purple Dome'.

ASSOCIATIONS: As a design element, this can be considered a large-scale plant of medium textures and indistinct form. Adjacent hues of light red-violet and light violet blend nicely when using *Heliotropium* 'Marine' and *Monarda didyma* 'Bluestocking' (1:3:2). Varied forms contribute interest for very light shade in this medium-scale grouping with overlapping bloom. *Chelone*'s small blooms are scattered above excellent dark foliage and contrast the denser *Monarda* flower clusters and *Heliotropium*'s horizontal, dark flowers.

Chrysanthemum frutescens

See *Argyranthemum frutescens*

Chrysanthemum frutescens **'Mary Wootton'**

See *Argyranthemum* 'Mary Wootton'

Chrysanthemum leucanthemum

See *Leucanthemum vulgare*

Chrysanthemum pacificum,

gold and silver chrysanthemum

Herbaceous perennial, 9–12 × 12 in (25–30 × 30 cm), blooms light yellow, summer to fall, foliage dark yellow-green with pale edging, late spring to fall. Does well in average soil and moisture in sun or part shade. USDA Zones 5–9. Photo 87. See also discussion under *Tagetes* 'Golden Gem'.

ASSOCIATIONS: *Aster novae-angliae* 'Purple Dome' and *Solidago* 'Crown of Rays', photo 87.

Use two of these planted with one *Hemerocallis* 'Gala Bells', two *Tagetes* 'Golden Gem', one *Salvia officinalis* 'Aurea', and one *Solidago* 'Cloth of Gold' (2:1:2:1:1), to form a small-scale grouping highlighting yellow flowers. It will bring brightness to a very lightly shaded space or one with late afternoon shade. Flowering is generally successive, although all companions overlap the long-blooming *Tagetes*. Forms and scales vary between large *Hemerocallis* heads, puffs of tiny *Tagetes*, and plumes of *Solidago*. Foliage is also distinctly varied in form and texture.

Chrysanthemum parthenium

See *Tanacetum parthenium*

Chrysogonum virginianum, goldenstar

Herbaceous perennial, 6–8 × 12 in (15–20 × 30 cm), blooms yellow-orange, mid to late spring, dark yellow-green foliage, spring to fall. Does well in average soil with moist to average conditions in sun or part shade. USDA Zones 5–9. Cooler weather will encourage bloom into fall.

ASSOCIATIONS: Goldenstar is a small-scale plant of medium textures and prostrate habit. One placed with three *Myosotis sylvatica* completes a small-scale spring combination thriving in light shade. Tiny, light blue *Myosotis* blossoms rise above the scattered, near-complementary, starry yellow-orange *Chrysogonum* flowers. This pair makes an excellent groundcover base for flowering bulbs, such as alliums, yellow tulips, or lilies.

Cimicifuga racemosa, black cohosh, snakeroot

Herbaceous perennial, 36–60 × 24 in (90–150 × 60 cm), blooms white, late spring to summer, dark yellow-green foliage, summer to fall. Prefers rich to average soil with moist to average conditions in sun or part shade. USDA Zones 3–8. Photo 26. See also discussions under *Aquilegia* 'Olympia' and *Iris sibirica* 'White Swirl'.

ASSOCIATIONS: *Aquilegia* 'Rose Queen', *Dicentra eximia* 'Luxuriant', *Hosta fortunei* 'Marginato-alba', *Thalictrum aquilegifolium* 'Album', photo 26.

Combine in an easily maintained grouping with one *Ligularia dentata* 'Desdemona' and three *Hyacinthoides hispanica* (1:1:3). Excellent foliage forms contrast between straplike *Hyacinthoides*, feathery *Cimicifuga*, and broad *Ligularia*. Note that there is no particular floral color association at play between the flowers, which appear in near-white, light blue-violet, and yellow-orange at different times. Fine for the woodland garden or large, lightly shaded mixed border.

Clematis × *jackmanii*

Vine, 6–10 ft (1.8–3.0 m), blooms very deep red-violet, late spring to summer, dark yellow-green foliage, late spring to summer. Does well in average soil with average to greater moisture in sun or very light shade. USDA Zones 5–7. See also discussion under photo 27.

ASSOCIATIONS: This clematis is most often used as a medium-scale element as it offers broad-textured flowers and medium-textured foliage. Its deep red-violet blooms make an excellent backdrop for complementary and adjacent-hued companions. For a refined association, allow one specimen to decorate a wall, fence, or trellis behind two *Campanula glomerata* 'Joan Elliot', four *Digitalis grandiflora*, and one *Geranium* 'Johnson's Blue' (1:2:4:1). Suits small spaces and designs establishing a tranquil mood. Pale yellow *Digitalis* spikes rise behind the mound of the *Geranium*'s light violet flowers. *Clematis* and *Campanula* bloom for some weeks after *Geranium* has ceased flowering.

Cleome spinosa 'Helen Campbell'

Generally grown as an annual in all zones, 24–60 × 12 in (60–150 × 30 cm), blooms white, fragrant, late spring to fall, dark yellow-green foliage, late spring to fall. Needs only average to lean soil with average to less moisture and sun. Photos 17, 37, 39. See also discussions under *Gladiolus callianthus*, *Nicotiana sylvestris*, and text reference in photo 24.

ASSOCIATIONS: *Ageratum houstonianum* 'Southern Cross', photo 39; *Antirrhinum majus* ' White Rocket', photo 39; *Argyranthemum frutescens*, photo 39; *Celosia elegans* 'Pink Tassles', photo 37; *Cleome spinosa* 'Violet Queen', photo 39; *Gladiolus callianthus*, photo 17; *Monarda didyma* 'Cambridge Scarlet', photo 24; *Nicotiana sylvestris*, photos 17, 39; *Tagetes* 'Primrose Lady', photo 17; *Verbena bonariensis*, photo 37; *Zinnia* 'Dreamland Ivory', photo 17; *Zinnia elegans* 'Silver Sun', photo 37.

For a long season of cool-hued effects in white, violet, and blue-violet, join with the annual *Nicotiana sylvestris*, *Salvia farinacea* 'Victoria', and *Salvia guaranitica* in a ratio of 3:1:5:2. This large-scale grouping requires sun or very light shade and is most effective in late summer and fall. Unlike many annual compositions, foliage and bloom forms are varied and distinctive.

Cleome spinosa 'Pink Queen'

Generally grown as an annual in all zones, 24–60 × 12 in (60–150 × 30 cm), blooms pale red, fragrant, late spring to fall, dark yellow-green foliage, late spring to fall. Needs only average to lean soil with average to less moisture and sun. Photo 28. See also discussions under *Celosia elegans* 'Pink Tassles' and *Miscanthus sinensis* 'Variegatus'.

ASSOCIATIONS: *Astrantia major* and *Cosmos* 'Pinkie', photo 28.

Cleome spinosa 'Violet Queen'

Generally grown as an annual in all zones, 24–60 × 12 in (60–150 × 30 cm), blooms red-violet, fragrant, late spring to fall, dark yellow-green foliage, late spring to fall. Needs only average to lean soil with average to less moisture and sun. Photo 39. See also discussion under *Aster novae-angliae* 'Purple Dome'.

ASSOCIATIONS: *Ageratum houstonianum* 'Southern Cross', *Antirrhinum* 'White Rocket', *Argyranthemum frutescens*, *Cleome spinosa* 'Helen Campbell', *Nicotiana sylvestris*, photo 39.

Convallaria majalis, lily-of-the-valley

Herbaceous perennial, 6–8 × 12 in (15–20 × 30 cm), blooms fragrant, white, mid spring, dark yellow-green foliage, mid spring to late summer. Prefers average to poor soil with moist to average conditions and shade or part shade. USDA Zones 2–7. May be invasive. All plant parts are poisonous. See also discussion under *Osmunda claytoniana*.

ASSOCIATIONS: This is a small-scale element contributing vertical form through its flowers and an indistinct foliage mass. Flowers are fine-textured and foliage is broad-textured. *Galium odoratum* and *Hosta sieboldiana* (5:3:1) can complete a trio of white and light violet blooms for light shade. They will be most useful for fronting shrub bases or in lightly wooded areas where the invasive nature of *Convallaria* will not be troublesome. *Hosta*'s stunning blue-green leaves and later pale violet blooms carry the composition as *Convallaria* foliage starts to wither. Foliage forms and tints are distinctive and effective in drifts.

Convolvulus cneorum

Shrub, 12–24 × 18 in (30–60 × 45 cm), blooms white, late spring to summer, foliage very gray yellow-green, mid spring to fall. Does well in average soil with little moisture in sun. USDA Zones 8–10. Photo 5. Prune to maintain compact growth.

ASSOCIATIONS: *Buddleja fallowiana* 'Lochinch', *Helichrysum angustifolium*, *Onopordum acanthium*, *Potentilla flamea*, *Stachys byzantina*, photo 5.

An association with less complex forms and somewhat reduced scale than that seen in photo 5 employs one *Buddleja fallowiana* 'Lochinch' as a background for five midground *Lavandula angustifolia* 'Hidcote', while two *Artemisia schmidtiana* 'Silver Mound' and three *Convolvulus cneorum* cluster in the foreground (3:1:5:2).

Coreopsis auriculata 'Nana'

Herbaceous perennial, 6–12 × 18 in (15–30 × 45 cm), blooms yellow-orange, late spring to late summer, foliage very dark yellow-green, mid spring to late summer. Does well in average soil and moisture in sun. USDA Zones 5–9. Pinch faded flowers to maintain long bloom season. May self-sow.

ASSOCIATIONS: 'Nana' is a small-scale plant of medium textures with daisy-type blooms rising above a mound of foliage. Blooms for many weeks with the near-complementary blue-violet *Veronica spicata* 'Blue Fox' (1:2). This relatively small-scale association looks well at the front of a border or along a path where the brilliant yellow-orange *Coreopsis* flowers attract attention. Color clashes may develop if this pair is placed near pink or red-violet blooms.

Coreopsis 'Sunray'

Herbaceous perennial, 18–24 × 12 in (45–60 × 30 cm), blooms yellow-orange, late spring to late summer, foliage very dark yellow-green, late spring to late summer. Does well in average soil and moisture in sun. USDA Zones 5–9. Photos 64,

145. See also discussion under *Achillea* 'Coronation Gold'.

ASSOCIATIONS: *Celosia cristata* 'Sparkler Mix', photo 64; *Gomphrena* 'Strawberry Fields', photo 64; *Heliotropium* 'Marine', photo 145; *Salvia farinacea* 'Victoria', photo 145; *Verbena canadensis* 'Homestead Purple', photo 145.

Adding two each of *Crocosmia* 'Lucifer', *Helenium autumnale* 'Brilliant', and *Tagetes* 'Golden Gem' completes a bold, mid to late summer display featuring yellow-orange, dark red-orange, red, and yellow (3:2:2:2). This grouping is not for the faint-hearted. It may settle in a fairly small space as long as other colors are not very pale or do not include red-violet. A wonderful group for drawing attention across a large space. Flowering season is successive and quite long, with greatest impact in summer and late summer.

Association with one *Heliopsis scabra*, five *Iris kaempferi*, three *Lilium* 'Enchantment', and two *Lysimachia ciliata* 'Purpurea' (2:1:5:3:2) produces a large-scale planting that blooms from late spring into summer. Initially warm colors contrast with the cool dark violet *Iris*. Later, as the irises fade, *Coreopsis* blooms harmonize with the bold yellow *Heliopsis* daisies, orange *Lilium*, and scattered, delicate yellow *Lysimachia* flowers and dark reddish foliage. This bold, large-scale group is best sited against a mass of neutralizing dark green foliage or with other similarly powerful dark violet, dark blue-violet, or warm hues.

Coreopsis verticillata, thread-leaf tickseed

Herbaceous perennial, 18–36 × 24 in (45–90 × 60 cm), blooms yellow, late spring to late summer, dark yellow-green foliage, late spring to fall. Does well in average soil and moisture in sun. USDA Zones 3–9. Drought-tolerant once plant is established. Tends to self-sow. See also discussions under *Campanula carpatica* 'Blue Clips' and *Gaillardia* × *grandiflora* 'Goblin'.

ASSOCIATIONS: Although this is one of the taller *Coreopsis*, it is still of medium scale and fine textures. It is very striking when planted with *Gom-phrena globosa* 'Strawberry Fields' (1:2). The slight red-orange tone in the *Gomphrena* flowers and the similar degree of tinting in the *Coreopsis* permit a very harmonious association. Although both are medium-scale plants, their powerful colors explode over a distance. The daisy-type *Coreopsis* flowers are also similar in size to the *Gomphrena* globes, but the differing forms avoid monotony. This is one of my favorite warm-hued associations. The strong colors need thoughtful siting.

Coreopsis verticillata 'Moonbeam'

Herbaceous perennial, 15–24 × 24 in (40–60 × 60 cm), blooms pale yellow, late spring to fall, dark yellow-green foliage, late spring to fall. Does well in average soil and moisture in sun or part shade. USDA Zones 3–9. Drought-tolerant once plant is established. Tends to self-sow. Photos 85, 89. See also discussions under *Cosmos sulphureus* 'Sunset' and *Veronica spicata* 'Blue Fox'.

ASSOCIATIONS: *Achillea* 'Coronation Gold', photo 89; *Achillea* 'Moonshine', photo 85; *Heliopsis scabra*, photo 89; *Hemerocallis* cultivars, photo 89; *Lavandula angustifolia* 'Hidcote', photo 85; *Lysimachia punctata*, photo 89; *Veronica spicata* 'Blue Charm', photo 89.

This plant is traditionally associated with *Salvia farinacea* 'Victoria' (1:2). The familiar blend of violet and yellow is considerably softened by the pale yellow *Coreopsis* flowers. The effect is very pleasing and lasts a very long period in summer. The small starry *Coreopsis* flowers contrast strikingly with the violet spires of *Salvia*. Foliar effect is not particularly inspiring, but the floral association is strong enough to eclipse this deficiency.

Siting with *Gaillardia* × *grandiflora* 'Goblin' and *Tagetes* 'Lemon Gem' produces another long-blooming, predominantly yellow association (1:1:1). Since flowers are small in *Tagetes* and *Coreopsis*, their brightness is not overwhelming. *Gaillardia*'s larger bloom contributes touches of red and preserves the group from the dullness risked by combining three daisy-type flower forms. The relatively small scale makes it useful as a focus in limited spaces. Foliage is unexciting. If this disadvantage is troubling, site this group near broad foliaged plants.

Corydalis lutea

Herbaceous perennial, 9–15 × 12 in (25–40 × 30 cm), blooms fragrant, very light yellow, early spring to fall, yellow green foliage, early spring to fall. Does well in average soil with moist to average conditions and part shade or sun. USDA Zones 5–7. Tends to self-sow. Photos 15, 57, 82, 90, 99. See also discussions under *Aquilegia vulgaris*, *Ceratostigma plumbaginoides*, and photo 86.

ASSOCIATIONS: *Achillea* 'Coronation Gold', photo 86; *Alchemilla mollis*, photos 15, 82; *Argyranthemum frutescens*, photo 15; *Brunnera macrophylla*, photo 99; *Campanula portenschlagiana*, photo 82; *Cosmos sulphureus* 'Sunny Red', photo 57; *Helichrysum petiolare*, photo 15; *Hyacinthoides hispanica*, photo 90; *Lavandula angustifolia* 'Munstead', photo 82; *Ruta graveolens*, photo 57; *Salvia* × *superba* 'East Friesland', photo 86.

Association with *Lamiastrum galeobdolon* 'Herman's Pride' and *Viola corsica* (1:1:5) offers a spring repetition of yellow blooms in *Corydalis* and *Lamiastrum* and color contrast with a near-complementary violet. The scale is very small. *Corydalis* flowers from early spring to late fall and the *Viola* for several months in spring. *Lamiastrum* contributes its spiky mid to late spring blooms, and its small variegated leaves brighten the composition until fall.

Cosmos bipinnatus 'Early Sensation'

Generally grown as an annual in all zones, 36–48 × 18 in (90–120 × 45 cm), blooms very light red-violet, summer to fall, dark yellow-green foliage, summer to fall. Does well with average to lean soil with average to less moisture in sun.

ASSOCIATIONS: 'Early Sensation' is a large-scale element. Its flowers are medium-textured while the foliage contributes an indistinct mass with its fine texture. See also discussion under *Phlox maculata* 'Alpha'.

Cosmos bipinnatus 'Pinkie'

Generally grown as an annual in all zones, 36–48 × 18 in (90–120 × 45 cm), blooms pale red to pale red-violet, summer to fall, dark yellow-green foliage, summer to fall. Does well with average to lean soil with average to less moisture in sun. Photo 28.

ASSOCIATIONS: *Astrantia major* and *Cleome spinosa* 'Pink Queen', photo 28.

Cosmos bipinnatus 'Sonata White'

Generally grown as an annual in all zones, 20–24 × 15 in (50–60 × 40 cm), blooms white, summer to fall, dark yellow-green foliage, summer to fall. Does well with average to lean soil with average to less moisture in sun. See also discussion under photo 24.

ASSOCIATIONS: 'Sonata White' can act as a medium-scale element of mixed texture typical of *Cosmos*. Flowers have a medium texture while foliage is fine-textured. See discussion for pairing with *Salvia* 'Lady in Red', photo 24.

Cosmos bipinnatus 'Versailles Tetra'

Generally grown as an annual in all zones, 36–48 × 18 in (90–120 × 45 cm), blooms very dark red-violet, summer to fall, dark yellow-green foliage, summer to fall. Does well with average to lean soil with average to less moisture in sun. Photo 18.

ASSOCIATIONS: *Perilla frutescens*, *Prunus cistena*, *Rosa* 'Prospero', *Knautia macedonica*, photo 18.

Cosmos sulphureus 'Sunny Red'

Generally grown as an annual in all zones, 15–18 × 15 in (40–45 × 40 cm), blooms light orange to light red-orange, late spring to fall, dark yellow-green foliage, late spring to fall. Does well in average to lean soil with average to less moisture in sun. Photos 57, 65. See also discussions under *Cer-*

atostigma plumbaginoides, *Lilium* 'Fireball', and *Monarda didyma* 'Mahogany'.

ASSOCIATIONS: *Corydalis lutea*, photo 57; *Iris pseudacorus*, photo 65; *Lobelia cardinalis*, photo 65; *Rudbeckia* 'Goldsturm', photo 65; *Ruta graveolens*, photo 57; *Salvia* 'Lady in Red', photo 65.

Use with *Achillea millefolium* 'Paprika' and *Tropaeolum majus* 'Gleam Mixture' in a planting ratio of 1:1:2. The resulting combination of red, red-orange, orange, and yellow is arresting, but not overwhelming since the blooms are lightly scattered on the plants. The attractive foliage of the nasturtium (*Tropaeolum*) makes a fine base for its companions. Flowering season is long. The group will benefit visually from a dark green background.

Cosmos sulphureus 'Sunset'

Generally grown as an annual in all zones, 24–36 × 18 in (60–90 × 45 cm), blooms red-orange, late spring to fall, dark yellow-green foliage, late spring to fall. Does well in average to lean soil with average to less moisture in sun.

ASSOCIATIONS: 'Sunset' is a medium-scale plant providing an indistinct mass due to its fine-textured foliage. Flowers are daisy-like and of medium texture. See also discussion under *Campanula carpatica* 'Blue Clips'.

A powerful, near-complementary floral association is created by joining the orange of one 'Sunset', the light violet of three *Campanula carpatica* 'Blue Clips', the pure strong yellow of one *Coreopsis verticillata*, and light blue-violet of two *Veronica* 'Sunny Border Blue' (1:3:1:2). The purer, brighter colors and vibrant warm/cool contrasts in this medium-scale group make a bold, eye-catching statement which fits a warm-hued border. A long flowering season is an added reason to try this assocation.

Cotinus coggygria 'Royal Purple'

Shrub, 10–15 × 5 ft (3.0–4.6 × 1.5 m), blooms pale red-violet, summer, foliage very dark red-violet, mid spring to fall. Does well with average soil and moisture in sun. USDA Zones 5–9. Hard annual pruning maintains the shrub at a scale suitable for smaller mixed plantings.

ASSOCIATIONS: 'Royal Purple' is a large-scale element of mixed textures that can contribute an indistinct mass in the garden landscape. See also discussion under *Salvia officinalis* 'Purpurea'.

As with many dark red-violet foliage plants, this one makes a harmonious background for blooms in adjacent blue-violet and foliage in complementary pale grayish yellow-green hues. This complementary foliage could be supplied by *Artemisia* 'Powis Castle' and *Artemisia schmidtiana* 'Silver Mound', the blue-violet bloom by *Veronica spicata* 'Blue Charm'. Repeating the dark red-violet foliage hue by using *Heuchera* 'Palace Purple' will strengthen the statement. The association is subtle, yet captivating (1:3:3:5:5).

Crambe cordifolia, colewort

Herbaceous perennial, 4–7 × 4 ft (1.2–2.1 × 1.2 m), blooms white, late spring to summer, dark yellow-green foliage, late spring to fall. Plant in average to poor soil, supply average to less moisture, and site in sun or part shade. USDA Zones 6–9. Photo 7.

ASSOCIATIONS: *Asteromoea mongolica, Miscanthus sinensis* 'Zebrinus', *Polygonatum odoratum* 'Variegatum', photo 7.

Crocosmia 'Lucifer'

Bulb, 24–48 × 12 in (60–120 × 30 cm), blooms dark red-orange, summer, dark yellow-green foliage, mid spring to fall. Does well in average soil and moisture in sun or part shade. USDA Zones 5–9. Photo 67. See also discussion under *Coreopsis* 'Sunray'.

ASSOCIATIONS: *Achillea* 'Coronation Gold', photo 67.

Cynoglossum amabile

Biennial frequently grown as an annual, 15–18 × 12 in (40–45 × 30 cm), blooms light blue, late spring to late summer, dark yellow-green foliage, late spring to fall. Does well with average soil and moisture in sun or part shade. Sow seed in fall or early spring where plants will flower their first season. Self-sows.

ASSOCIATIONS: This is a plant of small scale and mixed textures. Flowers are fine-textured and foliage medium-textured. To establish a planting with complementary yellow, use three *Cynoglossum amabile* with one *Achillea* 'Moonshine', adding five *Linum perenne* to strengthen the small quantity of pure light blue present (3:1:5). *Linum* needs to be massed so its delicate flowers are not visually overwhelmed by the stronger *Cynoglossum* foliage texture or the advancing bloom color of *Achillea* corymbs. When *Linum* and *Achillea* start to fade, cut back to about 6 in (15 cm) to encourage a renewed flowering.

Dahlia 'Ellen Houston'

Perennial, often grown as an annual, 36 × 24 in (90 × 60 cm), blooms red, summer to fall, foliage dark yellow-green with red tones, summer to fall. Plant in average to rich soil, ensure average to greater moisture in a sunny location. USDA Zones 9–10. Tubers may be lifted in fall. Store in a frost-free location for replanting in the following spring. Photo 58.

ASSOCIATIONS: *Hemerocallis* 'Sammy Russell' and *Ligularia stenocephala* 'The Rocket', photo 58.

Delphinium belladona

Herbaceous perennial, 36–48 × 36 in (90–120 × 90 cm), blooms blue-violet, late spring, dark yellow-green foliage, mid spring to late summer. Suitable for rich to average soil and moisture in sun. USDA Zones 3–9. A sturdy, hardy *Delphinium* species. Photo 91

ASSOCIATIONS: *Achillea* 'Coronation Gold', *Tanacetum parthenium, Rosa* 'New Dawn', photo 91.

Delphinium 'Charles Gregory Broan'

Herbaceous perennial, 60–84 × 36 in (150–215 × 90 cm), blooms violet, late spring to summer, dark

yellow-green foliage, mid spring to fall. Suitable for rich to average soil and moisture in sun. USDA Zones 3–7. Photo 143.

ASSOCIATIONS: *Lychnis chalcedonica* and *Buphthalmum speciosum*, photo 143.

Surrounding this bold form with *Eryngium amethystinum* and *Perovskia atriplicifolia* provides harmonizing light violet and blue-violet flower hues and contrasting plant forms (1:2:3). Useful for powerful repetitions in a large border or for establishing strong focus in a smaller area.

Delphinium 'Connecticut Yankee'

Herbaceous perennial, 36–48 × 36 in (90–120 × 90 cm), blooms light blue-violet, late spring to summer, dark yellow-green foliage, mid spring to fall. Suitable for rich to average soil and moisture, and sun. USDA Zones 3–7. See also discussion under *Leucanthemum × superbum* 'Alaska'.

ASSOCIATIONS: 'Connecticut Yankee' is of large scale and medium textures. Flowering spires develop above its indistinct mass of foliage. The pale yellow blooms in *Achillea taygetea* and *Lilium* 'French Vanilla' complement its light blue-violet blooms (1:1:2). Foliage textures are varied and bracket the late spring and early summer bloom.

Delphinium grandiflorum 'Blue Butterfly'

Herbaceous perennial, 24 × 15 in (60 × 40 cm), blooms blue-violet, late spring to summer, dark yellow-green foliage, mid spring to summer. Suitable for rich to average soil and moisture in sun. USDA Zones 4–8. Photo 93.

ASSOCIATIONS: *Achillea* 'Moonshine', *Nepeta* 'Six Hills Giant', *Oenothera tetragona*, photo 93.

Dennstaedtia punctiloba, hayscented fern

Fern, 18–36 × 24 in (45–90 × 60 cm), flowers absent, foliage fragrant, dark gray yellow-green, mid spring to fall. Does well in average to lean soil with average moisture and part shade, although it tolerates some sun. USDA Zones 3–8. See also discussion under *Leucojum aestivum* 'Gravetye Giant'.

ASSOCIATIONS: This is a medium-scale element of medium texture. Its neutral, grayish dark green foliage makes a fine contrast for strong colors or to frame distinctive flower forms. Pair with the bright, speckled orange *Lilium lancifolium* (1:2). Used in masses or drifts, they make a long-lived underplanting for shrubs or small trees and extend an informal design in light shade.

Dianthus plumarius, cottage pink, grass pink

Herbaceous perennial, 6–12 × 8 in (15–31 × 20 cm), blooms fragrant, very pale red-violet, late spring, very gray yellow-green foliage, mid spring to fall. Plant in average to poor soil, allow only dry to average conditions, and site in sun. USDA Zones 3–9.

ASSOCIATIONS: For garden design purposes, this is a small-scale element having medium texture in its flowers and fine-textured foliage. Flowers are flat and foliage appears as a spiky mass. See also discussions under *Ageratum houstonianum* 'Blue Puffs' and *Aquilegia alpina*.

Dianthus × allwoodii 'Essex Witch'

Herbaceous perennial, 12–18 × 12 in (30–45 × 30 cm), blooms fragrant, bicolored, dark red-violet and very pale red or white, late spring to summer and scattered bloom in late summer, foliage very gray yellow-green, mid spring to fall. Plant in average to poor soil with dry to average conditions in sun. USDA Zones 4–8. Photos 80, 131. See also discussion under *Leucanthemum × superbum* 'Alaska'.

ASSOCIATIONS: *Aquilegia* 'Heavenly Blue', photo 80; *Dicentra eximia* 'Luxuriant', photo 131; *Elymus arenarius*, photo 131; *Sedum* 'Ruby Glow', photo 131; *Veronica latifolia* 'Crater Lake Blue', photo 80.

Its blue-gray foliage harmonizes well with the blue-green of *Festuca glauca* and both can complement the dark red tones of another grassy form, *Imperata cylindrica* 'Red Baron' (2:1:3). This small-scale foliage composition has a long, effec-

tive season, enlivened in late spring by the appearance of fragrant red-violet and white *Dianthus* blooms.

Dicentra eximia 'Alba'

Herbaceous perennial, 12–18 x 12 in (30–45 × 30 cm), blooms white, mid spring to summer, foliage dark gray yellow-green, spring to fall. Suitable for rich to average soil with moist to average conditions and part shade or sun. USDA Zones 3–9. Photo 4.

ASSOCIATIONS: *Adiantum pedatum* and *Polygonatum biflorum*, photo 4.

Use two of these in light shade with one of the taller *Dicentra spectabilis* 'Alba' to mirror the characteristic white foliage speckles of three *Pulmonaria saccharata* 'Mrs. Moon'. This trio creates a pale variation of the combination illustrated in Photo 34. Add one *Geranium* 'Johnson's Blue' for the strong contribution its violet flowers make to the pure blue *Pulmonaria* flowers even as they fade (2:1:3:1). 'Alba' foliage declines in summer, but the remaining foliages combine pleasingly for the rest of the season.

Dicentra eximia 'Luxuriant'

Herbaceous perennial, 12–18 × 12 in (30–45 × 30 cm), blooms light red to light red-violet, mid spring to fall, foliage dark gray yellow-green, spring to fall. Suitable for rich to average soil, moist to average conditions, and part shade or sun. USDA Zones 3–7. Shear after first bloom to encourage fresh foliage and flowers. Photos 26, 34. See also discussions under *Aquilegia vulgaris*, *Astilbe chinensis* 'Pumila', *Centaurea montana*, and photo 131.

ASSOCIATIONS: *Aquilegia* 'Rose Queen', photo 26; *Cimicifuga racemosa*, photo 26; *Dianthus × allwoodii* 'Essex Witch', photo 131; *Dicentra spectabilis* 'Alba', photo 34; *Elymus arenarius*, photo 131; *Hosta fortunei* 'Marginato-alba', photo 26; *Pulmonaria saccharata* 'Mrs. Moon', photo 34; *Sedum* 'Ruby Glow', photo 131; *Thalictrum aquilegifolium* 'Album', photo 26.

Can make an effortless groundcover planting with *Iberis sempervirens* 'Snowflake' (2:1). Bear in mind that woody *Iberis* can spread to 3 ft (0.9m) over several years. I've seen this pair blooming splendidly under *Cercis canadensis* (eastern redbud) in spring. *Dicentra* flowers play against the tree's rosy bloom color while *Iberis*'s white-flowering mats enliven the scene. *Dicentra* blooms in light shade for many months, even without shearing, slowing only in hot periods.

Red-violet, blue, and blue-violet form a spring connection between this plant, *Mertensia virginica*, and *Muscari armeniacum* (1:1:3). Blooming is slightly successive and as the more transient *Mertensia* dies to the ground, *Dicentra* helps mask its decline. Small white daffodils and red-violet tulips also blend nicely with this trio. Note that by late spring or early summer, *Dicentra* is the only plant in this group to maintain form.

Dicentra spectabilis, common bleeding heart

Herbaceous perennial, 24–36 × 18 in (60–90 × 45 cm), blooms bicolored, pale red and white, mid to late spring, dark yellow-green foliage, mid spring to summer. Suitable for rich to average soil with moist to average conditions and part shade, shade, or morning sun. USDA Zones 2–9. Photo 25. See also discussions under *Brunnera macrophylla* and *Geranium sylvaticum* 'Mayflower'.

ASSOCIATIONS: *Leucojum aestivum* 'Gravetye Giant', photo 25.

Connects easily with *Muscari armeniacum*, *Myosotis sylvatica*, and *Narcissus* 'Mount Hood' (1:3:5:3) for a perennial, medium-scale ephemeral spring display in pink, blue-violet, blue, and white. This quartet is very effective for underplanting the hollow bases of shrubs such as early-blooming *Viburnum*. The foliar decline in *Dicentra* and *Narcissus* is conspicuous, so site where attention can later be diverted. Using a smaller *Narcissus* with finer-textured foliage, such as *Narcissus* 'Thalia', would lessen the impact of foliar decline, but would also reduce scale and visibility.

Dicentra spectabilis 'Alba'

Herbaceous perennial, 24–36 × 18 in (60–90 × 45 cm), blooms white, mid to late spring, dark yellow-green foliage, spring to summer. Suitable for rich to average soil with moist to average conditions and part shade, shade, or morning sun. USDA Zones 2–9. Photos 6, 34, 50. See also discussions under *Brunnera macrophylla*, *Centaurea montana*, *Dicentra eximia* 'Alba'.

ASSOCIATIONS: *Astilbe× arendsii* 'Deutschland', photo 50; *Dicentra eximia* 'Luxuriant', photo 34; *Digitalis purpurea* 'Excelsior', photo 6; *Hosta fortunei* 'Marginato-alba', photo 50; *Iris sibirica*, photo 50; *Lamium maculatum* 'White Nancy', photo 6; *Mertensia virginica*, photo 50; *Phalaris arundinacea* var. *picta*, photo 6; *Pulmonaria saccharata* 'Mrs. Moon', photo 34; *Tiarella cordifolia*, photo 6.

The lily-flowered tulip 'White Triumphator' blooms strikingly with this tall *Dicentra* (1:5). *Dicentra* blooms are small and lightly scattered among the foliage and permit the solid white and distinctive form of this flawless tulip to shine. The triumphant effect of the association is sometimes brief, although *Dicentra* continues blooming for several weeks. In a conspicuous location, provision should be made for other groundcover plants to mask the decline of this pair. See suggestions under photo 78.

Digitalis ambigua
See *D. grandiflora*

Digitalis grandiflora (*D. ambigua*), yellow foxglove

Herbaceous perennial, 24–36 × 18 in (60–90 × 45 cm), blooms pale yellow, late spring to summer, dark yellow-green foliage, late spring to fall. Requires average to rich soil with average to moist conditions and part shade or sun. USDA Zones 3–8. Cut back after flowering for re-bloom in late summer. Flowers and leaves poisonous. Photos 14, 83, 84. See also discussions under *Clematis× jackmanii*, *Kirengeshoma palmata*, *Paeonia lactiflora* 'Miss America', and photo 69.

ASSOCIATIONS: *Argyranthemum frutescens*, photo 14; *Aruncus dioicus*, photo 14; *Geranium* × *magnificum*, photos 83, 84; *Iris pseudacorus*, photos 14, 83, 84; *Nepeta mussinii*, photo 69; *Pulmonaria saccharata* 'Mrs. Moon', photos 83, 84; *Salvia* × *superba* 'May Night', photo 69; *Solidago* 'Cloth of Gold', photo 14; *Weigela florida* 'Variegata', photo 14.

Baptisia australis makes a simple and effective companion when planted in a ratio of 3:1. Pale yellow *Digitalis* and the taller light blue-violet *Baptisia* blooms are near-complementary and combine beautifully, if briefly. Later, the fresh, second-bloom *Digitalis* spires show to advantage against *Baptisia* foliage. Foliage of both plants is grayish yellow-green and their different forms and textures contrast attractively.

Digitalis purpurea 'Excelsior'

Biennial, sometimes naturalizes in shade, 36–60 × 18 in (90–150 × 45 cm), blooms various tints of red-violet and white, late spring to summer, dark yellow-green foliage, late spring to late summer. Requires rich to average soil with moist to average conditions and part shade or sun. USDA Zones 4–9. Flowers and leaves poisonous. Photo 77. See also discussions under *Geranium* 'Johnson's Blue' and photo 6.

ASSOCIATIONS: *Aquilegia alpina*, photo 77; *Dicentra spectabilis* 'Alba', photo 6; *Geranium macrorrhizum*, photo 77; *Lamium maculatum* 'White Nancy', photo 6; *Phalaris arundinacea* var. *picta*, photo 6; *Tiarella cordifolia*, photo 6; *Veronica latifolia* 'Crater Lake Blue', photo 77.

The many tints of red-violet and white commonly found in this foxglove's spires form a fine composition with the complementary dark yellow-green fronds of *Matteuccia struthiopteris*, with the tiny, light yellow blooms of *Primula vulgaris*, and with the yellow and white in *Primula japonica* 'Postford White' (2:1:2:2:). This standard spring association grows well with plenty of moisture in the light shade of deciduous trees.

Plant forms and textures which contrast strikingly with the foxglove's flowering spires include *Hosta fortunei* 'Marginato-alba' and *Polygonatum biflorum* (2:1:3). This trio will also flourish in light shade and depends on the dramatic form contrast between ascending *Digitalis*, slightly arching, smaller *Polygonatum*, and spreading *Hosta* with its distinctive, broad heart-shaped leaves. In moist and shady conditions *Digitalis* will self-seed and continue to produce yearly variations on this otherwise perennial composition.

Digitalis × *mertonensis*, strawberry foxglove

Herbaceous perennial, 30–48 × 18 in (75–120 × 45 cm), blooms pale red and pale red-orange, late spring to summer, foliage very dark yellow-green, mid spring to fall. Requires average to rich soil with average to moist conditions and part shade or sun. Flowers and leaves poisonous. USDA Zones 4–8. Photo 66. See also discussions under *Baptisia australis* and *Ruta graveolens*.

ASSOCIATIONS: *Achillea millefolium* 'Salmon Beauty', *Geranium endressii* 'Wargrave Pink', *Potentilla* 'Tangerine', photo 66.

Doronicum cordatum 'Magnificum'

Herbaceous perennial, 12–24 × 12 in (30–60 × 30 cm), blooms light yellow, mid to late spring, dark yellow-green foliage, mid to late spring. Does well in average soil with average to greater moisture in sun or part shade. Foliar dieback in summer. USDA Zones 4–7.

ASSOCIATIONS: 'Magnificum' is a small-scale plant with medium-textured flowers rising above an indistinct basal mass of broad-textured foliage. *Brunnera macrophylla*'s pure blue blooms offer the opportunity to attempt the blissful complementary color scheme of blue and yellow (1:2). *Doronicum*'s daisy-shaped blooms rise above the blue haze of *Brunnera* flowers in light shade or morning sun. Its summer disappearance is masked by the expansion of *Brunnera*'s broad leaves. Excellent pair for massing around lightly shaded shrubs.

Dryopteris noveboracensis (*Thelypteris noveboracensis*), New York fern

Fern, 12–24 × 24 in (30–60 × 60 cm), flowers absent, foliage very dark gray yellow-green, mid spring to fall. Suited to average to poor soil with average moisture in sun or part shade. USDA Zones 2–8. May be invasive.

ASSOCIATIONS: This is a medium-scale fern of medium texture. Where an informal, naturalistic planting in part shade is desired, its young foliage contrasts well with the form of *Alchemilla mollis* and with the clustered violet blooms of mid-size *Campanula glomerata* 'Joan Elliot' (1:1:3). This grouping is rather ragged for the formal flower border, but is a lovely combination for underplanting trees and shrubs and for a woodland garden.

Echinacea purpurea 'Bright Star'

Herbaceous perennial, 24–36 × 18 in (60–90 × 45 cm), blooms very light red-violet, mid to late summer, dark yellow-green foliage, summer to fall. Does well in average soil and moisture in sun. USDA Zones 3–8. Photos 73, 147. See also discussions under *Allium sphaerocephalon*, *Anemone vitifolia* 'Robustissima', *Foeniculum vulgare* 'Purpureum', *Thalictrum rochebrunianum*, and *Veronica* 'Sunny Border Blue'.

ASSOCIATIONS: *Anemone vitifolia* 'Robustissima', photo 73; *Aster frikartii* 'Mönch', photo 73; *Heliopsis scabra*, photo 147; *Rudbeckia* 'Goldsturm', photo 147; *Sedum* 'Autumn Joy', photo 73.

Harmonious adjacent hues and coincidental bloom suggest frequent association with *Sedum* 'Autumn Joy'. The excellent variation in flower form between the two is enhanced by adding the tinted red-violet, grassy tufts of pendulous *Pennisetum alopecuroides*. Including three *Stachys byzantina* as a foreground base for *Sedum*'s rather bare stems earlier in the season will ensure a pleasing connection (1:1:1:3).

It can also be linked effortlessly with the red-violet flower spikes of *Liatris spicata* 'Kobold', lacy

clusters of annual *Monarda didyma* 'Violet Queen', and loose, pale violet *Perovskia atriplicifolia* wands (1:2:2:2). The color harmony is quite subtle. Scale is medium to large with undistinguished foliage textures.

Echinops 'Taplow Blue'

Herbaceous perennial, 24–48 × 24 in (60–120 × 60 cm), blooms pale blue-violet, late spring to late summer, dark yellow-green foliage, late spring to fall. Does well in average soil and moisture in sun. USDA Zones 3–8. Photo 95. See also discussions under *Agastache foeniculum*, *Anaphalis margaritacea*, *Artemisia* 'Powis Castle', and *Eryngium amethystinum*.

ASSOCIATIONS: *Achillea* 'Moonshine', *Jasminum officinale*, *Lavandula angustifolia* 'Hidcote', photo 95.

Its pale blue-violet globes make a fine duo with pale yellow *Hemerocallis lilioasphodelus* flowers (1:1). Adding *Malva alcea* 'Fastigiata', with its delicate, pinkish flower clusters, expands the pair to a pleasing pastel-tinted grouping with distinctively attractive flower forms and leaf textures. Since *Malva* contributes quite a strong vertical element, double the quantities of 'Taplow Blue' (2:1:1). Sun or very light shade will suit this association.

Elymus arenarius (*Leymus arenarius*) lyme grass.

Grass, 18–24 × 15 in (45–60 × 40 cm), seedheads insignificant, foliage very pale blue-green, late spring to fall. Plant in poor to average soil with dry to average conditions in sun. USDA Zones 3–8. Can be invasive in richer soil and planting in a container is often recommended to restrain its vigor. Photos 55, 130. See also discussions under *Achillea millefolium* 'Weser River Sandstone', *Anaphalis triplinervis* 'Summer Snow', *Osteospermum* 'Salmon Queen', and photo texts 131, 132, and 133.

ASSOCIATIONS: *Alstroemeria* Ligtu Hybrids, photo 132; *Berberis thunbergii* 'Atropurpurea', photo 133; *Berberis thunbergii* 'Atropurpurea Nana', photo

130; *Dianthus* × *allwoodii* 'Essex Witch', photo 131; *Dicentra eximia* 'Luxuriant', photo 131; *Hemerocallis* 'Ed Murray', photo 133; *Heuchera* 'Palace Purple', photo 130; *Hosta montana* 'Aureomarginata', photo 55; *Hosta sieboldiana*, photo 133; *Macleaya microcarpa*, photo 132; *Polystichum setiferum* 'Divisilobum', photo 132; *Sedum* 'Ruby Glow', photo 131.

Endymion hispanicus

See *Hyacinthoides hispanica*

Epimedium × versicolor 'Sulphureum'

Herbaceous perennial, 12 × 12 in (30 × 30 cm), blooms very pale yellow, spring, dark yellow-green foliage, mid spring to fall. Does well in average soil with average to dry conditions, in shade or part shade. USDA Zones 5–8. Photo 8. See also discussion under photo 25.

ASSOCIATIONS: *Gladiolus callianthus, Hedera helix, Tulipa* 'White Triumphator', photo 8.

Myosotis sylvatica and *Muscari armeniacum* (3:5:3) offer another spring variation on the popular pale yellow and blue or blue-violet complementary association. Overlapping bloom shows the tiny pale yellow *Epimedium* flowers to advantage against the similarly minute *Myosotis* blooms and bolder *Muscari* spikes. The excellent, heart-shaped *Epimedium* foliage persists all summer. Later flowering bulbs may be added to this composition.

A larger-scale, pleasing spring association of light and pale yellow blooms is produced when this *Epimedium* mingles with *Lamiastrum galeobdolon* 'Herman's Pride' in the foreground and *Stylophorum diphyllum* in background (1:2:1). Flowering takes place from early spring to late spring. Either of the preceding compositions performs well in light shade or a north or east exposure.

Erigeron karvinskianus (E. mucronatus), Mexican daisy

Half-hardy perennial or annual, 9–18 × 12 in (25–45 × 30 cm), blooms pale red-violet and white, summer to fall, dark yellow-green foliage, mid spring to fall. Does well in average soil with dry to average conditions in sun or part shade. Perennial in USDA Zones 9–10. Photo 33.

ASSOCIATIONS: *Lavandula stoechas* and *Rosa* 'Chaucer', photo 33.

Erigeron mucronatus

See *E. karvinskianus*

Eryngium amethystinum

Herbaceous perennial, 24–30 × 18 in (60–75 × 45 cm), blooms pale blue-violet, mid to late summer, dark yellow-green foliage, late spring to fall. Plant in average to poor soil with average to dry conditions and sun. USDA Zones 2–8. Species typically confused in the trade. Photo 44. See also comments under *Cerastium tomentosum, Delphinium* 'Charles Gregory Broan', and *Lobelia erinus* 'Cambridge Blue'.

ASSOCIATIONS: *Liatris spicata, Physostegia virginiana* 'Summer Snow', *Platycodon grandiflorus*, photo 44.

Delicate, misty hues, brightened with white and an array of diffuse forms are emphasized when *Eryngium amethystinum* is associated with one *Echinops* 'Taplow Blue', one *Lavandula angustifolia* 'Hidcote', two *Lavandula stoechas*, one *Phlox maculata* 'Miss Lingard', and three *Tanacetum parthenium* (1:1:1:2:1:3). Useful for rock, border, patio, or wall plantings in full sun. Such delicate hues and forms do not compete successfully with strong warm hues and much bolder forms in the same view.

Eryngium giganteum, giant sea holly

Biennial, 36–48 × 36 in (90–120 × 90 cm), blooms pale blue-violet, mid to late summer, foliage pale gray yellow-green, late spring to fall. Prefers average to poor soil with average to dry conditions and sun. USDA Zones 4–8. Photo 31.

ASSOCIATIONS: *Agastache foeniculum* and *Malva moschata*, photo 31.

Erythronium 'Pagoda'

Bulb, 12–18 × 6 in (30–45 × 15 cm), blooms pale yellow, mid spring, foliage dark-yellow green, mottled, mid to late spring. Plant in average to rich soil with average to moist conditions and site in part shade or sun. USDA Zones 3–8. See also discussion under *Vinca minor*.

ASSOCIATIONS: 'Pagoda' can be a small-scale element offering a broad-textured foliage mass at its base and medium-textured flowers. Its bell-like flowers develop on upstanding stems and give a vertical emphasis. It combines with *Podophyllum peltatum* and *Stylophorum diphyllum* to make a fine successive association for light shade in spring (3:2:1). Its captivating pale yellow blooms are large enough to compete visually with the broad, decorative *Podophyllum* leaves. *Stylophorum* contributes a larger scale and its own scattered and broader light yellow blooms. Foliage persists in contrasting forms for some months. The composition's scale is small to medium and a single group demands an easily viewed location. Makes a fine association for early flowering shrubs, such as *Corylopsis pauciflora*.

Grouping with *Brunnera macrophylla* offers a small-scale, simple complementary association of pale yellow and light blue (3:1). *Brunnera*'s expanding foliage can cover *Erythronium*'s decline. Useful in the woodland garden, massed at the base of spring-flowering shrubs, or placed at the edge of a lightly-shaded patio.

Eschscholzia californica, California poppy

Half-hardy perennial or annual, 8–18 × 12 in (20–45 × 30 cm), blooms light yellow-orange and pale yellow, mid spring to late summer, gray yellow-green foliage, mid spring to fall. Prefers poor to average soil with dry to average conditions in sun. USDA Zones 8–10. Annual in colder zones, but self-seeds readily. However, pinch faded flowers to maintain current season's vigor. Photo 127.

ASSOCIATIONS: *Nepeta mussinii*, photo 127.

Blue *Linum perenne* blooms are a close complement for the California poppy's light yellow and yellow-orange flowers (1:3) and make a small-scale, ambrosial display. Since these are among my favorite bloom colors, I find this association enchanting. The grayed yellow-green foliages harmonize well, but are not an outstanding foliage association.

Eupatorium coelestinum, hardy ageratum

Herbaceous perennial, 24–36 × 18 in (60–90 × 45 cm), blooms very light violet, late summer to fall, dark yellow-green foliage, summer to fall. Does well in average soil with average to greater moisture in sun or part shade. USDA Zones 6–10. See also discussions under *Anemone hupehensis* 'September Charm', *Aster frikartii* 'Mönch', and *Caryopteris* × *clandonensis* 'Heavenly Blue'.

ASSOCIATIONS: Hardy ageratum contributes a medium to large scale and medium textures. Flowers are clustered above a mass of indistinct foliage. Its late light violet blooms harmonize with a similar floral hue in *Aster frikartii* 'Mönch', a darker violet in *Heliotropium* 'Marine', and light-blue violet in *Veronica* 'Sunny Border Blue' (2:2:2:1). The annual *Heliotropium* and perennial *Veronica* begin blooming months earlier and lead in to their companions.

Euphorbia epithymoides
See *E. polychroma*

Euphorbia polychroma (*E. epithymoides*), cushion spurge

Herbaceous perennial, 12–18 × 18 in (30–45 × 45 cm), blooms yellow, mid to late spring, dark yellow-green foliage, mid spring to fall. Does well in average soil with dry to average conditions in sun or part shade. USDA Zones 4–8. Photo 101.

ASSOCIATIONS: *Brunnera macrophylla* and *Hemerocallis* cultivars, photo 101.

A planting with a yellow-flowering *Hemerocallis* cultivar, *Lamiastrum galeobdolon* 'Herman's Pride', and *Lilium* 'Fireball' produces a successively flowering association for sun or light shade (1:1: 1:2). Attractive foliage textures and forms sustain the group throughout the growing season. The yellow daylily continues the color theme begun with *Euphorbia* and *Lamiastrum*. The red *Lilium* brings hint of summer fire, but a yellow or orange lily could substitute for a slightly less fiery display.

Festuca glauca (*F. ovina* 'Glauca'), blue fescue

Grass, 9–12 × 12 in (20–30 × 30 cm), seedheads pale yellow-orange, summer, pale blue-green foliage, early spring to fall. Suitable for average soil with average to dry conditions in sun. USDA Zones 4–9. May need division every two or three years. Clip flowering seed heads to control spread. Cut back to encourage fresh foliage. See also discussions under *Dianthus* × *allwoodii* 'Essex Witch' and *Stachys byzantina*.

ASSOCIATIONS: Blue fescue is a small-scale plant with vertical flowers topping its spiky mound of foliage. Both flowers and foliage are fine-textured. Its pale foliage hue associates well with similar pastels, including the late summer blooms of *Allium cernuum* and *Limonium latifolium* (1:1:1). Their different flower and foliage forms are very striking, and unified by their gentle pallor. This small-scale association needs sun or very light shade and careful siting to display its receding colors to advantage.

Festuca ovina 'Glauca'
See *F. glauca*

Filipendula hexapetala
See *F. vulgaris*

Filipendula vulgaris (*F. hexapetala*), dropwort

Herbaceous perennial, 24–36 × 24 in (60–90 × 60 cm), blooms whitish yellow, mid to late summer, foliage, very dark yellow-green, mid spring to fall. Does well in average soil with moist to average conditions in sun or part shade. USDA Zones 3–8.

ASSOCIATIONS: Dropwort matures to become a medium- to large-scale garden element. Both flowers and foliage are medium-textured and form an indistinct mass. Associate two of these with three *Lilium regale*, one *Macleaya microcarpa*, two *Malva sylvestris* 'Mauritiana', two *Monarda didyma* 'Croftway Pink', and two *Phlox maculata* 'Miss Lingard' (2:3:1:2:2:2) to produce a large-scale composition in near-white, light red-orange, and pale and dark red-violet. *Malva* flowers repeat the dark red hue present in the lily buds. Avoid too strong a concentration of *Phlox*'s deadening white flower clusters by siting the two separately. Much of the foliage is undistinguished, but large bold *Macleaya* leaves at the rear of the composition structure the group.

Less complicated associations which benefit from dropwort's long blooming season and dark foliage color could be made with a blend with any light or pale, cool-hued summer-blooming plants. For instance, *Eryngium giganteum* or *Eryngium amethystinum* and *Argyranthemum* 'Mary Wootton' (2:1:2).

Foeniculum vulgare 'Purpureum'

Perennial, often grown as an annual, 36–60 × 18 in (90–150 × 45 cm), blooms pale yellow-green, mid to late summer, foliage pale gray yellow-green with deep red tints, late spring to fall. Does well in average soil and moisture in sun. USDA Zones 5–9. See also discussions under *Allium giganteum* and *Salvia officinalis* 'Purpurea'.

ASSOCIATIONS: 'Purpureum' is a large-scale, fine-textured plant. Its flat-topped, umbellate flowers mingle amid its nebulous foliage. Use it to supply a delicate, tall element as a contrast to the broad, light red-violet, daisy-type flowers of *Echinacea purpurea* 'Bright Star' and low broad foliage of *Heuchera* 'Palace Purple' (1:3:2). *Heuchera*'s dark red leaves echo tints in *Foeniculum*.

Gaillardia × *grandiflora* 'Goblin'

Generally grown as an annual in all zones, 9–12 × 12 in (25–30 × 30 cm), blooms red, red-orange, and yellow, late spring to fall, dark yellow-green foliage, late spring to fall. Does well in average soil and moisture in sun. USDA Zones 2–10. See also discussions under *Asclepias tuberosa* 'Gay Butterflies' and *Coreopsis verticillata* 'Moonbeam'.

ASSOCIATIONS: 'Goblin' can contribute a small-scale, medium-textured element. Its flat blooms rise above an indistinct foliage mound. Use two of these in a complex, though small-scale grouping with one *Asclepias tuberosa* 'Gay Butterflies', one *Coreopsis verticillata*, one *Hemerocallis* cultivar, and five *Salvia farinacea* 'Victoria' (2:1:1:1:5). Enhanced by summer's bright reds and oranges in the *Gaillardia*, this predominantly violet and yellow grouping is rather eye-catching. Both flower and foliage forms are varied yet are unified by the dominant mass of violet *Salvia*.

Galium odoratum (*Asperula odorata*), sweet woodruff

Herbaceous perennial, 6–12 × 12 in (15–30 × 30 cm), blooms white, sweet-smelling, mid to late spring, foliage fragrant, very dark yellow-green, mid spring to fall. Does best with average soil and moisture in shade or part shade. USDA Zones 4–8. May be considered invasive if planted in rich soil under moist conditions. Freely self-sows. Photo 3. See also discussions under *Aquilegia* 'Olympia', *Convallaria majalis*, and *Phlox divaricata*.

ASSOCIATIONS: *Alchemilla mollis* and *Hosta fortunei* 'Marginato-alba', photo 3.

Blooms coincide with those of *Primula japonica* 'Postford White' to make a showy groundcover with yellow-centered white *Primula* blooms rising above mats of white *Galium* flowers (2:1). Flowering lasts several weeks. Later, its fine-textured foliage contrasts unobtrusively with *Primula*'s broad leaves. Large groups underplanting shrubs in light shade make the best use of this pairing.

Geranium 'Anne Folkard'.

Herbaceous perennial, 18–24 × 24 in (45–60 × 60 cm), blooms red-violet with dark red-violet cen-

ters, late spring to summer, dark yellow-green foliage, late spring to fall. Plant in average to rich soil, supply average moisture, and site in part shade or sun. USDA Zones 5–8. Photo 146.

ASSOCIATIONS: *Achillea taygetea* and *Lysimachia punctata*, photo 146.

Geranium armenum
See *G. psilostemon*

Geranium endressii 'Wargrave Pink'

Herbaceous perennial, 12–24 × 24 in (30–60 × 60 cm), blooms pale red, late spring to summer, dark yellow-green foliage, mid spring to fall. Does well in average soil with average to dry conditions in sun or part shade. USDA Zones 4–8. Photos 19, 76, 144. See also discussions under *Achillea* 'Moonshine', *Aquilegia alpina*, *Heliotropium* 'Marine', *Tiarella cordifolia*, and photo 66.

ASSOCIATIONS: *Alchemilla mollis*, photo 144; *Achillea millefolium* 'Salmon Beauty', photo 66; *Amsonia tabernaemontana*, photo 76; *Aquilegia* 'McKana Giants', photo 144; *Astilbe* × *arendsii* 'Cattleya', photo 19; *Brunnera macrophylla*, photo 76; *Campanula glomerata* 'Joan Elliot', photo 144; *Digitalis* × *mertonensis*, photo 66; *Geranium* 'Johnson's Blue', photo 144; *Iris sibirica*, photo 76; *Potentilla* 'Tangerine', photo 66.

Associates smoothly with *Achillea* 'Moonshine', *Iris kaempferi*, and *Salvia* × *superba* 'East Friesland' (1:2:2:2). Small, pale yellow *Achillea* blooms mix well with its pastel tints and with the intense, near-complementary colors in medium-sized, violet-spiked *Salvia* × *superba* 'East Friesland'. Almost any color *Iris kaempferi* cultivar would enhance the grouping, or even a bi-color, such as *Iris kaempferi* 'Nikko'.

Geranium 'Johnson's Blue'

Herbaceous perennial, 12–24 × 24 in (30–60 × 60 cm), blooms light violet, late spring, dark yellow-green foliage, mid spring to fall. Does well in average soil with average to less moisture in sun or part shade. USDA Zones 4–8. See also discussions under *Baptisia australis, Centranthus ruber, Clematis* × *jackmanii, Dicentra eximia* 'Alba', and photos 45, 108, and 144.

ASSOCIATIONS: 'Johnson's Blue' is of medium scale within our garden design considerations. Its flower texture is medium, its foliage is fine-textured, and together they contribute an indistinct form. Also see text references relating it to *Alchemilla mollis,* photos 108 and 144, *Aquilegia* 'McKana Giants' or *Aquilegia vulgaris, Campanula glomerata* 'Joan Elliot', and *Geranium endressii* 'Wargrave Pink', photo 144, *Penstemon* 'Rose Elf', photo 108, and *Salvia haematodes* and *Stachys byzantina,* photo 45.

Blooms harmonize delightfully with the light red flowers developing on *Penstemon* 'Rose Elf' and the violet-flowered *Salvia* × *superba* 'East Friesland' (1:2:3). Its flat, scattered blossoms enhance the *Salvia* spires and bright *Penstemon* clusters. When flowering is finished, the *Geranium* foliage remains outstanding and partially compensates for the weaker foliage forms of its companions.

A larger association of violet hues includes a foreground planting of five *Allium karataviense,* two midground *Geranium* 'Johnson's Blue', and one tall, blue-violet *Baptisia australis* and three *Digitalis purpurea* 'Excelsior' placed behind (2:5:1:3). Blooming persists for several weeks and *Geranium, Digitalis,* and *Baptisia* foliages combine well for much of the summer.

Geranium macrorrhizum, bigroot geranium

Herbaceous perennial, 12–18 × 18 in (30–45 × 45 cm), blooms light red-violet, mid to late spring, foliage fragrant, dark green with red tones, mid spring to fall. Does well in average soil with average to less moisture in sun or part shade. USDA Zones 3–8. Photo 77. See also discussions under *Astilbe* × *arendsii* 'Deutschland' and *Trillium grandiflorum.*

ASSOCIATIONS: *Aquilegia alpina, Digitalis purpurea* 'Excelsior', *Veronica latifolia* 'Crater Lake Blue', photo 77.

Associates effortlessly with *Astilbe* × *arendsii* 'Deutschland' in light shade (1:2). Such a compact unit fits the smaller, light-shade garden, yet this duo easily allows for planting in large drifts under deciduous trees or shrubs. Flowering is successive, with some overlap, but throughout the growing season there is a pleasing contrast between the broad, red-tinted *Geranium* leaves and finer, feathery *Astilbe* foliage.

Geranium psilostemon (G. armenum)

Herbaceous perennial, 24–48 × 24 in (60–120 × 60 cm), blooms red-violet with dark red-violet centers, late spring to summer, dark yellow-green foliage, mid spring to fall. Suitable for rich to average soil with moist to average conditions in sun or part shade. USDA Zones 5–8. Photos 136, 138.

ASSOCIATIONS: *Beta vulgaris* subsp. *cicla,* photo 136; *Knautia macedonica,* photo 136; *Kniphofia* 'Atlanta', photo 138; *Malva sylvestris* 'Mauritiana', photo 136; *Papaver somniferum,* photo 138; *Rosa,* photo 136; *Salvia officinalis* 'Purpurea', photo 136.

A fetching trio is possible by using the blue-violet spikes in *Veronica spicata* 'Blue Fox' to harmonize with the dark red-violet in the bi-toned geranium flowers, and the light red-violet plumes of *Astilbe* × *arendsii* 'Cattleya' to introduce a different bloom form and lighter hue. Use three 'Blue Fox' to balance the red-violet (1:3:1). Flowering is sustained longer in light shade and foliage forms are distinctive for many months.

Geranium sanguineum, bloody cranesbill

Herbaceous perennial, 12 × 18 in (30 × 45 cm), blooms dark red-violet, mid spring to summer, dark yellow-green foliage, mid spring to fall. Does well in average soil and moisture in sun or part shade. USDA Zones 3–8. See also discussion under *Alchemilla mollis.*

ASSOCIATIONS: This is a small-scale geranium with medium-textured flowers and fine-textured foliage. Its flowers blend with the near-adjacent hues in light red *Centranthus ruber* and blue-violet

Nepeta mussinii blooms (1:2:1). The soft gray quality in *Centranthus ruber* blooms is nicely appreciated when seen with the grayed foliage of *Nepeta mussinii*. *Geranium*'s red-violet flower hue also does much to enliven the recessive blue-violet in *Nepeta* flowers. This smaller-scale composition lacks the dynamism of groups with strongly ascending forms, but its compact forms and imprecise tints suit it to many quiet, cool-hued garden schemes.

Geranium sanguineum 'Album'

Herbaceous perennial, 12–24 × 24 in (30–60 × 60 cm), blooms white, mid to late spring, dark yellow-green foliage, mid spring to fall. Does well in average soil and moisture in sun or part shade. USDA Zones 3–8. Photo 2. See also discussions under *Centaurea montana*, *Iris sibirica* 'White Swirl', and *Myrrhis odorata*.

ASSOCIATIONS: *Iris sibirica* 'White Swirl' and *Paeonia lactiflora* 'Festiva Maxima', photo 2.

An uncommon pastel association can be produced with *Stachys byzantina* and *Helictotrichon sempervirens* (1:2:1). During the geranium's late-spring blooming, its white blossoms harmonize easily with the soft, silvery gray *Stachys* foliage and stiff, pale blue-green, grassy *Helictotrichon* foliage. After blooming, the geranium's attractive dark gray-green foliage blends subtly with its companions.

Geranium sanguineum var. lancastriense

See *G. s.* var. *striatum*

Geranium sanguineum var. striatum

(*G. s.* var. *lancastriense*)

Herbaceous perennial, 12 × 18 in (30 × 45 cm), blooms very pale red-violet with light red-violet stripes, mid spring to summer, dark yellow-green foliage, late spring to fall. Does well in average soil and moisture in sun or part shade. USDA Zones 3–8. Photo 115. See also discussions under *Geranium sanguineum* and *Leucanthemum* × *superbum* 'Alaska'.

ASSOCIATIONS: *Allium christophii* and *Astilbe* × *arendsii* 'Bridal Veil', photo 115.

Geranium sylvaticum 'Mayflower'

Herbaceous perennial, 24 × 24 in (60 × 60 cm), blooms very light red-violet with white center, mid to late spring, dark yellow-green foliage, mid spring to fall. Suitable for rich to average soil with moist to average conditions in sun or part shade. USDA Zones 4–8. Photo 38. See also discussion under *Cerastium tomentosum*.

ASSOCIATIONS: *Nepeta mussinii* 'White Wonder' and *Viola* 'Baby Lucia', photo 38.

For light shade, *Dicentra spectabilis*'s white and light red-violet flowers harmonize well with this geranium. As the *Dicentra* blooms fade, a differing foliage form and another harmonious color can be contributed by a violet-flowered *Iris sibirica* cultivar (1:1:3).

Geranium × magnificum, showy geranium

Herbaceous perennial, 18–24 × 24 in (45–60 × 60 cm), blooms light violet, late spring to summer, dark yellow-green foliage, mid spring to fall. Does well in average soil with average to less moisture and part shade or sun. USDA Zones 4–8. Photos 83, 84. See also discussion following photo 108.

ASSOCIATIONS: *Alchemilla mollis*, photo 108; *Digitalis grandiflora*, photos 83, 84; *Geranium* 'Johnson's Blue', photo 108; *Iris pseudacorus*, photos 83, 84; *Penstemon* 'Rose Elf', photo 108; *Pulmonaria saccharata* 'Mrs. Moon', photos 83, 84.

A simple, stunning pairing with *Stachys byzantina* (1:3) illustrates the affinity of light violet with gray, provided here by foliage. Even when the violet and gray affinity fades out, the geranium's exceptional foliage blends unobtrusively with its brighter companion.

Geum × borisii

Herbaceous perennial, 9–12 × 12 in (25–30 × 30 cm), blooms red-orange, mid to late spring, dark yellow-green foliage, mid spring to summer. Does well in average soil with average to greater moisture in sun or part shade. USDA Zones 3–7. See also discussion under *Aurinia saxatilis*.

ASSOCIATIONS: This plant can be used as a small-scale element of medium textures. Its small, brilliant red-orange blooms make a fine complementary contrast for the bluish green tones of broad *Hosta × tardiana* 'Halcyon' leaves in late spring (1:2). Light shade with good moisture suits both plants and intensifies the important grayish quality of the hosta's foliage. The geum's bright blooms are sufficiently random and do not overwhelm the hosta's contribution to the association. Foliage continues in a pleasing association of different scales and textures once bloom is finished.

Gladiolus callianthus (*Acidanthera bicolor*), Abyssinian gladiolus, peacock orchid

Bulb, 24–36 × 6 in (60–90 × 15 cm), blooms fragrant, white with very deep red throat, mid to late summer, foliage dark yellow-green, mid to late summer. Does well in average soil and moisture in sun or part shade. USDA Zones 8–10. See also discussions under photos 8 and 17.

ASSOCIATIONS: As a design element the peacock orchid's scale is medium to large and its texture medium, with flat flowers and vertical foliage. Suggested associations are given in the photo texts for *Cleome spinosa* 'Helen Campbell', photo 17; *Epimedium × versicolor* 'Sulphureum', photo 8; *Hedera helix*, photo 8; *Nicotiana sylvestris*, photo 17; *Tagetes* 'Primrose Lady', photo 17; *Tulipa* 'White Triumphator', photo 8; *Zinnia* 'Dreamland Ivory', and photo 17.

A subtle dark red and white combination can be gained by using *Cleome spinosa* 'Helen Campbell' and *Monarda* 'Adam' (6:2:1). The dark red of *Monarda* blooms repeats in the fragrant red and white flowers of *Gladiolus*. Subtle fragrance is also contributed by *Monarda* and *Cleome*. *Gladiolus* and *Cleome* will continue to bloom together for some weeks after *Monarda*.

Gomphrena globosa 'Lavender Lady'

Generally grown as an annual in all zones, 18–24 × 18 in (45–60 × 45 cm), blooms very light red-violet, summer to fall, dark yellow-green foliage, summer to fall. Does well in average soil with average to less moisture in sun. Photos 35, 112, 140. See also discussions under *Allium tuberosum* and *Artemisia* 'Powis Castle'.

ASSOCIATIONS: *Allium tuberosum*, photo 35; *Anemone vitifolia* 'Robustissima', photo 35; *Berberis thunbergii* 'Atropurpurea', photo 35; *Gomphrena globosa* 'Rosy', photo 140; *Helichrysum petiolare*, photo 112; *Nicotiana alata* 'Lime Green', photo 140; *Nicotiana alata* 'Nicki Pink', photo 140; *Salvia farinacea* 'Victoria', photos 112, 140; *Sedum* 'Vera Jameson', photo 35.

Verbena 'Amor Light Pink' contributes to an appealing, long-blooming arrangement of pastel red-violet and blue-violet annuals when sited with three *Gomphrena globosa* 'Lavender Lady' in the rear and three *Ageratum houstonianum* 'Blue Horizon' in the midground (3:2:3).

Gomphrena globosa 'Pomponette White'

Generally grown as an annual in all zones, 12 × 12 in (30 × 30 cm), blooms white, summer to fall, dark yellow-green foliage, summer to fall. Does well in average soil with average or less moisture in sun.

ASSOCIATIONS: For design purposes, 'Pomponette White' is of small scale and medium textures. Its spherical flowers top a rather indistinct foliage mass. See also comments under *Ageratum houstonianum* 'Blue Puffs' and *Allium tuberosum*.

Gomphrena globosa 'Rosy'

Generally grown as an annual in all zones, 8–12 × 12 in (20–30 × 30 cm), blooms pale red-violet, summer to fall, dark yellow-green foliage, summer to fall. Plant in average soil with average or less moisture in sun. Photos 111, 140.

ASSOCIATIONS: *Gomphrena globosa* 'Lavender Lady, *Nicotiana alata* 'Lime Green, *Nicotiana alata*

'Nicki Pink, and *Salvia farinacea* 'Victoria', photo 140; *Stachys byzantina*, photo 111.

Gomphrena globosa 'Strawberry Fields'

Generally grown as an annual in all zones, 12–24 × 12 in (30–60 × 30 cm), blooms very dark red-orange, summer to fall, dark yellow-green foliage, late spring to fall. Does well in average soil with average or less moisture in sun. Photo 20. See also comments under *Coreopsis verticillata*, *Melampodium paludosum* 'Medallion', *Solidago* 'Crown of Rays', and photo 64.

ASSOCIATIONS: *Coreopsis* 'Sunray' and *Celosia cristata* 'Sparkler Mix', photo 64; *Perilla frutescens* and *Zinnia elegans* 'Red Sun', photo 20.

In New York City's Central Park I've often seen a striking association of hues. Red-orange, dark violet, yellow-green, and red-violet create a garden composition of adjacent and complementary hues which is not for those of a nervous disposition. *Gomphrena* supplies the red-orange in its globular flowers, *Heliotropium* 'Marine' the dark violet, *Nicotiana alata* 'Lime Green' the yellow-green, and *Perilla frutescens* foliage contributes a dark red-violet. Use a ratio of 1:2:1:2 for maximum effect. Note that transitions to nearby compositions will be challenging.

Gunnera brasiliensis

See *G. manicata*

Gunnera manicata (*G. brasiliensis*)

Herbaceous perennial, 6–7× 6 ft (1.8–2.1 × 1.8 m), blooms yellow-green, summer, very deep yellow-green foliage, mid spring to fall. Does well in average soil and moist conditions in sun or part shade. USDA Zones 7–10. Photo 12.

ASSOCIATIONS: *Iris pseudacorus*, *Ligularia dentata* 'Desdemona', *Ligularia stenocephala* 'The Rocket', photo 12.

Hakonechloa macra 'Aureola'

Japanese forest grass

Grass, 12–18 × 15 in (30–45 × 40 cm), seedheads dark red-orange, summer, foliage pale yellow-green, mid spring to summer. Suitable for rich to average soil with average or greater moisture in part shade or shade. USDA Zones 5–8. Photo 54.

ASSOCIATIONS: *Sanguinaria canadensis*, photo 54.

Hedera helix, English ivy

Vine, 72 in (1.8 m), blooms white, late spring, foliage very dark gray yellow-green, evergreen. Does well in average soil with average or greater moisture and part shade or morning sun. USDA Zones 5–8. Photo 8.

ASSOCIATIONS: *Epimedium* × *versicolor* 'Sulphureum, *Gladiolus callianthus*, and *Tulipa* 'White Triumphator', photo 8.

Helenium autumnale 'Brilliant'

Herbaceous perennial, 36 × 18 in (90 × 45 cm), blooms very dark red-orange, late summer to fall, dark yellow-green foliage, summer to fall. Does well in average soil with moist to average conditions in sun. USDA Zones 3–8. Photo 60. See also discussion under *Coreopsis* 'Sunray'.

ASSOCIATIONS: *Helenium autumnale* 'Riverton', *Solidago* 'Crown of Rays', *Zinnia elegans* 'Red Sun', photo 60.

Helenium autumnale 'Riverton'

Herbaceous perennial, 36–48 × 18 in (90–120 × 45 cm), blooms yellow with dark red center, late summer to fall, dark yellow-green foliage, summer to fall. Does well in average soil with moist to average conditions in sun. USDA Zones 3–8. Photo 60.

ASSOCIATIONS: *Helenium autumnale* 'Brilliant', *Solidago* 'Crown of Rays', *Zinnia elegans* 'Red Sun', photo 60.

Helichrysum angustifolium, curry plant

Annual or half-hardy perennial, 12–18 × 12 in (30–45 × 30 cm), blooms yellow, summer, foliage very gray yellow-green, late spring to fall. Does well in average soil with less than average moisture in sun. USDA Zones 8–10. Photo 5.

ASSOCIATIONS: *Buddleja fallowiana* 'Lochinch', *Convolvulus cneorum*, *Onopordum acanthium*, *Potentilla flamea*, *Stachys byzantina*, photo 5.

Helichrysum petiolare (*H. petiolatum*), licorice plant

Half-hardy perennial or annual, 12–24 × 24 in (30–60 × 60 cm), blooms occasional, pale yellow, summer, foliage very gray yellow-green, mid spring to fall. Does well in average soil and moisture in sun. USDA Zones 7–9. Photos 15, 71, 112. See also discussion under *Argyranthemum* 'Mary Wootton'.

ASSOCIATIONS: *Alchemilla mollis*, photo 15; *Anemone hupehensis* 'September Charm', photo 71; *Argyranthemum frutescens*, photo 15; *Campanula portenschlagiana*, photo 71; *Corydalis lutea*, photo 15; *Gomphrena globosa* 'Lavender Lady', photo 112; *Salvia farinacea* 'Victoria', photo 112; *Verbena* 'Amethyst', photo 71.

The licorice plant's small, rounded, light gray leaves contrast beautifully with the complementary hue in light blue-violet *Ageratum houstonianum* 'Blue Horizon' blooms. Both in turn harmonize and contrast with the darker violet spires of *Salvia farinacea* 'Victoria' (1:1:2). In combination, the three provide a subtle, long-blooming, predominantly cool-hued composition.

Helichrysum petiolatum

See *H. petiolare*

Helictotrichon sempervirens, blue oat grass

Grass, 18–30 × 18 in (45–75 × 45 cm), seedheads pale yellow-orange, late summer, foliage very pale green to blue-green, late spring to fall. Suitable for rich to average soil with average or less moisture in sun or very light shade. May require frequent division to maintain form. USDA Zones 4–8.

ASSOCIATIONS: For the garden considerations entertained here, blue oat grass can be viewed as a medium-scale element. It is fine-textured and foliage develops as a spiky mound. The text of photo 130 discusses its use in combination with *Elymus arenarius*, *Berberis thunbergii* 'Crimson Pigmy', and *Heuchera* 'Palace Purple'. See also discussions under *Artemisia* 'Powis Castle', *Geranium sanguineum* 'Album', and *Imperata cylindrica* 'Red Baron'.

Its pale blue-green foliage harmonizes nicely with pale violet *Perovskia atriplicifolia* blooms. Both contrast well with the pale warm pink, summer stage of *Sedum* 'Autumn Joy' (2:1:2). While the blending of tints is enticing, it is the layered contrast of forms which makes this composition exceptional. Spiky *Helictotrichon* can be placed in front of the solid, horizontal *Sedum* flower heads, with ethereal *Perovskia* as a background for both.

Heliopsis scabra

Herbaceous perennial, 36–60 × 24 in (90–150 × 60 cm), blooms yellow-orange, late spring to summer, very dark yellow-green foliage, late spring to fall. Does well in average soil with average or less moisture in sun. USDA Zones 3–9. Photos 13, 89. See also discussions under *Asclepias tuberosa* 'Gay Butterflies', *Coreopsis* 'Sunray', and *Oenothera tetragona*.

ASSOCIATIONS: *Achillea* 'Coronation Gold', photo 89; *Coreopsis verticillata* 'Moonbeam', photo 89; *Hemerocallis* cultivars, photo 89; *Lysimachia punctata*, photos 13, 89; *Oenothera tetragona*, photo 13; *Tanacetum parthenium*, photo 13; *Veronica spicata* 'Blue Charm', photo 89.

A bold, vibrant, large-scale composition combines *Heliopsis scabra*'s yellow-orange blooms with those of *Liatris spicata* 'Kobold' in light red-violet and those of *Monarda* 'Adam' in dark red (1:3:3). This warm/cool association uses plants of near-adjacent colors with overlapping flowering periods. *Heliopsis* blooms first with the *Liatris* spires and has started to fade when the subdued dark red *Monarda* clusters appear. The coarse mass of dark *Heliopsis* foliage is useful in the landscape until fall.

Heliotropium 'Marine'

Perennial, usually grown as an annual, 12–18 × 12 in (30–45 × 30 cm), blooms fragrant, violet, late spring to late summer, foliage very dark yellow-green, late spring to late summer. Suitable for rich to average soil and moisture and sun. Photo 42. See also discussions under *Ageratum houstonianum* 'Southern Cross', *Chelone lyonii*, *Eupatorium coelestinum*, *Gomphrena globosa* 'Strawberry Fields', *Verbena* 'Amor Light Pink', and photo 88.

ASSOCIATIONS: *Ageratum houstonianum* 'Blue Puffs', photo 42; *Coreopsis* 'Sunray', photo 145; *Lobelia erinus* 'White Cascade', photo 42; *Nierembergia hippomanica* var. *violacea* 'Purple Robe', photo 42; *Salvia farinacea* 'Victoria', photos 88, 145; *Tagetes patula*, photo 88; *Verbena canadensis* 'Homestead Purple', photo 145.

To take advantage of the opportunities for light/dark contrasts, try combining this heliotrope's violet blooms with brilliant, reflective *Artemisia schmidtiana* 'Silver Mound' foliage. Diffusing qualities in the flowers of light-tinted *Baptisia australis*, *Geranium endressii* 'Wargrave Pink', and *Nepeta mussinii* add complexity to the original pair and will enlarge the association's scale (3:1:1:1:1). Flowering begins in late spring and develops through the summer.

Helleborus foetidus, stinking hellebore

Herbaceous perennial, 18–24 × 18 in (45–60 × 45 cm), blooms very pale yellow-green, early to late spring, foliage persistent, dark yellow-green. Does well in average soil and moisture and part shade. USDA Zones 5–9. Poisonous. Freely self-sows. Photo 126. See also discussion under *Vinca minor*.

ASSOCIATIONS: *Leucojum aestivum* 'Gravetye Giant', photo 126; *Tulipa* 'Spring Green', photo 126; *Vinca minor*, photo 126.

Helleborus orientalis, lenten rose

Herbaceous perennial, 12–24 × 24 in (30–60 × 60 cm), blooms very pale yellow-green to pale red-violet, early to mid spring, dark yellow-green foliage, early spring to fall. Does well in average soil and moisture and shade to part shade. USDA Zones 4–9. Poisonous. Freely self-sows. Photos 51, 105. See also discussion under *Vinca minor*.

ASSOCIATIONS: *Astilbe chinensis* 'Pumila', photo 105; *Hosta plantaginea* 'Royal Standard', photo 51.

Hemerocallis 'Colonial Dame'

Herbaceous perennial, 18 × 12 in (45 × 30 cm), blooms very pale yellow-orange, summer, dark yellow-green foliage, late spring to fall. Does well in average soil and moisture in sun or part shade. USDA Zones 3–9. Photos 10, 62. See also discussion under *Hemerocallis* 'Hyperion'.

ASSOCIATIONS: *Achillea millefolium* 'Weser River Sandstone', photo 62; *Alchemilla mollis*, *Iris pseudacorus*, *Lilium* 'French Vanilla', *Lysimachia punctata*, *Phalaris arundinacea* var. *picta*, and *Verbascum chaixii*, photo 10.

Hemerocallis 'Ed Murray'

Herbaceous perennial, 24–36 × 18 in (60–90 × 45 cm), blooms deep red-orange, late spring to summer, dark yellow-green foliage, mid spring to fall. Does well in average soil and moisture in sun or part shade. USDA Zones 3–9. Photo 133.

ASSOCIATIONS: *Berberis thunbergii* 'Atropurpurea', *Elymus arenarius*, *Hosta sieboldiana*, photo 133.

Hemerocallis flava

See *H. lilioasphodelus*

Hemerocallis fulva 'Kwanso Flore Plena'

Herbaceous perennial, 24–36 × 18 in (60 × 45 cm), blooms orange, mid to late summer, dark yellow-green foliage, mid spring to fall. Suited to average soil and moisture in sun or part shade. USDA Zones 3–9.

ASSOCIATIONS: This daylily is of medium to large scale with broad-textured flowers and medium-textured foliage. Leaves are weeping and straplike. See also design connections given under *Aconitum napellus*.

Hemerocallis 'Gala Bells'

Herbaceous perennial, 18 × 12 in (45 × 30 cm), blooms very light yellow, summer, dark yellow-green foliage, late spring to fall. Suited to average soil and moisture in sun or part shade. USDA Zones 3–9.

ASSOCIATIONS: 'Gala Bells' can be used as a small-scale element. Its flower texture is broad, its foliage medium-textured. Flowers develop on vertical stems above the weeping, straplike foliage. See discussion under *Chrysanthemum pacificum* for including this in a small-scale grouping highlighting yellow flowers.

Hemerocallis 'Hyperion'

Herbaceous perennial, 36 × 18 in (90 × 45 cm), blooms light yellow, summer, dark yellow-green foliage, late spring to fall. Suited to average soil and moisture in sun or part shade. USDA Zones 3–9. Clonal variety. See also discussion under photo 81.

ASSOCIATIONS: 'Hyperion' can act as a large-scale element of mixed textures. Flowers are broad-textured. Foliage is weeping, straplike, and of medium texture. Use three tucked against the background of one dark-foliaged and creamy white blooming *Hydrangea quercifolia* and with the pale yellow-orange flowers of three *Hemerocallis* 'Colonial Dame' and two white *Astilbe* × *arendsii* 'Deutschland' to create a beautiful display (3:1: 3:2). A succession of bloom over several weeks is created with very little effort. *Hydrangea* makes this a large-scale association useful in the mixed border, at the edge of woodland, or for a lightly shaded display beneath deciduous trees.

Hemerocallis lilioasphodelus (*H. flava*), lemon daylily

Herbaceous perennial, 24–36 × 18 in (60–90 × 45 cm), blooms pale yellow, late spring to summer, dark yellow-green foliage, late spring to fall. Suited to average soil and moisture in sun or part shade. USDA Zones 3–9. Photo 81. See also discussions under *Argyranthemum frutescens*, *Borago officinalis*, *Echinops* 'Taplow Blue', and photo 101.

ASSOCIATIONS: This daylily pairs well with the light red-violet spires of *Lythrum salicaria* 'Morden Pink' (1:1). Flower forms are varied and although the tints in both blooms are light enough to avoid dissonance, they also have enough strength to demand attention. *Hemerocallis* foliage is often attractive and useful after blooming is finished.

Contrasting foliage forms are one of the focuses of an association using *Hosta* 'Krossa Regal' due to the hosta's stunning, large, broad leaves (2:1). Pale yellow *Hemerocallis* blooms complement the bluish green tones in *Hosta*'s foliage and any lingering *Hemerocallis* blossoms accord with its pale violet blooms. Best in light shade.

Hemerocallis 'Mayan Gold'

Herbaceous perennial, 15–18 × 12 in (40–45 × 30 cm), blooms light yellow-orange, late spring to summer, dark yellow-green foliage, late spring to fall. Suited to average soil and moisture in sun or part shade. USDA Zones 3–9.

ASSOCIATIONS: 'Mayan Gold' can be used as a small-scale element of medium textures. Flowers develop on vertical stems above the weeping, straplike foliage. See text of photo 68, where this is a suggested alternate to be planted with *Lilium lancifolium* and *Potentilla flamea*.

Hemerocallis 'Sammy Russell'

Herbaceous perennial, 24–36 × 18 in (60–90 × 45 cm), blooms very deep red and very deep red-orange, late spring to summer, dark yellow-green foliage, late spring to fall. Suited to average soil and moisture in sun or part shade. USDA Zones 3–9. Photo 58.

ASSOCIATIONS: *Dahlia* 'Ellen Houston' and *Ligularia stenocephala* 'The Rocket', photo 58.

Hemerocallis 'Sombrero'

Herbaceous perennial, 24–36 × 18 in (60–90 × 45 cm), blooms very dark orange, late spring to summer, dark yellow-green foliage, late spring to fall. Suited to average soil and moisture in sun or part shade. USDA Zones 3–9. Photo 63.

ASSOCIATIONS: *Zinnia* 'Old Mexico', photo 63.

Hemerocallis 'Stella d'Oro'

Herbaceous perennial, 12–15 × 15 in (30–45 × 45 cm), blooms light yellow-orange, late spring to fall, dark yellow-green foliage, late spring to fall. Suited to average soil and moisture in sun or part shade. USDA Zones 3–9.

ASSOCIATIONS: 'Stella d'Oro' can be considered a small-scale element of medium textures. Very long-blooming, its flowers develop on vertical stems above the weeping, straplike foliage. See text of photo 68 where this is a suggested alternate to be planted with *Lilium lancifolium* and *Potentilla flamea*.

Its rather strident bloom color benefits from the softening effects of paler blooms in *Lantana* 'Confetti' and *Tagetes* 'Lemon Gem' (1:2:2).

Hemerocallis cultivars, daylilies

In several instances I have not specified a particular daylily. A cultivar can be found to fit most situations as there are hundreds to choose from and hybridizing continues. A general description is that of a herbaceous perennial, 18–48 × 12 in (45–120 × 30 cm), blooms in tints and shadings of yellow, orange, or red, late spring to late summer, dark yellow-green foliage, late spring to fall. Suited to average soil and moisture in sun or part shade. USDA

Zones 3–9. Photos 68, 79, 81, 89, 101. See also discussions under *Euphorbia polychroma*, *Gaillardia* × *grandiflora* 'Goblin', *Leucojum aestivum* 'Gravetye Giant', and *Monarda didyma* 'Mahogany'.

ASSOCIATIONS: *Achillea* 'Coronation Gold', photo 89; *Ajuga reptans* 'Alba' and *Ajuga reptans* 'Atropurpurea', photo 79; *Brunnera macrophylla*, photo 101; *Coreopsis verticillata* 'Moonbeam', photo 89; *Euphorbia polychroma*, photo 101; *Heliopsis scabra*, photo 89; *Hemerocallis* 'Hyperion', photo 81; *Lilium lancifolium*, photo 68; *Lysimachia punctata*, photo 89; *Mertensia virginica*, photo 79; *Perovskia atriplicifolia*, photo 81; *Potentilla flamea*, photo 68; *Veronica spicata* 'Blue Charm', photo 89.

Heuchera 'Palace Purple'

Herbaceous perennial, 12–24 × 12 in (30–60 × 30 cm), blooms very pale red-orange, mid to late summer, foliage deep red-orange to red-violet tinged green, mid spring to late summer. Does well in average soil with moist to average conditions in sun or part shade. USDA Zones 4–8. Photo 139. See also comments under *Cotinus coggygria* 'Royal Purple', *Foeniculum vulgare* 'Purpureum', *Iris* × *germanica* 'Sultan's Beauty', and photos 110 and 130.

ASSOCIATIONS: *Alchemilla mollis*, photo 139; *Berberis thunbergii* 'Atropurpurea Nana', photo 130; *Elymus arenarius*, photo 130; *Nicotiana langsdorffii*, photo 139; *Polygonatum odoratum* 'Variegatum', photo 139; *Salvia guaranitica*, photo 139; *Salvia officinalis* 'Aurea', photos 110, 139; *Salvia officinalis* 'Purpurea', photo 110; *Veronica spicata* 'Blue Charm', photo 110.

This *Heuchera*'s dark warm hues contrast beautifully with the light blue-violet flowers in *Camassia quamash* and *Phlox divaricata* and the pale red-orange of the spring-blooming *Tulipa* 'Apricot Beauty' (1:1:2:4). This compact group needs some sun for the *Camassia* and *Tulipa*. Adjacent colors of red-orange, red-violet, and blue-violet are linked but contrasted in their light and dark tones. *Tuli-*

pa flowers at the same time as *Phlox*, but offers contrasting height and form, and subtle color. *Heuchera* produces small, pale red-orange, fairly insignificant flowers in summer, and is used here for the tonal contrast of its stunning dark red foliage.

Hosta albomarginata

See *H. sieboldii*

Hosta fortunei

Herbaceous perennial, 12–18 × 24 in (30–45 × 60 cm), blooms pale violet, summer, gray yellow-green foliage, mid spring to fall. Suitable for rich to average soil with moist to average conditions and shade or part shade. USDA Zones 3–8. Photo 52.

ASSOCIATIONS: *Ajuga reptans, Athyrium nipponicum, Polygonatum odoratum* 'Variegatum', photo 52.

Interplanting with *Iris sibirica* 'White Swirl' (1:2) forms a pair that makes an effortless groundcover for light shade. Vertical *Iris* foliage and blooms contrast the hosta's broad leaves in late spring and are highlighted against their smooth darkness. *Iris* foliage persists and its form mirrors *Hosta*'s pale violet, ascending flower spikes in midsummer. I've had this long-lasting groundcover in place for fifteen years without maintenance attention. Most effective viewed from above.

Hosta fortunei 'Aurea'

Herbaceous perennial, 15–24 × 24 in (40–60 × 60 cm), blooms pale violet, summer, light yellow-green foliage, mid spring to fall. Suitable for rich to average soil in moist to average conditions and shade or part shade. USDA Zones 3–8. Photo 92.

ASSOCIATIONS: *Rhododendron* 'Golden Dream' and *Hyacinthoides hispanica*, photo 92.

Hosta fortunei 'Marginato-alba'

Herbaceous perennial, 12–18 × 24 in (30–45 × 60 cm), blooms pale violet, summer, foliage gray yel-

low-green edged white, mid spring to fall. Suitable for rich to average soil with moist to average conditions and shade or part shade. USDA Zones 3–8. Photos 3, 26. See also discussions under *Astilbe* × *arendsii* 'Deutschland', *Digitalis purpurea* 'Excelsior', and photos 50 and 55.

ASSOCIATIONS: *Alchemilla mollis*, photo 3; *Aquilegia* 'Rose Queen', photo 26; *Astilbe* × *arendsii* 'Deutschland', photo 50; *Cimicifuga racemosa*, photo 26; *Dicentra eximia* 'Luxuriant', photo 26; *Dicentra spectabilis* 'Alba', photo 50; *Elymus arenarius*, photo 55; *Galium odoratum*, photo 3; *Iris sibirica*, photo 50; *Mertensia virginica*, photo 50; *Thalictrum aquilegifolium* 'Album', photo 26.

For a medium-scale composition this hosta combines nicely with *Astilbe* × *arendsii* 'Deutschland' and *Lamium maculatum* 'White Nancy' (1:2:5). The trio will thrive in light shade and features white and green juxtapositions. *Hosta* and *Lamium* both have white leaf variegation in distinctly contrasting forms and sizes. The late white spring blooms of *Astilbe* and *Lamium* are followed in summer by the pale violet *Hosta* spikes.

Hosta glauca

See *H. sieboldiana*

Hosta 'Krossa Regal' (*H. nigrescens* 'Krossa Regal')

Herbaceous perennial, 48–60 × 36 in (1.2–1.5 × 0.9 m), blooms pale violet, late summer, foliage very gray yellow-green, mid spring to fall. Suitable for rich to average soil with moist to average conditions and part shade or shade. USDA Zones 3–8. See also discussions under *Anemone vitifolia* 'Robustissima', *Hemerocallis lilioasphodelus*, *Macleaya microcarpa*, and *Ruta graveolens*.

ASSOCIATIONS: This hosta can provide a large-scale element in the garden with its broad-textured leaves and medium-textured flower spires. Its strong foliage form is shown to advantage in light shade against the feathery foliage in *Astilbe* × *arendsii* 'Deutschland' and *Astilbe* × *arendsii* 'Cattleya' and the narrow leaves of *Tradescantia* × *andersoniana* 'Blue Stone' (1:1:1:1). Blooming is successive: near-white *Astilbe* × *arendsii* 'Deutschland' flowers emerge with blue-violet *Tradescantia* clusters in late spring and light red *Astilbe* × *arendsii* 'Cattleya' blooms follow with pale violet *Hosta* spikes in summer.

Hosta montana 'Aureo-marginata'

Herbaceous perennial, 24–36 × 36 in (60–90 × 90 cm), blooms pale violet, summer, dark yellow-green foliage with pale yellow-green margins, mid spring to fall. Suitable for rich to average soil with moist to average conditions and shade or part shade. USDA Zones 3–9. Photo 55. See also discussion under *Ruta graveolens*.

ASSOCIATIONS: *Elymus arenarius*, photo 55.

Hosta nigrescens 'Krossa Regal'

See *H.* 'Krossa Regal'

Hosta plantaginea 'Royal Standard'

Herbaceous perennial, 24–36 in × 24 in (60–90 × 60 cm), blooms fragrant, white, mid to late summer, dark yellow-green foliage, mid spring to fall. Suitable for rich to average soil with moist to average conditions and shade to part shade or morning sun. USDA Zones 3–8. Photos 43, 51, 107. See also discussions under *Aquilegia* 'Black Star', *Anemone hupehensis* 'September Charm', *Imperata cylindrica* 'Red Baron', *Lamium maculatum* 'White Nancy', *Nicotiana sylvestris*, and *Thalictrum rochebrunianum*.

ASSOCIATIONS: *Astilbe* × *arendsii* 'Fanal', photo 107; *Brunnera macrophylla*, photo 43; *Helleborus orientalis*, photo 51; *Viola* × *wittrockiana*, photo 43.

Hosta sieboldiana (*H. glauca*)

Herbaceous perennial, 30 × 30 in (75 × 75 cm), blooms very pale violet, late spring, very gray yellow-green foliage, mid spring to fall. Suitable for rich to average soil with moist to average conditions and shade or part shade. USDA Zones 3–8. Photos 119, 124. See also discussions under *Convallaria majalis* and photo 133.

ASSOCIATIONS: *Aquilegia* 'Olympia', photo 124; *Athyrium filix-femina*, photo 124; *Berberis thunbergii* 'Atropurpurea', photos 119, 133; *Elymus arenarius*, photo 133; *Hemerocallis* 'Ed Murray', photo 133; *Tulipa* 'Queen of Night', photo 119.

Hosta sieboldiana 'Frances Williams'

Herbaceous perennial, 30–36 × 36 in (75–90 × 90 cm), blooms very pale violet, late spring to summer, foliage very gray yellow-green with yellow-green edge, mid spring to fall. Suitable for rich to average soil with average to moist conditions and part shade or shade. USDA Zones 3–8. Photo 56.

ASSOCIATIONS: *Astilbe* × *arendsii* 'Deutschland' and *Athyrium nipponicum* 'Pictum', photo 56.

Hosta sieboldii (*Hosta albomarginata*)

Herbaceous perennial, 12–24 × 18 in (30–60 × 45 cm), blooms very light violet, summer, dark yellow-green foliage with narrow white margins, mid spring to fall. Suitable for rich to average soil with moist to average conditions and shade or part shade. USDA Zones 3–8.

ASSOCIATIONS: This species hosta can be used for its small to medium scale, medium-textured flowers, and broad-textured foliage. Flowers develop as spires above the mass of foliage. For associations in light shade see discussion under *Matteuccia struthiopteris*.

Hosta × *tardiana* 'Halcyon'

Herbaceous perennial, 18–24 × 24 in (45–60 × 60 cm), blooms very pale violet, late summer, foliage dark gray yellow-green, mid spring to fall. Suitable for rich to average soil with moist to average conditions and part shade or morning sun. USDA Zones 3–8. See also discussions under *Brunnera macrophylla* and *Geum* × *borisii*.

ASSOCIATIONS: As a garden design element, 'Halcyon' is very similar to the preceding hostas. Other cultivars of *Hosta* × *tardiana*, such as 'Blue Wedgewood' or 'Hadspen Blue', are perhaps more readily available and could substitute.

Kirengeshoma palmata makes an unusual companion in a light shade setting (1:1). For much of the growing season, the two distinct foliages, *Kirengeshoma*'s deeply lobed and *Hosta*'s broad and bluish, are sufficiently engaging. The pale yellow *Kirengeshoma* blooms discretely complement the *Hosta*'s pale violet spikes in late summer. This is not a showy association and should be sited with equally subtle companions.

Hyacinthoides hispanica (*Endymion hispanicus, Scilla campanulata, Scilla hispanica*)

Bulb, 15 × 6 in (40 × 15 cm), blooms fragrant, light blue-violet, mid to late spring, dark yellow-green foliage, mid spring to summer. Does well in average soil and moisture in sun or part shade. USDA Zones 4–7. Photos 90, 92. See also discussions under *Cimicifuga racemosa, Stylophorum diphyllum,* and *Tiarella cordifolia.*

ASSOCIATIONS: *Corydalis lutea*, photo 90; *Hosta fortunei* 'Aurea', photo 92; *Rhododendron* 'Golden Dream', photo 92.

Best suited to light shade, a simple foliage composition highlights the contrasting forms and textures of *Hyacinthoides hispanica*'s shiny, straplike foliage, *Ajuga reptans*'s broad leaves, and *Athyrium filix-femina*'s fine texture (3:1:3). Spiked blooms in the light violet *Ajuga* and blue-violet *Hyacinthoides* are complemented by the bright yellow-green *Athyrium* foliage. *Hyacinthoides* foliage persists for several months. Useful group for massing around shrubs in lightly shaded areas.

Hydrangea quercifolia, oak-leaf hydrangea

Shrub, 6 × 6 ft (1.8 × 1.8 m), blooms white, late spring to summer, foliage dark yellow-green turning dark red in fall, late spring to fall. Does well in average soil and moisture in sun or part shade.

USDA Zones 5–8. Prune to ground in spring to keep a compact 36 in (90 cm) form. Photo 53. See also discussion under *Hemerocallis* 'Hyperion'.

ASSOCIATIONS: *Lysimachia ciliata* 'Purpurea' and *Nepeta mussinii*, photo 53.

Iberis sempervirens 'Snowflake'

Herbaceous perennial, 8–10 × 18 in (20–25 × 45 cm), blooms white, early to late spring, dark yellow-green foliage, evergreen. Does well in average soil with average to dry conditions in sun or part shade. USDA Zones 3–9. Prune faded flowers to stimulate new growth. Photo 16. See also comments under *Dicentra eximia* 'Luxuriant'.

ASSOCIATIONS: *Aurinia saxatilis*, photo 16.

Plant in small quantities with *Brunnera macrophylla* to gain a simple blue and white scheme for the spring garden (1:3). *Iberis* bloom is intense and tends to dominate the tiny *Brunnera* blooms. After bloom, the fine *Iberis* foliage contrasts attractively with broad, heart-shaped *Brunnera* leaves. Useful for rock gardens or to decorate lightly shaded gentle slopes.

Impatiens 'Tempo Hybrid Red'

Generally grown as an annual in all zones, 8–12 × 12 in (20–30 × 30 cm), blooms red, late spring to fall, dark yellow-green foliage, late spring to fall. Does well in average soil with moist to average conditions in sun or part shade. Photo 134.

ASSOCIATIONS: *Achillea millefolium* 'Paprika' and *Callistephus chinensis* 'Deep Red', photo 134.

Imperata cylindrica 'Red Baron'

Grass, 12–18 × 15 in (30–45 × 40 cm), seedheads insignificant, foliage dark red with dark gray yellow-green base, summer to fall. Does well in average soil with moist to average conditions and part shade or sun. USDA Zones 5–9. See also discussion under *Dianthus* × *allwoodii* 'Essex Witch'.

ASSOCIATIONS: For design purposes, 'Red Baron' can be viewed as a small-scale element, with spiky, fine-textured foliage. Contrasting textures provide the design key in placing two of these with one each of *Anemone vitifolia* 'Robustissima', *Helictotrichon sempervirens*, and *Hosta plantaginea* 'Royal Standard', and three *Sedum* 'Ruby Glow' (2:1:1:1:3). Red and red-violet juxtapose with blue-green and dark yellowish green in both foliage and flowers in this near-complementary grouping. The foliage textures supply a long, interesting season starring the stiff, grassy, *Imperata* and *Helictotrichon* forms. Morning sun is tolerated, but light shade is best.

Iris ensata

See *I. kaempferi*

Iris kaempferi (*I. ensata*), Japanese iris

Herbaceous perennial, 24–36 × 12 in (60–90 × 30 cm), bloom colors variously violet, blue-violet, red-violet, and white, late spring to summer, dark yellow-green foliage, mid spring to fall. Suitable for rich to average soil with moist to average conditions in sun or part shade. USDA Zones 4–9. See also discussions under *Achillea* 'Coronation Gold', *Coreopsis* 'Sunray', and *Geranium endressii* 'Wargrave Pink'.

ASSOCIATIONS: This species iris enters our design considerations as a medium- to large-scale element of mixed textures. Flowers are broad-textured and foliage is medium-textured and vertical. A simple near-complementary, easily grown association uses two yellow-flowering *Lysimachia punctata* and one *Oenothera tetragona*, combined with four dark violet-flowered *Iris kaempferi*. Simultaneous blooming may last only a week or two if the weather is very hot, but even this somewhat transient effect is riveting. Plant in a ratio of 4:2:1 to balance the iris's violet hue and the advancing yellows of its companions.

Iris pseudacorus, yellow flag

Herbaceous perennial, 24–36 × 18 in (60–90 × 45 cm), blooms yellow, late spring, foliage very dark yellow-green, spring to fall. Suitable for rich to average soil with moist to average conditions in sun or part shade. USDA Zones 5–9. Photos 10, 14, 65, 83, 84, 98. See also discussions under *Allium moly* and photo 12.

ASSOCIATIONS: *Alchemilla mollis*, photo 10; *Argyranthemum frutescens*, photo 14; *Aruncus dioicus*, photo 14; *Cosmos sulphureus* 'Sunny Red', photo 65; *Digitalis grandiflora*, photos 14, 83, 84; *Geranium × magnificum*, photos 83, 84; *Gunnera manicata*, photo 12; *Hemerocallis* 'Colonial Dame', photo 10; *Ligularia dentata* 'Desdemona' and *L. stenocephala* 'The Rocket', photo 12; *Lilium* 'French Vanilla', photo 10; *Lobelia cardinalis*, photo 65; *Lysimachia punctata*, photo 10; *Myosotis sylvatica*, photo 98; *Phalaris arundinacea* var. *picta*, photo 10; *Pulmonaria saccharata* 'Mrs. Moon', photos 83, 84; *Rudbeckia* 'Goldsturm', photo 65; *Salvia* 'Lady in Red', photo 65; *Solidago* 'Cloth of Gold', photo 14; *Verbascum chaixii*, photo 10; *Weigela florida* 'Variegata', photo 14.

Iris sibirica

Herbaceous perennial, 18–36 × 9 in (45–90 × 25 cm), bloom colors vary, generally violet to light violet and white, late spring, dark yellow-green foliage, mid spring to fall. Does well in average soil with moist to average conditions in sun or part shade. USDA Zones 3–9. Photo 76. See also discussions under *Baptisia australis*, *Geranium sylvaticum* 'Mayflower', *Matteuccia struthiopteris*, and photo 50.

ASSOCIATIONS: *Amsonia tabernaemontana*, photo 76; *Astilbe × arendsii* 'Deutschland', photo 50 ; *Brunnera macrophylla*, photo 76; *Dicentra spectabilis* 'Alba', photo 50; *Geranium endressii* 'Wargrave Pink', photo 76; *Hosta fortunei* 'Marginato-alba' and *Mertensia virginica*, photo 50.

Associations: The yellow blooms of *Stylophorum diphyllum* are lightly scattered over its mounding foliage, making a well-balanced near-complementary companion for violet *Iris* and light blue-violet *Centaurea montana* blooms (2:1:1).

Stylophorum blooms first with *Centaurea* and later highlights the brief *Iris* flowering. *Centaurea* should be cut down after first flowers fade and will re-bloom within just a few weeks. For several weeks the spiked *Iris* contributes to a pleasing foliar association with *Centaurea* and the shorter, broader *Stylophorum*. *Stylophorum* foliage is more persistent when the plant is grown in light shade or morning sun with plenty of moisture.

Iris sibirica 'White Swirl'

Herbaceous perennial, 18–36 × 9 in (45–90 × 25 cm), blooms white with a yellow throat, late spring, dark yellow-green foliage, late spring to late summer. Does well in average soil with moist to average conditions in sun or part shade. USDA Zones 3–9. Photo 2. See also discussions under *Hosta fortunei, Lamium maculatum* 'White Nancy', *Leucanthemum × superbum* 'Alaska', and *Rodgersia aesculifolia*.

ASSOCIATIONS: *Geranium sanguineum* 'Album' and *Paeonia lactiflora* 'Festiva Maxima', photo 2.

The fine texture of *Cimicifuga racemosa* and *Geranium sanguineum* 'Album' leaves and the vertical *Iris* juxtapose the broad *Rodgersia aesculifolia* foliage (4:1:1:1) and make a dramatic statement for areas in very light shade. Successive white or near-white blooms in the four plants are useful in any shaded composition.

Iris × germanica, German iris

Herbaceous perennial, 18–24 × 12 in (45–60 × 30 cm), bloom color varies, late spring, dark yellow-green foliage, late spring to summer. Does well in average soil with average or less moisture and sun. USDA Zones 3–10. Photo 41. See also discussion under *Aquilegia alpina*.

ASSOCIATIONS: *Amsonia tabernaemontana, Aquilegia vulgaris, Leucanthemum × superbum* 'Alaska', *Nepeta mussinii, Tradescantia × andersoniana* 'Blue Stone', photo 41.

Iris × germanica 'Sultan's Beauty'

Herbaceous perennial, 18–24 × 12 in (45–60 × 30 cm), blooms deep red, late spring, dark yellow-green foliage, late spring to summer. Does well in average soil with average or less moisture and sun. USDA Zones 3–10. See also discussion under *Ajuga reptans* 'Atropurpurea'.

ASSOCIATIONS: 'Sultan's Beauty' is a medium-scale iris with broad textures and vertical foliage. Blooms harmonize well with similar dark red and red-violet tones in the foliages of *Ajuga reptans* 'Atropurpurea' and *Heuchera* 'Palace Purple'. Use two *Iris* with three *Ajuga* and one *Heuchera*. Adding five *Viola corsica* to the group brings enough violet blooms to coincide with the *Ajuga* flowers (2:3:1:5). After flowering, foliage hues and forms continue a fine association suited to very light shade or sun.

Jasminum officinale, common jasmine

Vine, semi-evergreen to deciduous, to 40 ft (12 m), blooms fragrant, white, summer, foliage very dark yellow-green, late spring to fall. Does well in average soil and moisture in sun. USDA Zones 7–9. Needs frequent light pruning to maintain healthy growth. Photo 95.

ASSOCIATIONS: *Echinops* 'Taplow Blue', *Lavandula angustifolia* 'Hidcote', *Achillea* 'Moonshine', photo 95.

Kirengeshoma palmata, yellow waxbells

Herbaceous perennial, 36–48 × 36 in (90–120 × 90 cm), blooms light yellow, late summer to fall, dark yellow-green foliage, summer to fall. Suitable for rich to average soil, moist to average conditions, and part shade. USDA Zones 5–8. See also discussions under *Ceratostigma plumbaginoides* and *Hosta × tardiana* 'Halcyon'.

ASSOCIATIONS: Yellow waxbells have small to medium-textured flowers and broad-textured foliage in a shrub-like mound that can be used as a large-scale element. *Alchemilla mollis* and *Digitalis grandiflora* associate smoothly (2:4:1), offering a successive association of pale yellow and yellow-green in light shade. *Kirengeshoma palmata*'s fine broad foliage makes an excellent spring backdrop for the *Digitalis* spires, and it contributes its own pale blossoms in summer. The composition has a subtle and subdued impact and should be used where these qualities are appreciated or as a calm oasis between showier associations. Cut back *Digitalis* after flowering for later re-bloom.

Knautia macedonica (*Scabiosa macedonica, S. rumelica*)

Herbaceous perennial, 24 × 18 in (60 × 45 cm), blooms very dark red, mid to late summer, dark yellow-green foliage, summer to fall. Prefers average to rich soil with average moisture in sun or part shade. USDA Zones 5–9. Add lime if soil is acidic. Remove spent flowers to prolong bloom. Photos 18, 22, 136.

ASSOCIATIONS: *Antirrhinum majus* 'Frontier Crimson', photo 22; *Beta vulgaris* subsp. *cicla*, photo 136; *Centranthus ruber*, photo 22; *Cosmos bipinnatus* 'Versailles Tetra', photo 18; *Geranium psilostemon*, photo 136; *Malva sylvestris* 'Mauritiana', photo 136; *Perilla frutescens*, photo 18; *Prunus × cistena*, photo 18; *Rosa*, photo 136; *Rosa* 'Prospero', photo 18; *Salvia officinalis* 'Purpurea', photo 136.

Kniphofia 'Atlanta'

Herbaceous perennial, 36 × 18 in (90 × 45 cm), blooms light yellow and dark red-orange, summer, foliage very dark yellow-green, late spring to late summer. Does well in average soil with average or less moisture in sun or part shade. USDA Zones 5–9. Photo 138. See also discussions under *Monarda didyma* 'Cambridge Scarlet' and *Potentilla* 'Tangerine'.

ASSOCIATIONS: *Papaver somniferum* and *Geranium psilostemon*, photo 138.

Lamiastrum galeobdolon 'Herman's Pride'

Herbaceous perennial, 12 × 18 in (30 × 45 cm), blooms light yellow, spring, foliage very dark yellow-green with white variegations, spring to fall. Does well in average soil with average or greater moisture and part shade or sun. USDA Zones 5–9. See also discussions under *Aquilegia vulgaris*, *Corydalis lutea*, *Epimedium × versicolor* 'Sulphureum', *Euphorbia polychroma*, and *Tulipa* 'White Triumphator'.

ASSOCIATIONS: 'Herman's Pride' is of small scale and medium textures. Foliage develops as a mound and flowers are held vertically above the foliage. To make a simple blue-violet, white, and yellow successive spring association, join one with five *Muscari armeniacum*, three *M. botryoides* 'Album', and five *Narcissus* 'Hawera' (1:5:3:5). Charming and effective in masses under deciduous trees, it will effortlessly knit together disparate shrubs. *Lamiastrum* foliage helps mask the foliar decline of its companions and persists into late fall.

Linking with one of the later season *Hosta fortunei* 'Marginato-alba' compositions would cause a strong repetition of white leaf markings.

Lamium maculatum 'Shell Pink'

Herbaceous perennial, 8 × 12 in (20 × 30 cm), blooms very pale red, mid to late spring, dark yellow-green foliage, mid spring to fall. Does well in average soil with average to moist conditions and part shade or morning sun. USDA Zones 3–8. Less invasive than the species.

ASSOCIATIONS: 'Shell Pink' is a small-scale plant of generally fine textures creating an indistinct horizontal mass. See comments under *Ajuga reptans* 'Alba' and photo 25 for suggested connections.

Lamium maculatum 'White Nancy'

Herbaceous perennial, 8 × 12 in (20 × 30 cm), blooms white, late spring, foliage dark yellow-green with white variegations, mid spring to fall. Does well in average soil with average to moist conditions and part shade or morning sun. USDA Zones 3–8. Less invasive than the species. See also discussions under *Astilbe* × *arendsii* 'Deutschland', *Tulipa* 'West Point', and photos 6 and 25.

ASSOCIATIONS: 'White Nancy' has design traits identical to 'Shell Pink', but it develops white flowers and white variegation on its leaves. See text of photo 6 for connections with *Dicentra spectabilis* 'Alba', *Digitalis purpurea* 'Excelsior', *Phalaris arundinacea* var. *picta*, and *Tiarella cordifolia*.

For a medium-scale association with good sun tolerance, combine three with the white and pale violet blooms of two *Aquilegia* 'Olympia', include one *Hosta plantaginea* 'Royal Standard', three *Iris sibirica* 'White Swirl', and two *Pulmonaria saccharata* 'Mrs. Moon' (3:2:1:3:2). This predominantly white and green planting offers successive flowering from early spring to late summer, with white speckles and striations evident in both foliage and flowers.

Lantana 'Confetti'

Usually grown as an annual in all zones or overwintered indoors, 12–15 × 15 in (30–40 × 40 cm), blooms fragrant, light yellow, yellow-orange, orange, red, and red-violet, late spring to fall, foliage pungent, dark yellow-green, late spring to fall. Does well in average soil and moisture in sun or very light shade. Photo 59. See also discussion under *Hemerocallis* 'Stella d'Oro' and *Tagetes* 'Primrose Lady'.

ASSOCIATIONS: *Lonicera periclymenum* 'Graham Thomas', photo 59.

Lavandula angustifolia 'Hidcote'

Herbaceous perennial, 18 × 12 in (45 × 30 cm), blooms fragrant, light violet, late spring to summer, foliage grayed deep yellow-green, late spring to fall. Does well in average soil with average or less moisture in sun. USDA Zones 5–9. Prune faded flowers to keep growth compact. Photos 85, 95. See also discussions under *Convolvulus cneorum*,

Eryngium amethystinum, *Limonium latifolium*, *Lychnis coronaria*, and photo 29.

ASSOCIATIONS: *Achillea* 'Moonshine', photos 85, 95; *Coreopsis verticillata* 'Moonbeam', photo 85; *Echinops* 'Taplow Blue', photo 95; *Jasminum officinale*, photo 95; *Papaver somniferum* and *Salvia sclarea*, photo 29.

Lavandula angustifolia 'Munstead'

Herbaceous perennial, 12 × 12 in (30 × 30 cm), blooms fragrant, light violet, late spring to summer, foliage grayed deep yellow-green, late spring to fall. Does well in average soil with average or less moisture in sun. USDA Zones 5–9. Prune faded flowers to keep growth compact. Photo 74. See also discussions under *Artemisia schmidtiana* 'Silver Mound' and *Campanula portenschlagiana*.

ASSOCIATIONS: *Ballota pseudodictamnus*, *Berberis thunbergii* 'Atropurpurea Nana', *Santolina chamaecyparissus*, *Teucrium chamaedrys*, photo 74.

Lavandula stoechas, Spanish lavender

Herbaceous perennial, 12–15 × 15 in (30–40 × 40 cm), blooms light red-violet, late spring to summer, deep yellow-green foliage, mid spring to fall. Does well in average soil with average or less moisture in sun. USDA Zones 6–9. Prune faded flowers to keep growth compact. Photo 33. See also discussion under *Eryngium amethystinum*.

ASSOCIATIONS: *Erigeron karvinskianus* and *Rosa* 'Chaucer', photo 33.

Leucanthemum vulgare (Chrysanthemum leucanthemum), ox-eye daisy

Herbaceous perennial, 12–30 × 12 in (30–75 × 30 cm), blooms white with yellow center, late spring to late summer, dark yellow-green foliage, late spring to fall. Plant in average to lean soil, supply dry to average moisture and site in sun. USDA Zones 4–9. Photo 24.

ASSOCIATIONS: *Cleome spinosa* 'Helen Campbell',

Cosmos 'Sonata White' and *Monarda didyma* 'Cambridge Scarlet', *Papaver rhoeas*, and *Salvia* 'Lady in Red', photo 24.

Leucanthemum × *superbum* 'Alaska'

Herbaceous perennial, 24 × 18 in (60 × 45 cm), blooms white with yellow center, late spring to summer, foliage very dark yellow-green, late spring to late summer. Does well in average soil with average or less moisture and sun or part shade. USDA Zones 4–9. Photo 41. See also discussions under *Achillea* 'Coronation Gold' and *Achillea millefolium* 'White Beauty'.

ASSOCIATIONS: *Aquilegia vulgaris, Amsonia tabernaemontana, Iris × germanica, Nepeta mussinii, Tradescantia × andersoniana* 'Blue Stone', photo 41.

Although commonly linked with yellow, *Leucanthemum* × *superbum* 'Alaska' connects very well with blue-violet and red-violet tints. Grouping one with two *Dianthus × allwoodii* 'Essex Witch', two *Delphinium* 'Connecticut Yankee', one *Geranium sanguineum* var. *striatum*, three *Iris sibirica* 'White Swirl', and one *Nepeta mussinii* (1:2:2:1:3:1) gives a traditional near-pastel association. Scale is medium and bloom persists for several weeks, with the most powerful effect in late spring. Fine foliage forms and textures and sporadic flowering from *Geranium* and *Nepeta* sustain the group through the summer.

Leucojum aestivum 'Gravetye Giant'

Bulb, 24 × 4 in (60 × 10 cm), blooms white, early to late spring, dark yellow-green foliage, early to late spring. Does well in average soil and moisture in sun or part shade. USDA Zones 4–9. Winter blooming in mild climates. Photos 25, 126. See also comments under *Ajuga reptans* 'Alba' and *Osmunda claytoniana*.

ASSOCIATIONS: *Dicentra spectabilis, Helleborus foetidus, Tulipa* 'Spring Green', and *Vinca minor*, photo 126.

Use one *Dennstaedtia punctiloba* to cover spaces left by the fading foliage of three *Leucojum* bulbs. Adding five *Ajuga reptans* 'Alba', one *Hemerocallis* cultivar, and two *Mertensia virginica* produces a long-blooming group ideal in the woodland border or as groundcover for shrubs and deciduous trees (3:1:5:1:2). The white-flowering form of *Ajuga* mingles nicely with white-blooming *Leucojum* and blue *Mertensia* in a partly shaded location. *Hemerocallis* bloom may be any color and, with the *Dennstaedtia*, the specimen fills the spaces left by *Leucojum* and *Mertensia*.

Leymus arenarius

See *Elymus arenarius*

Liatris spicata 'Kobold'

Herbaceous perennial, 18 × 12 in (45 × 30 cm), blooms very light red-violet, mid to late summer, dark yellow-green foliage, summer to fall. Does well in average soil and moisture in sun or very light shade. USDA Zones 3–9. See also discussions under *Echinacea purpurea* 'Bright Star', *Heliopsis scabra*, and photo 44.

ASSOCIATIONS: This liatris can be used as a medium-scale element of mixed textures. Its spire form is created by medium-textured flowers and fine-textured foliage. See text of photo 44 for connections with *Eryngium amethystinum, Physostegia virginiana* 'Summer Snow', and *Platycodon grandiflorus*.

A successively blooming summer association which uses harmoniously adjacent colors of light blue-violet and light red is *Liatris spicata* 'Kobold', *Caryopteris × clandonensis* 'Heavenly Blue', *Monarda didyma* 'Croftway Pink', and *Veronica spicata* 'Blue Fox'. Use a ratio of 3:1:2:3. The group thrives in sun or very light shade.

Ligularia dentata 'Desdemona'

Herbaceous perennial, 36 × 24 in (90 × 60 cm), blooms yellow-orange, summer, dark yellow-green foliage, late spring to fall. Does well in average soil with average to greater moisture in sun or part shade. USDA Zones 5–8. Photo 12. See also comments under *Cimicifuga racemosa*.

ASSOCIATIONS: *Gunnera manicata*, *Iris pseudacorus*, *Ligularia stenocephala* 'The Rocket', photo 12.

Ligularia stenocephala 'The Rocket'

Herbaceous perennial, 48–60 × 24 in (120–150 × 60 cm), blooms dark yellow, summer, dark yellow-green foliage, late spring to fall. Does well in average soil with average or greater moisture in sun or part shade. USDA Zones 5–8. Photos 12, 58. See also discussion under *Monarda didyma* 'Mahogany'.

ASSOCIATIONS: *Dahlia* 'Ellen Houston', photo 58; *Gunnera manicata*, photo 12; *Hemerocallis* 'Sammy Russell', photo 58; *Iris pseudacorus*, photo 12; *Ligularia dentata* 'Desdemona', photo 12.

Readily associated with *Alchemilla mollis*, *Astilbe* × *arendsii* 'Deutschland', and *Phalaris arundinacea* var. *picta* (1:3:2:1). Dark yellow and white spires and plumes of *Ligularia* and *Phalaris* offer striking ascending summer forms. *Astilbe* plumes unite the compact *Alchemilla* with its taller companions. Foliage composition remains outstanding before and after bloom. A lightly shaded mixed border or woodland edge will suit this quartet.

Lilium 'Casa Blanca'

Bulb, 24–36 × 12 in (60–90 × 30 cm), blooms fragrant, white, mid to late summer, very dark yellow-green foliage, late spring to late summer. Suitable for rich to average well-drained soil with average moisture in part shade or morning sun. USDA Zones 3–9. Vigorous. An oriental-type lily.

ASSOCIATIONS: This lily offers medium to large scale, a broad flower texture, and medium-textured foliage. See discussions under *Limonium latifolium* and *Nicotiana sylvestris* for suggestions on associations.

Lilium 'Enchantment'

Bulb, 24 × 12 in (60 × 30 cm), blooms dark orange, mid to late summer, foliage very dark yellow-green, late spring to late summer. Suitable for rich to average soil and moisture in part shade or morning sun. USDA Zones 3–9. Vigorous. Asiatic hybrid. Photo 61. See also discussion under *Coreopsis* 'Sunray'.

ASSOCIATIONS: *Oenothera tetragona* and *Tropaeolum majus* 'Alaska', photo 61.

Lilium 'Fireball'

Bulb, 24–36 × 12 in (60–90 × 30 cm), blooms red, mid to late summer, foliage very dark yellow-green, late spring to late summer. Suitable for average to rich, well-drained soil with average moisture in light shade or morning sun (not full sun). USDA Zones 3–9. Vigorous. Asiatic hybrid. See also discussion under *Euphorbia polychroma*.

ASSOCIATIONS: 'Fireball' combines well with *Cosmos sulphureus* 'Sunny Red' and the allied hues in the bi-colored red and yellow *Zinnia* 'Old Mexico' (2:2:1). The annuals *Zinnia* and *Cosmos* bloom for many months. Their dark red hues are captivating, but the blooms are sufficiently small and scattered on the plants that they do not dominate a small garden space. The red lily fires the group to new heights in midsummer. Foliage is unremarkable and an inoffensive foil for the long-lived blooms. Grow in light shade or morning sun.

Lilium 'French Vanilla'

Bulb, 36 × 12 in (90 × 30 cm), blooms pale yellow, late spring to summer, dark yellow-green foliage, late spring to late summer. Suitable for rich to average well-drained soil with average moisture in part shade or sun. USDA Zones 3–9. Aurelian hybrid type. Photo 10. See also discussion under *Delphinium* 'Connecticut Yankee'.

ASSOCIATIONS: *Alchemilla mollis*, *Hemerocallis* 'Colonial Dame', *Iris pseudacorus*, *Lysimachia punctata*, *Phalaris arundinacea* var. *picta*, *Verbascum chaixii*, photo 10.

Lilium lancifolium (*L. tigrinum*), tiger lily

Bulb, 24–48 × 12 in (60–120 × 30 cm), blooms dark orange and spotted black, summer, foliage very dark yellow-green, late spring to late summer. Suitable for rich to average soil and moisture in sun or part shade. USDA Zones 3–9. Flowers pendulous. Photo 68. See also discussions under *Aconitum napellus* and *Dennstaedtia punctiloba*.

ASSOCIATIONS: *Hemerocallis* cultivars and *Potentilla flamea*, photo 68.

Lilium regale, regal lily

Bulb, 48–72 × 12 in (120–180 × 30 cm), blooms fragrant, forming from dark red buds opening white, with light yellow throat, late spring to summer, very dark yellow-green foliage, late spring to late summer. Suitable for rich to average well-drained soil with average moisture in part shade or morning sun. USDA Zones 3–8. Trumpet-type lily. Introduced in 1903.

ASSOCIATIONS: This is a large-scale species lily with classic broad-textured flowers and medium-textured foliage. See discussion under *Filipendula vulgaris* for suggested use in a near-white and red-violet composition.

Lilium tigrinum

See *L. lancifolium*

***Lilium* 'Silver Elegance Strain'**

Bulb, 48–60 × 18 in (120–150 × 45 cm), blooms fragrant, white with red-violet spots, mid to late summer, foliage very dark yellow-green, late spring to late summer. Suitable for rich to average well-drained soil with average moisture in sun. USDA Zones 3–9. An oriental-type lily.

ASSOCIATIONS: This lily would constitute a large-scale element for our garden design purposes. Typically its flower is broad-textured and foliage medium-textured. Such a textural mix typifies most garden-grown lilies. See text of photo 28 for connections with *Astrantia major*, *Cleome spinosa* 'Pink Queen', and *Cosmos bipinnatus* 'Pinkie'.

Limonium latifolium (*Statice latifolia*), sea lavender, statice

Herbaceous perennial, 24–30 × 24 in (60–75 × 60 cm), blooms very light violet, mid to late summer, dark yellow-green foliage, late spring to fall. Does well in average soil with average or less moisture in sun. USDA Zones 3–9. See also discussions under *Achillea filipendulina* 'Gold Plate', *Agastache foeniculum*, and *Festuca glauca*.

ASSOCIATIONS: This can be considered a medium-scale element with fine-textured flowers and broad-textured foliage. Flowers develop as a horizontal cluster and foliage as a basal mass. For a largely successively blooming composition use with *Artemisia* 'Powis Castle' and *Lavandula angustifolia* 'Hidcote' (2:1:2). Light blue-violet and violet flower hues blend particularly well with the pale grayed foliage of the *Artemisia*. A grayed quality in *Lavandula* foliage enhances this connection. *Lavandula* also lends the group a wonderful fragrance when in bloom.

Broad *Limonium* foliage can serve to shade the roots of late-blooming, fragrant, white-flowered *Lilium* 'Casa Blanca'. Add a background of *Monarda fistulosa* and a foreground of earlier-flowering *Nepeta mussinii* for simultaneous flowering in harmonious tints of violet and blue-violet with white (3:1:2:2).

Linum perenne, perennial blue flax

Herbaceous perennial, 15–18 × 12 in (40–45 × 30 cm), blooms light blue, late spring to summer, foliage very dark yellow-green, late spring to late summer. Does well in average soil with dry to average conditions in sun or part shade. *Linum narbonnense* 'Heavenly Blue' is an excellent alternative and offers larger and more numerous flowers in a darker blue with white center. USDA Zones 4–9.

ASSOCIATIONS: This is a small-scale plant with fine textures. See discussions under *Cynoglossum amabile* and *Eschscholzia californica* for connections with complementary yellows in floral hues.

Liriope muscari, big blue lily-turf

Herbaceous perennial, 12–18 × 12 in (30–45 × 30 cm), blooms very light violet, late summer, dark yellow-green foliage, spring to fall. Does well in average soil with average or less moisture and part shade or morning sun. USDA Zones 6–9. Cut back old foliage in early spring to generate new growth.

ASSOCIATIONS: This species liriope can contribute small scale, medium textures, flowering spikes, and a mound of weeping straplike foliage. An easily maintained, monochromatic groundcover composition for shrub borders develops when associated with *Muscari armeniacum* and *Vinca minor* (1:2:3). *Vinca* is evergreen except in the very coldest areas and provides a fine-textured base for the *Liriope* foliage. All plants have light blue-violet or violet flowers. *Vinca* blooms in early spring with *Muscari* spikes in the same tint and hue. *Liriope's* light violet spikes develop in late summer. Light shade or a sunny space with afternoon shade suits all three. Useful under early spring-flowering trees, such as *Magnolia kobus* var. *stellata* (*Magnolia tomentosa*) which is hardy and flowers in USDA Zones 4–7.

Lobelia cardinalis, cardinal flower

Herbaceous perennial, 30–42 × 12 in (75–110 × 30 cm), blooms red, late summer to fall, dark yellow-green foliage, late spring to fall. Suitable for rich to average soil with moist to average conditions in morning sun, part shade, or shade. USDA Zones 2–9. Photos 65, 104.

ASSOCIATIONS: *Cosmos sulphureus* 'Sunny Red', *Iris pseudacorus*, *Rudbeckia* 'Goldsturm', and *Salvia* 'Lady in Red', photo 65; *Zinnia elegans* 'Red Sun', photo 104.

Lobelia erinus 'Cambridge Blue'

Generally grown as an annual in all zones, 4 × 6 in (10 × 15 cm), blooms pale blue, late spring to late summer, foliage very dark yellow-green, late spring to late summer. Does well in average soil and moisture in sun or part shade. May overwin-

ter in mild climates. Self-sows if conditions are favorable. See also discussion under *Artemisia schmidtiana* 'Silver Mound'.

ASSOCIATIONS: This plant can be used as a small-scale element offering fine textures and indistinct horizontal form. It can be linked to large-scale plantings by combining with pastel-toned foliage or flowers in a graduated scale. Siting four with the grayish foliages and pale blooms of one *Eryngium amethystinum* and two each of *Lychnis coronaria* 'Alba' and *Stachys byzantina* produces a subdued and soothing composition (4:1:2:2).

Lobelia erinus 'White Cascade'

Generally grown as an annual in all zones, 4 × 6 in (10 × 15 cm), blooms white, late spring to late summer, foliage very dark yellow-green, late spring to late summer. Does well in average soil and moisture in sun or part shade. May overwinter in mild climates. Self-sows if conditions are favorable. Photo 42. See also discussion under *Antirrhinum majus* 'White Rocket'.

ASSOCIATIONS: *Ageratum houstonianum* 'Blue Puffs', *Heliotropium* 'Marine', *Nierembergia hippomanica* var. *violacea* 'Purple Robe', photo 42.

Lobularia maritima 'Carpet of Snow'

Generally grown as an annual in all zones, 3 × 12 in (10 × 30 cm), blooms fragrant, white, mid spring to fall, dark yellow-green foliage, mid spring to fall. Does well in average soil and moisture in sun or part shade. Winter annual in mild climates. Self-sows. Photos 32, 40.

ASSOCIATIONS: *Antirrhinum majus* 'Princess White with Purple Eye', photo 40; *Lobularia maritima* 'Easter Bonnet Deep Pink', photo 40; *Lobularia maritima* 'Royal Carpet', *Petunia* 'Burgundy Madness', and *Salvia splendens* 'Laser Purple', photo 32.

Lobularia maritima 'Easter Bonnet Deep Pink'

Generally grown as an annual in all zones, 3 × 12 in (10 × 30 cm), blooms fragrant, very light red-violet, mid spring to fall, dark yellow-green foliage, mid spring to fall. Does well in average soil, average or less moisture, in sun or part shade. Winter annual in mild climates. Self-sows. Photo 40.

ASSOCIATIONS: *Antirrhinum majus* 'Princess White with Purple Eye' and *Lobularia maritima* 'Carpet of Snow', photo 40.

Lobularia maritima 'Royal Carpet'

Generally grown as an annual in all zones, 3 × 12 in (10 × 30 cm), blooms fragrant, violet, mid spring to fall, dark yellow-green foliage, mid spring to fall. Does well in average soil, average or less moisture, in sun or part shade. Winter annual in mild climates. Self-sows. Photo 32.

ASSOCIATIONS: *Lobularia maritima* 'Carpet of Snow', *Petunia* 'Burgundy Madness', *Salvia splendens* 'Laser Purple', photo 32.

Lonicera periclymenum 'Graham Thomas'

Vine, 12 ft (4 m), blooms fragrant, pale yellow, late spring to fall, dark yellow-green foliage, mid spring to fall. Does well in average soil and moisture in sun or part shade. USDA Zones 5–9. Evergreen in mild climates. Will twine around structures, nearby plants or itself. Photo 59.

ASSOCIATIONS: *Lantana* 'Confetti', photo 59.

Lychnis chalcedonica, Maltese cross

Herbaceous perennial, 24–36 × 18 in (60–90 × 45 cm), blooms red, late spring to summer, dark yellow-green foliage, late spring to fall. Does well in average soil with average to greater moisture in sun or part shade. USDA Zones 3–9. May need staking. Photo 143. See also discussion under *Oenothera tetragona.*

ASSOCIATIONS: *Delphinium* 'Charles Gregory Broan' and *Buphthalmum speciosum*, photo 143.

Lychnis coronaria, rose campion

Herbaceous perennial, 24–36 × 18 in (60–90 × 45 cm), blooms light red-violet, late spring, foliage

very light gray yellow-green, late spring to fall. Does well in average soil with average to dry conditions in sun. USDA Zones 4–8.

ASSOCIATIONS: Rose campion has medium to large scale, fine flower texture, and medium foliage texture. Flowers are disk-shaped and foliage contributes an indistinct mass. See discussion under photo 69 for connections with *Nepeta mussinii* and *Salvia × superba* 'May Night'.

Equal quantities of *Lavandula angustifolia* 'Hidcote' and *Salvia × superba* 'East Friesland' (1:1:1) are useful in making the transition from predominantly strong-hued, red-violet color schemes to cooler and paler hues. Intense, bright red-violet *Lychnis* blooms enliven the receding violet tones of *Salvia* and *Lavandula* flowers.

Lychnis coronaria 'Alba'

Herbaceous perennial, 24–36 × 18 in (60–90 × 45 cm), blooms white, late spring, foliage very light gray yellow-green, late spring to fall. Does well in average soil with average to dry conditions in sun. USDA Zones 4–8.

ASSOCIATIONS: Can be used for its design traits exactly as described under the species. The difference between the two lies only in floral color. See discussion under *Lobelia erinus* 'Cambridge Blue' for associating its white flowers and discreet foliage color in a soothing composition.

Lysimachia ciliata 'Purpurea'

Herbaceous perennial, 30–36 × 24 in (75–90 × 60 cm), blooms yellow, late spring to summer, foliage very deep red-orange, mid spring to fall. Does well in average soil with average or greater moisture in sun or part shade. USDA Zones 4–8. Photo 53. See also discussion under *Coreopsis* 'Sunray'.

ASSOCIATIONS: *Hydrangea quercifolia* and *Nepeta mussinii*, photo 53.

Lysimachia clethroides, gooseneck loosestrife

Herbaceous perennial, 18–36 × 24 in (45–90 × 60 cm), blooms white, summer, foliage very dark yellow-green, mid spring to fall. Does well in average soil with average to greater moisture in morning sun or part shade. USDA Zones 3–8. May be considered invasive when grown in moist conditions.

ASSOCIATIONS: Gooseneck loosestrife can add a medium- to large-scale element to the garden landscape. Both flower and foliage are medium-textured. Distinctive flowers form a swooping terminal cluster well above the foliage mass. See discussions under *Allium moly* and *Phalaris arundinacea* var. *picta* for specific recommendations on associations.

Lysimachia punctata, yellow loosestrife

Herbaceous perennial, 18–30 × 24 in (45–75 × 60 cm), blooms yellow, late spring to summer, dark yellow-green foliage, mid spring to fall. Does well in average soil and moisture in sun or part shade. Can be invasive. USDA Zones 4–8. Photos 10, 13, 89, 146. See also discussions under *Iris kaempferi* and *Potentilla* 'Tangerine'.

ASSOCIATIONS: *Achillea* 'Coronation Gold', photo 89; *Alchemilla mollis*, photo 10; *Achillea taygetea*, photo 146; *Coreopsis verticillata* 'Moonbeam', photo 89; *Geranium* 'Anne Folkard', photo 146; *Heliopsis scabra*, photos 13, 89; *Hemerocallis* 'Colonial Dame', photo 10; *Hemerocallis* cultivars, photo 89; *Iris pseudacorus*, photo 10; *Lilium* 'French Vanilla', photo 10; *Oenothera tetragona*, photo 13; *Phalaris arundinacea* var. *picta*, photo 10; *Tanacetum parthenium*, photo 13; *Verbascum chaixii*, photo 10; *Veronica spicata* 'Blue Charm', photo 89.

Lythrum salicaria 'Dropmore Purple',
(*L. virgatum* 'Dropmore Purple')

Herbaceous perennial, 24–36 × 24 in (60–90 × 60 cm), blooms light violet, late spring to late summer, dark yellow-green foliage, late spring to fall. Does well in average soil and moisture in sun or part shade. USDA Zones 3–9. Freely self-sows. Photo 148.

ASSOCIATIONS: *Achillea* 'Coronation Gold' and *Catananche caerulea*, photo 148.

Lythrum salicaria 'Morden Pink',
(*L. virgatum* 'Morden Pink')

Herbaceous perennial, 24–36 × 24 in (60–90 × 60 cm), blooms light red-violet, late spring to late summer, dark yellow-green foliage, mid spring to fall. Does well in average soil and moisture in sun or part shade. USDA Zones 3–9. Substitute shorter *Liatris spicata* 'Kobold' where any form of *Lythrum* is considered invasive. Freely self-sows. Photos 123, 135, 149. See also discussions under *Allium sphaerocephalon, Centranthus ruber,* and *Hemerocallis lilioaspodelus*.

ASSOCIATIONS: *Achillea filipendulina* 'Gold Plate', photo 149; *Asteromoea mongolica*, photos 123, 135; *Centranthus ruber*, photo 135; *Miscanthus sinensis* 'Gracillimus', photo 123; *Salvia guaranitica*, photo 135; *Salvia* × *superba* 'East Friesland', photo 149; *Verbena bonariensis*, photo 123; *Veronica spicata* 'Blue Fox', photo 123.

Lythrum virgatum 'Dropmore Purple'
See *L. salicaria* 'Dropmore Purple'

Lythrum virgatum 'Morden Pink'
See *L. salicaria* 'Morden Pink'

Macleaya microcarpa

Herbaceous perennial, 5–8 × 4 ft (1.5–2.4 × 1.2 m), blooms very light red-orange, late spring to summer, foliage dark gray yellow-green, late spring to fall. Prefers average to poor soil, dry to average conditions, sun or part shade. USDA Zones 3–8. Can be invasive. Photo 132. See also discussion under *Filipendula vulgaris*.

ASSOCIATIONS: *Alstroemeria* Ligtu Hybrids, *Elymus arenarius,* and *Polystichum setiferum* 'Divisilobum', photo 132.

Its distinctive grayish foliage is further enhanced by being sited with the bluish gray-green leaves of *Hosta* 'Krossa Regal'. The light undersides of its leaves also mirror a similar pallor in blooms of one *Aruncus dioicus* and foliage of two *Phalaris arundinacea* var. *picta* (1:2:1:2). This large-scale grouping does best in a lightly shaded space.

Malva alcea 'Fastigiata'

Herbaceous perennial, 36–48 × 15 in (90–120 × 40 cm), blooms pale red, summer, dark yellow-green foliage, late spring to fall. Does well in average soil with average or less moisture in sun or part shade. USDA Zones 4–8.

ASSOCIATIONS: 'Fastigiata' is a large-scale, vertical element of medium textures. See discussions under *Allium christophii* and *Echinops* 'Taplow Blue' for details on associating with five plant types in sun and with two companions in sun or light shade.

Malva moschata, musk mallow

Herbaceous perennial, 24–36 × 18 in (60–90 × 45 cm), blooms very light red, late spring to summer, dark yellow-green foliage, late spring to fall. Does well in average soil with average to dry conditions in sun or part shade. USDA Zones 3–7. Photo 31. See also discussion under *Salvia sclarea.*

ASSOCIATIONS: *Agastache foeniculum* and *Eryngium giganteum*, photo 31.

Planting one of these with one perennial *Monarda didyma* 'Croftway Pink' in the background and three annual *Nicotiana alata* 'Nicki Pink' in the midground offers a light-tinted composition which fits easily into a pastel or cool-hued border. Placing five violet *Verbena canadensis* 'Homestead Purple' in the foreground adds a stronger, yet still harmonious hue to this long-blooming association (1:1:3:5:).

Malva moschata 'Alba'

Herbaceous perennial, 24–36 × 18 in (60–90 × 45 cm), blooms white, late spring to summer, dark yellow-green foliage, late spring to fall. Does well in average soil with average to dry conditions in sun or part shade. USDA Zones 3–7. Photo 47. See also discussions under *Allium christophii* and *Cerastium tomentosum.*

ASSOCIATIONS: *Alchemilla mollis* and *Nigella damescena* 'Miss Jekyll', photo 47.

Malva sylvestris 'Mauritiana'

Herbaceous perennial, 36–72 × 24 in (90–185 × 60 cm), blooms deep red-violet, summer to fall, dark yellow-green foliage, late spring to fall. Does well in average soil and moisture in sun or part shade. USDA Zones 3–9. Photo 136. See also discussion under *Filipendula vulgaris.*

ASSOCIATIONS: *Beta vulgaris* subsp. *cicla, Geranium psilostemon, Knautia macedonica, Rosa* 'Prospero', *Salvia officinalis* 'Purpurea', photo 136.

Matteuccia struthiopteris, ostrich fern

Fern, 24–60 × 24 in (60–150 × 60 cm), flowers absent, foliage dark yellow-green, late spring to fall. Plant in average to rich soil with average or more moisture in shade or part shade. USDA Zones 2–7. Performs best in cold-winter climates. See also discussion under *Digitalis purpurea* 'Excelsior'.

ASSOCIATIONS: Ostrich fern is so named for the resemblance of its leaves to ostrich feathers. It contributes a medium- to large-scale element of medium texture. Plant base is narrow, with foliage spreading out gradually to form a large nebulous mass. It links easily with *Aruncus dioicus, Hosta sieboldii*, and *Iris sibirica* in light shade (1:1:1:5). This large-scale association exploits a variety of foliage forms while binding the tall, feathery, *Aruncus* foliage and flowers to the low, white-edged broad *Hosta* leaves, intermediate *Iris* spikes, and feathery *Matteuccia*. Flowering is successive and predominantly pale unless a violet or blue-violet iris is selected.

Melampodium paludosum 'Medallion'

Short-lived perennial usually grown as annual in all zones, 12–18 × 15 in (30–45 × 40 cm), blooms yellow-orange, late spring to fall, dark yellow-green foliage, late spring to fall. Plant in average to poor soil, supply average or less moisture, and site in sun. Photo 137.

ASSOCIATIONS: *Celosia elegans* 'Pink Tassles', photo 137.

An orange-red tone in the flowers of *Gomphrena globosa* 'Strawberry Fields' allows easy blending with companions developing in adjacent warm hues. A single *Melampodium* with its scattered, small, daisy-like yellow-orange blossoms is a perfect companion for two *Gomphrena* (1:2). The strong color mix makes a powerful accent and should be positioned by itself or accompanied by similarly powerful warm hues.

Mertensia virginica, Virginia bluebells

Herbaceous perennial, 12–24 × 12 in (30–60 × 30 cm), blooms very light blue to pale red-violet, early to mid spring, gray yellow-green foliage, early to late spring. Does well in average soil with moist to average conditions in shade or part shade. USDA Zones 3–9. May self-sow in favorable garden conditions. Photos 49, 50, 79, 97. See also discussions under *Brunnera macrophylla, Dicentra eximia* 'Luxuriant', and *Leucojum aestivum* 'Gravetye Giant'.

ASSOCIATIONS: *Ajuga reptans*, photo 97; *Ajuga reptans* 'Alba' and *Ajuga reptans* 'Atropurpurea', photo 79; *Astilbe* × *arendsii* 'Deutschland', photo 50; *Dicentra spectabilis* 'Alba', photo 50; *Hemerocallis* cultivars, photo 79; *Hosta fortunei* 'Marginato-alba', photo 50; *Iris sibirica*, photo 50; *Narcissus* 'Clare', photo 97; *Podophyllum peltatum*, photo 49.

Miscanthus sinensis 'Gracillimus'

Grass, 4–7 × 5 ft (1.2–2.1 × 1.5 m), seedheads very pale red-orange, fall, foliage light, very gray yellow-green, summer to fall. Does well in average soil and moisture in sun or part shade. USDA Zones 4–8. Photos 11, 120, 123.

ASSOCIATIONS: *Anemone vitifolia* 'Robustissima', photo 120; *Asteromoea mongolica*, photo 123;

Lythrum salicaria 'Morden Pink', photo 123; *Phlox paniculata* 'Bright Eyes', photo 120; *Rudbeckia* 'Goldsturm', photo 11; *Silphium perfoliatum*, photo 11; *Thalictrum rochebrunianum*, photo 120; *Verbena bonariensis*, photo 123; *Veronica spicata* 'Blue Fox', photo 123.

Miscanthus sinensis 'Variegatus',
striped eulalia grass

Grass, 4–7 × 5 ft (1.2–2.1 × 1.5 m), seedheads very pale yellow-orange, fall, foliage light, gray yellow-green, with very pale yellow stripe, summer to fall. Does well in average soil and moisture in sun or part shade. USDA Zones 4–8. See also discussion under *Achillea filipendulina* 'Gold Plate'.

ASSOCIATIONS: This becomes a large-scale vertical element in fall garden design considerations. Flowers develop on upright stalks while foliage assumes a weeping habit. Flower texture is medium and foliage is fine-textured. Its pale striped, grayish green, pendulous foliage provides an elegant backdrop for the distinctive blue-violet flowering globes of *Agapanthus praecox* and flower clusters of *Cleome spinosa* 'Pink Queen'. *Nepeta* 'Six Hills Giant' in the foreground brings earlier, light blue-violet bloom and harmonizing grayish green foliage (1:3:3:1).

Miscanthus sinensis 'Zebrinus'

Grass, 60–72 × 36 in (150–185 × 90 cm), seedheads very pale yellow-orange, fall, foliage light gray yellow-green with horizontal, pale yellow bands, summer to fall. Does well in average soil and moisture in sun or part shade. USDA Zones 4–8. Photo 7.

ASSOCIATIONS: *Asteromoea mongolica, Crambe cordifolia, Polygonatum odoratum* 'Variegatum', photo 7.

Monarda 'Adam'

Herbaceous perennial, 24–36 in × 15 in (60–90 × 40 cm), blooms dark red, mid to late summer, foliage fragrant, dark yellow-green, late spring to fall. Does well in average soil with average or greater moisture in sun or part shade. USDA Zones 4–9. May be invasive. Cut back hard in fall.

ASSOCIATIONS: 'Adam' can contribute a medium- to large-scale form of medium textures. Flowers develop above a crest of indistinct foliage. See discussions under *Gladiolus callianthus*, *Heliopsis scabra*, and *Veronica* 'Sunny Border Blue' for specific suggestions on associations.

Monarda didyma 'Bluestocking'

Herbaceous perennial, 30–36 × 15 in (75–90 × 40 cm), blooms light violet, mid to late summer, foliage fragrant, dark yellow-green, late spring to fall. Does well in average soil with average or greater moisture in sun or part shade. USDA Zones 4–9. May be invasive. Cut back hard in fall.

ASSOCIATIONS: Its design contribution is quite similar to that of *Monarda* 'Adam', which typifies the ornamental *Monarda*. The light violet blooms of 'Bluestocking', however, suggest other potential companions. See discussions under *Achillea filipendulina* 'Gold Plate', *Chelone Lyonii*, and *Phlox maculata* 'Alpha' for details.

Monarda didyma 'Cambridge Scarlet'

Herbaceous perennial, 30–36 × 15 in (75–90 × 40 cm), blooms red, mid to late summer, foliage fragrant, dark yellow-green, late spring to fall. Does well in average soil with average or greater moisture in sun or part shade. USDA Zones 4–9. May be invasive. Cut back hard in fall.

ASSOCIATIONS: 'Cambridge Scarlet' is fast becoming a classic *Monarda* cultivar of medium to large scale, medium textures, and reliable bloom. See other suggestions for its use in the text for *Verbascum chaixii* and photo 24.

Creates a vivid association with *Kniphofia* 'Atlanta' and *Rudbeckia* 'Goldsturm', featuring harmonious, near-adjacent pure red, red-orange, and yellow-orange flowers (3:3:1). Blooming for the entire group is quite lengthy, largely because *Rudbeckia* blooms are so persistent. Flower forms are noticeably varied between *Monarda* clusters, *Kniphofia* spires, and large *Rudbeckia* daisy forms. Foliage is undistinguished. Choose a sunny area in a space large enough to accommodate the potency of vivid hues.

Monarda didyma 'Croftway Pink'

Herbaceous perennial, 30–36 × 15 in (75–90 × 40 cm), blooms pale red, mid to late summer, foliage fragrant, dark yellow-green, late spring to fall. Does well in average soil with average or greater moisture in sun or part shade. USDA Zones 4–9. May be invasive. Cut back hard in fall.

ASSOCIATIONS: This can be seen as a medium- to large-scale element displaying medium textures and indistinct mass of foliage. See discussions under *Allium senescens*, *Filipendula vulgaris*, *Liatris spicata* 'Kobold', and *Malva moschata* for specific associates.

Monarda didyma 'Mahogany'

Herbaceous perennial, 24–36 × 15 in (60–90 × 40 cm), blooms deep red, mid to late summer, foliage fragrant, dark yellow-green, late spring to fall. Does well in average soil with average or greater moisture in sun or part shade. USDA Zones 4–9. May be invasive. Cut back hard in fall.

ASSOCIATIONS: 'Mahogany' develops deep red flowers. It is of medium to large scale with medium textures. A large-scale successively flowering group with bold foliage can be contrived when placed with *Cosmos sulphureus* 'Sunny Red', *Hemerocallis* cultivars, and *Ligularia stenocephala* 'The Rocket' (2:2:1:1). Any strong-hued, yellow-to-red flowering *Hemerocallis* will associate well with the long-blooming *Cosmos*. Mid-season sees *Cosmos* linked with yellow *Ligularia* spires and in summer with deep red *Monarda* clusters. Foliage texture varies from fine to medium to broad, enhancing the blooming succession.

Monarda didyma 'Violet Queen'

Herbaceous perennial, 24–36 × 15 in (60–90 × 40 cm), blooms red-violet, mid to late summer, foliage fragrant, dark yellow-green, late spring to fall. Does well in average soil with average or greater moisture in sun or part shade. USDA Zones 4–9. May be invasive. Cut back hard in fall. Photo 116. See also discussions under *Echinacea purpurea* 'Bright Star' and *Salvia guaranitica*.

ASSOCIATIONS: *Sedum* 'Autumn Joy', photo 116.

Monarda fistulosa

Herbaceous perennial, 36–48 × 18 in (90–120 × 45 cm), blooms pale red-violet, late summer, foliage fragrant, dark yellow-green, late spring to fall. Does well with average to poor soil with average moisture in sun or part shade. USDA Zones 3–9. May be invasive. Cut back hard in fall. Photo 117. See also discussion under *Limonium latifolium*.

ASSOCIATIONS: *Artemisia lactiflora*, *Pennisetum alopecuroides*, *Sedum* 'Autumn Joy', photo 117.

Muscari armeniacum

Bulb, 6–8 × 4 in (15–20 × 10 cm), blooms fragrant, light blue-violet, mid spring, dark yellow-green foliage, mid to late spring. Does well in average soil with average or less moisture and sun. USDA Zones 4–8. Companions for masking foliar decline are suggested in the text of photo 78. Photos 46, 70, 96, 128. See also discussions under *Dicentra eximia* 'Luxuriant', *Dicentra spectabilis*, *Epimedium* × *versicolor* 'Sulphureum', *Lamiastrum galeobdolon* 'Herman's Pride', *Liriope muscari*, *Phlox subulata*, and *Polemonium reptans* 'Blue Pearl'.

ASSOCIATIONS: *Arabis caucasica*, photo 46; *Narcissus* 'Trevithian', photo 96; *Narcissus tazetta* 'Geranium', photo 128; *Narcissus* 'Thalia', photo 46; *Tulipa* 'Pink Impression', photo 70; *Viola cucullata*, photo 46.

Muscari botryoides 'Album'

Bulb, 6–8 × 6 in (15–20 × 15 cm), fragrant white blooms, mid spring, dark yellow-green foliage, mid to late spring. Does well in average soil with average or less moisture in sun or part shade. USDA Zones 4–8. Companions for masking foliar decline are suggested in the text of photo 78.

ASSOCIATIONS: 'Album' lends small scale, medium textures, stalked flowers, and straplike foliage to the spring garden composition. See discussion under *Lamiastrum galeobdolon* 'Herman's Pride' for a specific association.

Myosotis alpestris

See *M. sylvatica*

Myosotis palustris

See *M. sylvatica*

Myosotis sylvatica (*M. alpestris*, *M. palustris*)

Biennial treated as herbaceous perennial, 6–8 × 8 in (15–20 × 20 cm), blooms light blue, early to late spring, dark yellow-green foliage, early spring to summer. Does well with average soil and moisture in part shade or sun. USDA Zones 3–8. Photos 48, 98. See also discussions under *Aurinia saxatilis* 'Citrinum', *Chrysogonum virginianum*, *Dicentra spectabilis*, *Epimedium* × *versicolor* 'Sulphureum', *Polemonium reptans* 'Blue Pearl', *Stylophorum diphyllum*, *Tulipa* 'West Point', and photo 25.

ASSOCIATIONS: *Iris pseudacorus*, photo 98; *Trillium grandiflorum*, photo 48.

Frequently planted as a base to display violet *Aquilegia vulgaris* blooms (1:4). Dark, nodding *Aquilegia* flowers are well highlighted against the hazy base of pale *Myosotis sylvatica* blooms. Especially effective underplanting a flowering pale yellow azalea or red-violet rhododendron in lightly shaded woodlands.

Myrrhis odorata, sweet Cicely

Herbaceous perennial, 36–60 × 24 in (90–150 × 60 cm), blooms white, late spring, dark yellow-green foliage, fragrant, mid spring to fall. Does well in average soil and moisture in part shade or filtered sun. USDA Zones 4–8.

ASSOCIATIONS: Sweet Cicely can be a large-scale element offering an indistinct mass of fine textures. Use with *Geranium sanguineum* 'Album' and *Polygonatum biflorum* to create a successive white-flowering composition for light shade (1:3:1). Flowering begins in spring with tiny white *Polygonatum* bells, continues with *Geranium sanguineum* 'Album' blooms, and concludes with tall, sweet Cicely clusters. The foliage composition is captivating during and after these charming floral periods. Feathery *Myrrhis* foliage can stand behind the slender *Polygonatum* arching towards broad mounds of *Geranium* leaves. The group is captivating in a lightly shaded location.

Narcissus 'Clare'

Bulb, 12–18 × 6 in (30–45 × 15 cm), blooms fragrant, pale yellow, mid spring, dark yellow-green foliage, mid to late spring. Does well in average soil with average or less moisture in sun or part shade. USDA Zones 4–9. Needs well-drained soil. A jonquilla hybrid daffodil introduced 1968. Photo 97. Companions for masking foliage decline are suggested in text of photo 78.

ASSOCIATIONS: *Ajuga reptans* and *Mertensia virginica*, photo 97.

Narcissus 'Geranium'

Bulb, 12–18 × 6 in (30–45 × 15 cm), blooms fragrant, white with red-orange center, mid spring, dark yellow-green foliage, early to late spring. Does well in average soil with average or less moisture in sun or part shade. USDA Zones 6–10. Needs well-drained soil. A tazetta-type daffodil, develops flowers in clusters. Photo 128. Companions for masking foliage decline are suggested in text of photo 78.

ASSOCIATIONS: *Muscari armeniacum*, photo 128.

Narcissus 'Hawera'

Bulb, 12 × 6 in (30 × 15 cm), fragrant yellow blooms, mid spring, dark yellow-green foliage, mid to late spring. Does well in average soil with average or less moisture in sun or part shade. USDA Zones 4–9. Needs well-drained soil. A triandrus-jonquilla hybrid daffodil with several flowers per stem. Companions for masking foliage decline are suggested in text of photo 78.

ASSOCIATIONS: 'Hawera' offers small scale and vertical emphasis. Foliage is fine- to medium-textured and flowers develop a medium-sized cup. See discussion under *Lamiastrum galeobdolon* 'Herman's Pride' for specific suggestions in landscape use.

Narcissus 'Mount Hood'

Bulb, 14 × 6 in (35 × 15 cm), blooms very pale yellow opening white, mid spring, dark yellow-green foliage, mid to late spring. Does well in average soil with average or less moisture in sun or part shade. USDA Zones 4–9. Needs well-drained soil. A vigorous trumpet-type daffodil. Companions for masking foliage decline are suggested in text of photo 78.

ASSOCIATIONS: 'Mount Hood' develops as a small-scale element with vertical growth habit. Foliage is medium-textured and large flowers develop a deep cup form behind the petals. See discussion under *Dicentra spectabilis* for joining with other spring-blooming plants.

Narcissus 'Thalia'

Bulb, 15–18 × 6 in (40–45 × 15 cm), fragrant white blooms, mid spring, dark yellow-green foliage, mid to late spring. Does well in average soil with average or less moisture in sun or part shade. USDA Zones 4–10. Needs well-drained soil. A triandrus-type daffodil sometimes referred to as "The Orchid Narcissus." Several flowers per stem. Companions for masking foliage decline are suggested in text of photo 78.

ASSOCIATIONS: *Arabis caucasica*, *Muscari armeniacum*, and *Viola cucullata*, photo 46.

'Thalia' can be introduced as a small-scale element of mixed textures. Foliage is vertical and fine-textured, while its flowers display medium texture and develop medium-sized cups. For specific design connections, see discussion under *Dicentra spectabilis* and *Trillium grandiflorum*, and text of photo 46.

Narcissus 'Trevithian'

Bulb, 12–18 × 6 in (30–45 × 15 cm), blooms fragrant, light yellow, mid spring, dark yellow-green foliage, mid to late spring. Does well in average soil with average or less moisture in sun or part shade. USDA Zones 4–9. Needs well-drained soil. A jonquilla-type daffodil. Photo 96. Companions for masking foliage decline are suggested in text of photo 78.

ASSOCIATIONS: *Muscari armeniacum*, photo 96.

A fine complementary spring association of light blue and light yellow results from association with *Brunnera macrophylla* and *Stylophorum diphyllum* (4:3:1). Foliage and flower forms are complex and *Brunnera* and *Stylophorum* blooms continue long after *Narcissus* fades. The expanding *Brunnera* foliage masks *Narcissus* dieback.

Nepeta mussinii

Herbaceous perennial, 12–18 × 18 in (30–45 × 45 cm), blooms light blue-violet, mid spring to summer, foliage fragrant, dark gray yellow-green, mid spring to fall. Does well in average soil with average or less moisture and sun. USDA Zones 3–8. Cut back after bloom to encourage fresh foliage and a compact second flowering. Self-sows freely. *Nepeta* × *faassenii* is an excellent substitute with finer leaf texture, neater form, and less inclination to self-sow. Photos 53, 69, 127. See also discussions under *Ajuga reptans* 'Atropurpurea', *Anaphalis margaritacea*, *Geranium sanguineum*, *Heliotropium* 'Marine', *Leucanthemum* × *superbum* 'Alaska', *Limonium latifolium*, and photo 41.

ASSOCIATIONS: *Allium giganteum*, photo 69; *Amsonia tabernaemontana* and *Aquilegia vulgaris*, photo 41; *Eschscholzia californica*, photo 127; *Hydrangea quercifolia*, photo 53; *Iris* × *germanica*, photo 41; *Leucanthemum* × *superbum* 'Alaska',

photo 41; *Lysimachia ciliata* 'Purpurea', photo 53; *Perilla frutescens*, photo 53; *Salvia* × *superba* 'May Night', photo 69.

Its light blue-violet blooms harmonize splendidly with the pastel tones in adjacent pale red *Nicotiana alata* 'Nicki Pink' blooms and in the complementary pale yellow-green flower heads of *Sedum* 'Autumn Joy' (2:4:1). By sheering *Nepeta* after its first bloom it can continue to associate well with *Sedum*'s maturing light red in late summer. The annual *Nicotiana* may also be cut back slightly if appearance deteriorates in summer, and it will bloom more or less continuously until fall.

Nepeta mussinii 'White Wonder'

Herbaceous perennial, 12–15 × 18 in (30–40 × 45 cm), blooms white, mid spring to summer, foliage fragrant, dark yellow-green, mid spring to fall. Does well in average soil with average or less moisture in sun or part shade. USDA Zones 3–8. Develops a more compact form than the species. Photo 38.

ASSOCIATIONS: *Geranium sylvaticum* 'Mayflower' and *Viola* 'Baby Lucia', photo 38.

Nepeta 'Six Hills Giant'

Herbaceous perennial, 24–36 × 36 in (60–90 × 90 cm), blooms very light blue-violet, late spring to summer, foliage fragrant, dark yellow-green, mid spring to fall. Does well in average soil with average or less moisture in sun. USDA Zones 4–8.

ASSOCIATIONS: This *Nepeta* cultivar can be considered a medium- to large-scale plant with fine textures. See discussion under *Miscanthus sinensis* 'Variegatus' for ideas to incorporate its design traits with grayish green foliage. See also text of photo 93 for further suggestions.

Nicotiana alata 'Lime Green'

Perennial, generally grown as an annual, 18–30 x 12 in (45–75 × 30 cm), blooms noticeably fragrant at night, pale yellow-green, late spring to fall, dark yellow-green foliage, spring to fall. Does well in average soil and moisture in sun or part shade. Photo 140. Hardy only in frost-free areas. See also discussion under *Gomphrena* 'Strawberry Fields'.

ASSOCIATIONS: *Gomphrena globosa* 'Lavender Lady', *Gomphrena globosa* 'Rosy', *Nicotiana alata* 'Nicki Pink', *Salvia farinacea* 'Victoria', photo 140.

Nicotiana alata 'Nicki Lime'

Perennial, generally grown as an annual, 15–18 × 12 in (40–45 × 30 cm), blooms noticeably fragrant at night, pale yellow-green, late spring to fall, dark yellow-green foliage, late spring to fall. Does well in average soil and moisture in sun or part shade. Hardy only in frost-free areas. Self sows.

ASSOCIATIONS: 'Nicki Lime' can be treated as a small-scale element of medium textures, with flowers developing in vertical clusters above a mass of foliage. See also discussions under *Salvia* 'Lady in Red' and *Salvia superba* 'May Night'.

One can produce a stunning association of complementary yellow-green and violet by using 'Nicki Lime' with violet-flowered *Petunia* 'Purple Robe' and *Salvia farinacea* 'Victoria' (2:2:3). Flower forms vary between the *Nicotiana* clusters, *Salvia* spires, and large, trumpet-shaped *Petunia* blooms. Foliage is rather uninteresting, but this annual association's almost continuous blooming from late spring to fall makes it invaluable for containers and borders.

Nicotiana alata 'Nicki Pink'

Perennial, generally grown as an annual, 15–18 × 12 in (40–45 × 30 cm), blooms noticeably fragrant at night, light to pale red, late spring to fall, dark yellow-green foliage, late spring to fall. Does well in average soil and moisture in sun or part shade. Photo 140. Hardy only in frost-free areas. Self-sows. See also discussions under *Campanula carpatica* 'Blue Clips', *Celosia elegans* 'Pink Tassles', *Malva moschata*, *Nepeta mussinii*, and *Senecio cineraria* 'Silver Queen'.

ASSOCIATIONS: *Gomphrena globosa* 'Lavender La-

dy', *Gomphrena globosa* 'Rosy', *Nicotiana alata* 'Lime Green', and *Salvia farinacea* 'Victoria', photo 140.

Nicotiana langsdorffii

Perennial, generally grown as an annual, 36–48 × 18 in (90–120 × 45 cm), blooms noticeably fragrant at night, very pale yellow-green, late spring to fall, dark yellow-green foliage, late spring to fall. Does well in average soil and moisture in sun or part shade. Photo 139. Hardy only in frost-free areas. Self-sows. See also discussion under *Verbena* 'Amor Light Pink'.

ASSOCIATIONS: *Alchemilla mollis*, *Heuchera* 'Palace Purple', *Polygonatum odoratum* 'Variegatum', *Salvia guaranitica*, *Salvia officinalis* 'Aurea', photo 139.

Blends well with the unusual forms and near-complementary deep red hue in grassy *Pennisetum* 'Burgundy Giant', dark blue-violet *Salvia guaranitica*, and light violet *Verbena bonariensis* (3:1:1:2). Sometimes used in large containers, this long-blooming combination of a grass and three annuals is easily assembled and also very effective in the border.

Nicotiana sylvestris, fragrant tobacco plant

Perennial, generally grown as an annual, 48–60 × 18 in (120–150 × 45 cm), white blooms noticeably fragrant at night, summer to fall, dark yellow-green foliage, late spring to fall. Does well in average soil and moisture in sun or very light shade. Photo 39. Hardy only in frost-free areas. Self-sows. See also discussions under *Cleome spinosa* 'Helen Campbell' and photo 17.

ASSOCIATIONS: *Ageratum houstonianum* 'Southern Cross', *Antirrhinum* 'White Rocket', *Argyranthemum frutescens*, *Cleome spinosa* 'Helen Campbell' and *Cleome spinosa* 'Violet Queen', photo 39; *Gladiolus callianthus*, *Tagetes* 'Primrose Lady', and *Zinnia* 'Dreamland Ivory', photo 17.

Associate one with three *Cleome spinosa* 'Helen Campbell', one *Hosta plantaginea* 'Royal Standard', and two *Lilium* 'Casa Blanca' to create a large-scale, long-blooming composition (1:3:1:2). These all-white blooms are particularly valuable in shaded spaces or night gardens where the fragrance in all four plants may be appreciated.

Nierembergia hippomanica var. *violacea* 'Purple Robe'

Half-hardy perennial, usually grown as an annual, 6–8 × 6 in (15–20 × 15 cm), blooms violet, late spring to summer, foliage very dark yellow-green, late spring to late summer. Does well in average soil with average or greater moisture in sun or part shade. USDA Zones 7–10. Remove spent flowers to encourage re-bloom. When grown as a perennial, cut back growth at end of growing season to promote compact growth. Photo 42.

ASSOCIATIONS: *Ageratum houstonianum* 'Blue Puffs', *Heliotropium* 'Marine', *Lobelia erinus* 'White Cascade', photo 42.

Nigella damescena 'Miss Jekyll'

Annual, 15–24 × 12 in (40–60 × 30 cm), blooms light blue to light blue-violet, late spring to summer, dark yellow-green foliage, late spring to fall. Does well in average soil and moisture in sun. Self-sows. Photo 47.

ASSOCIATIONS: *Alchemilla mollis* and *Malva moschata* 'Alba', photo 47.

The light red and light red-violet floral tints in *Papaver somniferum* and *Penstemon* 'Rose Elf' harmonize easily with the light blue blooms of 'Miss Jekyll' (3:1:1). The *Papaver* juxtaposes a valuable broad flower form against the more diffuse blooms of its companions.

Oenothera fruticosa

See *O. tetragona*

Oenothera tetragona (*O. fruticosa*), sundrops

Herbaceous perennial, 18 × 12 in (45 × 30 cm), blooms light yellow, late spring to summer, dark yellow-green foliage, mid spring to fall. Does well in average soil with average or less moisture and sun. USDA Zones 4–8. Photos 13, 61, 93. See also discussions under *Iris kaempferi*, *Salvia × superba* 'East Friesland', and *Zinnia* 'Old Mexico'.

ASSOCIATIONS: *Achillea* 'Moonshine', photo 93; *Delphinium grandiflorum* 'Blue Butterfly', photo 93; *Heliopsis scabra*, photo 13; *Lilium* 'Enchantment', photo 61; *Lysimachia punctata*, photo 13; *Nepeta* 'Six Hills Giant', photo 93; *Tanacetum parthenium*, photo 13; *Tropaeolum majus* 'Alaska', photo 61.

Association with the yellow-flowering *Heliopsis scabra* and red blooms of *Lychnis chalcedonica* produces a bold and bright large-scale grouping suitable for the warm-hued border (2:1:3). The effect of this primary color grouping is fairly brief, since *Oenothera* and *Lychnis* are not particularly long-blooming, but *Heliopsis* continues to offer its yellow daisy-type flowers and bold textured foliage for several weeks longer.

Onopordum acanthium,
cotton thistle, Scotch thistle

Biennial, 72 × 36 in (185 × 90 cm), blooms light red-violet, summer, foliage light, very gray yellow-green, late spring to late summer. Does well in average soil under dry to average conditions in sun. Photo 5.

ASSOCIATIONS: *Buddleja fallowiana* 'Lochinch', *Convolvulus cneorum*, *Helichrysum angustifolium*, *Potentilla flamea*, *Stachys byzantina*, photo 5.

Ornithogalum umbellatum, star-of-Bethlehem

Bulb, 6–9 × 6 in (15–25 × 15 cm), blooms white, mid to late spring, dark yellow-green foliage with pale stripe, mid spring to summer. Does well in average soil with average or less moisture in sun or part shade. USDA Zones 4–9. May naturalize to invasive proportions.

ASSOCIATIONS: Star-of-Bethlehem is a small-scale element of fine textures and straplike foliage. Its common name derives from its star-shaped flowers, although flowers typically close at night. See discussion under *Polygonatum odoratum* 'Variegatum' for a specific spring plant display.

Osmunda claytoniana, interrupted fern

Fern, 36–60 × 24 in (90–150 × 60 cm), flowers absent, foliage gray yellow-green, late spring to fall. Does well in average soil with moist conditions and shade. USDA Zones 3–8.

ASSOCIATIONS: This fern presents a large-scale mass of medium-textured foliage. A quartet for light shade adds six *Convallaria majalis,* four *Leucojum aestivum* 'Gravetye Giant', and four *Polygonatum biflorum* (1:6:4:4). The play of different plant forms establishes this group as a valuable garden accent. Small, white, bell-like blooms repeat in *Convallaria, Leucojum,* and *Polygonatum* and are best viewed at close range. Unlike other associations with *Convallaria majalis,* this group does not translate well to drift planting, where the delicate details of *Leucojum* and *Polygonatum* blooms may be lost.

Osteospermum 'Salmon Queen'

Perennial, usual grown as annual, 12 × 12 in (30 × 30 cm), blooms pale orange and pale yellow-orange, late spring to late summer, dark yellow-green foliage, late spring to fall. Does well with average to lean, well-drained soil and average moisture in sun. USDA Zones 8–10.

ASSOCIATIONS: This is a small-scale element with medium-textured flowers and fine-textured foliage. Its daisy-like flowers mingle and rise above the indistinct mass of leaves and stems. For specific companions see also discussions under photos 127 and 130.

The light red-orange and light orange tints in *Achillea millefolium* 'Weser River Sandstone' blooms harmonize with *Osteospermum*'s pale yellow-orange flowers and complement the light blue-green of *Elymus arenarius* foliage (2:1:1). *Osteospermum* and *Achillea* have a long bloom season which makes this association especially valu-

able. The trio is also well suited for designs featuring warm pastel hues.

Paeonia lactiflora 'Festiva Maxima'

Herbaceous perennial, 30–36 × 36 in (75–90 × 90 cm), blooms fragrant, white with dark red splash, late spring, dark yellow-green foliage, mid spring to fall. Does well in average soil and moisture, and sun. USDA Zones 3–7. Photo 2. See also discussion under *Celosia plumosa* 'New Look'.

ASSOCIATIONS: *Geranium sanguineum* 'Album' and *Iris sibirica* 'White Swirl', photo 2.

Paeonia lactiflora 'Miss America'

Herbaceous perennial, 18–36 × 36 in (45–90 × 90 cm), blooms white with yellow stamens, late spring, dark yellow-green foliage, mid spring to fall. Does well in average soil and moisture in sun. USDA Zones 3–7.

ASSOCIATIONS: 'Miss America' can act as a medium- to large-scale element for garden design purposes. Flowers are broad and broad-textured, foliage is medium-textured and visually an indistinct mass. Site one with two *Alchemilla mollis,* three *Digitalis grandiflora,* one *Thalictrum speciocissimum,* and two *Trollius* 'Alabaster' (1:2:3:1:2) to make a large-scale grouping for the pastel or warm-hued mixed border, or even as a pale complement for cool-hued groupings. Overlapping flowering occurs in late spring and summer in tones of light yellow to very pale yellow verging on white. Varied foliage forms and tones remain captivating after the long flowering period. Flourishes in sun or light shade.

Paeonia suffruticosa, tree peony

Shrub, 4–5 × 4 ft (1.2 –1.5 × 1.2 m), blooms light yellow, pale red, light red-violet, and white, mid spring, dark yellow-green foliage, mid spring to fall. Does well in average soil, average or less moisture, and part shade or sun. USDA Zones 3–7. Many hybrid cultivars available. Photo 9.

ASSOCIATIONS: *Trollius europeus* 'Superbus' and *Tulipa* 'Golden Artist', photo 9.

Papaver rhoeas, corn poppy

Generally grown as an annual in all zones, 12–24 × 12 in (30–60 × 30 cm), blooms red, late spring to late summer, foliage very dark yellow-green, late spring to late summer. Plant in average to poor soil, supply average or less moisture and site in full sun. Leaves poisonous. Photo 24.

ASSOCIATIONS: *Leucanthemum vulgare* and *Tanacetum parthenium*, photo 24.

Papaver somniferum, opium poppy

Generally grown as an annual in all zones, 30 × 12 in (75 × 30 cm), blooms pale red-violet, summer, foliage dark, very gray yellow-green, mid to late summer. Does well in average soil with average or less moisture in sun. Fruits and sap are poisonous. Photos 29, 138. See also discussion under *Nigella damescena* 'Miss Jekyll'.

ASSOCIATIONS: *Geranium psilostemon*, photo 138; *Kniphofia* 'Atlanta', photo 138; *Lavandula angustifolia* 'Hidcote', photo 29; *Salvia sclarea*, photo 29.

Pennisetum alopecuroides, fountain grass

Perennial grass, 36 × 60 in (90 × 150 cm), seedheads gray yellow-green to dark red-violet, summer to fall, dark yellow-green foliage, late spring to fall. Does well in average soil with average to greater moisture in sun. USDA Zones 4–9. Photos 117, 118. See also discussion under *Echinacea purpurea* 'Bright Star'.

ASSOCIATIONS: *Artemisia lactiflora*, photo 117; *Monarda fistulosa*, photo 117; *Sedum* 'Autumn Joy', photos 117, 118; *Stachys byzantina*, photo 118.

The distinctive form and near effortless culture of fountain grass promote its frequent use in gardens and larger landscapes. A principal attraction is its late-season plumes, their color beginning as a light grayish green which gradually develops a dark reddish hue. Joining such hues with the long-blooming, pale yellow flowers of *Tagetes* 'Primrose Lady' and tall, light-violet flowered *Verbena bonariensis* allows a near-complementary, low-maintenance association for sun (1:2:4). *Pennisetum*'s loose, active form also mitigates the dull solidity of *Tagetes* blooms.

Pennisetum 'Burgundy Giant'

Perennial grass, usually treated as an annual, 5 × 7 ft (1.5 × 2.1 m), seedheads deep red, summer to fall, deep red foliage, late spring to fall. Does well in average soil with average to greater moisture in sun. USDA Zones 9–10.

ASSOCIATIONS: 'Burgundy Giant' offers large scale with fine-textured flowers and foliage. Flowers assume the form of an arching plume while foliage is slightly weeping. See discussions under *Celosia elegans* 'Pink Tassles', *Nicotiana langsdorffii*, and *Thalictrum rochebrunianum* for specific landscape connections.

Penstemon hirsutus 'Pygmaeus'

Herbaceous perennial, 9 × 12 in (25 × 30 cm), blooms pale violet, late spring to summer, foliage very dark yellow-green, late spring to late summer. Does well in average soil with average or less moisture in sun. USDA Zones 4–9. Requires well-drained soil. Photo 113.

ASSOCIATIONS: *Allium schoenoprasum*, *Artemisia* 'Powis Castle', *Cerastium tomentosum*, *Veronica spicata* subsp. *incana*, photo 113.

Penstemon 'Rose Elf'

Herbaceous perennial, 18 × 12 in (45 × 30 cm), blooms very light red, late spring to summer, dark yellow-green foliage, late spring to fall. Does well in average soil with average or less moisture in sun. USDA Zones 5–8. Requires well-drained soil. See discussion under photo 108.

ASSOCIATIONS: 'Rose Elf' is a small-scale design element with medium-textured flowers and foliage.

Flowers are clustered above indistinct foliage. For specific companions see discussions under *Geranium* 'Johnson's Blue', *Nigella damescena* 'Miss Jekyll', and photo 108.

Perilla frutescens

Generally grown as an annual in all zones, 24–36 × 18 in (60–90 × 45 cm), blooms white, summer, foliage very deep red-violet, summer to fall. Does well in average soil with average or less moisture in sun. Photos 18, 20, 94, 121. See also discussions under *Asteromoea mongolica*, *Gomphrena globosa* 'Strawberry Fields', *Salvia farinacea* 'Victoria', and photo 53.

ASSOCIATIONS: *Allium sphaerocephalon*, photo 121; *Artemisia* 'Powis Castle', photo 121; *Aster frickartii* 'Mönch', photo 94; *Cosmos bipinnatus* 'Versailles Tetra', photo 18; *Gomphrena globosa* 'Strawberry Fields', photo 20; *Hydrangea quercifolia*, photo 53; *Knautia macedonica*, photo 18; *Nepeta mussinii*, photo 53; *Prunus cistena*, photo 18; *Rosa* 'Prospero', photo 18; *Sedum* 'Ruby Glow', photo 121; *Solidago* 'Crown of Rays', photo 94; *Zinnia elegans* 'Red Sun', photo 20.

Perovskia atriplicifolia, Russian sage

Herbaceous perennial, 36 × 18 in (90 × 45 cm), blooms pale violet, mid to late summer, foliage very gray yellow-green, summer to fall. Prefers average to lean soil with average or less moisture and sun. USDA Zones 3–9. May require staking when planted in rich soil. Photo 81. See also discussions under *Campanula carpatica* 'Blue Clips', *Delphinium* 'Charles Gregory Broan', *Echinacea purpurea* 'Bright Star', *Helictotrichon sempervirens*, and *Veronica spicata* 'Blue Fox'.

ASSOCIATIONS: *Hemerocallis* cultivars, photo 81.

Petunia 'Burgundy Madness'

Annual, 9–12 × 12 in (25–30 × 30 cm), blooms dark red-violet, late spring to summer, dark yellow-green foliage, late spring to fall. Does well in av-

erage soil with average to greater moisture in sun or part shade. Photo 32. See also discussion under *Antirrhinum majus* 'White Rocket'.

ASSOCIATIONS: *Lobularia maritima* 'Carpet of Snow', *Lobularia maritima* 'Royal Carpet', *Salvia splendens* 'Laser Purple', photo 32.

Petunia 'Purple Robe'

Annual, 9–12 × 12 in (25–30 × 30 cm), blooms dark violet, late spring to fall, dark yellow-green foliage, late spring to summer. Does well in average soil with average to greater moisture in sun or part shade. *Petunia* 'Royal Cascade' is another fine cultivar.

ASSOCIATIONS: See *Nicotiana alata* 'Nicki Lime' and *Salvia argentea* for associations with yellow-green blooms and silvery foliage.

Phalaris arundinacea var. picta, ribbon grass

Grass, 18–36 × 18 in (45–90 × 45 cm), seedheads insignificant , very pale red, summer, foliage light gray yellow-green with pale yellow stripes, late spring to late summer. Does well in average or lean soil with average moisture in sun or part shade. USDA Zones 4–8. May be invasive. Cut back and fertilize if brown and spindly in summer. Photo 10. See also comments under *Anemone* 'Honorine Jobert', *Aruncus dioicus*, *Astilbe × arendsii* 'Deutschland', *Ligularia stenocephala* 'The Rocket', *Macleaya microcarpa*, and photo 6.

ASSOCIATIONS: *Alchemilla mollis*, photo 10; *Dicentra spectabilis* 'Alba', photo 6; *Digitalis purpurea* 'Excelsior', photo 6; *Hemerocallis* 'Colonial Dame', photo 10; *Iris pseudacorus*, photo 10; *Lilium* 'French Vanilla', photo 10; *Lysimachia punctata*, photo 10; *Phalaris arundinacea* var. *picta*, photos 6, 10; *Tiarella cordifolia*, photo 6; *Verbascum chaixii*, photo 10.

This perennial grass is often linked in light shade with *Aruncus dioicus* because of the advantage of juxtaposing near-white and green in blooms and foliage. This theme can continue by adding the smaller, later, white-blooming *Lysimachia cleth-*

roides (1:1:5). Foliage hues vary between very pale and very dark green and excellent textures range from feathery to grassy to lance-shaped.

A fairly precisely detailed and ornamental effect for light shade is obtained when one is planted with one *Astilbe* × *arendsii* 'Deutschland', three *Polygonatum biflorum*, and three *Tiarella cordifolia* (1:1:3:3). Flower and leaf forms and textures are captivatingly varied. All-white blooms, which will be clearly visible in light shade, occur successively in *Tiarella*, *Polygonatum*, and *Astilbe*, followed later by *Phalaris*.

Phlox caroliniana **'Miss Lingard'**

See *P. maculata* 'Miss Lingard'

Phlox divaricata, woodland phlox

Herbaceous perennial, 12–15 × 12 in (30–40 × 30 cm), blooms very pale blue-violet, mid to late spring, dark yellow-green foliage, mid spring to summer. Plant in average to rich soil with average to greater moisture and part shade or morning sun. USDA Zones 3–9. See also comments under *Heuchera* 'Palace Purple' and *Phlox subulata*.

ASSOCIATIONS: Woodland phlox can be considered a small-scale element with medium-textured flowers and fine-textured foliage. Flowers develop in clusters above a nebulous mass of foliage. A bright, small-scale ornamental grouping for early spring in light shade can be completed with *Galium odoratum*, *Polygonatum odoratum* 'Variegatum', and *Tiarella cordifolia* (2:2:5:3). The white blooms in these companions are allied with the phlox's nodding, blue-violet clusters for several weeks. *Galium*'s fine-textured, prostrate, bright yellow-green foliage contrasts with the broader form in the mounded *Tiarella* and arching, white-edged, *Polygonatum* leaves.

Also associates well with *Stylophorum diphyllum* in light shade. The purer, more powerful yellow floral hue of *Stylophorum* readily swamps its delicate color unless care is taken to proportion the two plants so *Phlox* quantities are strongly evident. A ratio of 4:1 allows the *Phlox* to partici-

pate successfully. Particularly effective underplanting for shrubs or small trees.

Phlox maculata **'Alpha'**

Herbaceous perennial, 30–36 × 24 in (75–90 × 60 cm), blooms light red-violet, late spring to summer, dark yellow-green foliage, mid spring to fall. Prefers average to rich soil with average or greater moisture in sun or part shade. USDA Zones 3–9. Cut back faded flowers to encourage re-bloom.

ASSOCIATIONS: 'Alpha' is a medium-scale planting design element with uniform, medium textures. Site with *Cosmos bipinnatus* 'Early Sensation' and *Monarda didyma* 'Bluestocking' (1:1:1) to make excellent use of its red-violet flower color. Combined with the harmonious, adjacent light violet in *Monarda* 'Bluestocking' and the light red-violet to white in *Cosmos*, *Phlox*'s sometimes jarring floral hue is subdued. Summer flower forms range from dense *Phlox* panicles, to scattered daisy-like *Cosmos*, to globular *Monarda* clusters. Similar heights allow them to intermingle smoothly.

Phlox maculata **'Miss Lingard',**
(*P. caroliniana* 'Miss Lingard')

Herbaceous perennial, 24–30 × 24 in (60–75 × 60 cm), blooms white, late spring to summer, dark yellow-green foliage, spring to fall. Plant in average to rich soil with average or greater moisture in sun or part shade. USDA Zones 3–9. Cut back faded flowers to encourage re-bloom.

ASSOCIATIONS: This is a medium-scale plant, and both flowers and foliage display medium textures. See discussions under *Eryngium amethystinum* and *Filipendula vulgaris* for details on its use in a sunny situation or in part shade.

Phlox paniculata **'Bright Eyes'**

Herbaceous perennial, 24 × 18 in (60 × 45 cm), blooms very pale red with light red-violet eye, mid to late summer, dark yellow-green foliage, late spring to fall. Prefers average to rich soil, average or greater moisture, in sun or part shade. USDA Zones 3–9. Thin in spring, leaving only about five strong shoots. Remove faded flowers. Self-sows, but seedlings are not true. Photo 120. See also comments under *Allium sphaerocephalon*.

ASSOCIATIONS: *Anemone vitifolia* 'Robustissima', *Miscanthus sinensis* 'Gracillimus', *Thalictrum rochebrunianum*, photo 120.

Phlox subulata, moss phlox

Herbaceous perennial, 3–6 × 12 in (10–15 × 30 cm), blooms pale violet, pale red-violet and white, early to mid spring, dark yellow-green foliage, early spring to late summer. Does well in average soil with average or less moisture in sun. USDA Zones 3–9. Leaves evergreen in mild climates. Cut back after first bloom.

ASSOCIATIONS: Moss phlox is of small scale, fine textures, and horizontal emphasis in its growth habit. One *Arabis caucasica* associates well with two of these prolifically flowering *Phlox* and three of the more subtle *Phlox divaricata* (2:1:3). Pale blue-violet, light violet, and white can graciously welcome spring, particularly if these color masses are balanced so that *Phlox divaricata* flowers are not eclipsed by its companions' more dense and striking bloom. A lightly shaded space or one with morning sun and well-drained soil will suit this group. Foliage is uninteresting after bloom.

Muscari armeniacum is a popular companion due to its blue-violet blooms, and together with *Phlox subulata* makes a particularly harmonious underplanting for common lilac (*Syringa vulgaris*). The repetition of similar floral hues at the lilac's base can make a compelling visual anchor. *Muscari* and *Phlox* should be interplanted in roughly equal proportions and massed beneath the shrub. A minimal underplanting would extend from the shrub's trunk to its drip line.

Phlox 'Chattahoochee'

Herbaceous perennial, 10–15 × 12 in (25–40 × 30 cm), blooms pale blue-violet with light red-violet center, late spring to summer, dark yellow-green foliage, mid spring to late summer. Does well in average soil with average or less moisture in sun. USDA Zones 3–9.

ASSOCIATIONS: 'Chattahoochee' can be considered a small-scale element of indistinct form. Its flowers are medium-textured while foliage presents a fine texture. See comments under *Allium karataviense* for use in a spring trio highlighted by silvery foliage.

Physostegia virginiana 'Summer Snow'

Herbaceous perennial, 30–48 × 18 in (75–120 × 45 cm), blooms white, mid to late summer, foliage very dark yellow-green, late spring to fall. Does well in average soil and moisture in sun or part shade. USDA Zones 2–9. Photo 44. See also discussion under *Achillea millefolium* 'White Beauty'.

ASSOCIATIONS: *Eryngium amethystinum*, *Liatris spicata* 'Kobold', *Platycodon grandiflorus*, photo 44.

Platycodon grandiflorus, balloon flower

Herbaceous perennial, 18–24 × 12 in (45–60 × 30 cm), blooms light blue-violet, summer, dark yellow-green foliage, mid to late summer. Does well in average soil and moisture in sun or part shade. USDA Zones 3–8. Emerges late in spring. Photo 44. See also discussion under *Achillea millefolium* 'Weser River Sandstone'.

ASSOCIATIONS: *Eryngium amethystinum*, *Liatris spicata* 'Kobold', *Physostegia virginiana* 'Summer Snow', photo 44.

Plumbago larpentiae
See *Ceratostigma plumbaginoides*

Podophyllum peltatum, mandrake, mayapple

Herbaceous perennial, 12–18 × 12 in (30–45 × 30 cm), blooms white, mid spring, dark yellow-green foliage, early spring to late summer. Prefers average to rich soil with average to greater moisture and part shade. USDA Zones 3–9. Leaves, roots, and seeds poisonous. Spreads readily. Photo 49. See also discussion under *Erythronium* 'Pagoda'.

ASSOCIATIONS: *Mertensia virginica*, photo 49.

Composition with other natives, such as *Stylophorum diphyllum* and *Trillium grandiflorum* (2:1:1), can create an early spring attraction of excellent foliage forms. This trio is especially appealing when planted in informal drifts under trees and shrubs. Heights and plant forms are all rather similar and lend a unifying, soothing elegance to the landscape. Light shade, rich soil, and moisture are essential to their success. The pleasing foliage association is brightened by interruptions of yellow *Stylophorum* blooms, white to pink *Trillium*, and discrete white *Podophyllum* flowers.

Polemonium reptans 'Blue Pearl'

Herbaceous perennial, 12 × 12 in (30 × 30 cm), blooms very light blue-violet, mid spring, foliage very dark yellow-green, mid spring to fall. Does well in average soil with average or greater moisture and part shade or sun. USDA Zones 3–9. Self-sows. Will not tolerate full sun and high temperatures.

ASSOCIATIONS: For design purposes this plant can be described as small scale, of medium textures, and with an indistinct outline. Together with *Muscari armeniacum* and *Myosotis sylvatica* (2:4:2) it produces a compact and delightful composition. All plants will do well in a situation offering morning sun or very light shade and well-drained soil. This small-scale group offers a delicate cluster of light blue amid dominating blue-violet flowers, and all bloom together over a very long period in spring.

Polygonatum biflorum, small Solomon's seal

Herbaceous perennial, 12–24 × 12 in (30–60 × 30 cm), blooms white with very pale yellow-green band, mid to late spring, dark yellow-green foliage, mid spring to fall. Plant in average to rich soil, supply average or greater moisture, in part shade

or shade. USDA Zones 4–9. Photo 4. See also discussions under *Aquilegia* 'Olympia', *Brunnera macrophylla*, *Digitalis purpurea* 'Excelsior', *Myrrhis odorata*, *Osmunda claytoniana*, *Phalaris arundinacea* var. *picta*, and *Stylophorum diphyllum*.

ASSOCIATIONS: *Adiantum pedatum* and *Dicentra eximia* 'Alba', photo 4.

A cultural affinity for ferns in lightly shaded spaces suggests association with the delicate *Athyrium filix-femina*. Adding a foreground planting of *Ajuga reptans* 'Atropurpurea' brings textural contrast and complementary deep-red violet foliage and light violet blooms (2:1:5). *Polygonatum biflorum* gently arches over its diminutive companions.

Polygonatum odoratum 'Variegatum'

Herbaceous perennial, 12–24 × 12 in (30–60 × 30 cm), blooms white, mid to late spring, foliage yellow-green with white edge, mid spring to fall. Plant in average to rich soil, supply average or greater moisture, in part shade or shade. USDA Zones 4–9. Photos 7, 52, 125, 139. See also discussion under *Phlox divaricata*.

ASSOCIATIONS: *Ajuga reptans*, photo 52; *Ajuga reptans* 'Atropurpurea', photo 125; *Alchemilla mollis*, photos 125, 139; *Aruncus dioicus*, photo 125; *Asteromoea mongolica*, photo 7; *Athyrium nipponicum*, photo 52; *Crambe cordifolia*, photo 7; *Heuchera* 'Palace Purple', photo 139; *Hosta fortunei*, photo 52; *Miscanthus sinensis* 'Zebrinus', photo 7; *Nicotiana langsdorffii*, photo 139; *Salvia guaranitica*, photo 139; *Salvia officinalis* 'Aurea', photo 139.

Presents a striking repetition of grayed yellow-green and white variegation when placed with *Ornithogalum umbellatum*, *Tulipa* 'Greenland', and *Tulipa* 'Spring Green' (2:2:3:3). The pale gray yellow-green and white *Ornithogalum* flowers are about 9 in (23 cm) high and the stems, flowers, and variegated leaves of the taller *Polygonatum* arch over while the tulips rise behind the entire group. A touch of complementary and brightening red-violet is present in the *Tulipa* 'Greenland' blooms.

Polystichum setiferum 'Divisilobum'

Fern, 24 × 24 in (60 × 60 cm), flowers absent, foliage very dark yellow-green, mid spring to fall. Prefers average soil and moisture in either part shade or sun. USDA Zones 5–8. Photo 132.

ASSOCIATIONS: *Alstroemeria* Ligtu Hybrids, *Elymus arenarius*, *Macleaya microcarpa*, photo 132.

Potentilla flamea

Herbaceous perennial, 12 × 12 in (30 × 30 cm), blooms red, summer, foliage very dark yellow-green, late spring to late summer. Does well in average soil and moisture in sun. USDA Zones 3–8. Photos 5, 68.

ASSOCIATIONS: *Buddleja fallowiana* 'Lochinch', photo 5; *Convolvulus cneorum*, photo 5; *Helichrysum angustifolium*, photo 5; *Hemerocallis* cultivars, photo 68; *Lilium lancifolium*, photo 68; *Onopordum acanthium*, photo 5; *Stachys byzantina*, photo 5.

Potentilla 'Tangerine'

Shrub, 36 × 36 in (90 × 90 cm), blooms light orange or yellow, summer, foliage very dark yellow-green, late spring to late summer. Does well in average soil and moisture, and sun. USDA Zones 3–8. Blooms yellow if planted in full sun. Will require occasional pruning to maintain a size appropriate to small-scale compositions. Photo 66.

ASSOCIATIONS: *Achillea millefolium* 'Salmon Beauty', *Digitalis mertonensis*, *Geranium endressii* 'Wargrave Pink', photo 66.

A strong yellow, orange, and yellow-orange composition includes one *Achillea* 'Coronation Gold', two *Alstroemeria* Ligtu Hybrids, three *Kniphofia* 'Atlanta', and three *Lysimachia punctata* (1:1:2:3:3). Flower forms and foliage textures are pleasingly varied. The strength of the colors demands an open space, probably in a long, warm-hued border.

Primula japonica, Japanese primrose

Herbaceous perennial, 12–18 × 12 in (30–45 × 30 cm), blooms light red-violet, mid to late spring, dark yellow-green foliage, early spring to summer. Does well in average soil with moist to very moist conditions in part shade. USDA Zones 5–7.

ASSOCIATIONS: Japanese primrose design traits identify it as a small-scale element with medium-textured flowers and broad-textured foliage. Flowers develop as a long-stemmed vertical cluster while foliage remains a basal mass. See discussion under *Athyrium nipponicum* 'Pictum' for joining in light shade as a shrub underplanting.

It contrasts well with the fine foliage texture of *Adiantum pedatum* and spring emergence of *Rodgersia aesculifolia* (10:3:1). Spring will also initiate a stunning color contrast between the light red-violet *Primula* blooms and the yellow green of the companion foliage. Light shade will suit this trio best and it is ornamental enough for a formal shaded border. Provide more moisture than average and the foliage of all three will thrive and harmonize effortlessly for several months.

Primula japonica 'Postford White'

Herbaceous perennial, 12–18 × 12 in (30–45 × 30 cm), blooms white with a light yellow center, mid to late spring, dark yellow-green foliage, early to late spring. Does well in average soil with moist to very moist conditions in part shade. USDA Zones 5–7.

ASSOCIATIONS: 'Postford White' is of small scale and mixed textures. Flowers are medium-textured and develop as a vertical cluster. Foliage is broad-textured, developing as a foliage mass at the plant's base. See discussions under *Digitalis purpurea* 'Excelsior' and *Galium odoratum* for details on popular spring associations.

Primula vulgaris, English primrose

Herbaceous perennial, 8 × 8 in (20 × 20 cm), blooms fragrant, light yellow, mid to late spring, dark yellow-green foliage, early spring to summer.

Does well in average soil with moist to very moist conditions in part shade. USDA Zones 5–8.

ASSOCIATIONS: The English primrose is of smaller scale than the two preceding species. Flowers and foliage are both medium-textured and conform to the stemmed floral cluster rising from a mass of basal leaves. See discussion on *Digitalis purpurea* 'Excelsior' for a composition using foxgloves, ferns, and primroses.

Prunus × cistena, purpleleaf sand cherry

Shrub, 4–7 × 5 ft (1–2 × 2 m), blooms light red-violet and white, mid spring, deep red-violet foliage, mid spring to fall. Does well in average soil and moisture in sun. USDA Zones 2–7. Photo 18. See also discussion under *Aquilegia* 'Black Star'.

ASSOCIATIONS: *Cosmos bipinnatus* 'Versailles Tetra', *Perilla frutescens*, *Rosa* 'Prospero', *Knautia macedonica*, photo 18.

Pulmonaria saccharata 'Mrs. Moon'

Herbaceous perennial, 10 × 15 in (25 × 40 cm), blooms light blue to light violet, early to late spring, foliage dark yellow-green with white speckles, early spring to late summer. Does well in average soil with moist to average conditions, in shade or part shade. USDA Zones 3–8. Photos 34, 83, 84. See also discussions under *Dicentra eximia* 'Alba' and *Lamium maculatum* 'White Nancy'.

ASSOCIATIONS: *Dicentra eximia* 'Luxuriant', photo 34; *Dicentra spectabilis* 'Alba', photo 34; *Digitalis grandiflora*, photos 83, 84; *Geranium × magnificum*, photos 83, 84; *Iris pseudacorus*, photos 83, 84.

Rhododendron 'Golden Dream'

Deciduous shrub, 5–7 × 5 ft (1.5–2.1 × 1.5 m), blooms light yellow, late spring, dark yellow-green foliage, mid spring to fall. Plant in average to rich acid soil, supply average moisture, and site in part shade or filtered sun. USDA Zones 6–9. See discussion under *Aquilegia vulgaris* and photo 92.

ASSOCIATIONS: 'Golden Dream' is large-scale with medium textures and abundant flowers. See text of photo 92 where this is a suggested alternate planted with *Hosta fortunei* 'Aurea' and *Hyacinthoides hispanica*.

Rodgersia aesculifolia, fingerleaf rodgersia

Herbaceous perennial, 36–48 × 24 in (90–120 × 60 cm), blooms white, summer, foliage very dark yellow-green, late spring to late summer. Suitable for rich to average soil in moist conditions and part shade or sun. USDA Zones 5–7. See also discussions under *Aruncus dioicus*, *Iris sibirica* 'White Swirl', and *Primula japonica*.

ASSOCIATIONS: This plant is of large scale and broad textures. Flowers evolve as airy plumes topping an exuberant mass of foliage. To produce a subtle play of white or creamy white with yellow-green, associate with *Alchemilla mollis*, *Astilbe × arendsii* 'Deutschland', and *Iris sibirica* 'White Swirl' (1:2:1:3). Light shade is most suitable and will permit the white blooms to glow and persist. *Rodgersia* enlarges the scale of this group. Differences in foliage forms create an arresting composition from spring to late summer.

Rosa 'Chaucer'

David Austin rose, introduced 1970. Shrub, 36 × 36 in (90 × 90 cm), blooms fragrant, pale red, summer, foliage very dark yellow-green, late spring to late summer. Suitable for rich to average soil and moisture in sun. USDA Zones 5–9.

ASSOCIATIONS: 'Chaucer' is large-scale with medium textures and abundant flowers. See text of photo 33, where this is a suggested alternate planted with *Erigeron karvinskianus* and *Lavandula stoechas*.

Rosa 'New Dawn'

Climbing rose, introduced 1930. Shrub, 20 ft (6 m), blooms fragrant, pale red, late spring to late summer, foliage very dark yellow-green, late spring to fall. Suitable for rich to average soil and moisture in sun. USDA Zones 5–9.

ASSOCIATIONS: 'New Dawn' is large-scale with medium textures and abundant flowers. See text of photo 91 where this is a suggested alternate planted with *Achillea* 'Coronation Gold', *Delphinium belladona*, and *Tanacetum parthenium*.

Rosa 'Prospero'

David Austin rose, introduced 1982. Shrub, 30 × 30 in (75 × 75 cm), fragrant dark red blooms summer, foliage very dark yellow-green, late spring to late summer. Suitable for rich to average soil and moisture in sun. USDA Zones 5–9. Photos 18, 136.

ASSOCIATIONS: *Beta vulgaris* subsp. *cicla*, photo 136; *Cosmos bipinnatus* 'Versailles Tetra', photo 18; *Geranium psilostemon*, photo 136; *Knautia macedonica*, photos 18, 136; *Malva sylvestris* 'Mauritiana', photo 136; *Perilla frutescens* and *Prunus cistena*, photo 18; *Salvia officinalis* 'Purpurea', photo 136.

Rudbeckia 'Goldsturm'

Herbaceous perennial, 18–24 × 18 in (45–60 × 45 cm), blooms yellow-orange, mid to late summer, dark yellow-green foliage, late spring to fall. Does well in average soil and moisture and sun. USDA Zones 3–9. Photos 11, 65, 147. See also discussions under *Asclepias tuberosa* 'Gay Butterflies' and *Monarda didyma* 'Cambridge Scarlet'.

ASSOCIATIONS: *Cosmos sulphureus* 'Sunny Red', photo 65; *Echinacea purpurea* 'Bright Star', photo 147; *Iris pseudacorus*, photo 65; *Lobelia cardinalis*, photo 65; *Miscanthus sinensis* 'Gracillimus', photo 11; *Salvia* 'Lady in Red', photo 65; *Silphium perfoliatum*, photo 11.

Rudbeckia hirta 'Goldilocks'

Short-lived perennial, usually grown as an annual, 18–24 × 18 in (45–60 × 45 cm), blooms yellow-orange, mid to late summer, dark yellow-green foliage, late spring to fall. Does well in average soil and moisture, and sun.

ASSOCIATIONS: 'Goldilocks' functions as a medium-scale element of mixed textures in our garden connections survey. Flowers are broad-textured, developing as numerous, flat, daisy-like forms. Foliage is medium-textured and abundant, yielding a mass of dark yellow-green. See discussions under *Salvia officinalis* 'Aurea' and *Tagetes* 'Golden Gem' for details on joining with yellow-green and yellows.

Ruta graveolens, rue

Herbaceous perennial, 24–36 × 15 in (60–90 × 40 cm), blooms pale yellow, summer, foliage dark gray yellow-green, mid spring to fall or evergreen in mild climates. Does well in average soil and moisture, and sun. USDA Zones 4–9. Plant parts may be irritating to the skin. Photos 57, 141.

ASSOCIATIONS: *Alchemilla alpina*, photo 141; *Astilbe* × *arendsii* 'Fanal', photo 141; *Campanula poscharkyana*, photo 141; *Corydalis lutea*, photo 57; *Cosmos sulphureus* 'Sunny Red', photo 57.

Similar foliage color in a different form occurs in *Hosta* 'Krossa Regal' and *Thalictrum speciocissimum*. Use one of each and expand on the notion that this slightly bluish gray green can complement pale red and red-orange tints by adding two *Digitalis* × *mertonensis* and three of the later-blooming pale red-violet *Astilbe chinensis* 'Pumila' (1:1: 1:2:3). Morning sun or very light partial shade is ideal for this successively flowering group.

Salvia argentea, silver sage

Biennial or short-lived perennial, 18–36 × 24 in (45–90 × 60 cm), blooms white, summer, foliage very pale, gray yellow-green, late spring to fall. Does well in average soil with average or less moisture and sun. USDA Zones 5–9. Flowers rather uninteresting; remove flowering stems to favor foliage development.

ASSOCIATIONS: Silver sage offers medium- to large-scale, fine-textured flowers developing in a branching cluster, and broad-textured foliage expanding as a basal mass. Its striking, broad silvery foliage associates pleasingly in planters or borders with the complementary dark violet hues in *Petunia* 'Purple Robe' and *Salvia farinacea* 'Victoria' (1:5:3). The mass of silver foliage in this annual combination presents a strong focus for many months. Care should be taken to avoid conflicting hues or strong visual competition when positioning within a border.

Salvia farinacea 'Victoria'

Half-hardy perennial, usually grown as an annual, 18–24 × 12 in (45–60 × 30 cm), blooms violet, late spring to fall, dark yellow-green foliage, late spring to fall. Does well in average soil and moisture in sun or part shade. Perennial in USDA Zones 7–10. Photos 88, 112, 140, 142. See also discussions under *Achillea* 'Moonshine', *Ageratum houstonianum* 'Blue Horizon', *Cleome spinosa* 'Helen Campbell', *Coreopsis verticillata* 'Moonbeam', *Gaillardia* × *grandiflora* 'Goblin', *Helichrysum petiolare*, *Nicotiana alata* 'Nicki Lime', *Salvia argentea*, and photo 145.

ASSOCIATIONS: *Coreopsis grandiflora* 'Sunray', photo 145; *Gomphrena globosa* 'Lavender Lady', photos 112, 140; *Gomphrena globosa* 'Rosy', photo 140; *Helichrysum petiolare*, photo 112; *Heliotropium* 'Marine', photo 88; *Nicotiana alata* 'Lime Green' and *Nicotiana alata* 'Nicki Pink', photo 140; *Tagetes patula*, photo 88; *Tagetes* 'Primrose Lady', photo 142; *Zinnia elegans* 'Red Sun', photo 142; *Verbena canadensis* 'Homestead Purple', photo 145.

Its violet blooms and excellent, medium-textured foliage mingle well with broad, deep red-violet *Perilla frutescens* leaves, producing a striking, but relatively effortless annual combination (2:1).

Salvia guaranitica, blue sage

Half-hardy perennial, usually grown as an annual, 36–60 × 24 in (90–150 × 60 cm), blooms dark blue-violet, late summer to fall, dark yellow-green foliage, summer to fall. Does well in average soil and moisture in sun. USDA Zones 8–10. Photos 135.

See also discussions under *Cleome spinosa* 'Helen Campbell', *Nicotiana langsdorffii*, and photo 139.

ASSOCIATIONS: *Alchemilla mollis*, photo 139; *Asteromoea mongolica*, photo 135; *Centranthus ruber*, photo 135; *Heuchera* 'Palace Purple', photo 139; *Lythrum salicaria* 'Morden Pink', photo 135; *Nicotiana langsdorffii*, photo 139; *Polygonatum odoratum* 'Variegatum', photo 139; *Salvia officinalis* 'Aurea', photo 139.

Rather dark cool hues are stressed with its dark violet flowers associating with *Monarda didyma* 'Violet Queen' and *Veronica* 'Sunny Border Blue' (2:3:2). The blue-violet spires of *Veronica* and dark violet *Salvia* juxtapose pleasingly with red-violet *Monarda* clusters. The somber, somewhat receding colors are best viewed at close quarters. Foliage is varied and pleasing.

Salvia haematodes

Herbaceous perennial, 36 × 18 in (90 × 45 cm), blooms light blue-violet, late spring to summer, dark yellow-green foliage, mid spring to fall. Does well in average soil and moisture in sun. USDA Zones 6–9. See discussion under photo 45.

ASSOCIATIONS: *Salvia haematodes* can be developed as a relatively large-scale design element of medium textures. Its abundant flowers develop in a vertical cluster above indistinct foliage mass. See text of photo 45 for associating with *Geranium* 'Johnson's Blue' and *Stachys byzantina*.

Salvia icterina

See *S. officinalis* 'Aurea'

Salvia 'Lady in Red'

Generally grown as an annual in all zones, 12–15 × 12 in (30–40 × 30 cm), blooms red, late spring to fall, dark yellow-green foliage, late spring to fall. Does well in average soil and moisture in sun. USDA Zones 9–10. Photo 65. See also discussions under *Tagetes* 'Primrose Lady' and photo 24.

ASSOCIATIONS: *Cosmos bipinnatus* 'Sonata White', photo 24; *Cosmos sulphureus* 'Sunny Red', photo

65; *Iris pseudacorus*, photo 65; *Lobelia cardinalis*, photo 65; *Rudbeckia* 'Goldsturm', photo 65.

Its lightly distributed red blooms associate well with the pale yellow-green in *Alchemilla mollis* and *Nicotiana alata* 'Nicki Lime' blooms (3:1:2). *Nicotiana* and *Salvia* continue blooming together for many weeks after *Alchemilla* flowers fade. Their finer foliage textures serve as contrast for the broad *Alchemilla* leaves.

Salvia nemerosa

See *S.* × *superba*

Salvia officinalis 'Aurea' (*S. icterina*)

Half-hardy perennial, usually grown as an annual, 12–18 × 12 in (30–45 × 30 cm), occasional blooms light red-violet, summer, foliage very gray yellow-green with light yellow-green markings, late spring to fall. Does well in average soil and moisture in sun. USDA Zones 7–10. Long season foliage accent. Photos 110, 139. See also discussions under *Ajuga reptans* and *Chrysanthemum pacificum*.

ASSOCIATIONS: *Alchemilla mollis*, photo 139; *Heuchera* 'Palace Purple', photos 110, 139; *Nicotiana langsdorffii*, photo 139; *Polygonatum odoratum* 'Variegatum', photo 139; *Salvia guaranitica*, photo 139; *Salvia officinalis* 'Purpurea', photo 110; *Veronica spicata* 'Blue Charm', photo 110.

Makes a fine foreground planting for similar and near-adjacent hues in yellow-green flowering *Alchemilla mollis* and taller, yellow-orange blooming *Rudbeckia hirta* 'Goldilocks' (3:1:1). *Rudbeckia*'s long bloom season sustains this eye-catching composition for many weeks.

Salvia officinalis 'Purpurea'

Half-hardy perennial, usually grown as an annual, 12–18 × 12 in (30–45 × 30 cm), blooms light red-violet, summer, foliage very deep red-violet with gray yellow-green markings, late spring to fall. Does well in average soil and moisture in sun. USDA Zones 7–10. Long season foliage accent. Photos 30, 110, 136.

ASSOCIATIONS: *Beta vulgaris* subsp. *cicla*, photo 136; *Geranium psilostemon*, photo 136; *Heuchera* 'Palace Purple', photo 110; *Knautia macedonica*, photo 136; *Malva sylvestris* 'Mauritiana', photo 136; *Rosa* 'Prospero', photo 136; *Salvia officinalis* 'Aurea', photo 110; *Symphytum officinale*, photo 30; *Syringa microphylla* 'Superba', photo 30; *Veronica spicata* 'Blue Charm', photo 110.

Its deep red violet foliage shows dramatically against the pale gray leaves of *Artemisia* 'Powis Castle', which in turn contrast the dark foliar hues in *Cotinus coggygria* 'Royal Purple' and *Foeniculum vulgare* 'Purpureum' (5:3:1:1). Flowering is insignificant in this striking foliage composition of outstanding color and textural contrasts that are effective from late spring to fall.

Salvia sclarea, clary sage

Biennial, 36–60 × 36 in (90–150 × 90 cm), blooms pale red-violet, summer to fall, foliage dark gray yellow-green, late spring to fall. Does well in average soil and moisture in sun. USDA Zones 7–10. Photos 29, 36. See also discussion under *Alcea rosea* 'Single Mix'.

ASSOCIATIONS: *Alcea rosea* 'Single Mix', photo 36; *Lavandula angustifolia* 'Hidcote', photo 29; *Papaver somniferum*, photo 29; *Verbena bonariensis*, photo 36.

Pale red-violet tints in the nebulous spires of *Salvia sclarea* harmonize with similar hues in *Malva moschata*. These two plants make a fine background for the distinctively globular, light blue-violet *Agapanthus praecox* blooms (1:2:4). Although these receding colors are less visible over large distances, the striking flower forms and large scale are nonetheless eye-catching.

Salvia splendens 'Laser Purple'

Annual, 12 × 12 in (30 × 30 cm), blooms red-violet to violet, late spring to fall, dark yellow-green foliage, late spring to fall. Does well in average soil and moisture in sun. USDA Zones 9–10.

ASSOCIATIONS: 'Laser Purple' is a small-scale design element with medium textures and abundant flowers developing in a vertical cluster above indistinct foliage mass. See text of photo 32 for associating with *Lobularia maritima* 'Carpet of Snow', *Lobularia maritima* 'Royal Carpet', and *Petunia* 'Burgundy Madness'.

Salvia × superba (*S. nemerosa*)

Herbaceous perennial, 18–36 × 18 in (45–90 × 45 cm), blooms violet, late spring to summer, dark yellow-green foliage, mid spring to fall. Does well in average soil and moisture in sun. USDA Zones 5–9. Cut back after bloom to encourage a second flowering. Photo 129. See also discussion under *Tradescantia × andersoniana* 'Blue Stone'.

ASSOCIATIONS: *Calendula officinalis*, photo 129.

Salvia × superba 'East Friesland'

Herbaceous perennial, 15–18 × 18 in (40–45 × 45 cm), blooms violet, late spring to summer, dark yellow-green foliage, late spring to fall. Does well in average soil and moisture in sun. USDA Zones 5–9. Cut back after bloom to encourage a second flowering. Photos 86, 149. See also discussions under *Centranthus ruber*, *Geranium endressii* 'Wargrave Pink', *Geranium* 'Johnson's Blue', and *Lychnis coronaria*.

ASSOCIATIONS: *Achillea* 'Coronation Gold', photo 86; *Achillea filipendulina* 'Gold Plate', photo 149; *Corydalis lutea*, photo 86; *Lythrum salicaria* 'Morden Pink', photo 149.

Associates splendidly with the near-complementary colors present in *Achillea* 'Moonshine' and *Oenothera tetragona* (3:2:1). This association emphasizes strong, bold, intense floral hues by combining the bright yellow *Oenothera* with this pure violet *Salvia*. The flat, horizontal *Achillea* blooms increase form complexity and mitigate the almost strident color intensity of its companions.

Salvia × superba 'May Night'

Herbaceous perennial, 18 × 18 in (45 × 45 cm), blooms dark violet, late spring to summer, dark yellow-green foliage, late spring to fall. Does well in average soil and moisture in sun. USDA Zones 5–9. Cut back after bloom to encourage a second flowering. Photo 69. See also discussion under *Veronica spicata* subsp. *incana*.

ASSOCIATIONS: *Allium giganteum*, *Centranthus ruber*, *Digitalis grandiflora*, *Lychnis coronaria*, *Nepeta mussinii*, photo 69.

Planted with one *Alchemilla mollis* in the foreground and two *Nicotiana alata* 'Nicki Lime' in the midground, the slightly taller and darker *Salvia* creates a stunning, bold association of complementary violet and yellow-green (3:1:2). *Nicotiana* has a long flowering season, especially if cut back during mid-season. Re-bloom in *Nicotiana* and *Salvia* may coincide in late summer.

Sanguinaria canadensis, bloodroot

Herbaceous perennial, 6–9 × 12 in (15–25 × 30 cm), blooms white, early spring, dark gray yellow-green foliage, early spring to late summer. Prefers average to rich soil with average or greater moisture in either part shade or shade. USDA Zones 3–9. Plants should not be allowed to dry out. Photo 54.

ASSOCIATIONS: *Hakonechloa macra* 'Aureola', photo 54.

Santolina chamaecyparissus, lavender cotton

Shrub, 18–24 × 24 in (45–60 × 60 cm), blooms light yellow, summer, foliage fragrant, whitish gray yellow-green, early spring to winter. Does well in average soil with dry conditions and sun. USDA Zones 6–8. Prune faded flowers.

ASSOCIATIONS: Lavender cotton has medium scale, fine textures, and small globular flowers. Foliage develops as a compact, indistinct mass of color. See text of photo 74, where this is a suggested alternate planted with *Berberis thunbergii* 'Atropurpurea Nana', *Lavandula angustifolia* 'Munstead', and *Teucrium chamaedrys*.

Scabiosa macedonica

See *Knautia macedonica*

Scabiosa rumelica

See *Knautia macedonica*

Scilla campanulata

See *Hyacinthoides hispanica*

Scilla hispanica

See *Hyacinthoides hispanica*

***Sedum* 'Autumn Joy'**

Herbaceous perennial, 18–24 × 24 in (45–60 × 60 cm), blooms evolve from pale yellow-green to light red to very deep red, summer to fall, foliage dark gray yellow-green, summer to fall. Does well in average soil with average or less moisture in sun or part shade. USDA Zones 3–8. Photos 1, 73, 114, 116, 117, 118. See also discussions under *Anaphalis margaritacea*, *Artemisia* 'Powis Castle', *Aster frikartii* 'Mönch', *Echinacea purpurea* 'Bright Star', *Helictotrichon sempervirens*, *Nepeta mussinii*, and *Stachys byzantina*.

ASSOCIATIONS: *Allium giganteum*, photo 114; *Allium tuberosum*, photo 1; *Anemone vitifolia* 'Robustissima', photo 73; *Artemisia lactiflora*, photos 117, 118; *Aster frikartii* 'Mönch', photo 73; *Echinacea purpurea* 'Bright Star', photo 73; *Monarda didyma* 'Violet Queen', photo 116; *Monarda fistulosa*, photos 117, 118; *Pennisetum alopecuroides*, photos 117, 118; *Stachys byzantina*, photo 118; *Yucca filamentosa*, photo 114.

***Sedum* 'Rosy Glow'**

Herbaceous perennial, 6–12 × 15 in (15–30 × 40 cm), blooms red to red-violet, developing from light red-violet buds, late summer to fall, foliage dark gray yellow-green, late spring to fall, dark red-violet stems. Does well in average soil with average or less moisture in sun or part shade. USDA Zones 3–8. Photo 103. See also discussions under *Astilbe chinensis* 'Pumila' and *Stachys byzantina*.

ASSOCIATIONS: *Alchemilla mollis*, photo 103.

***Sedum* 'Ruby Glow'**

Herbaceous perennial, 6–12 × 15 in (15–30 × 40 cm), blooms dark red, summer to fall, foliage dark gray yellow-green, late spring to fall, dark red-violet stems. Does well in average soil with average or less moisture in sun or part shade. USDA Zones 3–8. Photos 121, 131. See also discussion under *Imperata cylindrica* 'Red Baron'.

ASSOCIATIONS: *Allium sphaerocephalon*, photo 121; *Artemisia* 'Powis Castle', photo 121; *Dianthus* × *allwoodii* 'Essex Witch', photo 131; *Dicentra eximia* 'Luxuriant', photo 131; *Elymus arenarius*, photo 131; *Perilla frutescens*, photo 121.

***Sedum* 'Vera Jameson'**

Herbaceous perennial, 10–15 × 12 in (25–40 × 30 cm), blooms dark grayish red, late summer to fall, dark gray yellow-green foliage edged dark grayish red-violet, late spring to fall, dark grayish red-violet stems. Does well in average soil with average or less moisture in sun or part shade. USDA Zones 3–8. Photos 35, 122. See also discussion under *Ageratum houstonianum* 'Blue Horizon'.

ASSOCIATIONS: *Allium senescens* 'Glaucum', photo 122; *Allium tuberosum*, photo 35; *Anemone vitifolia* 'Robustissima', photo 35; *Berberis thunbergii* 'Atropurpurea', photo 35; *Gomphrena globosa* 'Lavender Lady', photo 35; *Verbascum chaixii*, photo 122.

Emphasis is placed on its dusky foliage when associated with gray-foliaged *Artemisia* 'Powis Castle' and the darker gray-green foliage of *Caryopteris* × *clandonensis* 'Heavenly Blue' (1:1:2). The grayed, dusky red-violet *Sedum* blooms harmonize beautifully with this *Artemisia*, as do the blue-violet clusters of late summer *Caryopteris* blooms. Sun and good drainage will suit all three.

***Senecio cineraria* 'Silver Queen'**

Perennial, usually grown as an annual, 8 × 8 in (20 × 20 cm), blooms pale yellow, summer, foliage very pale gray yellow-green, mid spring to fall. Does well in average soil, less than average moisture and sun. Perennial in USDA Zones 8–10. Photo 23.

ASSOCIATIONS: *Celosia plumosa* 'New Look', photo 23.

Associating one pale pink blooming *Nicotiana alata* 'Nicki Pink' and two *Verbena* 'Amor Light Pink' with the pale grayed foliage of 'Silver Queen' shows both pastel hues to great advantage. *Nicotiana* slightly enlarges the scale of the association while adding textural complexity and light fragrance (3:1:2).

Silphium perfoliatum, cup plant

Herbaceous perennial, 48–96 × 24 in (120–245 × 60 cm), blooms yellow, late summer to fall, dark yellow-green foliage, summer to fall. Does well in average soil and moisture in sun. USDA Zones 3–10. See discussion under photo 11.

ASSOCIATIONS: Cup plant can contribute large scale, fine-textured flowers, and medium-textured foliage. Its daisy-like flowers top a strongly vertical mass of foliage. See text of photo 11 for grouping with *Miscanthus sinensis* 'Gracillimus' and *Rudbeckia* 'Goldsturm'.

Solidago 'Cloth of Gold'

Herbaceous perennial, 20 × 12 in (50 × 30 cm), blooms very dark yellow, late summer to fall, dark yellow-green foliage, summer to fall. Does well in average soil and moisture in sun or part shade. USDA Zones 3–10. May be invasive. Photo 14. See also discussion under *Chrysanthemum pacificum*.

ASSOCIATIONS: *Argyranthemum frutescens*, *Aruncus dioicus*, *Digitalis grandiflora*, *Iris pseudacorus*, *Weigela florida* 'Variegata', photo 14.

Solidago 'Crown of Rays'

Herbaceous perennial, 18–24 × 12 in (45–60 × 30 cm), blooms dark yellow, late summer to fall, dark yellow-green foliage, summer to fall. Does well in average soil and moisture in sun or part shade. USDA Zones 3–10. May be invasive. Photos 87, 94.

See also discussions under *Tagetes* 'Golden Gem' and photo 60.

ASSOCIATIONS: *Aster frickartii* 'Mönch', photo 94; *Aster novae-angliae* 'Purple Dome', photo 87; *Chrysanthemum pacificum*, photo 87; *Helenium autumnale* 'Brilliant' and ; *Helenium autumnale* 'Riverton', photo 60; *Perilla frutescens*, photo 94; *Zinnia elegans* 'Red Sun', photo 60.

Its bright yellow flower tuft contrasts in form while harmonizing in color with the red-orange hue of *Gomphrena globosa* 'Strawberry Fields'. Plant in a ratio of 1:2. Use this pairing to augment other warm-hued summer associations or to stand alone where a small- to medium-scale planting focus is needed.

Spiraea aruncus

See *Aruncus dioicus*

Stachys byzantina (*S. lanata*), lamb's ears

Herbaceous perennial, 12–15 × 12 in (30–40 × 30 cm), blooms light red-violet, late spring, foliage very pale gray yellow-green, spring to fall. Does well in average soil and moisture in sun. USDA Zones 4–8. Blooms insignificant. Long season foliage accent. Photos 5, 45, 111. See also discussions under *Ageratum houstonianum* 'Southern Cross', *Allium karataviense*, *Allium christophii*, *Anaphalis margaritacea*, *Artemisia schmidtiana* 'Silver Mound', *Baptisia australis*, *Cerastium tomentosum*, *Echinacea purpurea* 'Bright Star', *Geranium* × *magnificum*, *Geranium sanguineum* 'Album', *Lobelia erinus* 'Cambridge Blue', and photo 118.

ASSOCIATIONS: *Buddleja fallowiana* 'Lochinch', photo 5; *Convolvulus cneorum*, photo 5; *Geranium* 'Johnson's Blue', photo 45; *Gomphrena globosa* 'Rosy', photo 111; *Helichrysum angustifolium*, photo 5; *Onopordum acanthium*, photo 5; *Pennisetum alopecuroides*, photo 118; *Potentilla flamea*, photo 5; *Salvia haematodes*, photo 45, *Sedum* 'Autumn Joy', photo 118.

Associates well with many sedums, especially the tall *Sedum* 'Autumn Joy' with its grayed reddish hues, and the prostrate *Sedum* 'Rosy Glow'.

This simple association is further enhanced by adding a blue-green grassy *Festuca glauca*. Use one *Sedum* 'Autumn Joy' in the background, one *Festuca* in midground, and two *Stachys* with one *Sedum* 'Rosy Glow' in the foreground (2:1:1:1).

Stachys grandiflora

See *S. macrantha* 'Robusta'

Stachys lanata

See *S. byzantina*

Stachys macrantha 'Robusta' (*S. grandiflora*)

Herbaceous perennial, 15–24 × 12 in (40–60 × 30 cm), blooms light red-violet, mid to late summer, dark yellow-green foliage, late spring to fall. Does well in average soil and moisture in sun. USDA Zones 2–8.

ASSOCIATIONS: 'Robusta' can be termed a small to medium-scale plant element of medium textures, mounding foliage, and vertical emphasis with flower development. See discussion under *Argyranthemum* 'Mary Wootton' for using in a calming summer association.

Statice latifolia

See *Limonium latifolium*

Stylophorum diphyllum, celandine poppy

Herbaceous perennial, 18–24 × 12 in (45–60 × 30 cm), blooms yellow, early spring to late summer, dark yellow-green foliage, early spring to fall. Does well with average to rich soil with average or greater moisture in morning sun or part to full shade. USDA Zones 4–9. See also discussions under *Epimedium* × *versicolor* 'Sulphureum', *Erythronium* 'Pagoda', *Iris sibirica*, *Narcissus* 'Trevithian', *Phlox divaricata*, and *Podophyllum peltatum*.

ASSOCIATIONS: Garden design uses for the celandine poppy begin by recognizing its medium scale and mixed textures. Flowers are medium-textured and open, foliage is broad-textured with a mounding habit. It is commonly planted with *Myosotis*

sylvatica (1:5) for an effective spring association of light blue and yellow blooms. Because its blooms are intermittent and scattered over the broad foliage, they accord nicely without overwhelming the carpets of tiny *Mysosotis* blooms. The pair is wonderful as an underplanting for small trees or large shrubs in the lightly shaded informal garden.

Another light shade shrub or tree underplanting with more structure and formality can be produced by association with *Hyacinthoides hispanica* and *Polygonatum biflorum* (1:3:2). The mounded plant form and loosely distributed *Stylophorum* blooms lend an informal appearance, but the vertical spires of the blue-violet *Hyacinthoides* blooms and the taller, slightly pendulous *Polygonatum* form create a structured composition of distinct forms and textures absent in the preceding association.

Symphytum officinale, comfrey

Herbaceous perennial, 36 × 36 in (90 × 90 cm), blooms light and dark red-violet, late spring, foliage very dark yellow-green, mid spring to fall. Does well in average soil with average or greater moisture in sun or part shade. USDA Zones 3–9. May be difficult to eradicate. Photo 30.

ASSOCIATIONS: *Salvia officinalis* 'Purpurea' and *Syringa microphylla* 'Superba', photo 30.

Syringa microphylla 'Superba'

Shrub, 4–6 × 6 ft (1.2–1.8 × 1.8 m), blooms fragrant, light red-violet, mid to late spring, dark yellow-green foliage, mid spring to fall. Does well in average soil and moisture in sun. USDA Zones 5–7. Photo 30.

ASSOCIATIONS: *Salvia officinalis* 'Purpurea' and *Symphytum officinale*, photo 30.

Tagetes 'Golden Gem'

Generally grown as an annual in all zones, 9–15 × 12 in (25–40 × 30 cm), blooms fragrant, yellow, late spring to fall, dark yellow-green foliage, late spring to fall. Does well with average soil and moisture in sun. Remove spent flowers to prolong bloom. See also discussions under *Chrysanthemum pacificum* and *Coreopsis* 'Sunray'.

ASSOCIATIONS: *Tagetes* 'Golden Gem' can be used as a small-scale element of indistinct form. Its fine texture in both flowers and foliage shows well against the broader, bolder form of *Rudbeckia hirta* 'Goldilocks', and the intermediate textures of *Solidago* 'Cloth of Gold' and *Chrysanthemum pacificum* (2:1:2:2). This successive, strong-hued, yellow-flowering composition blooms for several months, with the boldest effects occurring in summer and late summer.

Tagetes 'Lemon Gem'

Generally grown as an annual in all zones, 9–15 × 12 in (25–40 × 30 cm), blooms fragrant, very light yellow, late spring to fall, dark yellow-green foliage, late spring to fall. Does well with average soil and moisture in sun. Remove spent flowers to prolong bloom. See discussion under *Hemerocallis* 'Stella d'Oro' for use in moderating a potentially strident yellow-orange.

ASSOCIATIONS: 'Lemon Gem' offers the same design considerations as the preceding cultivar, differing only in bloom color. See discussions under *Coreopsis verticillata* 'Moonbeam' and *Veronica latifolia* 'Crater Lake Blue' for details on compositions in yellows and blue-violet.

Tagetes patula, French marigold

Generally grown as an annual in all zones, 10–12 × 12 in (25–30 × 30 cm), blooms fragrant, yellow, late spring to fall, dark yellow-green foliage, late spring to fall. Does well with average soil and moisture in sun. Remove spent flowers to prolong bloom. Photo 88.

ASSOCIATIONS: *Heliotropium* 'Marine' and *Salvia farinacea* 'Victoria', photo 88.

Tagetes 'Primrose Lady'

Generally grown as an annual in all zones, 15 × 15 in (40 × 40 cm), blooms fragrant, pale greenish yellow, late spring to fall, dark yellow-green foliage, late spring to fall. Does well with average soil and moisture in sun. Remove spent flowers to prolong bloom. Photos 17, 142. See also discussions under *Ceratostigma plumbaginoides, Pennisetum alopecuroides, Tropaeolum* 'Gleam Mixture', and *Verbascum chaixii.*

ASSOCIATIONS: *Cleome spinosa* 'Helen Campbell', *Gladiolus callianthus, Nicotiana sylvestris,* photo 17; *Salvia farinacea* 'Victoria', photo 142; *Zinnia* 'Dreamland Ivory', photo 17; *Zinnia elegans* 'Red Sun', photo 142.

General design benefits are gained from association with other warm-hued blooms in lighter, indistinct textures. It combines pleasingly with the bi-colored *Lantana* 'Confetti' and *Salvia* 'Lady in Red' (1:2:3). As all three annuals flower over several months, these smaller companion blooms gradually expand loosely around the solid *Tagetes* form.

Tanacetum parthenium (*Chrysanthemum parthenium*)

Herbaceous perennial, 12–36 × 12 in (30–90 × 30 cm), blooms white with yellow center, summer to fall, dark yellow-green foliage, late spring to fall. Does well in average soil with average or less moisture in sun or part shade. USDA Zones 6–8. Typically short-lived, but freely self-sows. Photos 13, 91. See also discussions under *Allium senescens, Eryngium amethystinum,* and photo 24.

ASSOCIATIONS: *Achillea* 'Coronation Gold', photo 91; *Delphinium belladona,* photo 91; *Heliopsis scabra,* photo 13; *Lysimachia punctata,* photo 13; *Oenothera tetragona,* photo 13; *Papaver rhoeas,* photo 24 ; *Rosa* 'New Dawn', photo 91.

Telekia speciosa

See *Buphthalmum speciosum*

Teucrium chamaedrys

Herbaceous perennial, 12–18 × 12–18 in (30–45 × 30–45 cm), blooms light red-violet, mid to late summer, dark yellow-green foliage, mid spring to fall. Does well in average, well-drained soil and average to less moisture in sun or part shade. USDA Zones 4–9. Shear to keep growth habit compact. Photo 74.

ASSOCIATIONS: *Berberis thunbergii* 'Atropurpurea Nana', *Ballota pseudodictamnus*, *Lavandula angustifolia* 'Munstead', *Santolina chamaecyparissus*, photo 74.

Thalictrum aquilegifolium 'Album'

Herbaceous perennial, 36–48 × 36 in (90–120 × 90 cm), blooms white, late spring to mid summer, foliage dark gray yellow-green, mid spring to fall. Requires rich soil, plenty of moisture, and part shade. USDA Zones 5–8. May need protection from strong winds. Growth will be weak if plant is over-fertilized. Photo 26.

ASSOCIATIONS: *Aquilegia* 'Rose Queen', *Cimicifuga racemosa*, *Dicentra eximia* 'Luxuriant', *Hosta fortunei* 'Marginato-alba', photo 26.

Thalictrum rochebrunianum

Herbaceous perennial, 36–60 × 36 in (90–150 × 90 cm), blooms very light violet, mid to late summer, very dark gray yellow-green foliage, late spring to late summer. Does well with average soil and moisture in sun or part shade. USDA Zones 5–9.

ASSOCIATIONS: The primary design trait difference between this and the preceding entry is in its light violet floral color, as its large scale, vertical form, and fine textures provide similar design opportunities. See discussions under *Alcea rosea* 'Single Mix', *Anemone vitifolia* 'Robustissima', and photo 120 for specific suggestions.

One can also create a large-scale grouping in harmonious tones of red, red-violet, and violet when two *Thalictrum rochebrunianum* are used as background for the daisy-form flowers of two

Echinacea purpurea 'Bright Star' and one grassy *Pennisetum* 'Burgundy Giant'. Contrasting this trio with a distinctly different leaf texture in a foreground *Hosta plantaginea* 'Royal Standard' emboldens the composition (2:2:1:1). *Hosta*'s bright yellow-green leaves complement the cool hues of its companions' blooms and foliage. It also contributes its own fragrant white spires in late summer.

Thalictrum speciocissimum

Herbaceous perennial, 36–60 × 36 in (90–150 × 90 cm), blooms very light yellow, mid summer, foliage dark gray yellow-green, late spring to late summer. Does well with average soil and moisture in sun or part shade. USDA Zones 5–9.

ASSOCIATIONS: This can be viewed as a large-scale vertical element of fine textures sporting tall, airy flower clusters. Foliage is lush yet not dense. See discussions under *Paeonia lactiflora* 'Miss America' and *Ruta graveolens* for associations highlighting its pastel floral hue and foliage color.

Thelypteris noveboracensis

See *Dryopteris noveboracensis*

Tiarella cordifolia, foamflower

Herbaceous perennial, 8–12 × 12 in (20–30 × 30 cm), blooms white to very pale yellow, late spring, dark yellow-green foliage, mid spring to late summer. Prefers average to rich soil, damp to average moisture, and full or part shade. USDA Zones 3–8. Photo 6. See also discussions under *Ajuga reptans*, *Phalaris arundinacea* var. *picta*, and *Phlox divaricata*.

ASSOCIATIONS: *Dicentra spectabilis* 'Alba', *Digitalis purpurea* 'Excelsior', *Lamium maculatum* 'White Nancy', *Phalaris arundinacea* var. *picta*, photo 6.

In part or filtered shade, combine two foamflowers with three *Ajuga reptans*, one *Geranium endressii* 'Wargrave Pink', and three *Hyacinthoides hispanica* (2:3:1:3). The association offers a light-tinted and therefore easily harmonized grouping. Blooming is successive from spring to summer. Floral colors include light blue-violet *Ajuga* and *Scilla*, near-white *Tiarella* and pink in *Geranium*. Foliage composition is pleasing for the entire growing season.

Tradescantia × andersoniana 'Blue Stone'

Herbaceous perennial, 18–36 × 18 in (45–90 × 45 cm), blooms light blue-violet, late spring to summer, dark yellow-green foliage, late spring to fall. Does well with average soil and moisture in sun or part shade. USDA Zones 4–9.

ASSOCIATIONS: 'Blue Stone' displays medium to large scale, medium textures, and flowers that top a sprawl of clean-edged, straplike foliage. See discussions under *Centaurea montana* for a fine grouping of blue-violet with white, and under *Hosta* 'Krossa Regal' for a foliar design connection. See also text of photo 41 for relating to *Amsonia tabernaemontana*, *Aquilegia vulgaris*, *Iris × germanica*, *Leucanthemum × superbum*, and *Nepeta mussinii*. Text of photo 69 also discusses its possible use with *Nepeta mussinii* while adding the dark violet-flowered *Salvia × superba* 'May Night'.

Violet *Salvia × superba* spires harmonize with the adjacent light blue-violet flower clusters of 'Blue Stone' and both contribute to a delicate light/dark contrast with pale hued, horizontal *Achillea taygetea* blooms (1:2:1). Flowering persists for several weeks and all will re-bloom sparsely in late summer if cut back after first flowering.

Tradescantia × andersoniana 'Innocence'

Herbaceous perennial, 18–36 × 18 in (45–90 × 45 cm), blooms white, late spring to summer, dark yellow-green foliage, late spring to fall. Does well with average soil and moisture in sun or part shade. USDA Zones 4–9.

ASSOCIATIONS: 'Innocence' can function as a medium- to large-scale element of medium textures. Its flowers develop in vertical clusters above strap-

like foliage. See discussion under *Achillea millefolium* 'White Beauty' for connections with other whites and yellows.

Trillium grandiflorum, great white trillium

Herbaceous perennial, 12–18 × 12 in (30–45 × 30 cm), blooms white, mid spring, foliage very dark yellow-green, mid spring to summer. Suitable for rich to average soil, damp to average moisture, and shade or part shade. USDA Zones 4–9. Adequate moisture will prevent premature summer dormancy. Photo 48. See also discussion under *Podophyllum peltatum*.

ASSOCIATIONS: *Myosotis sylvatica*, photo 48.

To create a successively blooming association suitable for the light shade of deciduous trees, use one with one *Geranium macrorrhizum* and five *Narcissus* 'Thalia' (1:1:5). *Trillium* blooms as the *Narcissus* and *Geranium* foliage is emerging. *Trillium* and white *Narcissus* blooms fade as *Geranium* foliage and blooms expand and mask the decline of its companions. *Narcissus* and *Geranium* also contribute distinctive fragrances.

Trollius 'Alabaster'

Herbaceous perennial, 24 × 24 in (60 × 60 cm), blooms pale yellow, mid to late spring, foliage very dark yellow-green, mid spring to summer. Does well in average soil with average or greater moisture in sun or part shade. USDA Zones 3–6. Remove spent blooms to prolong flowering.

ASSOCIATIONS: 'Alabaster' is of medium scale and textures with vertically held, globular flowers escaping its nebulous mass of foliage. See discussions under *Paeonia lactiflora* 'Miss America' and *Tulipa* 'White Triumphator' for design connection suggestions.

Trollius europeus 'Superbus'

Herbaceous perennial, 12–24 × 12 in (30–60 × 30 cm), blooms yellow, mid spring to summer, foliage very dark yellow-green, late spring to summer.

Does well in average soil with average or greater moisture in sun or part shade. USDA Zones 3–6. Remove spent blooms to prolong flowering. Photo 9.

ASSOCIATIONS: *Paeonia suffruticosa* and *Tulipa* 'Golden Artist', photo 9.

Tropaeolum majus 'Alaska'

Perennial, usually grown as an annual, 12 × 12 in (30 × 30 cm), blooms fragrant, orange, yellow-orange, or dark red, late spring to fall, foliage yellow-green with pale yellow stripe, late spring to fall. Does well in average soil with average or less moisture in sun. Photo 61. Flowers edible.

ASSOCIATIONS: *Lilium* 'Enchantment' and *Oenothera tetragona*, photo 61.

Tropaeolum majus 'Gleam Series'

Perennial, usually grown as an annual, 12–15 × 12 in (30–40 × 30 cm), blooms fragrant, orange, yellow-orange, or red, late spring to fall, yellow-green foliage, late spring to fall. Does well in average soil with average or less moisture in sun. Flowers edible.

ASSOCIATIONS: This 'Gleam Series' nasturtium displays small scale, medium-textured flowers, and a broad-textured, mounding mass of foliage. See discussion under *Achillea millefolium* 'Paprika' for joining in a bright, strong trio.

Its flowers harmonize easily with the pale yellow blooms of another easily grown, long-blooming annual, *Tagetes* 'Primrose Lady' (2:1). The broad *Tropaeolum* foliage is an excellent contrast for the finer *Tagetes* foliage. Its relaxed, spreading form reduces the stiffness apparent in most *Tagetes*, while its scattered, warm-hued blooms interrupt the often rigid display of *Tagetes* flowers. Both plants contribute distinct fragrance.

Tulipa 'Apricot Beauty'

Bulb, 14 × 6 in (35 × 15 cm), blooms very pale red-orange, mid spring, dark yellow-green foliage, mid

to late spring. Does well in average soil and moisture in sun. USDA Zones 2–8. A Single Early tulip.

ASSOCIATIONS: 'Apricot Beauty' can be seen as a medium-scale element of mixed textures. Flowers are broad-textured and oval-shaped, and lend vertical emphasis. Foliage is medium-textured, strap-like, and only slightly less transient than the bloom. See discussions under *Heuchera* 'Palace Purple' and photo 98 for ideas on association.

Tulipa 'Arabian Mystery'

Bulb, 18–24 × 6 in (45–60 × 15 cm), blooms deep red-violet and white, mid spring, dark yellow-green foliage, mid to late spring. Does well in average soil and moisture in sun. USDA Zones 2–8. A Darwin tulip. Photo 78.

ASSOCIATIONS: *Tulipa* 'Negrita' and *Viola* × *wittrockiana*, photo 78.

Tulipa 'Golden Artist'

Bulb, 14 × 6 in (35 × 15 cm), blooms yellow, mid spring, dark yellow-green foliage, mid to late spring. Does well in average soil and moisture in sun. USDA Zones 2–8. A Viridiflora tulip. Photo 9.

ASSOCIATIONS: *Paeonia suffruticosa* and *Trollius europeus* 'Superbus', photo 9;

Tulipa 'Greenland'

Bulb, 18–24 × 6 in (45–60 × 15 cm), blooms light red-violet with yellow-green stripe, mid spring, dark yellow-green foliage, mid to late spring. Does well in average soil and moisture in sun. USDA Zones 2–8. A Viridiflora tulip. Photo 75. See also discussion under *Polygonatum odoratum* 'Variegatum'.

ASSOCIATIONS: *Allium aflatuense* and *Viola* × *wittrockiana*, photo 75.

Tulipa 'Negrita'

Bulb, 18–24 × 6 in (45–60 × 15 cm), blooms dark red-violet, mid spring, dark yellow-green foliage, mid to late spring. Does well in average soil and moisture in sun. USDA Zones 2–8. A mid-season Triumph tulip. Photo 78. See also discussion under photo 72.

ASSOCIATIONS: *Tulipa* 'Arabian Mystery' and *Viola* × *wittrockiana*, photo 78.

Tulipa 'Pink Impression'

Bulb, 18–24 × 6 in (45–60 × 15 cm), blooms pale red or pale red-violet, mid spring, dark yellow-green foliage, mid to late spring. Does well in average soil and moisture in sun. USDA Zones 2–8. A Darwin type tulip. Photo 70.

ASSOCIATIONS: *Muscari armeniacum*, photo 70.

Tulipa 'Purple Rain'

Bulb, 18–24 × 6 in (45–60 × 15 cm), blooms dark red-violet, mid spring, dark yellow-green foliage, mid to late spring. Does well in average soil and moisture in sun. USDA Zones 2–8. A Darwin tulip. Photo 72.

ASSOCIATIONS: *Allium aflatuense* 'Purple Sensation' and *Camassia quamash*, photo 72.

Tulipa 'Queen of Night'

Bulb, 24 × 6 in (60 × 15 cm), blooms very deep red-violet, late spring, dark yellow-green foliage, late spring to summer. Does well in average soil and moisture in sun. USDA Zones 2–8. A Single Late tulip. Photos 21, 119. See also discussion under *Aquilegia* 'Black Star'.

ASSOCIATIONS: *Berberis thunbergii* 'Atropurpurea', photos 21, 119; *Hosta sieboldiana*, photo 119; *Tulipa* 'Red Shine', photo 21.

Forms a pleasing yellow-green and deep red-violet association with *Adiantum pedatum* (5:1). This pairing is ideal for a very lightly shaded location where *Adiantum* can enjoy somewhat moist conditions. The power of this planting derives from the use of dark against light and complementary colors, and the juxtaposition of prostrate and rising forms. Also sits well amid a groundcover of *Galium odoratum* or *Hedera helix*.

Tulipa 'Red Shine'

Bulb, 24 × 6 in (60 × 15 cm), blooms dark red, late spring, dark yellow-green foliage, late spring to summer. Does well in average soil and moisture in sun. USDA Zones 2–8. A Lily-flowered tulip, mid- to late-season. Photo 21.

ASSOCIATIONS: *Berberis thunbergii* 'Atropurpurea' and *Tulipa* 'Queen of Night', photo 21.

Tulipa 'Spring Green'

Bulb, 18–24 × 6 in (45–60 × 15 cm), blooms white and yellow-green, mid spring, dark yellow-green foliage, late spring. Does well in average soil and moisture in sun. USDA Zones 2–8. A Viridiflora tulip.

ASSOCIATIONS: 'Spring Green' has medium scale, broad flower texture, and medium foliage texture. Flower stems establish a vertical emphasis above the straplike foliage and terminate with an oval-shaped flower. See discussion under *Polygonatum odoratum* 'Variegatum' and photo 126 for design extension in yellow-green and white. See also text of photo 126 for joining with *Helleborus foetidus*, *Leucojum aestivum* 'Gravetye Giant', and *Vinca minor*.

Tulipa 'West Point'

Bulb, 18–24 × 6 in (45–60 × 15 cm), blooms light yellow, late spring, dark yellow-green foliage, late spring. Does well in average soil and moisture in sun. USDA Zones 2–8. A Lily-flowered tulip.

ASSOCIATIONS: 'West Point' shares design traits similar to *Tulipa* 'Spring Green' in terms of scale and texture, differing primarily in its lily-like flower shape. *Brunnera macrophylla* is frequently planted with spring-flowering bulbs because its strikingly dark, heart-shaped foliage expands to cover bulb decline. Use one here for the added highlight of its blue flowers, which would complement six of these yellow-flowered *Tulipa*. Adding three *Lamium maculatum* 'White Nancy' can increase later season interest when light variegated foliage can offer contrast to the dark *Brunnera* leaves. Include three *Myosotis sylvatica* to increase the light-blue flowering presence and enhance the dynamic quality of complementary color (6:1:3:3).

Tulipa 'White Triumphator'

Bulb, 18–24 × 6 in (45–60 × 15 cm), blooms white, mid spring, dark yellow-green foliage, mid to late spring. Does well in average soil and moisture in sun. USDA Zones 2–8. A Lily-flowered tulip. Photo 8. See also discussion under *Dicentra spectabilis* 'Alba'.

ASSOCIATIONS: *Epimedium* × *versicolor* 'Sulphureum', *Gladiolus callianthus*, *Hedera helix*, photo 8.

Intermingling an irregular cluster of these tulips among a couple of *Lamiastrum galeobdolon* 'Herman's Pride' and one *Trollius* 'Alabaster' provides a stunning white and pale yellow spring picture (5:2:1). *Lamiastrum* foliage provides a visual base for rising *Tulipa*. Also suitable as a groundcover for any spring-blooming shrubs flowering in warm hues or white. Particularly effective sited under *Cornus florida*, *Enkianthus campanulatus*, or *Viburnum plicatum* f. *tomentosum*.

Verbascum chaixii, nettle-leaved mullein

Herbaceous perennial, 30–60 × 18 in (75–150 × 45 cm), blooms very light yellow with dark red-violet center, late spring to summer, foliage dark yellow-green, late spring to fall. Does well in average soil and moisture in sun. Usually considered a short-lived perennial. Site in well-drained soil. Self-sows. Cut back after flowering to encourage repeat bloom in fall. USDA Zones 5–8. Photos 10, 122. See also discussions under *Achillea* 'Moonshine', *Achillea millefolium* 'White Beauty', and *Argyranthemum frutescens*.

ASSOCIATIONS: *Alchemilla mollis*, photo 10; *Allium senescens* 'Glaucum', photo 122; *Hemerocallis* 'Colonial Dame', photo 10; *Iris pseudacorus*, photo 10; *Lilium* 'French Vanilla', photo 10; *Lysimachia punctata*, photo 10; *Phalaris arundinacea*

var. *picta*, photo 10; *Sedum* 'Vera Jameson', photo 122.

Extended highlights from late spring through midsummer can be gained by joining this *Verbascum* with *Tagetes* and *Monarda*. *Tagetes* 'Primrose Lady' begins blooming in late spring and will complement the similar light yellow of the mullein's flowering spires. By mid summer *Monarda didyma* 'Cambridge Scarlet' will transform the composition into a bold, eye-catching association of red and yellow (3:2:3).

Verbena bonariensis (*V. patagonica*), tall verbena

Half-hardy perennial or annual, 36 × 12 in (90 × 30 cm), blooms light violet, summer to fall, dark yellow-green foliage, late spring to fall. Does well in average soil and moisture in sun or part shade. USDA Zones 7–10. Self-sows. Photos 36, 37, 123. See also discussions under *Aster novae-angliae* 'Purple Dome', *Nicotiana langsdorffii*, and *Pennisetum alopecuroides*.

ASSOCIATIONS: *Alcea rosea* 'Single Mix', photo 36; *Asteromoea mongolica*, photo 123; *Celosia elegans* 'Pink Tassles', photo 37; *Cleome spinosa* 'Helen Campbell', photo 37; *Lythrum salicaria* 'Morden Pink', photo 123; *Miscanthus sinensis* 'Gracillimus', photo 123; *Salvia sclarea*, photo 36; *Veronica spicata* 'Blue Fox', photo 123; *Zinnia elegans* 'Silver Sun', photo 37.

Makes a simple and effective combination with the pale complementary grayed yellow-green in the foliage of *Artemisia* 'Powis Castle'. Adding dark red-violet *Atriplex hortensis* 'Cupreata' foliage strengthens the light/dark juxtaposition (3:2:1). Textural and form variations are emphasized when *Verbena* sprays rise through the dense, broad *Atriplex* foliage and feathery *Artemisia* leaves.

Verbena canadensis 'Homestead Purple'

Half-hardy perennial or annual, 10 × 10 in (25 × 25 cm), blooms violet to red-violet, mid spring to late summer, foliage very dark yellow-green, mid spring to fall. Does well in average soil with dry to average conditions and sun. USDA Zones 6–10. Photo 145. See also discussion under *Malva moschata*.

ASSOCIATIONS: *Coreopsis* 'Sunray', *Heliotropium* 'Marine', *Salvia farinacea* 'Victoria', photo 145.

Verbena 'Amethyst'

Perennial, usually grown as an annual, 12 × 12 in (30 × 30 cm), blooms light violet, mid spring to fall, dark yellow-green foliage, mid spring to fall. Does well in average soil and moisture in sun. USDA Zones 8–10. Photo 71. See also discussion under *Antirrhinum majus* 'White Rocket'.

ASSOCIATIONS: *Anemone hupehensis* 'September Charm', *Campanula portenschlagiana*, *Helichrysum petiolare*, photo 71.

Verbena 'Amor Light Pink'

Perennial, usually grown as an annual, 10 × 10 in (25 × 25 cm), blooms very light red-violet and white, mid spring to fall, dark yellow-green foliage, mid spring to fall. Does well with average soil and moisture in sun. USDA Zones 8–10.

ASSOCIATIONS: 'Amor Light Pink' can be considered a small-scale element of medium-textured flowers and fine-textured foliage with flowers developing in small clusters above a mass of foliage. See discussions under *Gomphrena globosa* 'Lavender Lady' and *Senecio cineraria* 'Silver Queen' for combining with blue-violet, white, and gray and pink.

The pale yellow-green blooms of tall *Nicotiana langsdorffii* offer both a light complementary color and a contrasting form. Two mid-size *Heliotropium* 'Marine' placed in the midground will unite its companions with harmonizing violet, a broader flower form, and a light fragrance (3:1:2).

Veronica latifolia 'Crater Lake Blue'

Herbaceous perennial, 18 × 12 in (45 × 30 cm), blooms blue-violet, late spring, foliage very dark

yellow-green, late spring to late summer. Does well in average soil with average or less moisture in sun or part shade. USDA Zones 4–9. May be short-lived. Its tendency to flop may warrant some brush support. Photos 77, 80, 100.

ASSOCIATIONS: *Allium moly*, photo 100; *Aquilegia alpina*, photo 77; *Aquilegia* 'Heavenly Blue', photo 80; *Dianthus × allwoodii* 'Essex Witch', photo 80; *Digitalis purpurea* 'Excelsior', photo 77; *Geranium macrorrhizum*, photo 77.

Its strong blue-violet bloom combines well with the slightly lighter toned but powerful yellow in the annual *Tagetes* 'Lemon Gem' (2:3). The small-scale *Tagetes* flowers permit easy harmony with receding blue-violet *Veronica* blooms. *Tagetes* blooms for several months and this pairing may be extended after the relatively brief *Veronica* flowering.

Veronica spicata 'Blue Charm'

Herbaceous perennial, 24–30 × 12 in (60–75 × 30 cm), blooms very light blue-violet, late spring to summer, dark yellow-green foliage, late spring to fall. Does well in average soil with average to dry conditions in sun. USDA Zones 3–8. Photo 89. See also discussions under *Achillea millefolium* 'Appleblossom', *Alcea rosea* 'Single Mix', *Campanula carpatica* 'Blue Clips', *Cotinus coggygria* 'Royal Purple', and photo 110.

ASSOCIATIONS: *Achillea* 'Coronation Gold', photo 89; *Coreopsis verticillata* 'Moonbeam', photo 89; *Heliopsis scabra*, photo 89; *Hemerocallis* cultivar, photo 89; *Heuchera* 'Palace Purple', photo 110; *Lysimachia punctata*, photo 89; *Salvia officinalis* 'Aurea' and *Salvia officinalis* 'Purpurea', photo 110.

Veronica spicata 'Blue Fox'

Herbaceous perennial, 15–18 × 12 in (40–45 × 30 cm), blooms light blue-violet, late spring to late summer, dark yellow-green foliage, late spring to fall. Does well in average soil, with average or less moisture in sun. USDA Zones 3–8.

ASSOCIATIONS: This veronica offers small scale, medium textures, vertical emphasis with flower development, and a very long blooming period. For details on several associations see discussions under *Coreopsis auriculata* 'Nana', *Geranium psilostemon*, *Liatris spicata* 'Kobold', and photos 102 and 123.

Frequently seen in association with *Coreopsis verticillata* 'Moonbeam', as its pale yellow blooms are a near complement for the veronica's blue-violet flowers. Feathery, light violet background wands of *Perovskia atriplicifolia* flowers will add complexity to this long-blooming summer association (2:1:1).

Veronica spicata **subsp.** *incana,*
woolly speedwell

Herbaceous perennial, 6–12 × 12 in (15–30 × 30 cm), blooms blue-violet, late spring, foliage pale, very gray yellow-green, mid spring to fall. Does well in average soil, average or less moisture, in sun or part shade. USDA Zones 3–7. Photo 113.

ASSOCIATIONS: *Allium schoenoprasum*, *Artemisia* 'Powis Castle', *Cerastium tomentosum*, *Penstemon hirsutus* 'Pygmaeus', photo 113.

Siting in front of *Aquilegia vulgaris* and *Salvia* × *superba* 'May Night' offers a repetition of the spiked form in powerful tones of near-adjacent dark violet, violet, and blue-violet (3:2:3). Foliage textures are varied and the veronica's attractive grayed foliage persists through fall.

Veronica **'Sunny Border Blue'**

Herbaceous perennial, 18 × 18 in (45 × 45 cm), blooms light blue-violet, late spring to fall, dark yellow-green foliage, late spring to fall. Does well in average soil with average or less moisture in sun or filtered shade. USDA Zones 3–8.

ASSOCIATIONS: This veronica offers medium scale, medium textures, vertical emphasis with flower development, and a lush yet quiet mass of foliage. For details on various associations see discussions under *Ceratostigma plumbaginoides*, *Cosmos sulphureus* 'Sunset', *Eupatorium coelestinum*, and *Salvia guaranitica*.

Its exquisite blue-violet bloom color looks well in front of the near-adjacent floral hues of light red-violet *Echinacea purpurea* 'Bright Star' and dark red *Monarda* 'Adam' flower clusters (2:1:2). This fine late-summer association is effective for several weeks and does well in full sun.

Vinca minor,
common periwinkle, lesser periwinkle

Herbaceous perennial, 6 × 12 in (15 × 30 cm), blooms very light violet, early spring, dark yellow-green foliage, early spring to fall. Does well in average soil with average to moist conditions and part shade or morning sun. USDA Zones 4–9. Photo 126. See also discussions under *Allium ostrowskianum*, *Liriope muscari*, photo 25.

ASSOCIATIONS: *Helleborus foetidus*, *Leucojum aestivum* 'Gravetye Giant', *Tulipa* 'Spring Green', photo 126.

Vinca's light violet to blue-violet blooms create a fine early-spring groundcover when combined with the complementary hues in yellow *Erythronium* 'Pagoda', pale yellow-green *Helleborus foetidus*, and *Helleborus orientalis* (8:2:1:1). The varied forms and delicate tints of this group make an engaging underplanting for various *Corylopsis*, *Magnolia*, and *Viburnum* shrubs and trees.

Viola **'Baby Lucia'**

Herbaceous perennial, 4–6 × 9 in (10–15 × 25 cm), blooms violet, late spring to summer, foliage very dark yellow-green, mid spring to fall. Does well in average soil with average to moist conditions in sun or part shade. USDA Zones 6–9. Photo 38.

ASSOCIATIONS: *Geranium sylvaticum* 'Mayflower', *Nepeta mussinii* 'White Wonder', photo 38.

Viola corsica

Herbaceous perennial, 6 × 9 in (15 × 25 cm), blooms violet, late spring to summer, foliage very dark yellow-green, spring to fall. Does well in average soil with average to moist conditions in sun or part shade. USDA Zones 6–9. See also discussions under *Corydalis lutea* and *Iris* × *germanica* 'Sultan's Beauty'.

ASSOCIATIONS: This viola offers a small-scale garden design element of medium textures. Its disc-shaped flowers develop just above its mass of foliage. To emphasize its violet blooms, join five with the blue-violet flowering of three *Amsonia tabernaemontana* and supplement with two each of *Aquilegia vulgaris* and *Camassia quamash* (5:3:2:2). The spiked blue-violet flower form of *Camassia quamash* completes a tonal bouquet of violets and blue violets perfect for light shade. The receding quality of violet hues suggests positioning fairly close to view with *Viola* in the foreground to act as a unifying base.

Viola cucullata, marsh blue violet

Herbaceous perennial, 3 × 12 in (10 × 30 cm), blooms light violet, mid spring, dark yellow-green foliage, mid to late spring. Does well in average soil with average to moist conditions in sun or part shade. USDA Zones 4–8. May be invasive. See also discussion under photo 46.

ASSOCIATIONS: The marsh blue violet displays the same design traits of small scale and medium textures as other *Viola* mentioned. See text of photo 46 for connections with *Arabis caucasica*, *Muscari armeniacum*, and *Narcissus* 'Thalia'.

Viola tricolor 'Bowles' Black'

Generally grown as an annual in all zones, 6–9 × 9 in (15–25 × 25 cm), blooms very deep violet, mid spring to summer, foliage very dark yellow-green, mid spring to fall. Does well in average soil with average to moist conditions in sun or part shade. Self-sows.

ASSOCIATIONS: 'Bowles' Black' is of small scale and medium textures with disc-shaped flowers cresting an indistinct foliage mass. The deep red-violet tones in *Ajuga reptans* 'Atropurpurea' and dark reddish stems in *Athyrium nipponicum* 'Pictum'

foliage harmonize specifically with the deep tones of its blooms (6:3:2). Pale *Athyrium* foliage and light blue-violet *Ajuga* blooms also offer brightening contrast. Makes a particularly fine underplanting for a deep red-blooming *Rhododendron*.

Viola × *wittrockiana,* pansy

Perennial, usually grown as an annual, 6–8 × 9 in (15–20 × 25 cm), blooms blue-violet, late spring to summer, foliage very dark yellow-green, late spring to late summer. Does well in average soil with average to moist conditions in sun or part shade. Remove spent flowers to prolong blooming. 'Lac de Zurich' and 'Joker' are cultivars particularly suited to the suggested associations. Photos 43, 75, 78.

ASSOCIATIONS: *Allium aflatuense*, photo 75; *Brunnera macrophylla*, photo 43; *Hosta plantaginea* 'Royal Standard', photo 43; *Tulipa* 'Arabian Mystery', photo 78; *Tulipa* 'Greenland', photo 75; *Tulipa* 'Negrita', photo 78.

Weigela florida 'Variegata'

Shrub, 4–5 × 4 ft (1.2–1.5 × 1.2 m), blooms light red-violet, late spring, foliage yellow-green with light yellow edge, late spring to fall. Does well in average soil and moisture in sun. USDA Zones 5–7. Photo 14. See also discussion under *Antirrhinum majus* 'White Rocket'.

ASSOCIATIONS: *Aruncus dioicus*, *Argyranthemum frutescens*, *Digitalis grandiflora*, *Iris pseudacorus*, *Solidago* 'Cloth of Gold', photo 14.

Yucca filamentosa, Adam's-needle

Herbaceous perennial, 36–60 × 36 in (90–150 × 90 cm), blooms very pale yellow, mid to late summer, dark gray yellow-green foliage, late spring to fall. Plant in average to poor soil with average or less moisture and sun. USDA Zones 4–10. Photo 114.

ASSOCIATIONS: *Allium giganteum* and *Sedum* 'Autumn Joy', photo 114.

Zinnia 'Dreamland Ivory'

Generally grown as an annual in all zones, 12–15 × 12 in (30–40 × 30 cm), blooms very pale yellow, late spring to fall, dark yellow-green foliage, late spring to fall. Does well in average soil and moisture in sun. Photo 17.

ASSOCIATIONS: *Cleome spinosa* 'Helen Campbell', *Gladiolus callianthus*, *Nicotiana sylvestris*, *Tagetes* 'Primrose Lady', photo 17.

Zinnia elegans 'Red Sun'

Generally grown as an annual in all zones, 36 × 24 in (90 × 60 cm), blooms red, late spring to fall, dark yellow-green foliage, late spring to fall. Does well in average soil and moisture in sun. Photos 20, 60, 104, 142.

ASSOCIATIONS: *Gomphrena* 'Strawberry Fields', photo 20; *Helenium autumnale* 'Brilliant' and *Helenium autumnale* 'Riverton', photo 60; *Lobelia cardinalis*, photo 104; *Perilla frutescens*, photo 20; *Salvia farinacea* 'Victoria', *Tagetes* 'Primrose Lady', photo 142; *Solidago* 'Crown of Rays', photo 60.

Zinnia elegans 'Silver Sun'

Generally grown as an annual in all zones, 36 × 24 in (90 × 60 cm), blooms very pale yellow, late spring to fall, dark yellow-green foliage, late spring to fall. Does well in average soil and moisture in sun. Photo 37. See also discussion under *Antirrhinum majus* 'White Rocket'.

ASSOCIATIONS: *Celosia elegans* 'Pink Tassles', *Cleome spinosa* 'Helen Campbell', *Verbena bonariensis*, photo 37.

Zinnia 'Old Mexico'

Generally grown as an annual in all zones, 12–18 × 12 in (30–45 × 30 cm), blooms yellow and deep red-orange, late spring to fall, dark yellow-green foliage, late spring to fall. Does well in average soil and moisture in sun. Photo 63. See also discussion under *Lilium* 'Fireball'.

ASSOCIATIONS: *Hemerocallis* 'Sombrero', photo 63.

Another bright-hued, long-blooming association combines this zinnia with the multi-hued *Asclepias tuberosa* 'Gay Butterflies', annual *Cosmos sulphureus* 'Sunny Red', and yellow *Oenothera tetragona* (2:1:1:1). To provide a strong foliar background against which to contrast these bright hues, use a single *Heliopsis scabra* or *Miscanthus sinensis* 'Gracillimus', or place this group in front of an appropriately scaled smooth dark green hedge.

Bloom Options for Temperate Climates by Exposure, Season, and Color

EXPOSURE: SUN

Bloom Season: Early Spring

YELLOW
Aurinia saxatilis
Aurinia saxatilis 'Citrina'
Corydalis lutea
Stylophorum diphyllum

BLUE
Myosotis sylvatica

VIOLET
Phlox subulata
Vinca minor

RED-VIOLET
Phlox subulata

WHITE
Iberis sempervirens 'Snowflake'
Leucojum aestivum 'Gravetye Giant'
Phlox subulata

PASTEL TINTS
Aurinia saxatilis 'Citrina'
Phlox subulata

Bloom Season: Mid Spring

RED
Aquilegia 'Rose Queen'
Celosia plumosa 'New Look'
Dicentra eximia 'Luxuriant'
Dicentra spectabilis
Lamium maculatum 'Shell Pink'

Paeonia suffruticosa
Tulipa 'Pink Impression'

RED-ORANGE
Geum × borisii
Narcissus 'Geranium'
Tulipa 'Apricot Beauty'

ORANGE/YELLOW-ORANGE
Chrysogonum virginianum
Eschscholzia californica

YELLOW
Aquilegia 'McKana Giants'
Aurinia saxatilis
Aurinia saxatilis 'Citrina'
Corydalis lutea
Doronicum cordatum
Erythronium 'Pagoda'
Eschscholzia californica
Euphorbia polychroma
Lamiastrum galeobdolon 'Herman's Pride'
Lonicera periclymenum 'Graham Thomas'
Narcissus 'Clare'
Narcissus 'Hawera'
Narcissus 'Mount Hood'
Narcissus 'Trevithian'
Paeonia suffruticosa
Stylophorum diphyllum
Trollius 'Alabaster'
Trollius europeus 'Superbus'
Tulipa 'Golden Artist'

YELLOW-GREEN
Tulipa 'Greenland'
Tulipa 'Spring Green'

BLUE
Brunnera macrophylla
Myosotis sylvatica

BLUE-VIOLET
Ajuga reptans
Ajuga reptans 'Atropurpurea'
Aquilegia 'Heavenly Blue'
Baptisia australis
Camassia quamash
Centaurea montana
Hyacinthoides hispanica
Muscari armeniacum
Nepeta mussinii
Phlox divaricata
Polemonium reptans 'Blue Pearl'

VIOLET
Ajuga reptans
Ajuga reptans 'Atropurpurea'
Allium karataviense
Aquilegia alpina
Aquilegia 'McKana Giants'
Aquilegia 'Olympia'
Lobularia maritima 'Royal Carpet'
Phlox subulata
Verbena 'Amethyst'
Verbena canadensis 'Homestead Purple'
Viola corsica

Exposure: Sun, Bloom Season: Mid Spring, Color: Violet, *continued*

Viola cucullata
Viola tricolor 'Bowles Black'

RED-VIOLET
Allium giganteum
Antirrhinum majus 'Princess White with Purple Eye'
Aquilegia 'Black Star'
Aquilegia 'McKana Giants'
Dicentra eximia 'Luxuriant'
Geranium macrorrhizum
Geranium sanguineum
Geranium sanguineum var. *striatum*
Geranium sylvaticum 'Mayflower'
Lobularia maritima 'Easter Bonnet Deep Pink'
Paeonia suffruticosa
Phlox subulata
Prunus × *cistena*
Syringa microphylla 'Superba'
Tulipa 'Arabian Mystery'
Tulipa 'Greenland'
Tulipa 'Negrita'
Tulipa 'Pink Impression'
Tulipa 'Purple Rain'
Verbena 'Amor Light Pink'

WHITE
Ajuga reptans 'Alba'
Antirrhinum majus 'Princess White with Purple Eye'
Aquilegia 'Olympia'
Aquilegia 'Heavenly Blue'
Aquilegia 'McKana Giants'
Aquilegia 'Rose Queen'
Arabis caucasica
Cerastium tomentosum
Dicentra eximia 'Alba'
Dicentra spectabilis
Dicentra spectabilis 'Alba'
Geranium sanguineum 'Album'
Iberis sempervirens 'Snowflake'
Leucojum aestivum 'Gravetye Giant'
Lobularia maritima 'Carpet of Snow'
Muscari botryoides 'Album'
Narcissus 'Geranium'
Narcissus 'Mount Hood'
Narcissus 'Thalia'

Nepeta mussinii 'White Wonder'
Ornithogalum umbellatum
Paeonia suffruticosa
Phlox subulata
Polygonatum biflorum
Tulipa 'Spring Green'
Tulipa 'White Triumphator'
Verbena 'Amor Light Pink'

PASTEL TINTS
Allium karataviense
Aquilegia 'McKana Giants'
Aurinia saxatilis 'Citrina'
Camassia quamash
Dicentra spectabilis
Erythronium 'Pagoda'
Eschscholzia californica
Geranium sanguineum var. *striatum*
Lamium maculatum 'Shell Pink'
Lonicera periclymenum 'Graham Thomas'
Narcissus 'Clare'
Narcissus 'Mount Hood'
Phlox divaricata
Phlox subulata
Trollius 'Alabaster'
Tulipa 'Apricot Beauty'
Tulipa 'Pink Impression'

Bloom Season: Late Spring

RED
Antirrhinum 'Frontier Crimson'
Aquilegia 'Rose Queen'
Argyranthemum frutescens
Astilbe × *arendsii* 'Cattleya'
Astilbe × *arendsii* 'Fanal'
Celosia cristata 'Sparkler Mix'
Celosia plumosa 'New Look'
Centranthus ruber
Cleome spinosa 'Pink Queen'
Dicentra eximia 'Luxuriant'
Dicentra spectabilis
Digitalis × *mertonensis*
Gaillardia × *grandiflora* 'Goblin'
Geranium endressii 'Wargrave Pink'
Hemerocallis 'Sammy Russell'
Impatiens 'Tempo Hybrid Red'
Iris × *germanica* 'Sultan's Beauty'
Lamium maculatum 'Shell Pink'
Lantana 'Confetti'
Lychnis chalcedonica

Malva moschata
Nicotiana alata 'Nicki Pink'
Paeonia lactiflora 'Festiva Maxima'
Papaver rhoeas
Penstemon 'Rose Elf'
Rosa 'New Dawn'
Salvia 'Lady in Red'
Tropaeolum majus 'Alaska'
Tropaeolum majus 'Gleam Series'
Tulipa 'Red Shine'
Zinnia elegans 'Red Sun'

RED-ORANGE
Alstroemeria Ligtu Hybrids
Calendula officinalis
Celosia cristata 'Sparkler Mix'
Cosmos sulphureus 'Sunny Red'
Cosmos sulphureus 'Sunset'
Digitalis × *mertonensis*
Gaillardia × *grandiflora* 'Goblin'
Geum × *borisii*
Hemerocallis 'Ed Murray'
Hemerocallis 'Sammy Russell'
Heuchera 'Palace Purple'
Macleaya microcarpa
Zinnia 'Old Mexico'

ORANGE/YELLOW-ORANGE
Alstroemeria Ligtu Hybrids
Aruncus dioicus
Calendula officinalis
Celosia cristata 'Sparkler Mix'
Chrysogonum virginianum
Coreopsis auriculata 'Nana'
Coreopsis 'Sunray'
Cosmos sulphureus 'Sunny Red'
Eschscholzia californica
Heliopsis scabra
Hemerocallis 'Mayan Gold'
Hemerocallis 'Sombrero'
Hemerocallis 'Stella d'Oro'
Lantana 'Confetti'
Melampodium paludosum 'Medallion'
Osteospermum 'Salmon Queen'
Tropaeolum majus 'Alaska'
Tropaeolum majus 'Gleam Series'

YELLOW
Achillea 'Coronation Gold'
Achillea 'Moonshine'
Allium moly
Aquilegia 'McKana Giants'
Argyranthemum frutescens

Astilbe × *arendsii* 'Deutschland'
Celosia cristata 'Sparkler Mix'
Coreopsis verticillata
Coreopsis verticillata 'Moonbeam'
Corydalis lutea
Digitalis grandiflora
Doronicum cordatum
Eschscholzia californica
Euphorbia polychroma
Gaillardia × *grandiflora* 'Goblin'
Hemerocallis cultivars
Hemerocallis lilioasphodelus
Iris pseudacorus
Iris sibirica 'White Swirl'
Lantana 'Confetti'
Lilium 'French Vanilla'
Lonicera periclymenum 'Graham
   Thomas'
Lysimachia ciliata 'Purpurea'
Lysimachia punctata
Narcissus 'Mount Hood'
Oenothera tetragona
Rhododendron 'Golden Dream'
Stylophorum diphyllum
Tagetes 'Golden Gem'
Tagetes 'Lemon Gem'
Tagetes patula
Tagetes 'Primrose Lady'
Trollius 'Alabaster'
Trollius europeus 'Superbus'
Tulipa 'West Point'
Verbascum chaixii
Zinnia 'Dreamland Ivory'
Zinnia elegans 'Silver Sun'
Zinnia 'Old Mexico'

YELLOW-GREEN
Alchemilla alpina
Alchemilla mollis
Nicotiana alata 'Lime Green'
Nicotiana alata 'Nicki Lime'
Nicotiana langsdorffii

BLUE
Borago officinalis
Brunnera macrophylla
Cynoglossum amabile
Linum perenne
Lobelia erinus 'Cambridge Blue'
Myosotis sylvatica
Nigella damescena 'Miss Jekyll'

BLUE-VIOLET
Agapanthus praecox
Ageratum houstonianum 'Blue
   Horizon'

Ageratum houstonianum 'Blue
   Puffs'
Ageratum houstonianum
   'Southern Cross'
Ajuga reptans
Ajuga reptans 'Atropurpurea'
Amsonia tabernaemontana
Aquilegia 'Heavenly Blue'
Baptisia australis
Camassia quamash
Centaurea montana
Delphinium belladonna
Delphinium grandiflorum 'Blue
   Butterfly'
Delphinium 'Connecticut Yankee'
Echinops 'Taplow Blue'
Hyacinthoides hispanica
Iris kaempferi
Nepeta mussinii
Nepeta 'Six Hills Giant'
Nigella damescena 'Miss Jekyll'
Phlox divaricata
Phlox 'Chattahoochee'
Salvia haematodes
Tradescantia × *andersoniana*
   'Blue Stone'
Veronica latifolia 'Crater Lake
   Blue'
Veronica spicata 'Blue Charm'
Veronica spicata 'Blue Fox'
Veronica spicata subsp. *incana*
Veronica 'Sunny Border Blue'
Viola × *wittrockiana*

VIOLET
Ajuga reptans
Ajuga reptans 'Atropurpurea'
Allium karataviense
Allium schoenoprasum
Aquilegia alpina
Aquilegia 'McKana Giants'
Aquilegia 'Olympia'
Aquilegia vulgaris
Campanula carpatica 'Blue Clips'
Campanula glomerata 'Joan Elliot'
Campanula portenschlagiana
Campanula poscharkyana
Catananche caerulea
Delphinium 'Charles Gregory
   Broan'
Geranium 'Johnson's Blue'
Geranium × *magnificum*
Heliotropium 'Marine'
Iris kaempferi

Iris sibirica
Lavandula angustifolia 'Hidcote'
Lavandula angustifolia 'Munstead'
Lobularia maritima 'Royal Carpet'
Lythrum salicaria 'Dropmore
   Purple'
Nierembergia hippomanica var.
   violacea 'Purple Robe'
Penstemon hirsutus 'Pygmaeus'
Petunia 'Purple Robe'
Salvia farinacea 'Victoria'
Salvia × *superba*
Salvia × *superba* 'East Friesland'
Salvia × *superba* 'May Night'
Verbena 'Amethyst'
Verbena canadensis 'Homestead
   Purple'
Viola 'Baby Lucia'
Viola corsica
Viola tricolor 'Bowles Black'

RED-VIOLET
Allium aflatuense
Allium aflatuense 'Purple
   Sensation'
Allium christophii
Allium giganteum
Allium ostrowskianum
Antirrhinum majus 'Princess
   White with Purple Eye'
Aquilegia 'Black Star'
Aquilegia 'McKana Giants'
Aquilegia 'Rose Queen'
Clematis × *jackmanii*
Cleome spinosa 'Violet Queen'
Dianthus plumarius
Dianthus × *allwoodii* 'Essex Witch'
Digitalis purpurea 'Excelsior'
Geranium 'Ann Folkard'
Geranium macrorrhizum
Geranium psilostemon
Geranium sanguineum
Geranium sanguineum var.
   striatum
Geranium sylvaticum 'Mayflower'
Iris kaempferi
Lantana 'Confetti'
Lavandula stoechas
Lobularia maritima 'Easter Bonnet
   Deep Pink'
Lychnis coronaria
Lythrum salicaria 'Morden Pink'
Petunia 'Burgundy Madness'
Phlox maculata 'Alpha'

Exposure: Sun, Bloom Season: Late Spring, Color: Red-violet, *continued*

Prunus × *cistena*
Salvia splendens 'Laser Purple'
Stachys byzantina
Symphytum officinale
Syringa microphylla 'Superba'
Tulipa 'Queen of Night'
Verbena 'Amor Light Pink'
Weigela florida 'Variegata'

WHITE
Ajuga reptans 'Alba'
Antirrhinum majus 'Princess White with Purple Eye'
Antirrhinum majus 'White Rocket'
Aquilegia 'Heavenly Blue'
Aquilegia 'McKana Giants'
Aquilegia 'Olympia'
Aquilegia 'Rose Queen'
Aquilegia vulgaris
Argyranthemum frutescens
Astilbe × *arendsii* 'Bridal Veil'
Cerastium tomentosum
Cimicifuga racemosa
Cleome spinosa 'Helen Campbell'
Convolvulus cneorum
Crambe cordifolia
Dianthus × *allwoodii* 'Essex Witch'
Dicentra eximia 'Alba'
Dicentra spectabilis
Dicentra spectabilis 'Alba'
Digitalis purpurea 'Excelsior'
Geranium sanguineum 'Album'
Hedera helix
Hydrangea quercifolia
Iberis sempervirens 'Snowflake'
Iris kaempferi
Iris sibirica 'White Swirl'
Lamium maculatum 'White Nancy'
Leucanthemum vulgare
Leucanthemum × *superbum* 'Alaska'
Leucojum aestivum 'Gravetye Giant'
Lilium regale
Lobelia erinus 'White Cascade'
Lobularia maritima 'Carpet of Snow'
Lychnis coronaria 'Alba'
Malva moschata 'Alba'
Myrrhis odorata

Nepeta mussinii 'White Wonder'
Ornithogalum umbellatum
Paeonia lactiflora 'Festiva Maxima'
Paeonia lactiflora 'Miss America'
Phlox maculata 'Miss Lingard'
Prunus × *cistena*
Tradescantia × *andersoniana* 'Innocence'
Verbena 'Amor Light Pink'
Zinnia elegans 'Silver Sun'

PASTEL TINTS
Achillea 'Moonshine'
Ageratum houstonianum 'Blue Horizon'
Ageratum houstonianum 'Blue Puffs'
Ageratum houstonianum 'Southern Cross'
Alchemilla alpina
Alchemilla mollis
Allium christophii
Allium karataviense
Allium ostrowskianum
Allium schoenoprasum
Amsonia tabernaemontana
Aquilegia 'McKana Giants'
Aruncus dioicus
Astilbe × *arendsii* 'Cattleya'
Astilbe × *arendsii* 'Deutschland'
Camassia quamash
Cleome spinosa 'Pink Queen'
Coreopsis verticillata 'Moonbeam'
Dianthus plumarius
Dianthus × *allwoodii* 'Essex Witch'
Dicentra spectabilis
Digitalis grandiflora
Digitalis purpurea 'Excelsior'
Digitalis × *mertonensis*
Echinops 'Taplow Blue'
Eschscholzia californica
Geranium endressii 'Wargrave Pink'
Geranium sanguineum var. *striatum*
Hemerocallis lilioasphodelus
Heuchera 'Palace Purple'
Iris kaempferi
Lamium maculatum 'Shell Pink'
Lilium 'French Vanilla'
Lobelia erinus 'Cambridge Blue'
Lonicera periclymenum 'Graham Thomas'
Narcissus 'Mount Hood'

Nicotiana alata 'Lime Green'
Nicotiana alata 'Nicki Lime'
Nicotiana alata 'Nicki Pink'
Nicotiana langsdorffii
Osteospermum 'Salmon Queen'
Penstemon hirsutus 'Pygmaeus'
Phlox divaricata
Phlox 'Chattahoochee'
Prunus × *cistena*
Rosa 'New Dawn'
Tagetes 'Primrose Lady'
Trollius 'Alabaster'
Verbena 'Amor Light Pink'
Zinnia 'Dreamland Ivory'

Bloom Season: Summer

RED
Achillea millefolium 'Paprika'
Achillea millefolium 'Weser River Sandstone'
Antirrhinum 'Frontier Crimson'
Argyranthemum frutescens
Astilbe × *arendsii* 'Cattleya'
Astilbe × *arendsii* 'Fanal'
Astrantia major
Callistephus chinensis 'Deep Red'
Celosia cristata 'Sparkler Mix'
Celosia plumosa 'New Look'
Centranthus ruber
Chelone lyonii
Cleome spinosa 'Pink Queen'
Cosmos bipinnatus 'Pinkie'
Dahlia 'Ellen Houston'
Dicentra eximia 'Luxuriant'
Digitalis × *mertonensis*
Gaillardia × *grandiflora* 'Goblin'
Geranium endressii 'Wargrave Pink'
Gladiolus callianthus
Hemerocallis 'Sammy Russell'
Impatiens 'Tempo Hybrid Red'
Knautia macedonica
Lantana 'Confetti'
Lilium 'Fireball'
Lychnis chalcedonica
Malva alcea 'Fastigiata'
Malva moschata
Monarda 'Adam'
Monarda didyma 'Cambridge Scarlet'
Monarda didyma 'Croftway Pink'
Monarda didyma 'Mahogany'
Nicotiana alata 'Nicki Pink'

Papaver rhoeas
Pennisetum 'Burgundy Giant'
Penstemon 'Rose Elf'
Phalaris arundinacea var. *picta*
Phlox paniculata 'Bright Eyes'
Potentilla flamea
Rosa 'Chaucer'
Rosa 'New Dawn'
Rosa 'Prospero'
Salvia 'Lady in Red'
Sedum 'Ruby Glow'
Tropaeolum majus 'Alaska'
Tropaeolum majus 'Gleam Series'
Zinnia elegans 'Red Sun'

RED-ORANGE
Achillea millefolium 'Salmon
   Beauty'
Calendula officinalis
Celosia cristata 'Sparkler Mix'
Cosmos sulphureus 'Sunny Red'
Cosmos sulphureus 'Sunset'
Crocosmia 'Lucifer'
Digitalis × *mertonensis*
Gaillardia × *grandiflora* 'Goblin'
Gomphrena globosa 'Strawberry
   Fields'
Hemerocallis 'Ed Murray'
Heuchera 'Palace Purple'
Kniphofia 'Atlanta'
Lantana 'Confetti'
Macleaya microcarpa
Zinnia 'Old Mexico'

ORANGE/YELLOW-ORANGE
Achillea millefolium 'Salmon
   Beauty'
Achillea millefolium 'Weser River
   Sandstone'
Alstroemeria Ligtu Hybrids
Aruncus dioicus
Asclepias tuberosa 'Gay Butterflies'
Calendula officinalis
Celosia cristata 'Sparkler Mix'
Coreopsis auriculata 'Nana'
Coreopsis 'Sunray'
Cosmos sulphureus 'Sunny Red'
Eschscholzia californica
Festuca glauca
Heliopsis scabra
Hemerocallis 'Colonial Dame'
Hemerocallis fulva 'Kwanso Flore
   Plena'
Hemerocallis 'Mayan Gold'
Hemerocallis 'Sombrero'

Hemerocallis 'Stella d'Oro'
Lantana 'Confetti'
Ligularia dentata 'Desdemona'
Lilium 'Enchantment'
Lilium lancifolium
Melampodium paludosum
   'Medallion'
Osteospermum 'Salmon Queen'
Potentilla 'Tangerine'
Rudbeckia 'Goldsturm'
Rudbeckia hirta 'Goldilocks'
Tropaeolum majus 'Alaska'
Tropaeolum majus 'Gleam Series'

YELLOW
Achillea filipendulina 'Gold Plate'
Achillea taygetea
Argyranthemum frutescens
Asclepias tuberosa 'Gay Butterflies'
Astilbe × *arendsii* 'Deutschland'
Buphthalmum speciosum
Celosia cristata 'Sparkler Mix'
Chrysanthemum pacificum
Coreopsis verticillata
Coreopsis verticillata 'Moonbeam'
Corydalis lutea
Digitalis grandiflora
Eschscholzia californica
Filipendula vulgaris
Gaillardia × *grandiflora* 'Goblin'
Helichrysum angustifolium
Helichrysum petiolare
Hemerocallis cultivars
Hemerocallis 'Gala Bells'
Hemerocallis 'Hyperion'
Hemerocallis lilioasphodelus
Kniphofia 'Atlanta'
Lantana 'Confetti'
Ligularia stenocephala 'The
   Rocket'
Lilium 'French Vanilla'
Lonicera periclymenum 'Graham
   Thomas'
Lysimachia ciliata 'Purpurea'
Lysimachia punctata
Oenothera tetragona
Potentilla 'Tangerine'
Ruta graveolens
Santolina chamaecyparissus
Senecio cineraria 'Silver Queen'
Stylophorum diphyllum
Tagetes 'Golden Gem'
Tagetes 'Lemon Gem'
Tagetes patula

Tagetes 'Primrose Lady'
Thalictrum speciocissimum
Trollius europeus 'Superbus'
Tropaeolum majus 'Gleam Series'
Verbascum chaixii
Yucca filamentosa
Zinnia 'Dreamland Ivory'
Zinnia elegans 'Silver Sun'
Zinnia 'Old Mexico'

YELLOW-GREEN
Alchemilla mollis
Foeniculum vulgare 'Purpureum'
Gunnera manicata
Nicotiana alata 'Lime Green'
Nicotiana alata 'Nicki Lime'
Nicotiana langsdorffii
Pennisetum alopecuroides
Sedum 'Autumn Joy'

BLUE
Borago officinalis
Cynoglossum amabile
Linum perenne
Lobelia erinus 'Cambridge Blue'
Nigella damescena 'Miss Jekyll'

BLUE-VIOLET
Agapanthus praecox
Ageratum houstonianum 'Blue
   Horizon'
Ageratum houstonianum 'Blue
   Puffs'
Ageratum houstonianum
   'Southern Cross'
Centaurea montana
Delphinium 'Connecticut Yankee'
Delphinium grandiflorum 'Blue
   Butterfly'
Echinops 'Taplow Blue'
Eryngium amethystinum
Eryngium giganteum
Iris kaempferi
Nepeta mussinii
Nepeta 'Six Hills Giant'
Nigella damescena 'Miss Jekyll'
Phlox 'Chattahoochee'
Platycodon grandiflorus
Salvia haematodes
Tradescantia × *andersoniana*
   'Blue Stone'
Veronica spicata 'Blue Charm'
Veronica spicata 'Blue Fox'
Veronica 'Sunny Border Blue'
Viola × *wittrockiana*

Exposure: Sun, Bloom Season: Summer, *continued*

VIOLET

Aconitum napellus
Agastache foeniculum
Campanula carpatica 'Blue Clips'
Campanula glomerata 'Joan Elliot'
Campanula portenschlagiana
Campanula poscharkyana
Catananche caerulea
Delphinium 'Charles Gregory Broan'
Geranium × magnificum
Heliotropium 'Marine'
Iris kaempferi
Lavandula angustifolia 'Hidcote'
Lavandula angustifolia 'Munstead'
Limonium latifolium
Lobularia maritima 'Royal Carpet'
Lythrum salicaria 'Dropmore Purple'
Monarda didyma 'Bluestocking'
Nierembergia hippomanica var. *violacea* 'Purple Robe'
Penstemon hirsutus 'Pygmaeus'
Perovskia atriplicifolia
Petunia 'Purple Robe'
Salvia farinacea 'Victoria'
Salvia splendens 'Laser Purple'
Salvia × superba
Salvia × superba 'East Friesland'
Salvia × superba 'May Night'
Thalictrum rochebrunianum
Verbena 'Amethyst'
Verbena bonariensis
Verbena canadensis 'Homestead Purple'
Viola 'Baby Lucia'
Viola corsica
Viola tricolor 'Bowles Black'

RED-VIOLET

Achillea millefolium 'Appleblossom'
Alcea rosea 'Single Mix'
Allium cernuum
Allium christophii
Allium ostrowskianum
Allium senescens
Allium senescens 'Glaucum'
Allium sphaerocephalon
Antirrhinum majus 'Princess White with Purple Eye'

Argyranthemum 'Mary Wootton'
Astilbe chinensis 'Pumila'
Chelone lyonii
Clematis × jackmanii
Cleome spinosa 'Violet Queen'
Cosmos bipinnatus 'Early Sensation'
Cosmos bipinnatus 'Versailles Tetra'
Cotinus coggygria 'Royal Purple'
Dianthus × allwoodii 'Essex Witch'
Digitalis purpurea 'Excelsior'
Echinacea purpurea 'Bright Star'
Erigeron karvinskianus
Geranium 'Ann Folkard'
Geranium psilostemon
Geranium sanguineum
Geranium sanguineum var. *striatum*
Gomphrena globosa 'Lavender Lady'
Gomphrena globosa 'Rosy'
Iris kaempferi
Lantana 'Confetti'
Lavandula stoechas
Liatris spicata 'Kobold'
Lobularia maritima 'Easter Bonnet Deep Pink'
Lythrum salicaria 'Morden Pink'
Malva sylvestris 'Mauritiana'
Monarda didyma 'Violet Queen'
Onopordum acanthium
Papaver somniferum
Petunia 'Burgundy Madness'
Phlox maculata 'Alpha'
Salvia officinalis 'Aurea'
Salvia officinalis 'Purpurea'
Salvia sclarea
Salvia splendens 'Laser Purple'
Stachys macrantha 'Robusta'
Teucrium chamaedrys
Verbena 'Amor Light Pink'
Verbena canadensis 'Homestead Purple'

WHITE

Achillea millefolium 'White Beauty'
Anaphalis triplinervis 'Summer Snow'
Antirrhinum majus 'Princess White with Purple Eye'
Antirrhinum majus 'White Rocket'
Argyranthemum frutescens
Astilbe × arendsii 'Bridal Veil'

Astrantia major
Chrysanthemum leucanthemum
Chrysanthemum × superbum 'Alaska'
Cimicifuga racemosa
Cleome spinosa 'Helen Campbell'
Cosmos bipinnatus 'Sonata White'
Convolvulus cneorum
Crambe cordifolia
Dianthus × allwoodii 'Essex Witch'
Dicentra eximia 'Alba'
Digitalis purpurea 'Excelsior'
Filipendula vulgaris
Gladiolus callianthus
Gomphrena globosa 'Pomponette White'
Heuchera 'Palace Purple'
Hosta plantaginea 'Royal Standard'
Hydrangea quercifolia
Iris kaempferi
Jasminium officinale
Leucanthemum vulgare
Leucanthemum × superbum 'Alaska'
Lilium 'Casa Blanca'
Lilium regale
Lilium 'Silver Elegance Strain'
Lobelia erinus 'White Cascade'
Lobularia maritima 'Carpet of Snow'
Lysimachia clethroides
Malva moschata 'Alba'
Nepeta mussinii 'White Wonder'
Nicotiana sylvestris
Perilla frutescens
Phlox maculata 'Miss Lingard'
Physostegia virginiana 'Summer Snow'
Rodgersia aesculifolia
Salvia argentea
Tanacetum parthenium
Tradescantia × andersoniana 'Innocence'
Verbena 'Amor Light Pink'
Zinnia elegans 'Silver Sun'

PASTEL TINTS

Achillea millefolium 'Appleblossom'
Achillea millefolium 'Weser River Sandstone'
Achillea taygetea
Ageratum houstonianum 'Blue Horizon'

Ageratum houstonianum 'Blue
    Puffs'
Ageratum houstonianum
    'Southern Cross'
Alcea rosea 'Single Mix'
Alchemilla mollis
Allium cernuum
Allium christophii
Allium ostrowskianum
Argyranthemum 'Mary Wootton'
Aruncus dioicus
Astilbe chinensis 'Pumila'
Astilbe × arendsii 'Cattleya'
Astilbe × arendsii 'Deutschland'
Astrantia major
Cleome spinosa 'Pink Queen'
Coreopsis verticillata 'Moonbeam'
Cosmos bipinnatus 'Pinkie'
Cotinus coggygria 'Royal Purple'
Dianthus × allwoodii 'Essex Witch'
Digitalis grandiflora
Digitalis purpurea 'Excelsior'
Digitalis × mertonensis
Echinops 'Taplow Blue'
Erigeron karvinskianus
Eryngium amethystinum
Eryngium giganteum
Eschscholzia californica
Festuca glauca
Filipendula vulgaris
Foeniculum vulgare 'Purpureum'
Geranium endressii 'Wargrave
    Pink'
Geranium sanguineum var.
    striatum
Gomphrena globosa 'Rosy'
Hemerocallis lilioasphodelus
Hemerocallis 'Colonial Dame'
Heuchera 'Palace Purple'
Iris kaempferi
Lantana 'Confetti'
Lilium 'French Vanilla'
Lobelia erinus 'Cambridge Blue'
Lonicera periclymenum 'Graham
    Thomas'
Malva alcea 'Fastigiata'
Monarda didyma 'Croftway Pink'
Nicotiana alata 'Lime Green'
Nicotiana alata 'Nicki Lime'
Nicotiana alata 'Nicki Pink'
Nicotiana langsdorffii
Osteospermum 'Salmon Queen'
Papaver somniferum
Penstemon hirsutus 'Pygmaeus'

Perovskia atriplicifolia
Phalaris arundinacea var. *picta*
Phlox paniculata 'Bright Eyes'
Phlox 'Chattahoochee'
Rosa 'Chaucer'
Rosa 'New Dawn'
Ruta graveolens
Salvia sclarea
Sedum 'Autumn Joy'
Senecio cineraria 'Silver Queen'
Tagetes 'Primrose Lady'
Yucca filamentosa
Zinnia 'Dreamland Ivory'

Bloom Season: Late Summer
RED
Antirrhinum 'Frontier Crimson'
Argyranthemum frutescens
Astrantia major
Callistephus chinensis 'Deep Red'
Celosia cristata 'Sparkler Mix'
Celosia plumosa 'New Look'
Chelone lyonii
Cleome spinosa 'Pink Queen'
Cosmos bipinnatus 'Pinkie'
Dahlia 'Ellen Houston'
Dicentra eximia 'Luxuriant'
Gaillardia × grandiflora 'Goblin'
Gladiolus callianthus
Helenium autumnale 'Riverton'
Impatiens 'Tempo Hybrid Red'
Knautia macedonica
Lantana 'Confetti'
Lobelia cardinalis
Lilium 'Fireball'
Monarda didyma 'Cambridge
    Scarlet'
Monarda didyma 'Croftway Pink'
Monarda didyma 'Mahogany'
Monarda 'Adam'
Nicotiana alata 'Nicki Pink'
Papaver rhoeas
Pennisetum 'Burgundy Giant'
Phlox paniculata 'Bright Eyes'
Rosa 'New Dawn'
Salvia 'Lady in Red'
Sedum 'Autumn Joy'
Sedum 'Rosy Glow'
Sedum 'Ruby Glow'
Sedum 'Vera Jameson'
Tropaeolum majus 'Alaska'
Tropaeolum majus 'Gleam Series'
Zinnia elegans 'Red Sun'

RED-ORANGE
Celosia cristata 'Sparkler Mix'
Cosmos sulphureus 'Sunny Red'
Cosmos sulphureus 'Sunset'
Gaillardia × grandiflora 'Goblin'
Gomphrena globosa 'Strawberry
    Fields'
Helenium autumnale 'Brilliant'
Heuchera 'Palace Purple'
Zinnia 'Old Mexico'

ORANGE/YELLOW-ORANGE
Celosia cristata 'Sparkler Mix'
Coreopsis auriculata 'Nana'
Coreopsis 'Sunray'
Cosmos sulphureus 'Sunny Red'
Eschscholzia californica
Festuca glauca
Helictotrichon sempervirens
Hemerocallis fulva 'Kwanso Flore
    Plena'
Hemerocallis 'Stella d'Oro'
Lantana 'Confetti'
Lilium 'Enchantment'
Melampodium paludosum
    'Medallion'
Osteospermum 'Salmon Queen'
Rudbeckia 'Goldsturm'
Rudbeckia hirta 'Goldilocks'
Tropaeolum majus 'Alaska'
Tropaeolum majus 'Gleam Series'

YELLOW
Argyranthemum frutescens
Artemisia lactiflora
Celosia cristata 'Sparkler Mix'
Chrysanthemum pacificum
Coreopsis verticillata
Coreopsis verticillata 'Moonbeam'
Corydalis lutea
Eschscholzia californica
Filipendula vulgaris
Gaillardia × grandiflora 'Goblin'
Helenium autumnale 'Riverton'
Hemerocallis cultivars
Lantana 'Confetti'
Lonicera periclymenum 'Graham
    Thomas'
Silphium perfoliatum
Solidago 'Cloth of Gold'
Solidago 'Crown of Rays'
Stylophorum diphyllum
Tagetes 'Golden Gem'
Tagetes 'Lemon Gem'
Tagetes patula

Exposure: Sun, Bloom Season: Late Summer, Color: Yellow, *continued*

Tagetes 'Primrose Lady'
Verbascum chaixii
Yucca filamentosa
Zinnia 'Dreamland Ivory'
Zinnia elegans 'Silver Sun'
Zinnia 'Old Mexico'

YELLOW-GREEN
Foeniculum vulgare 'Purpureum'
Nicotiana alata 'Lime Green'
Nicotiana alata 'Nicki Lime'
Nicotiana langsdorffii
Pennisetum alopecuroides

BLUE
Cynoglossum amabile
Lobelia erinus 'Cambridge Blue'

BLUE-VIOLET
Agapanthus praecox
Ageratum houstonianum 'Blue Horizon'
Ageratum houstonianum 'Blue Puffs'
Ageratum houstonianum 'Southern Cross'
Aster frickartii 'Mönch'
Buddleja fallowiana 'Lochinch'
Caryopteris × *clandonensis* 'Heavenly Blue'
Centaurea montana
Ceratostigma plumbaginoides
Echinops 'Taplow Blue'
Eryngium amethystinum
Eryngium giganteum
Salvia guaranitica
Veronica spicata 'Blue Fox'
Veronica 'Sunny Border Blue'

VIOLET
Aconitum napellus
Agastache foeniculum
Aster novae-angliae 'Purple Dome'
Campanula carpatica 'Blue Clips'
Eupatorium coelestinum
Heliotropium 'Marine'
Hosta × *tardiana* 'Halcyon'
Limonium latifolium
Liriope muscari
Lobularia maritima 'Royal Carpet'

Lythrum salicaria 'Dropmore Purple'
Monarda didyma 'Bluestocking'
Perovskia atriplicifolia
Petunia 'Purple Robe'
Salvia farinacea 'Victoria'
Salvia splendens 'Laser Purple'
Thalictrum rochebrunianum
Verbena 'Amethyst'
Verbena bonariensis
Verbena canadensis 'Homestead Purple'

RED-VIOLET
Alcea rosea 'Single Mix'
Allium cernuum
Allium senescens
Allium senescens 'Glaucum'
Allium sphaerocephalon
Anemone hupehensis 'September Charm'
Anemone vitifolia 'Robustissima'
Aster novae-angliae 'Alma Potschke'
Astilbe chinensis 'Pumila'
Celosia elegans 'Pink Tassles'
Chelone lyonii
Cleome spinosa 'Violet Queen'
Cosmos bipinnatus 'Early Sensation'
Cosmos bipinnatus 'Versailles Tetra'
Echinacea purpurea 'Bright Star'
Erigeron karvinskianus
Gomphrena globosa 'Lavender Lady'
Gomphrena globosa 'Rosy'
Lantana 'Confetti'
Liatris spicata 'Kobold'
Lobularia maritima 'Easter Bonnet Deep Pink'
Lythrum salicaria 'Morden Pink'
Malva sylvestris 'Mauritiana'
Monarda didyma 'Violet Queen'
Monarda fistulosa
Petunia 'Burgundy Madness'
Salvia sclarea
Salvia splendens 'Laser Purple'
Sedum 'Rosy Glow'
Stachys macrantha 'Robusta'
Teucrium chamaedrys
Verbena 'Amor Light Pink'
Verbena canadensis 'Homestead Purple'

WHITE
Allium tuberosum
Anaphalis margaritacea
Anaphalis triplinervis 'Summer Snow'
Anemone 'Honorine Jobert'
Antirrhinum majus 'White Rocket'
Argyranthemum frutescens
Asteromoea mongolica
Astrantia major
Cleome spinosa 'Helen Campbell'
Cosmos bipinnatus 'Sonata White'
Filipendula vulgaris
Gladiolus callianthus
Gomphrena globosa 'Pomponette White'
Hosta plantaginea 'Royal Standard'
Leucanthemum vulgare
Lilium 'Casa Blanca'
Lilium 'Silver Elegance Strain'
Lobelia erinus 'White Cascade'
Lobularia maritima 'Carpet of Snow'
Nicotiana sylvestris
Physostegia virginiana 'Summer Snow'
Tanacetum parthenium
Verbena 'Amor Light Pink'

PASTEL TINTS
Ageratum houstonianum 'Blue Horizon'
Ageratum houstonianum 'Blue Puffs'
Ageratum houstonianum 'Southern Cross'
Alcea rosea 'Single Mix'
Allium cernuum
Anemone vitifolia 'Robustissima'
Artemisia lactiflora
Astilbe chinensis 'Pumila'
Astrantia major
Caryopteris × *clandonensis* 'Heavenly Blue'
Celosia elegans 'Pink Tassles'
Cleome spinosa 'Pink Queen'
Coreopsis verticillata 'Moonbeam'
Cosmos bipinnatus 'Pinkie'
Echinops 'Taplow Blue'
Erigeron karvinskianus
Eryngium amethystinum
Eryngium giganteum
Eschscholzia californica
Filipendula vulgaris

Foeniculum vulgare 'Purpureum'
Geranium endressii 'Wargrave
   Pink'
Geranium sanguineum var.
   striatum
Gomphrena globosa 'Rosy'
Helichrysum angustifolium
Helictotrichon sempervirens
Heuchera 'Palace Purple'
Hosta × *tardiana* 'Halcyon'
Lantana 'Confetti'
Lobelia erinus 'Cambridge Blue'
Lonicera periclymenum 'Graham
   Thomas'
Malva alcea 'Fastigiata'
Monarda didyma 'Croftway Pink'
Monarda fistulosa
Nicotiana alata 'Lime Green'
Nicotiana alata 'Nicki Lime'
Nicotiana alata 'Nicki Pink'
Nicotiana langsdorffii
Osteospermum 'Salmon Queen'
Perovskia atriplicifolia
Phlox paniculata 'Bright Eyes'
Rosa 'New Dawn'
Salvia sclarea
Sedum 'Autumn Joy'
Senecio cineraria 'Silver Queen'
Tagetes 'Primrose Lady'
Yucca filamentosa
Zinnia 'Dreamland Ivory'

Bloom Season: Fall

RED
Argyranthemum frutescens
Celosia cristata 'Sparkler Mix'
Celosia plumosa 'New Look'
Chelone lyonii
Cleome spinosa 'Pink Queen'
Cosmos bipinnatus 'Pinkie'
Dahlia 'Ellen Houston'
Dicentra eximia 'Luxuriant'
Gaillardia × *grandiflora* 'Goblin'
Helenium autumnale 'Riverton'
Impatiens 'Tempo Hybrid Red'
Lantana 'Confetti'
Lobelia cardinalis
Nicotiana alata 'Nicki Pink'
Pennisetum 'Burgundy Giant'
Salvia 'Lady in Red'
Sedum 'Autumn Joy'
Sedum 'Rosy Glow'

Sedum 'Ruby Glow'
Sedum 'Vera Jameson'
Tropaeolum majus 'Alaska'
Tropaeolum majus 'Gleam Series'
Zinnia elegans 'Red Sun'

RED-ORANGE
Celosia cristata 'Sparkler Mix'
Cosmos sulphureus 'Sunny Red'
Cosmos sulphureus 'Sunset'
Gaillardia × *grandiflora* 'Goblin'
Gomphrena globosa 'Strawberry
   Fields'
Helenium autumnale 'Brilliant'
Miscanthus sinensis 'Gracillimus'
Tropaeolum majus 'Alaska'
Tropaeolum majus 'Gleam Series'
Zinnia 'Old Mexico'

ORANGE/YELLOW-ORANGE
Celosia cristata 'Sparkler Mix'
Cosmos sulphureus 'Sunny Red'
Hemerocallis 'Stella d'Oro'
Lantana 'Confetti'
Miscanthus sinensis 'Variegatus'
Miscanthus sinensis 'Zebrinus'
Melampodium paludosum
   'Medallion'
Tropaeolum majus 'Alaska'
Tropaeolum majus 'Gleam Series'

YELLOW
Argyranthemum frutescens
Celosia cristata 'Sparkler Mix'
Chrysanthemum pacificum
Coreopsis verticillata 'Moonbeam'
Corydalis lutea
Gaillardia × *grandiflora* 'Goblin'
Helenium autumnale 'Riverton'
Lantana 'Confetti'
Lonicera periclymenum 'Graham
   Thomas'
Silphium perfoliatum
Solidago 'Cloth of Gold'
Solidago 'Crown of Rays'
Tagetes 'Golden Gem'
Tagetes 'Lemon Gem'
Tagetes patula
Tagetes 'Primrose Lady'
Verbascum chaixii
Zinnia 'Dreamland Ivory'
Zinnia elegans 'Silver Sun'
Zinnia 'Old Mexico'

YELLOW-GREEN
Nicotiana alata 'Lime Green'
Nicotiana alata 'Nicki Lime'
Nicotiana langsdorffii

BLUE-VIOLET
Ageratum houstonianum 'Blue
   Horizon'
Ageratum houstonianum
   'Southern Cross'
Aster frickartii 'Mönch'
Caryopteris × *clandonensis*
   'Heavenly Blue'
Centaurea montana
Ceratostigma plumbaginoides
Salvia guaranitica
Veronica 'Sunny Border Blue'

VIOLET
Agastache foeniculum
Aster novae-angliae 'Purple Dome'
Eupatorium coelestinum
Lobularia maritima 'Royal Carpet'
Petunia 'Purple Robe'
Salvia farinacea 'Victoria'
Salvia splendens 'Laser Purple'
Verbena 'Amethyst'
Verbena bonariensis

RED-VIOLET
Allium senescens
Allium senescens 'Glaucum'
Anemone vitifolia 'Robustissima'
Anemone hupehensis 'September
   Charm'
Aster novae-angliae 'Alma
   Potschke'
Celosia elegans 'Pink Tassles'
Chelone lyonii
Cleome spinosa 'Violet Queen'
Cosmos bipinnatus 'Early
   Sensation'
Cosmos bipinnatus 'Versailles
   Tetra'
Erigeron karvinskianus
Gomphrena globosa 'Lavender
   Lady'
Gomphrena globosa 'Rosy'
Lantana 'Confetti'
Lobularia maritima 'Easter Bonnet
   Deep Pink'
Malva sylvestris 'Mauritiana'
Pennisetum alopecuroides
Petunia 'Burgundy Madness'
Salvia sclarea

Exposure: Sun, Bloom Season: Fall, Color: Red-violet,

continued

Salvia splendens 'Laser Purple'
Sedum 'Rosy Glow'
Verbena 'Amor Light Pink'

WHITE
Anaphalis margaritacea
Anemone 'Honorine Jobert'
Argyranthemum frutescens
Asteromoea mongolica
Boltonia asteroides 'Snowbank'
Cleome spinosa 'Helen Campbell'
Cosmos bipinnatus 'Sonata White'
Gomphrena globosa 'Pomponette White'

Lobularia maritima 'Carpet of Snow'
Nicotiana sylvestris
Tanacetum parthenium
Verbena 'Amor Light Pink'

PASTEL TINTS
Ageratum houstonianum 'Blue Horizon'
Ageratum houstonianum 'Southern Cross'
Anemone vitifolia 'Robustissima'
Caryopteris × *clandonensis* 'Heavenly Blue'
Celosia elegans 'Pink Tassles'
Cleome spinosa 'Pink Queen'
Coreopsis verticillata 'Moonbeam'

Cosmos bipinnatus 'Pinkie'
Erigeron karvinskianus
Gomphrena globosa 'Rosy'
Lantana 'Confetti'
Lonicera periclymenum 'Graham Thomas'
Miscanthus sinensis 'Gracillimus'
Miscanthus sinensis 'Variegatus'
Miscanthus sinensis 'Zebrinus'
Nicotiana alata 'Lime Green'
Nicotiana alata 'Nicki Lime'
Nicotiana alata 'Nicki Pink'
Nicotiana langsdorffii
Salvia sclarea
Tagetes 'Primrose Lady'
Zinnia 'Dreamland Ivory'

EXPOSURE: PART SHADE

Bloom Season: Early Spring

YELLOW
Corydalis lutea
Stylophorum diphyllum

YELLOW-GREEN
Helleborus foetidus
Helleborus orientalis

BLUE
Mertensia virginica
Myosotis sylvatica
Pulmonaria saccharata 'Mrs. Moon'

BLUE-VIOLET
Mertensia virginica
Pulmonaria saccharata 'Mrs. Moon'

VIOLET
Pulmonaria saccharata 'Mrs. Moon'
Vinca minor

RED-VIOLET
Helleborus orientalis
Mertensia virginica

WHITE
Iberis sempervirens 'Snowflake'
Leucojum aestivum 'Gravetye Giant'
Sanguinaria canadensis

PASTEL TINTS
Helleborus foetidus
Helleborus orientalis
Mertensia virginica

Bloom Season: Mid Spring

RED
Aquilegia 'Rose Queen'
Dicentra eximia 'Luxuriant'
Dicentra spectabilis
Lamium maculatum 'Shell Pink'
Paeonia suffruticosa

RED-ORANGE
Geum × *borisii*
Narcissus 'Geranium'

ORANGE/YELLOW-ORANGE
Chrysogonum virginianum
Narcissus 'Geranium'

YELLOW
Aquilegia 'McKana Giants'
Corydalis lutea
Dicentra spectablis 'Alba'
Doronicum cordatum
Epimedium × *versicolor* 'Sulphureum'
Erythronium 'Pagoda'
Euphorbia polychroma
Lamiastrum galeobdolon 'Herman's Pride'

Lonicera periclymenum 'Graham Thomas'
Narcissus 'Clare'
Narcissus 'Hawera'
Narcissus 'Mount Hood'
Narcissus 'Trevithian'
Paeonia suffruticosa
Primula japonica 'Postford White'
Primula vulgaris
Stylophorum diphyllum
Trollius 'Alabaster'
Trollius europeus 'Superbus'

YELLOW-GREEN
Helleborus foetidus
Helleborus orientalis
Ornithogalum umbellatum
Polygonatum biflorum

BLUE
Brunnera macrophylla
Mertensia virginica
Myosotis sylvatica
Pulmonaria saccharata 'Mrs. Moon'

BLUE-VIOLET
Ajuga reptans
Ajuga reptans 'Atropurpurea'
Aquilegia 'Heavenly Blue'
Baptisia australis
Camassia quamash
Centaurea montana

Hyacinthoides hispanica
Mertensia virginica
Phlox divaricata
Polemonium reptans 'Blue Pearl'
Pulmonaria saccharata 'Mrs.
  Moon'

VIOLET
Ajuga reptans
Ajuga reptans 'Atropurpurea'
Allium karataviense
Aquilegia alpina
Aquilegia 'McKana Giants'
Aquilegia 'Olympia
Lobularia maritima 'Royal Carpet'
Pulmonaria saccharata 'Mrs.
  Moon'
Viola corsica
Viola cucullata
Viola tricolor 'Bowles Black'

RED-VIOLET
Antirrhinum majus 'Princess
  White with Purple Eye'
Aquilegia 'Black Star'
Aquilegia 'McKana Giants'
Geranium macrorrhizum
Geranium sanguineum
Geranium sanguineum var.
  striatum
Geranium sylvaticum 'Mayflower'
Helleborus orientalis
Lobularia maritima 'Easter Bonnet
  Deep Pink'
Mertensia virginica
Paeonia suffruticosa
Primula japonica

WHITE
Ajuga reptans 'Alba'
Antirrhinum majus 'Princess
  White with Purple Eye'
Aquilegia 'Heavenly Blue'
Aquilegia 'McKana Giants'
Aquilegia 'Olympia'
Aquilegia 'Rose Queen'
Convallaria majalis
Dicentra eximia 'Alba'
Dicentra spectabilis
Dicentra spectabilis 'Alba'
Galium odoratum
Geranium sanguineum 'Album'
Iberis sempervirens 'Snowflake'
Leucojum aestivum 'Gravetye
  Giant'

Lobularia maritima 'Carpet of
  Snow'
Muscari botryoides 'Album'
Narcissus 'Geranium'
Narcissus 'Mount Hood'
Narcissus 'Thalia'
Nepeta mussinii 'White Wonder'
Ornithogalum umbellatum
Paeonia suffruticosa
Podophyllum peltatum
Polygonatum biflorum
Polygonatum odoratum
  'Variegatum'
Primula japonica 'Postford White'
Trillium grandiflorum

PASTEL TINTS
Allium karataviense
Aquilegia 'McKana Giants'
Camassia quamash
Dicentra spectabilis
Epimedium × versicolor
  'Sulphureum'
Erythronium 'Pagoda'
Geranium sanguineum var.
  striatum
Helleborus foetidus
Helleborus orientalis
Lamium maculatum 'Shell Pink'
Lonicera periclymenum 'Graham
  Thomas'
Mertensia virginica
Narcissus 'Clare'
Narcissus 'Mount Hood'
Phlox divaricata
Polygonatum biflorum
Trollius 'Alabaster'

Bloom Season: Late Spring

RED
Antirrhinum 'Frontier Crimson'
Aquilegia 'Rose Queen'
Argyranthemum frutescens
Astilbe × *arendsii* 'Cattleya'
Astilbe × arendsii 'Fanal'
Centranthus ruber
Dicentra eximia 'Luxuriant'
Dicentra spectabilis
Digitalis × mertonensis
Geranium endressi 'Wargrave Pink'
Hemerocallis 'Sammy Russell'
Impatiens 'Tempo Hybrid Red'
Lamium maculatum 'Shell Pink'

Lantana 'Confetti'
Lychnis chalcedonica
Malva moschata
Nicotiana alata 'Nicki Pink'

RED-ORANGE
Alstroemeria Ligtu Hybrids
Calendula officinalis
Digitalis × mertonensis
Geum × borisii
Hemerocallis 'Ed Murray'
Hemerocallis 'Sammy Russell'
Heuchera 'Palace Purple'
Macleaya microcarpa

ORANGE/YELLOW-ORANGE
Alstroemeria Ligtu Hybrids
Aruncus dioicus
Calendula officinalis
Chrysogonum virginianum
Hemerocallis 'Mayan Gold'
Hemerocallis 'Sombrero'
Hemerocallis 'Stella d'Oro'
Lantana 'Confetti'

YELLOW
Allium moly
Aquilegia 'McKana Giants'
Argyranthemum frutescens
Astilbe × arendsii 'Deutschland'
Coreopsis verticillata 'Moonbeam'
Corydalis lutea
Digitalis grandiflora
Doronicum cordatum
Epimedium × versicolor
  'Sulphureum'
Erythronium 'Pagoda'
Euphorbia polychroma
Hemerocallis cultivars
Hemerocallis lilioasphodelus
Iris pseudacorus
Iris sibirica 'White Swirl'
Lamiastrum galeobdolon
  'Herman's Pride'
Lantana 'Confetti'
Lilium 'French Vanilla'
Lonicera periclymenum 'Graham
  Thomas'
Lysimachia ciliata 'Purpurea'
Lysimachia punctata
Narcissus 'Mount Hood'
Paeonia suffruticosa
Primula japonica 'Postford White'
Primula vulgaris
Rhododendron 'Golden Dream'

Exposure: Part Shade, Bloom Season: Late Spring, Color: Yellow, *continued*

Stylophorum diphyllum
Trollius 'Alabaster'
Trollius europeus 'Superbus'

YELLOW-GREEN

Alchemilla alpina
Alchemilla mollis
Helleborus foetidus
Nicotiana alata 'Lime Green'
Nicotiana alata 'Nicki Lime'
Nicotiana langsdorffii
Polygonatum biflorum

BLUE

Brunnera macrophylla
Cynoglossum amabile
Linum perenne
Lobelia erinus 'Cambridge Blue'
Myosotis sylvatica
Pulmonaria saccharata 'Mrs. Moon'

BLUE-VIOLET

Ajuga reptans
Ajuga reptans 'Atropurpurea'
Amsonia tabernaemonta
Aquilegia 'Heavenly Blue'
Baptisia australis
Camassia quamash
Centaurea montana
Hyacinthoides hispanica
Mertensia virginica
Nepeta 'Six Hills Giant'
Phlox divaricata
Polemonium reptans 'Blue Pearl'
Pulmonaria saccharata 'Mrs. Moon'
Tradescantia × andersonia 'Bluestone'
Veronica latifolia 'Crater Lake Blue'
Veronica spicata subsp. *incana*
Veronica 'Sunny Border Blue'
Viola × wittrockiana

VIOLET

Ajuga reptans
Ajuga reptans 'Atropurpurea'
Allium karataviense
Allium schoenoprasum
Aquilegia alpina
Aquilegia 'McKana Giants'

Aquilegia 'Olympia'
Aquilegia vulgaris
Campanula carpatica 'Blue Clips'
Campanula glomerata 'Joan Elliot'
Campanula portenschlagiana
Campanula poscharkyana
Geranium 'Johnson's Blue'
Geranium × magnificum
Hosta sieboldiana
Hosta sieboldiana 'Frances Williams'
Hyacinthoides hispanica
Iris kaempferi
Iris sibirica
Lobularia maritima 'Royal Carpet'
Lythrum salicaria 'Dropmore Purple'
Nierembergia hippomanica var. *violacea* 'Purple Robe'
Petunia 'Purple Robe'
Pulmonaria saccharata 'Mrs. Moon'
Salvia farinacea 'Victoria'
Viola 'Baby Lucia'
Viola corsica
Viola tricolor 'Bowles Black'

RED-VIOLET

Allium ostrowskianum
Antirrhinum majus 'Princess White with Purple Eye'
Aquilegia 'Black Star'
Aquilegia 'McKana Giants'
Aquilegia vulgaris
Clematis × jackmanii
Digitalis purpurea 'Excelsior'
Geranium 'Ann Folkard'
Geranium macrorrhizum
Geranium psilostemon
Geranium sanguineum
Geranium sanguineum var. *striatum*
Geranium sylvaticum 'Mayflower'
Hosta sieboldiana
Hosta sieboldiana 'Frances Williams'
Iris kaempferi
Lantana 'Confetti'
Lobularia maritima 'Easter Bonnet Deep Pink'
Lythrum salicaria 'Morden Pink'
Petunia 'Burgundy Madness'
Phlox maculata 'Alpha'
Primula japonica
Symphytum officinale

WHITE

Ajuga reptans 'Alba'
Antirrhinum majus 'Princess White with Purple Eye'
Antirrhinum majus 'White Rocket'
Aquilegia 'Olympia'
Aquilegia 'Heavenly Blue'
Aquilegia 'McKana Giants'
Aquilegia 'Rose Queen'
Aquilegia vulgaris
Argyranthemum frutescens
Astilbe × arendsii 'Bridal Veil'
Cimicifuga racemosa
Crambe cordifolia
Convallaria majalis
Dicentra eximia 'Alba'
Dicentra spectabilis
Dicentra spectabilis 'Alba'
Digitalis purpurea 'Excelsior'
Galium odoratum
Geranium sanguineum 'Album'
Hedera helix
Hydrangea quercifolia
Iberis sempervirens 'Snowflake'
Iris kaempferi
Iris sibirica 'White Swirl'
Lamium maculatum 'White Nancy'
Leucanthemum × superbum 'Alaska'
Leucojum aestivum 'Gravetye Giant'
Lilium regale
Lobelia erinus 'White Cascade'
Lobularia maritima 'Carpet of Snow'
Malva moschata 'Alba'
Muscari botryoides 'Album'
Myrrhis odorata
Narcissus 'Thalia'
Nepeta mussinii 'White Wonder'
Ornithogalum umbellatum
Phlox maculata 'Miss Lingard'
Podophyllum peltatum
Polygonatum biflorum
Polygonatum odoratum 'Variegatum'
Primula japonica 'Postford White'
Thalictrum aquilegifolium 'Album'
Tiarella cordifolia
Tradescantia × andersoniana 'Innocence'
Trillium grandiflorum

PASTEL TINTS

Alchemilla alpina
Alchemilla mollis
Allium karataviense

Allium ostrowskianum
Allium schoenoprasum
Amsonia tabernaemonta
Aquilegia 'McKana Giants'
Aruncus dioicus
Astilbe × arendsii 'Cattleya'
Astilbe × arendsii 'Deutschland'
Astilbe × arendsii 'Fanal'
Camassia quamash
Coreopsis verticillata 'Moonbeam'
Dicentra spectabilis
Digitalis grandiflora
Digitalis purpurea 'Excelsior'
Digitalis × mertonensis
Epimedium × versicolor 'Sulphureum'
Erythronium 'Pagoda'
Geranium endressi 'Wargrave Pink'
Geranium sanguineum var. *striatum*
Helleborus foetidus
Hemerocallis lilioasphodelus
Heuchera 'Palace Purple'
Hosta sieboldiana
Hosta *sieboldiana* 'Frances Williams'
Iris kaempferi
Lamium maculatum 'Shell Pink'
Lilium 'French Vanilla'
Lobelia erinus 'Cambridge Blue'
Lonicera periclymenum 'Graham Thomas'
Narcissus 'Mount Hood'
Nicotiana alata 'Lime Green'
Nicotiana alata 'Nicki Lime'
Nicotiana alata 'Nicki Pink'
Nicotiana langsdorffii
Phlox divaricata
Polygonatum biflorum
Trollius 'Alabaster'

Bloom Season: Summer

RED

Achillea millefolium 'Salmon Beauty'
Antirrhinum 'Frontier Crimson'
Argyranthemum frutescens
Astilbe × arendsii 'Cattleya'
Astilbe × arendsii 'Fanal'
Astrantia major
Centranthus ruber
Chelone lyonii
Cosmos bipinnatus 'Pinkie'

Dicentra eximia 'Luxuriant'
Digitalis × mertonensis
Geranium endressii 'Wargrave Pink'
Gladiolus callianthus
Hemerocallis 'Sammy Russell'
Impatiens 'Tempo Hybrid Red'
Knautia macedonica
Lantana 'Confetti'
Lilium 'Fireball'
Lychnis chalcedonica
Malva alcea 'Fastigiata'
Malva moschata
Malva sylvestris 'Mauritiana'
Monarda didyma 'Cambridge Scarlet'
Monarda didyma 'Croftway Pink'
Monarda didyma 'Mahogany'
Monarda 'Adam'
Nicotiana alata 'Nicki Pink'
Phalaris arundinacea var. *picta*
Phlox paniculata 'Bright Eyes'
Sedum 'Autumn Joy'
Sedum 'Ruby Glow'

RED-ORANGE

Achillea millefolium 'Salmon Beauty'
Alstroemeria Ligtu Hybrids
Calendula officinalis
Cosmos sulphureus 'Sunny Red'
Cosmos sulphureus 'Sunset'
Crocosmia 'Lucifer'
Digitalis × mertonensis
Hakonechloa macra 'Aureola'
Hemerocallis 'Ed Murray'
Hemerocallis 'Sammy Russell'
Heuchera 'Palace Purple'
Kniphofia 'Atlanta'
Macleaya microcarpa

ORANGE/YELLOW-ORANGE

Aruncus dioicus
Achillea millefolium 'Weser River Sandstone'
Alstroemeria Ligtu Hybrids
Calendula officinalis
Hemerocallis 'Colonial Dame'
Hemerocallis fulva 'Kwanso Flore Plena'
Hemerocallis 'Mayan Gold'
Hemerocallis 'Sombrero'
Hemerocallis 'Stella d'Oro'
Lantana 'Confetti'
Ligularia dentata 'Desdemona'

Lilium 'Enchantment'
Lilium lancifolium

YELLOW

Argyranthemum frutescens
Astilbe × arendsii 'Deutschland'
Chrysanthemum pacificum
Coreopsis verticillata 'Moonbeam'
Corydalis lutea
Digitalis grandiflora
Filipendula vulgaris
Hemerocallis cultivars
Hemerocallis 'Gala Bells'
Hemerocallis 'Hyperion'
Hemerocallis lilioasphodelus
Kniphofia 'Atlanta'
Lantana 'Confetti'
Ligularia stenocephala 'The Rocket'
Lilium 'French Vanilla'
Lonicera periclymenum 'Graham Thomas'
Lysimachia ciliata 'Purpurea'
Lysimachia punctata
Stylophorum diphyllum
Thalictrum speciocissimum
Trollius europeus 'Superbus'

YELLOW-GREEN

Alchemilla mollis
Gunnera manicata
Nicotiana alata 'Lime Green'
Nicotiana alata 'Nicki Lime'
Nicotiana langsdorffii
Sedum 'Autumn Joy'

BLUE

Cynoglossum amabile
Linum perenne
Lobelia erinus 'Cambridge Blue'

BLUE-VIOLET

Campanula poscharkyana
Centaurea montana
Iris kaempferi
Nepeta 'Six Hills Giant'
Platycodon grandiflorus
Tradescantia × andersoniana 'Blue Stone'
Veronica 'Sunny Border Blue'
Viola × wittrockiana

VIOLET

Aconitum napellus
Campanula carpatica 'Blue Clips'
Campanula glomerata 'Joan Elliot'

**Exposure: Part Shade, Bloom
Season: Summer, Color: Violet,**
continued

Campanula portenschlagiana
Campanula poscharkyana
Geranium 'Johnson's Blue'
Geranium × *magnificum*
Hosta fortunei
Hosta fortunei 'Aurea'
Hosta fortunei 'Marginato-alba'
Hosta montana 'Aureo-marginata'
Hosta sieboldiana 'Frances Williams'
Hosta sieboldii
Iris kaempferi
Lobularia maritima 'Royal Carpet'
Lythrum salicaria 'Dropmore
    Purple'
Monarda didyma 'Bluestocking'
Nierembergia hippomanica var.
    violacea 'Purple Robe'
Petunia 'Purple Robe'
Salvia farinacea 'Victoria'
Thalictrum rochebrunianum
Verbena bonariensis
Viola 'Baby Lucia'
Viola corsica
Viola tricolor 'Bowles Black'

RED-VIOLET
Allium ostrowskianum
Allium senescens
Allium senescens 'Glaucum'
Allium sphaerocephalon
Antirrhinum majus 'Princess
    White with Purple Eye'
Astilbe chinensis 'Pumila'
Chelone lyonii
Clematis × *jackmanii*
Dicentra eximia 'Luxuriant'
Digitalis purpurea 'Excelsior'
Erigeron karvinskianus
Geranium 'Ann Folkard'
Geranium psilostemon
Geranium sanguineum
Geranium sanguineum var.
    striatum
Iris kaempferi
Lantana 'Confetti'
Lobularia maritima 'Easter Bonnet
    Deep Pink'
Lythrum salicaria 'Morden Pink'
Malva sylvestris 'Mauritiana'
Monarda didyma 'Violet Queen'

Petunia 'Burgundy Madness'
Phlox maculata 'Alpha'
Stachys macrantha 'Robusta'
Teucrium chamaedrys

WHITE
Anaphalis triplinervis 'Summer
    Snow'
Antirrhinum majus 'Princess
    White with Purple Eye'
Antirrhinum majus 'White Rocket'
Argyranthemum frutescens
Astilbe × *arendsii* 'Bridal Veil'
Astrantia major
Cimicifuga racemosa
Crambe cordifolia
Dicentra eximia 'Alba'
Digitalis purpurea 'Excelsior'
Filipendula vulgaris
Gladiolus callianthus
Hosta plantaginea 'Royal Standard'
Hydrangea quercifolia
Iris kaempferi
Leucanthemum × *superbum* 'Alaska'
Lilium regale
Lilium 'Casa Blanca'
Lobelia erinus 'White Cascade'
Lobularia maritima 'Carpet of
    Snow'
Lysimachia clethroides
Malva moschata 'Alba'
Nepeta mussinii 'White Wonder'
Nicotiana sylvestris
Phlox maculata 'Miss Lingard'
Physostegia virginiana 'Summer
    Snow'
Rodgersia aesculifolia
Tanacetum parthenium
Thalictrum aquilegifolium 'Album'
Tradescantia × *andersoniana*
    'Innocence'

PASTEL TINTS
Alchemilla mollis
Allium ostrowskianum
Aruncus dioicus
Astilbe chinensis 'Pumila'
Astilbe × *arendsii* 'Cattleya'
Astilbe × *arendsii* 'Deutschland'
Astrantia major
Coreopsis verticillata 'Moonbeam'
Digitalis grandiflora
Digitalis purpurea 'Excelsior'
Digitalis × *mertonensis*
Erigeron karvinskianus

Filipendula vulgaris
Geranium endressii 'Wargrave
    Pink'
Geranium sanguineum var.
    striatum
Hemerocallis 'Colonial Dame'
Hemerocallis lilioasphodelus
Heuchera 'Palace Purple'
Hosta fortunei
Hosta fortunei 'Aurea'
Hosta fortunei 'Marginato-alba'
Hosta montana 'Aureo marginata'
Hosta sieboldiana 'Frances Williams'
Iris kaempferi
Lilium 'French Vanilla'
Lobelia erinus 'Cambridge Blue'
Lonicera periclymenum 'Graham
    Thomas'
Malva alcea 'Fastigiata'
Monarda didyma 'Croftway Pink'
Nicotiana alata 'Lime Green'
Nicotiana alata 'Nicki Lime'
Nicotiana alata 'Nicki Pink'
Nicotiana langsdorffii
Phalaris arundinacea var. *picta*
Phlox paniculata 'Bright Eyes'
Sedum 'Autumn Joy'

Bloom Season: Late Summer

RED
Antirrhinum 'Frontier Crimson'
Argyranthemum frutescens
Astrantia major
Chelone lyonii
Dicentra eximia 'Luxuriant'
Gladiolus callianthus
Impatiens 'Tempo Hybrid Red'
Knautia macedonica
Lantana 'Confetti'
Lilium 'Fireball'
Lobelia cardinalis
Malva sylvestris 'Mauritiana'
Monarda 'Adam'
Monarda didyma 'Cambridge
    Scarlet'
Monarda didyma 'Croftway Pink'
Monarda didyma 'Mahogany'
Nicotiana alata 'Nicki Pink'
Phlox paniculata 'Bright Eyes'
Sedum 'Autumn Joy'
Sedum 'Rosy Glow'
Sedum 'Ruby Glow'
Sedum 'Vera Jameson'

ORANGE/YELLOW-ORANGE

Helictotrichon sempervirens
Hemerocallis fulva 'Kwanso Flore Plena'
Hemerocallis 'Stella d'Oro'
Heuchera 'Palace Purple'
Lantana 'Confetti'
Lilium 'Enchantment'

YELLOW

Argyranthemum frutescens
Artemisia lactiflora
Chrysanthemum pacificum
Coreopsis verticillata 'Moonbeam'
Corydalis lutea
Filipendula vulgaris
Hemerocallis cultivars
Kirengeshoma palmata
Lantana 'Confetti'
Lonicera periclymenum 'Graham Thomas'
Solidago 'Cloth of Gold'
Solidago 'Crown of Rays'
Stylophorum diphyllum
Tanacetum parthenium 'Alba'

YELLOW-GREEN

Nicotiana alata 'Lime Green'
Nicotiana alata 'Nicki Lime'
Nicotiana langsdorffii
Sedum 'Autumn Joy'

BLUE

Cynoglossum amabile
Lobelia erinus 'Cambridge Blue'

BLUE-VIOLET

Centaurea montana
Ceratostigma plumbaginoides
Platycodon grandiflorus
Veronica 'Sunny Border Blue'

VIOLET

Aconitum napellus
Campanula carpatica 'Blue Clips'
Eupatorium coelestinum
Hosta 'Krossa Regal'
Hosta × *tardiana* 'Halcyon'
Liriope muscari
Lobularia maritima 'Royal Carpet'
Lythrum salicaria 'Dropmore Purple'
Monarda didyma 'Bluestocking'
Petunia 'Purple Robe'
Salvia farinacea 'Victoria'
Thalictrum rochebrunianum
Verbena bonariensis

RED-VIOLET

Allium senescens
Allium senescens 'Glaucum'
Allium sphaerocephalon
Anemone hupehensis 'September Charm'
Anemone vitifolia 'Robustissima'
Astilbe chinensis 'Pumila'
Chelone lyonii
Erigeron karvinskianus
Lantana 'Confetti'
Lobularia maritima 'Easter Bonnet Deep Pink'
Lythrum salicaria 'Morden Pink'
Malva sylvestris 'Mauritiana'
Monarda didyma 'Violet Queen'
Monarda fistulosa
Petunia 'Burgundy Madness'
Sedum 'Rosy Glow'
Sedum 'Vera Jameson'
Stachys macrantha 'Robusta'
Teucrium chamaedrys

WHITE

Allium tuberosum
Anaphalis margaritacea
Anaphalis triplinervis 'Summer Snow'
Anemone 'Honorine Jobert'
Antirrhinum majus 'White Rocket'
Argyranthemum frutescens
Astrantia major
Filipendula vulgaris
Gladiolus callianthus
Hosta plantaginea 'Royal Standard'
Lilium 'Casa Blanca'
Lobelia erinus 'White Cascade'
Lobularia maritima 'Carpet of Snow'
Nicotiana sylvestris
Physostegia virginiana 'Summer Snow'
Tanacetum parthenium

PASTEL TINTS

Anemone vitifolia 'Robustissima'
Artemisia lactiflora
Astilbe chinensis 'Pumila'
Astrantia major
Coreopsis verticillata 'Moonbeam'
Erigeron karvinskianus
Filipendula vulgaris
Helictotrichon sempervirens
Heuchera 'Palace Purple'
Hosta 'Krossa Regal'

Hosta × *tardiana* 'Halcyon'
Lobelia erinus 'Cambridge Blue'
Lonicera periclymenum 'Graham Thomas'
Monarda didyma 'Croftway Pink'
Monarda fistulosa
Nicotiana alata 'Lime Green'
Nicotiana alata 'Nicki Lime'
Nicotiana alata 'Nicki Pink'
Nicotiana langsdorffii
Sedum 'Autumn Joy'
Phlox paniculata 'Bright Eyes'

Bloom Season: Fall

RED

Argyranthemum frutescens
Chelone lyonii
Dicentra eximia 'Luxuriant'
Impatiens 'Tempo Hybrid Red'
Lantana 'Confetti'
Lobelia cardinalis
Nicotiana alata 'Nicki Pink'
Sedum 'Autumn Joy'
Sedum 'Rosy Glow'
Sedum 'Ruby Glow'
Sedum 'Vera Jameson'

RED-ORANGE

Miscanthus sinensis 'Gracillimus'

ORANGE/YELLOW-ORANGE

Hemerocallis 'Stella d'Oro'
Lantana 'Confetti'
Miscanthus sinensis 'Variegatus'
Miscanthus sinensis 'Zebrinus'

YELLOW

Argyranthemum frutescens
Chrysanthemum pacificum
Coreopsis verticillata 'Moonbeam'
Corydalis lutea
Kirengeshoma palmata
Lantana 'Confetti'
Lonicera periclymenum 'Graham Thomas'
Solidago 'Cloth of Gold'
Solidago 'Crown of Rays'

YELLOW-GREEN

Nicotiana alata 'Lime Green'
Nicotiana alata 'Nicki Lime'
Nicotiana langsdorffii

BLUE-VIOLET

Centaurea montana
Ceratostigma plumbaginoides
Veronica 'Sunny Border Blue'

Exposure: Part Shade, Bloom Season: Fall, *continued*

VIOLET
Eupatorium coelestinum
Lobularia maritima 'Royal Carpet'
Petunia 'Purple Robe'
Salvia farinacea 'Victoria'
Verbena bonariensis

RED-VIOLET
Allium senescens
Allium senescens 'Glaucum'
Anemone hupehensis 'September Charm'
Anemone vitifolia 'Robustissima'

Chelone lyonii
Erigeron karvinskianus
Lantana 'Confetti'
Lobularia maritima 'Easter Bonnet Deep Pink'
Malva sylvestris 'Mauritiana'
Petunia 'Burgundy Madness'
Sedum 'Vera Jameson'

WHITE
Anaphalis margaritacea
Anemone 'Honorine Jobert'
Argyranthemum frutescens
Boltonia asteroides 'Snowbank'
Lobularia maritima 'Carpet of Snow'

Nicotiana sylvestris
Tanacetum parthenium

PASTEL TINTS
Anemone vitifolia 'Robustissima'
Coreopsis verticillata 'Moonbeam'
Erigeron karvinskianus
Lonicera periclymenum 'Graham Thomas'
Miscanthus sinensis 'Gracillimus'
Miscanthus sinensis 'Variegatus'
Miscanthus sinensis 'Zebrinus'
Nicotiana alata 'Lime Green'
Nicotiana alata 'Nicki Lime'
Nicotiana alata 'Nicki Pink'
Nicotiana langsdorffii

EXPOSURE: SHADE

Bloom Season: Early Spring

YELLOW
Stylophorum diphyllum

YELLOW-GREEN
Helleborus orientalis

BLUE
Mertensia virginica
Pulmonaria saccharata 'Mrs. Moon'

BLUE-VIOLET
Mertensia virginica
Pulmonaria saccharata 'Mrs. Moon'

VIOLET
Pulmonaria saccharata 'Mrs. Moon'

RED-VIOLET
Helleborus orientalis
Mertensia virginica

WHITE
Sanguinaria canadensis

PASTEL TINTS
Helleborus orientalis
Mertensia virginica

Bloom Season: Mid Spring

RED
Dicentra spectabilis

YELLOW
Epimedium × *versicolor* 'Sulphureum'
Stylophorum diphyllum

YELLOW-GREEN
Helleborus orientalis
Polygonatum biflorum

BLUE
Mertensia virginica
Pulmonaria saccharata 'Mrs. Moon'

BLUE-VIOLET
Mertensia virginica
Phlox divaricata
Pulmonaria saccharata 'Mrs. Moon'

VIOLET
Pulmonaria saccharata 'Mrs. Moon'

RED-VIOLET
Helleborus orientalis
Mertensia virginica

WHITE
Convallaria majalis
Dicentra spectabilis
Dicentra spectabilis 'Alba'
Galium odoratum
Polygonatum biflorum
Polygonatum odoratum 'Variegatum'
Trillium grandiflorum

PASTEL TINTS
Dicentra spectabilis
Epimedium × *versicolor* 'Sulphureum'
Helleborus orientalis
Mertensia virginica
Phlox divaricata
Polygonatum biflorum

Bloom Season: Late Spring

RED
Dicentra spectabilis

YELLOW
Stylophorum diphyllum

YELLOW-GREEN
Polygonatum biflorum

BLUE
Pulmonaria saccharata 'Mrs. Moon'

BLUE-VIOLET
Pulmonaria saccharata 'Mrs. Moon'

VIOLET
Hosta sieboldiana
Hosta sieboldiana 'Frances Williams'
Pulmonaria saccharata 'Mrs. Moon'

WHITE
Dicentra spectabilis
Dicentra spectabilis 'Alba'
Galium odoratum
Polygonatum biflorum
Polygonatum odoratum
  'Variegatum'
Tiarella cordifolia

PASTEL TINTS
Dicentra spectabilis
Hosta sieboldiana
Hosta sieboldiana 'Frances
  Williams'
Polygonatum biflorum

Bloom Season: Summer

RED-ORANGE
Hakonechloa macra 'Aureola'

YELLOW
Stylophorum diphyllum

VIOLET
Hosta fortunei
Hosta fortunei 'Aurea'
Hosta fortunei 'Marginato-alba'
Hosta montana 'Aureo-marginata'
Hosta sieboldiana 'Frances Williams'
Hosta sieboldii

WHITE
Hosta plantaginea 'Royal Standard'

PASTEL TINTS
Hosta fortunei
Hosta fortunei 'Aurea'
Hosta fortunei 'Marginato-alba'
Hosta montana 'Aureo-marginata'
Hosta sieboldiana 'Frances Williams'
Hosta sieboldii

Bloom Season: Late Summer

RED
Lobelia cardinalis

YELLOW
Stylophorum diphyllum

VIOLET
Hosta 'Krossa Regal'

WHITE
Hosta plantaginea 'Royal Standard'

PASTEL TINTS
Hosta 'Krossa Regal'

Bloom Season: Fall

RED
Lobelia cardinalis

Foliar Options for Temperate Climates by Exposure, Season, and Color

EXPOSURE: SUN

Foliar Season: Early Spring

GREEN/BLUE-GREEN
Festuca glauca
Hedera helix
Vinca minor

GRAY-GREEN
Santolina chamaecyparissus

RED/RED-ORANGE/RED-VIOLET
Berberis thunbergii 'Atropurpurea'
Berberis thunbergii 'Atropurpurea Nana'

Foliar Season: Mid Spring

GREEN/BLUE-GREEN
Alchemilla mollis
Anemone vitifolia 'Robustissima'
Brunnera macrophylla
Dennstaedtia punctiloba
Dryopteris noveboracensis
Festuca glauca
Geranium macrorrhizum
Gunnera manicata
Hedera helix
Hosta plantaginea 'Royal Standard'
Hosta × tardiana 'Halcyon'
Polystichum setiferum 'Divisilobum'
Teucrium chamaedrys
Vinca minor

GRAY-GREEN
Ballota pseudodictamnus

Convolvulus cneorum
Helichrysum petiolare
Santolina chamaecyparissus
Senecio cineraria 'Silver Queen'
Stachys byzantina

RED/RED-ORANGE/RED-VIOLET
Berberis thunbergii 'Atropurpurea'
Berberis thunbergii 'Atropurpurea Nana'
Cotinus coggygria 'Royal Purple'
Heuchera 'Palace Purple'
Lysimachia ciliata 'Purpurea'
Prunus × cistena

Foliar Season: Late Spring

GREEN/BLUE-GREEN
Alchemilla mollis
Anemone vitifolia 'Robustissima'
Brunnera macrophylla
Dennstaedtia punctiloba
Dryopteris noveboracensis
Elymus arenarius
Festuca glauca
Geranium macrorrhizum
Gunnera manicata
Hedera helix
Helictotrichon sempervirens
Hosta plantaginea 'Royal Standard'
Hosta × tardiana 'Halcyon'
Hydrangea quercifolia
Pennisetum alopecuroides
Polystichum setiferum

'Divisilobum'
Teucrium chamaedrys
Vinca minor
Weigela florida 'Variegata'
Yucca filamentosa

GRAY-GREEN
Artemisia 'Powis Castle'
Artemisia schmidtiana 'Silver Mound'
Athyrium nipponicum 'Pictum'
Ballota pseudodictamnus
Convolvulus cneorum
Eryngium giganteum
Helichrysum angustifolium
Helichrysum petiolare
Onopordum acanthium
Phalaris arundinacea var. *picta*
Salvia argentea
Santolina chamaecyparissus
Senecio cineraria 'Silver Queen'
Stachys byzantina

RED/RED-ORANGE/RED-VIOLET
Berberis thunbergii 'Atropurpurea'
Berberis thunbergii 'Atropurpurea Nana'
Beta vulgaris subsp. *cicla*
Cotinus coggygria 'Royal Purple'
Foeniculum vulgare 'Purpureum'
Heuchera 'Palace Purple'
Lysimachia ciliata 'Purpurea'
Pennisetum setaceum 'Burgundy Giant'

Prunus × *cistena*
Salvia officinalis 'Purpurea'

YELLOW
Salvia officinalis 'Aurea'

Foliar Season: Summer

GREEN/BLUE-GREEN
Alchemilla mollis
Anemone vitifolia 'Robustissima'
Brunnera macrophylla
Dennstaedtia punctiloba
Dryopteris noveboracensis
Elymus arenarius
Festuca glauca
Geranium macrorrhizum
Gunnera manicata
Hedera helix
Helictotrichon sempervirens
Hosta plantaginea 'Royal Standard'
Hosta × *tardiana* 'Halcyon'
Hydrangea quercifolia
Imperata cylindrica 'Red Baron'
Miscanthus sinensis 'Gracillimus'
Miscanthus sinensis 'Variegatus'
Miscanthus sinensis 'Zebrinus'
Pennisetum alopecuroides
Polystichum setiferum
  'Divisilobum'
Teucrium chamaedrys
Vinca minor
Weigela florida 'Variegata'
Yucca filamentosa

GRAY-GREEN
Artemisia 'Powis Castle'
Artemisia schmidtiana 'Silver
  Mound'
Athyrium nipponicum 'Pictum'
Ballota pseudodictamnus
Convolvulus cneorum
Eryngium giganteum
Helichrysum angustifolium
Helichrysum petiolare
Onopordum acanthium
Phalaris arundinacea var. *picta*
Salvia argentea
Santolina chamaecyparissus
Senecio cineraria 'Silver Queen'
Stachys byzantina

RED/RED-ORANGE/RED-VIOLET
Atriplex hortensis 'Cupreata'
Berberis thunbergii 'Atropurpurea'

Berberis thunbergii 'Atropurpurea
  Nana'
Beta vulgaris subsp. *cicla*
Cotinus coggygria 'Royal Purple'
Foeniculum vulgare 'Purpureum'
Heuchera 'Palace Purple'
Imperata cylindrica 'Red Baron'
Lysimachia ciliata 'Purpurea'
Pennisetum setaceum 'Burgundy
  Giant'
Perilla frutescens
Prunus × *cistena*
Salvia officinalis 'Purpurea'

YELLOW
Salvia officinalis 'Aurea'

Foliar Season: Late Summer

GREEN/BLUE-GREEN
Alchemilla mollis
Anemone vitifolia 'Robustissima'
Brunnera macrophylla
Dennstaedtia punctiloba
Dryopteris noveboracensis
Elymus arenarius
Festuca glauca
Geranium macrorrhizum
Gunnera manicata
Hedera helix
Helictotrichon sempervirens
Hosta plantaginea 'Royal Standard'
Hosta × *tardiana* 'Halcyon'
Hydrangea quercifolia
Imperata cylindrica 'Red Baron'
Miscanthus sinensis 'Gracillimus'
Miscanthus sinensis 'Variegatus'
Miscanthus sinensis 'Zebrinus'
Pennisetum alopecuroides
Polystichum setiferum
  'Divisilobum'
Teucrium chamaedrys
Vinca minor
Weigela florida 'Variegata'
Yucca filamentosa

GRAY-GREEN
Artemisia 'Powis Castle'
Artemisia schmidtiana 'Silver
  Mound'
Athyrium nipponicum 'Pictum'
Ballota pseudodictamnus
Convolvulus cneorum
Eryngium giganteum
Helichrysum angustifolium

Helichrysum petiolare
Onopordum acanthium
Phalaris arundinacea var. *picta*
Salvia argentea
Santolina chamaecyparissus
Senecio cineraria 'Silver Queen'
Stachys byzantina

RED/RED-ORANGE/RED-VIOLET
Atriplex hortensis 'Cupreata'
Berberis thunbergii 'Atropurpurea'
Berberis thunbergii 'Atropurpurea
  Nana'
Beta vulgaris subsp. *cicla*
Cotinus coggygria 'Royal Purple'
Foeniculum vulgare 'Purpureum'
Heuchera 'Palace Purple'
Imperata cylindrica 'Red Baron'
Lysimachia ciliata 'Purpurea'
Pennisetum setaceum 'Burgundy
  Giant'
Perilla frutescens
Prunus × *cistena*
Salvia officinalis 'Purpurea'

YELLOW
Salvia officinalis 'Aurea'

Foliar Season: Fall

GREEN/BLUE-GREEN
Alchemilla mollis
Anemone vitifolia 'Robustissima'
Brunnera macrophylla
Dennstaedtia punctiloba
Dryopteris noveboracensis
Elymus arenarius
Festuca glauca
Geranium macrorrhizum
Gunnera manicata
Hedera helix
Helictotrichon sempervirens
Hosta plantaginea 'Royal Standard'
Hosta × *tardiana* 'Halcyon'
Hydrangea quercifolia
Imperata cylindrica 'Red Baron'
Miscanthus sinensis 'Gracillimus'
Miscanthus sinensis 'Variegatus'
Miscanthus sinensis 'Zebrinus'
Pennisetum alopecuroides
Polystichum setiferum 'Divisilobum'
Teucrium chamaedrys
Vinca minor
Weigela florida 'Variegata'
Yucca filamentosa

Exposure: Sun, Foliar Season: Fall, *continued*

GRAY-GREEN
Artemisia 'Powis Castle'
Artemisia schmidtiana 'Silver Mound'
Athyrium nipponicum 'Pictum'
Ballota pseudodictamnus
Convolvulus cneorum
Eryngium giganteum
Helichrysum angustifolium
Helichrysum petiolare

Salvia argentea
Santolina chamaecyparissus
Senecio cineraria 'Silver Queen'
Stachys byzantina

RED/RED-ORANGE/RED-VIOLET
Atriplex hortensis 'Cupreata'
Berberis thunbergii 'Atropurpurea'
Berberis thunbergii 'Atropurpurea Nana'
Cotinus coggygria 'Royal Purple'
Foeniculum vulgare 'Purpureum'
Geranium macrorrhizum

Heuchera 'Palace Purple'
Hydrangea quercifolia
Imperata cylindrica 'Red Baron'
Lysimachia ciliata 'Purpurea'
Pennisetum alopecuroides
Pennisetum setaceum 'Burgundy Giant'
Perilla frutescens
Prunus × *cistena*
Salvia officinalis 'Purpurea'

YELLOW
Salvia officinalis 'Aurea'

EXPOSURE: PART SHADE

Foliar Season: Early Spring

GREEN/BLUE-GREEN
Hedera helix
Podophyllum peltatum
Vinca minor

RED/RED-ORANGE/RED-VIOLET
Berberis thunbergii 'Atropurpurea'
Berberis thunbergii 'Atropurpurea Nana'

Foliar Season: Mid Spring

GREEN/BLUE-GREEN
Adiantum pedatum
Alchemilla mollis
Anemone vitifolia 'Robustissima'
Brunnera macrophylla
Dennstaedtia punctiloba
Dryopteris noveboracensis
Geranium macrorrhizum
Gunnera manicata
Hedera helix
Hosta fortunei
Hosta fortunei 'Aurea'
Hosta fortunei 'Marginato-alba'
Hosta 'Krossa Regal'
Hosta montana 'Aureo-marginata'
Hosta plantaginea 'Royal Standard'
Hosta sieboldiana
Hosta sieboldiana 'Frances Williams'
Hosta sieboldii
Hosta × *tardiana* 'Halcyon'
Podophyllum peltatum
Polystichum setiferum 'Divisilobum'
Teucrium chamaedrys
Vinca minor

RED/RED-ORANGE/RED-VIOLET
Berberis thunbergii 'Atropurpurea'
Berberis thunbergii 'Atropurpurea Nana'
Heuchera 'Palace Purple'

YELLOW
Hakonechloa macra 'Aureola'

Foliar Season: Late Spring

GREEN/BLUE-GREEN
Adiantum pedatum
Alchemilla mollis
Anemone vitifolia 'Robustissima'
Athyrium filix-femina
Brunnera macrophylla
Dennstaedtia punctiloba
Dryopteris noveboracensis
Geranium macrorrhizum
Gunnera manicata
Hedera helix
Helictotrichon sempervirens
Hosta fortunei
Hosta fortunei 'Aurea'
Hosta fortunei 'Marginato-alba'
Hosta 'Krossa Regal'
Hosta montana 'Aureo-marginata'
Hosta plantaginea 'Royal Standard'
Hosta sieboldiana
Hosta sieboldiana 'Frances Williams'
Hosta sieboldii
Hosta × *tardiana* 'Halcyon'
Hydrangea quercifolia
Matteuccia struthiopteris
Podophyllum peltatum
Polystichum setiferum 'Divisilobum'

Teucrium chamaedrys
Vinca minor

GRAY-GREEN
Athyrium nipponicum 'Pictum'
Phalaris arundinacea 'Picta'

RED/RED-ORANGE/RED-VIOLET
Athyrium nipponicum 'Pictum'
Berberis thunbergii 'Atropurpurea'
Berberis thunbergii 'Atropurpurea Nana'
Beta vulgaris subsp. *cicla*
Heuchera 'Palace Purple'
Lysimachia ciliata 'Purpurea'

YELLOW
Hakonechloa macra 'Aureola'

Foliar Season: Summer

GREEN/BLUE-GREEN
Adiantum pedatum
Alchemilla mollis
Anemone vitifolia 'Robustissima'
Athyrium filix-femina
Brunnera macrophylla
Dennstaedtia punctiloba
Dryopteris noveboracensis
Geranium macrorrhizum
Gunnera manicata
Hedera helix
Helictotrichon sempervirens
Hosta fortunei
Hosta fortunei 'Aurea'
Hosta fortunei 'Marginato-alba'
Hosta 'Krossa Regal'
Hosta montana 'Aureo-marginata'
Hosta plantaginea 'Royal Standard'

Hosta sieboldiana
Hosta sieboldiana 'Frances Williams'
Hosta sieboldii
Hosta × tardiana 'Halcyon'
Hydrangea quercifolia
Imperata cylindrica 'Red Baron'
Kirengeshoma palmata
Matteuccia struthiopteris
Miscanthus sinensis 'Gracillimus'
Miscanthus sinensis 'Variegatus'
Miscanthus sinensis 'Zebrinus'
Podophyllum peltatum
Polystichum setiferum 'Divisilobum'
Teucrium chamaedrys
Vinca minor

GRAY-GREEN
Athyrium nipponicum 'Pictum'
Phalaris arundinacea 'Picta'

RED/RED-ORANGE/RED-VIOLET
Athyrium nipponicum 'Pictum'
Berberis thunbergii 'Atropurpurea'
Berberis thunbergii 'Atropurpurea
  Nana'
Beta vulgaris subsp. *cicla*
Heuchera 'Palace Purple'
Imperata cylindrica 'Red Baron'
Lysimachia ciliata 'Purpurea'

YELLOW
Hakonechloa macra 'Aureola'

Foliar Season: Late Summer

GREEN/BLUE-GREEN
Adiantum pedatum
Alchemilla mollis
Anemone vitifolia 'Robustissima'
Athyrium filix-femina
Brunnera macrophylla
Dennstaedtia punctiloba
Dryopteris noveboracensis

Geranium macrorrhizum
Gunnera manicata
Hedera helix
Helictotrichon sempervirens
Hosta fortunei
Hosta fortunei 'Aurea'
Hosta fortunei 'Marginato-alba'
Hosta 'Krossa Regal'
Hosta montana 'Aureo-marginata'
Hosta plantaginea 'Royal Standard'
Hosta sieboldiana
Hosta sieboldiana 'Frances Williams'
Hosta sieboldii
Hosta × tardiana 'Halcyon'
Hydrangea quercifolia
Imperata cylindrica 'Red Baron'
Kirengeshoma palmata
Matteuccia struthiopteris
Miscanthus sinensis 'Gracillimus'
Miscanthus sinensis 'Variegatus'
Miscanthus sinensis 'Zebrinus'
Podophyllum peltatum
Polystichum setiferum 'Divisilobum'
Teucrium chamaedrys
Vinca minor

GRAY-GREEN
Athyrium nipponicum 'Pictum'
Phalaris arundinacea 'Picta'

RED/RED-ORANGE/RED-VIOLET
Athyrium nipponicum 'Pictum'
Berberis thunbergii 'Atropurpurea'
Berberis thunbergii 'Atropurpurea
  Nana'
Beta vulgaris subsp. *cicla*
Heuchera 'Palace Purple'
Imperata cylindrica 'Red Baron'
Lysimachia ciliata 'Purpurea'

YELLOW
Hakonechloa macra 'Aureola'

Foliar Season: Fall

GREEN/BLUE-GREEN
Alchemilla mollis
Anemone vitifolia 'Robustissima'
Athyrium filix-femina
Brunnera macrophylla
Dennstaedtia punctiloba
Dryopteris noveboracensis
Geranium macrorrhizum
Gunnera manicata
Hedera helix
Helictotrichon sempervirens
Hosta fortunei
Hosta fortunei 'Aurea'
Hosta fortunei 'Marginato-alba'
Hosta 'Krossa Regal'
Hosta montana 'Aureo-marginata'
Hosta plantaginea 'Royal Standard'
Hosta sieboldiana
Hosta sieboldiana 'Frances Williams'
Hosta sieboldii
Hosta × tardiana 'Halcyon'
Imperata cylindrica 'Red Baron'
Kirengeshoma palmata
Matteuccia struthiopteris
Phalaris arundinacea 'Picta'
Polystichum setiferum 'Divisilobum'

GRAY-GREEN
Athyrium nipponicum 'Pictum'

RED/RED-ORANGE/RED-VIOLET
Athyrium nipponicum 'Pictum'
Berberis thunbergii 'Atropurpurea'
Berberis thunbergii 'Atropurpurea
  Nana'
Geranium macrorrhizum
Heuchera 'Palace Purple'
Hydrangea quercifolia
Imperata cylindrica 'Red Baron'
Lysimachia ciliata 'Purpurea'
YELLOW
Hakonechloa macra 'Aureola'

EXPOSURE: SHADE

Foliar Season: Early Spring

GREEN/BLUE-GREEN
Adiantum pedatum

Foliar Season: Mid Spring

GREEN/BLUE-GREEN
Adiantum pedatum
Hosta fortunei

Hosta fortunei 'Aurea'
Hosta fortunei 'Marginato-alba'
Hosta 'Krossa Regal'
Hosta montana 'Aureo-marginata'
Hosta plantaginea 'Royal Standard'
Hosta sieboldiana
Hosta sieboldiana 'Frances Williams'
Hosta sieboldii

YELLOW
Hakonechloa macra 'Aureola'

Foliar Season: Late Spring

GREEN/BLUE-GREEN
Adiantum pedatum
Hosta fortunei
Hosta fortunei 'Aurea'
Hosta fortunei 'Marginato-alba'

Exposure: Shade, Foliar Season: Late Spring, Color: Green/Blue-green, *continued*

Hosta 'Krossa Regal'
Hosta montana 'Aureo-marginata'
Hosta plantaginea 'Royal Standard'
Hosta sieboldiana
Hosta sieboldiana 'Frances Williams'
Hosta sieboldii
Matteuccia struthiopteris
Osmunda claytoniana

YELLOW
Hakonechloa macra 'Aureola'

Foliar Season: Summer

GREEN/BLUE-GREEN
Adiantum pedatum
Hosta fortunei
Hosta fortunei 'Aurea'
Hosta fortunei 'Marginato-alba'

Hosta 'Krossa Regal'
Hosta montana 'Aureo-marginata'
Hosta plantaginea 'Royal Standard'
Hosta sieboldiana
Hosta sieboldiana 'Frances Williams'
Hosta sieboldii
Matteuccia struthiopteris
Osmunda claytoniana

YELLOW
Hakonechloa macra 'Aureola'

Foliar Season: Late Summer

GREEN/BLUE-GREEN
Adiantum pedatum
Hosta fortunei
Hosta fortunei 'Aurea'
Hosta fortunei 'Marginato-alba'
Hosta 'Krossa Regal'
Hosta montana 'Aureo-marginata'
Hosta plantaginea 'Royal Standard'
Hosta sieboldiana

Hosta sieboldiana 'Frances Williams'
Hosta sieboldii
Matteuccia struthiopteris
Osmunda claytoniana

YELLOW
Hakonechloa macra 'Aureola'

Foliar Season: Fall

GREEN/BLUE-GREEN
Hosta fortunei
Hosta fortunei 'Aurea'
Hosta fortunei 'Marginato-alba'
Hosta 'Krossa Regal'
Hosta montana 'Aureo-marginata'
Hosta plantaginea 'Royal Standard'
Hosta sieboldiana
Hosta sieboldiana 'Frances Williams'
Hosta sieboldii
Matteuccia struthiopteris

YELLOW
Hakonechloa macra 'Aureola'

Common Name Cross-Reference

Abyssinian gladiolus: *Gladiolus callianthus*
Adam's-needle: *Yucca filamentosa*
Alma Potschke aster: *Aster novae-angliae* 'Alma
  Potschke'
alpine columbine: *Aquilegia alpina*
alpine lady's mantle: *Alchemilla alpina*
alumroot: *Heuchera*
aster: *Aster, Callistephus*
august lily: *Hosta plantaginea*
avens: *Geum*
azalea: *Rhododendron*

balloon flower: *Platycodon grandiflorus*
barrenwort: *Epimedium*
basket-of-gold: *Aurinia saxatilis*
beard tongue: *Penstemon*
beebalm: *Monarda didyma*
bellflower: *Campanula*
bergamot: *Monarda*
Bethlehem sage: *Pulmonaria saccharata*
betony: *Stachys*
big blue lily-turf: *Liriope muscari*
bigroot geranium: *Geranium macrorrhizum*
black cohosh: *Cimicifuga racemosa*
blackeyed Susan: *Rudbeckia*
blanket flower: *Gaillardia*
blazing star: *Liatris*
bloodroot: *Sanguinaria canadensis*
bloody cranesbill: *Geranium sanguineum*
blue African lily: *Agapanthus praecox*
blue false indigo: *Baptisia australis*
blue fescue: *Festuca glauca*
blue mist shrub: *Caryopteris* × *clandonensis*
blue oat grass: *Helictotrichon sempervirens*

blue onion: *Allium senescens* 'Glaucum'
blue sage: *Salvia guaranitica*
blue star: *Amsonia tabernaemontana*
blue wild indigo: *Baptisia australis*
bluebeard: *Caryopteris*
boneset: *Eupatorium*
borage: *Borago officinalis*
bronze fennel: *Foeniculum vulgare* 'Purpureum'
busy Lizzie: *Impatiens*
butterfly bush: *Buddleja*
butterfly weed: *Asclepias tuberosa*

California poppy: *Eschscholzia californica*
campion: *Lychnis*
candytuft: *Iberis*
cardinal flower: *Lobelia cardinalis*
Carpathian bellflower: *Campanula carpatica*
catmint: *Nepeta*
celandine poppy: *Stylophorum diphyllum*
chard: *Beta vulgaris*
China aster: *Callistephus chinensis*
Chinese chives: *Allium tuberosum*
cinquefoil: *Potentilla*
clary sage: *Salvia sclarea*
colewort: *Crambe cordifolia*
comfrey: *Symphytum officinale*
common bleeding heart: *Dicentra spectabilis*
common bugle weed: *Ajuga reptans*
common jasmine: *Jasminum officinale*
common monkshood: *Aconitum napellus*
common pearly everlasting: *Anaphalis margaritacea*
common periwinkle: *Vinca minor*
common sneezeweed: *Helenium autumnale*
coneflower: *Echinacea, Rudbeckia*

corn poppy: *Papaver rhoeas*
cornflower: *Centaurea montana*
cottage pink: *Dianthus plumarius*
cotton thistle: *Onopordum acanthium*
cranesbill: *Geranium*
cup plant: *Silphium perfoliatum*
cupflower: *Nierembergia*
cupid's dart: *Catananche caerulea*
curry plant: *Helichrysum angustifolium*
cushion spurge: *Euphorbia polychroma*

daffodil: *Narcissus*
daisy: *Buphthalmum, Chrysanthemum, Erigeron*
Dalmatian bellflower: *Campanula portenschlagiana*
daylily: *Hemerocallis*
deadnettle: *Lamium*
downy onion: *Allium christophii*
dropwort: *Filipendula vulgaris*
drumstick onion: *Allium sphaerocephalon*
dusty meadowrue: *Thalictrum speciocissimum*
dusty miller: *Artemisia, Centaurea, Senecio*
dwarf red-leaf barberry: *Berberis thunbergii* 'Atropur-
    purea Nana'
dwarf tickseed: *Coreopsis auriculata* 'Nana'

endymion: *Hyacinthoides hispanica*
English ivy: *Hedera helix*
English lavender: *Lavandula angustifolia*
English primrose: *Primula vulgaris*

false dragonhead: *Physostegia virginiana*
fescue: *Festuca*
feverfew: *Tanacetum parthenium*
fingerleaf rodgersia: *Rodgersia aesculifolia*
flax: *Linum perenne*
fleabane: *Erigeron*
floss flower: *Ageratum houstonianum*
flowering tobacco: *Nicotiana alata*
foamflower: *Tiarella cordifolia*
forget-me-not: *Myosotis*
fountain grass: *Pennisetum alopecuroides*
foxglove: *Digitalis*
fragrant plantain lily: *Hosta plantaginea*
fragrant tobacco: *Nicotiana sylvestris*
French marigold: *Tagetes patula*
fringed loosestrife: *Lysimachia ciliata*

garden chives: *Allium schoenoprasum*
garden columbine: *Aquilegia vulgaris*
garden orach: *Atriplex*
garden phlox: *Phlox paniculata*
garden sage: *Salvia officinalis*

gayfeather: *Liatris*
German iris: *Iris* × *germanica*
germander: *Teucrium*
giant onion: *Allium giganteum*
giant sea holly: *Eryngium giganteum*
globe amaranth: *Gomphrena*
globe thistle: *Echinops*
globeflower: *Trollius*
goat's-beard: *Aruncus dioicus*
gold and silver chrysanthemum: *Chrysanthemum
    pacificum*
golden onion: *Allium moly*
goldenrod: *Solidago*
goldenstar: *Chrysogonum virginianum*
gooseneck loosestrife: *Lysimachia clethroides*
granny's bonnets: *Aquilegia vulgaris*
grape hyacinth: *Muscari*
grapeleaf anemone: *Anemone vitifolia*
grass pink: *Dianthus plumarius*
great white trillium: *Trillium grandiflorum*

hardy ageratum: *Eupatorium coelestinum*
hayscented fern: *Dennstaedtia punctiloba*
heliotrope: *Heliotropium*
hellebore: *Helleborus*
helmet flower: *Aconitum napellus*
high mallow: *Malva sylvestris*
hollyhock: *Alcea*
hollyhock mallow: *Malva alcea*
honeysuckle: *Lonicera*
Hungarian speedwell: *Veronica latifolia*
hybrid sage: *Salvia* × *superba*

indigo: *Baptisia*
interrupted fern: *Osmunda claytoniana*
ivy: *Hedera*

Jackman's clematis: *Clematis* × *jackmanii*
Jacob's ladder: *Polemonium*
Japanese anemone: *Anemone* × *hybrida*
Japanese barberry: *Berberis thunbergii*
Japanese blood grass: *Imperata cylindrica*
Japanese forest grass: *Hakonechloa macra* 'Aureola'
Japanese iris: *Iris kaempferi*
Japanese painted fern: *Athyrium nipponicum* 'Pictum'
Japanese primrose: *Primula japonica*
jasmine: *Jasminum officinale*

lady fern: *Athyrium filix-femina*
lady's mantle: *Alchemilla mollis*
lamb's ears: *Stachys byzantina*
larkspur: *Delphinium*

lavender cotton: *Santolina chamaecyparissus*
lavender: *Lavandula*
leadwort: *Ceratostigma plumbaginoides*
lemon daylily: *Hemerocallis lilioasphodelus*
lenten rose: *Helleborus orientalis*
leopard's bane: *Doronicum*
lesser periwinkle: *Vinca minor*
licorice plant: *Helichrysum petiolare*
lilac: *Syringa*
lily-of-the-valley: *Convallaria majalis*
lily-turf: *Liriope*
littleleaf lilac: *Syringa microphylla*
loosestrife: *Lysimachia, Lythrum*
love-in-a-mist: *Nigella damescena*
lungwort: *Pulmonaria*
lyme grass: *Elymus arenarius*

maiden grass: *Miscanthus sinensis*
maidenhair fern: *Adiantum pedatum*
mallow: *Malva*
maltese cross: *Lychnis chalcedonica*
mandrake: *Podophyllum peltatum*
Marguerite daisy: *Argyranthemum frutescens*
marigold: *Calendula, Tagetes*
marsh blue violet: *Viola cucullata*
masterwort: *Astrantia major*
mayapple: *Podophyllum peltatum*
meadowrue: *Thalictrum*
meadowsweet: *Filipendula*
mealycup sage: *Salvia farinacea*
Mexican daisy: *Erigeron karvinskianus*
Mexican giant hyssop: *Agastache foeniculum*
Michaelmas daisy: *Aster novae-angliae*
monkshood: *Aconitum napellus*
moss phlox: *Phlox subulata*
mugwort: *Artemisia*
mullein: *Verbascum*
musk mallow: *Malva moschata*
myrtle: *Vinca*

nasturtium: *Tropaeolum*
nettle-leaved mullein: *Verbascum chaixii*
New England aster: *Aster novae-angliae*
New York fern: *Dryopteris noveboracensis*
nodding onion: *Allium cernuum*

oak-leaf hydrangea: *Hydrangea quercifolia*
obedient plant: *Physostegia virginiana*
onion: *Allium*
opium poppy: *Papaver somniferum*
orach: *Atriplex*
orange geum: *Geum* × *borisii*

ornamental onion: *Allium senescens*
ostrich fern: *Matteuccia struthiopteris*
Ostrowsky onion: *Allium ostrowskianum*
Oswego tea: *Monarda didyma*
ox-eye daisy: *Buphthalmum speciosum, Leucanthemum vulgare*

painted fern: *Athyrium nipponicum* 'Pictum'
pansy: *Viola* × *wittrockiana*
peacock orchid: *Gladiolus callianthus*
pearly everlasting: *Anaphalis*
peony: *Paeonia*
perennial blue flax: *Linum perenne*
perennial candytuft: *Iberis sempervirens*
perennial cornflower: *Centaurea montana*
Persian onion: *Allium aflatuense*
Peruvian lily: *Alstroemeria*
pink: *Dianthus*
pink loosestrife: *Lythrum salicaria* 'Morden Pink'
pink turtlehead: *Chelone lyonii*
plantain lily: *Hosta*
plume celosia: *Celosia cristata*
plume poppy: *Macleaya*
poppy: *Eschscholzia, Papaver*
pot marigold: *Calendula officinalis*
primrose: *Primula*
purple coneflower: *Echinacea purpurea*
purple loosestrife: *Lythrum salicaria*
purple sage: *Salvia officinalis* 'Purpurea'
purpleleaf bugleweed: *Ajuga reptans* 'Atropurpurea'
purpleleaf sand cherry: *Prunus* × *cistena*

quamash: *Camassia quamash*

red-leaf Japanese barberry: *Berberis thunbergii* 'Atropurpurea'
red valerian: *Centranthus ruber*
regal lily: *Lilium regale*
ribbon grass: *Phalaris arundinacea* var. *picta*
rockcress: *Arabis caucasica*
rose campion: *Lychnis coronaria*
rose: *Rosa*
rosinweed: *Silphium perfoliatum*
rue: *Ruta graveolens*
Russian sage: *Perovskia atriplicifolia*

sage: *Salvia*
Scotch thistle: *Onopordum acanthium*
sea lavender: *Limonium latifolium*
Serbian bellflower: *Campanula poscharkyana*
shasta daisy: *Leucanthemum* × *superbum*
showy geranium: *Geranium* × *magnificum*

Siberian bugloss: *Brunnera macrophylla*
silver groundsel: *Senecio cineraria*
silver sage: *Salvia argentea*
small Solomon's seal: *Polygonatum biflorum*
smoke bush: *Cotinus coggygria*
snakeroot: *Cimicifuga racemosa*
snapdragon: *Antirrhinum majus*
snow-in-summer: *Cerastium tomentosum*
snowflake: *Leucojum aestivum*
soft shield fern: *Polystichum setiferum*
Solomon's seal: *Polygonatum*
Spanish bluebells: *Hyacinthoides hispanica*
Spanish lavender: *Lavandula stoechas*
spiderflower: *Cleome spinosa*
spiderwort: *Tradescantia*
spike gayfeather: *Liatris spicata*
spiked speedwell: *Veronica spicata*
spotted dead nettle: *Lamium maculatum*
star of the veldt: *Osteospermum*
star-of-Bethlehem: *Ornithogalum umbellatum*
statice: *Limonium latifolium*
stinking hellebore: *Helleborus foetidus*
stonecrop: *Sedum*
strawberry foxglove: *Digitalis* × *mertonensis*
striped eulalia grass: *Miscanthus sinensis* 'Variegatus'
sulphur yarrow: *Achillea taygetea*
sundrops: *Oenothera tetragona*
sweet alyssum: *Lobularia maritima*
sweet Cicely: *Myrrhis odorata*
sweet woodruff: *Galium odoratum*
Swiss chard: *Beta vulgaris* subsp. *cicla*

tall verbena: *Verbena bonariensis*
thread-leaf tickseed: *Coreopsis verticillata*
tickseed: *Coreopsis*
tiger lily: *Lilium lancifolium*
touch-me-not: *Impatiens*
tree peony: *Paeonia suffruticosa*
trout lily: *Erythronium*
tulip: *Tulipa*
Turkistan onion: *Allium karataviense*
turtlehead: *Chelone*

valerian: *Centranthus*
vervain: *Verbena*
violet: *Viola*
Virginia bluebells: *Mertensia virginica*

white campion: *Lychnis coronaria* 'Alba'
white mallow: *Malva moschata* 'Alba'
white mugwort: *Artemisia lactiflora*
wild bergamot: *Monarda*
woodbine: *Lonicera periclymenum*
woodland phlox: *Phlox divaricata*
woolly speedwell: *Veronica spicata* subsp. *incana*
wormwood: *Artemisia*

yarrow: *Achillea*
yellow archangel: *Lamiastrum galeobdolon*
yellow flag: *Iris pseudacorus*
yellow foxglove: *Digitalis grandiflora*
yellow loosestrife: *Lysimachia punctata*
yellow sage: *Salvia officinalis* 'Aurea'
yellow waxbells: *Kirengeshoma palmata*

APPENDIX D

Hardiness Zone Maps

HARDINESS ZONE
TEMPERATURE RANGES

°F	ZONE	°C
below −50	1	below −45
−50 to −40	2	−45 to −40
−40 to −30	3	−40 to −34
−30 to −20	4	−34 to −29
−20 to −10	5	−29 to −23
−10 to 0	6	−23 to −17
0 to 10	7	−17 to −12
10 to 20	8	−12 to −7
20 to 30	9	−7 to −1
30 to 40	10	−1 to 5

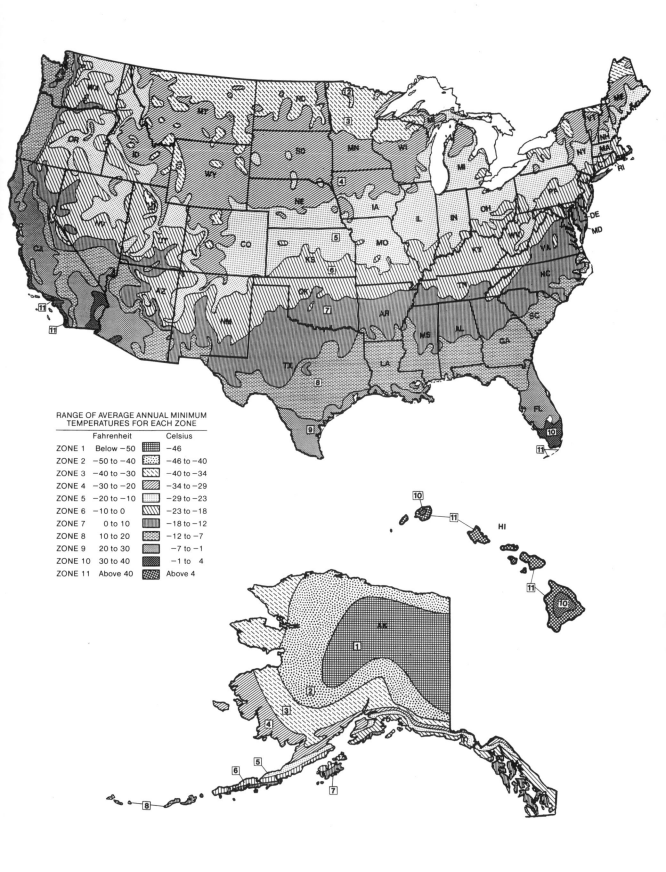

RANGE OF AVERAGE ANNUAL MINIMUM
TEMPERATURES FOR EACH ZONE

	Fahrenheit	Celsius
ZONE 1	Below −50	−46
ZONE 2	−50 to −40	−46 to −40
ZONE 3	−40 to −30	−40 to −34
ZONE 4	−30 to −20	−34 to −29
ZONE 5	−20 to −10	−29 to −23
ZONE 6	−10 to 0	−23 to −18
ZONE 7	0 to 10	−18 to −12
ZONE 8	10 to 20	−12 to −7
ZONE 9	20 to 30	−7 to −1
ZONE 10	30 to 40	−1 to 4
ZONE 11	Above 40	Above 4

Bibliography

Armitage, Allan M. 2000. *Armitage's Garden Perennials: A Color Encyclopedia*. Portland, Ore.: Timber Press.

Armitage, Allan M. 2001. *Armitage's Manual of Annuals, Biennials, and Half-Hardy Perennials*. Portland, Ore.: Timber Press.

Barash, Cathy Wilkinson. 2000. *The Climbing Garden*. New York: Friedman/Fairfax.

Brickell, Christopher, and Judith D. Zuk. 1997. *American Horticultural Society A–Z Encyclopedia of Garden Plants and Flowers*. New York: Dorling Kindersley.

Cox, Peter A., and Kenneth N. E. Cox. 1990. *Cox's Guide to Choosing Rhododendrons*. Portland, Ore.: Timber Press.

Darke, Rick. 1999. *The Color Encyclopedia of Ornamental Grasses: Sedges, Rushes, Restios, Cat-tails, and Selected Bamboos*. Portland, Ore.: Timber Press.

Druse, Ken. 1992. *The Natural Shade Garden*. New York: Clarkson Potter.

Ellis, Barbara W. 1999. *Taylor's Guide to Annuals*. New York: Houghton Mifflin.

Gleitman, Henry. 1991. *Psychology*. New York: W. W. Norton & Co.

Harper, Pamela J. 2001. *Designing with Perennials*. Asheville, N.C.: Lark Books.

Harper, Pamela, and Frederick McGourty. 1987. *Perennials: How to Select, Grow, and Enjoy*. Tucson, Ariz.: H.P. Books.

Hessayon, D. G. 1999. *The Bulb Expert*. New York: Sterling.

Hobhouse, Penelope. 1997. *Garden Style*. Minocqua, Wis.: Willow Creek Press.

Itten, Johannes. 1970. *The Elements of Color*. Edited by Faber Birren. New York: Van Nostrand Reinhold.

Jekyll, Gertrude. 1908. *Colour Schemes for the Flower Garden*. Introduced and revised by Graham Stuart Thomas. 1983. Salem, N.H.: Ayer.

Lacey, Stephen. 2000. *Scent in Your Garden*. London: Frances Lincoln Ltd.

Lloyd, Christopher. 2000. *Garden Flowers*. Portland, Ore.: Timber Press.

Martin, Clair G. 1997. *100 English Roses for the American Garden*. New York: Workman Publishing.

Phillips, Roger, and Martyn Rix. 2002. *Annuals and Biennials*. Toronto: Firefly Books.

Robinson, Florence. 1940. *Planting Design*. New York: McGraw-Hill.

Ruggiero, Michael A., and Tom Christopher. 2002. *Annuals with Style*. Newtown, Conn.: Taunton Press.

Thomas, Graham Stuart. 1990. *Perennial Garden Plants*. Portland, Ore.: Timber Press.

Wilder, Louise Beebe. 1990. *Color in My Garden*. New York: Atlantic Monthly Press.

Index of Plant Names